1980 Supplement

Law, Psychiatry and the Mental Health System

Alexander D. Brooks
Professor of Law
Rutgers Law School, Newark

Little, Brown and Company   *Boston and Toronto*

Library of Congress Catalog Card No. 74-7818

FG

Published simultaneously in Canada
by Little, Brown & Company (Canada) Limited

PRINTED IN THE UNITED STATES OF AMERICA

Table of Contents

Table of Cases

Principal cases in italics

Preface

The publication of this Supplement at this time has been made imperative in light of the extraordinary burgeoning of the law of the mental health system since the manuscript of this Casebook was originally completed in Spring, 1974. A number of areas, such as that of the right of hospitalized mental patients to refuse treatment, have substantially changed form in the last few years with new statutory, judicial, and regulatory developments that now require careful examination. A number of legal issues have emerged or have evolved in more refined and sophisticated ways.

In this Supplement I have tried to present as much material as is feasible bearing on these changes. But a Supplement is only a Supplement. This Supplement should be considered a stop-gap effort, to serve only until a substantially revised and restructured second edition appears within the next two years.

Accordingly, I have presented the more important recent cases and statutory material, together with a very considerable reference to the law review and psychiatric literature emphasizing the newer issues in the field. These materials should provide a basis for discussion of most of the important new problems. Moreover, I have stressed materials in those areas that seem most promising for stimulating seminar and classroom discussion, e.g., right to refuse treatment, privileges and confidentiality, the disposition of insanity acquittees, etc. I am, however, well aware that there is some material I simply have not been able to include in this temporary edition.

Inclusion of such additional materials, with appropriate discussion, will have to await the second edition of this book.

Alexander D. Brooks

September, 1979

Part 1
An Introduction and Overview

Chapter One

Psychiatrists and Lawyers

Page 15. After 4., A Selected List of Books on Law and Psychiatry, add:

1979

A. Watson, Psychiatry for Lawyers (2d ed. 1979).

T. Thornberry and J. Jacoby, The Criminally Insane: A Community Follow-Up of Mentally Ill Offenders (1979).

L. Plyushch, History's Carnival: A Dissident's Autobiography (1979).

D. Weisstub, ed., Law and Psychiatry II: Proceedings of the Second International Symposium Held at the Clarke Institute of Psychiatry (1979).

E. Fersch, Jr., Law, Psychology, and the Courts: Rethinking Treatment of the Young and Disturbed (1979).

G. Cooke, ed., The Role of the Forensic Psychologist (1979).

A. Scull, Museums of Madness: The Social Organization of Insanity in Nineteenth-Century England (1979).

A. Clare, ed., Psychiatry in Dissent: Controversial Issues in Thought and Practice (1979).

F. and E. Hartz, I Sometimes Wish God Had Freddie Hood: A Case History in Psychiatry and Law (1979).

D. Hogan, The Regulation of Psychotherapists, Vol. III: A Review of Malpractice Suits in the United States (1979).

N. Beran and B. Toomey, Mentally Ill Offenders and the Criminal Justice System: Issues in Forensic Services (1979).

1978

J. Chamberlin, On Our Own: Patient-Controlled Alternatives to the Mental Health System (1978).

B. Ennis and R. Emery, The Rights of Mental Patients (Rev. ed. 1978).

J. Rubin, ed., Litigation and the Mentally Disabled (1978).

R. Sadoff, ed., Violence and Responsibility: The Individual, the Family and Society (1978).

J. Wilson, The Rights of Adolescents in the Mental Health System (1978).

C. Steir, Blue Jolts: True Stories From the Cuckoo's Nest (1978).

W. Barton and C. Sanborn, Law and the Mental Health Professions: Friction at the Interface (1978).

W. Gaylin, I. Glasser, S. Marcus and D. Rothman, Doing Good: The Limits of Benevolence (1978).

J. Rubin, Economics, Mental Health, and the Law (1978).

S. Chavkin, The Mind Stealers: Psychosurgery and Mind Control (1978).

D. Gallant and R. Force, Legal and Ethical Issues in Human Research and Treatment—Psychopharmacologic Considerations (1978).

M. Schiffer, Mental Disorder and the Criminal Trial Process (1978).

R. Fox, So Far Disordered in Mind: Insanity in California, 1870-1930 (1978).

S. Pfohl, Predicting Dangerousness: The Social Construction of Psychiatric Reality (1978).

1977

D. West and A. Walk, eds., Daniel McNaughton, His Trial and Aftermath (1977).

E. Hayt, Medicolegal Aspects of Hospital Records (1977).

S. Shuman, Psychosurgery and the Medical Control of Violence (1977).

R. Bonnie, Psychiatrists and the Legal Process: Diagnosis and Debate (1977).

T. Szasz, Psychiatric Slavery (1977).

A. Scull, Decarceration: Community Treatment and the Deviant: A Radical View (1977).

L. Tancredi and A. Slaby, Ethical Policy in Mental Health Care—The Goals of Psychiatric Intervention (1977).

R. Roesch and S. Golding, A Systems Analysis of Competency to Stand Trial Procedures: Implications for Forensic Services in North Carolina (1977).

E. Bardach, The Implementation Game: What Happens After a Bill Becomes a Law (1977).

B. Sales, ed., Psychology and the Legal Process (1977).

S. Bloch and P. Reddaway, Psychiatric Terror: How Soviet Psychiatry Is Used to Suppress Dissent (1977).

J. Aker, A. Walsh, and J. Beam, Mental Capacity: Medical and Legal Aspects of the Aging (1977).

1976

S. Golann and W. Fremouw, eds., The Right to Treatment for Mental Patients (1976).
G. Koocher, Children's Rights and the Mental Health Professions (1976).
R. Scheerenberger, Deinstitutionalization and Institutional Reform (1976).
J. Feinberg and H. Gross, Responsibility: Selected Readings (1976).
W. Crain, The Psycho Squad (1976).
T. Szasz, Heresies (1976).
K. Donaldson, Insanity Inside Out (1976).
M. Kindred, J. Cohen, D. Penrod and T. Shaffer, eds., The Mentally Retarded Citizen and the Law (1976).
K. Miller, Managing Madness: The Case Against Civil Commitment (1976).
P. Friedman, The Rights of Mentally Retarded Persons (1976).
R. Bogomolny, Human Experimentation (1976).
F. Miller, R. Dawson, G. Dix and R. Parnas, The Mental Health Process (2d ed. 1976).
T. Szasz, Schizophrenia: The Sacred Symbol of Psychiatry (1976).
The Trial of Patty Hearst (1976).
S. Shuman, Psychosurgery and the Medical Control of Violence (1976).
W. Gaylin, J. Meister, and R. Neville, Operating on the Mind: The Psychosurgery Conflict (1976).
E. Asinof, The Fox is Crazy, Too (1976).
P. Mitchell, Act of Love: The Killing of George Zygmanik (1976).

1975

S. Yochelson and S. Samenow, The Criminal Personality, Vols. I and II (1975).
J. Ziskin, Coping with Psychiatric and Psychological Testimony (2d ed. 1975).
J. Neaman, Suggestion of the Devil: The Origins of Madness (1975).
R. Sadoff, Forensic Psychiatry: A Practical Guide for Lawyers of Psychiatrists (1975).
J. Gotkin and P. Gotkin, Too Much Anger, Too Many Tears: A Personal Triumph Over Psychiatry (1975).
R. Allen, E. Ferster, and J. Rubin, Readings in Law and Psychiatry (Revised and Expanded Edition, 1975).

M. Foucault, ed., I, Pierre Riviere, having slaughtered my mother, my sister, and my brother . . . A Case of Parricide in the 19th Century (1975).

G. Annas, The Rights of Hospital Patients (1975).

A. Stone, Mental Health and Law: A System in Transition (1975).

M. Peszke, Involuntary Treatment of the Mentally Ill: The Problem of Autonomy (1975).

J. Zusman and W. Carnahan, Mental Health: New York Law and Practice, 2 vols. (1975).

A. Brandt, Reality Police: The Experience of Insanity in America (1975).

G. Morris, The Insanity Defense: A Blueprint for Legislative Reform (1975).

E. Browne, The Right to Treatment Under Civil Commitment (1975).

1974

R. Perruci, Circle of Madness: On Being Insane and Institutionalized in America (1974).

F. Ayd, Jr., ed., Medical, Moral and Legal Issues in Mental Health Care (1974).

H. Steadman and J. Cocozza, Careers of the Criminally Insane: Excessive Control of Deviance (1974).

1973

G. Grob, Mental Institutions in America: Social Policy to 1875 (1973).

M. Blinder, Psychiatry in the Everyday Practice of Law (1973).

T. Szasz, The Age of Madness: The History of Involuntary Mental Hospitalization Presented in Selected Texts (1973).

1972

J. Katz, Experimentation With Human Beings (1972).

E. Hitchcock, L. Laitinen, and K. Vaernet, eds., Psychosurgery (1972).

S. Brodsky, Psychologists in the Criminal Justice System (1972).

Page 19. After 5., A Selected List of General Books on Psychiatry . . ., add:

A. Freedman, H. Kaplan and B. Sadock, Comprehensive Textbook of Psychiatry (2d ed. 1975) (2 vol.).

E. Torrey, The Death of Psychiatry (1974).

O. Friedrich, Going Crazy: An Inquiry Into Madness in Our Time (1976).

Neary, Whom the Gods Destroy (1976).

S. Halleck, The Treatment of Emotional Disorders (1978).

6. The Periodical Literature

The expansion of mental health law has brought about the emergence of a number of new periodicals dealing exclusively with law-psychiatry issues. The most valuable of these for the student and practicing lawyer is the Mental Disability Law Reporter, published six times a year by the Mental Disability Legal Resource Center of the American Bar Association. M.D.L.R. contains case law developments, legislative and regulatory developments, articles, bibliographies of articles, practice materials, and the like.

More traditional legal journals include the new International Journal of Law and Psychiatry; the Journal of Psychiatry and Law; and the Bulletin of the American Academy of Psychiatry and the Law. Another new periodical is Advocacy Now: The Journal of Patient Rights and Mental Health Advocacy. Law and Human Behavior often contains articles of interest in the law-psychiatry field.

Articles on law and psychiatry also appear frequently in several major psychiatric periodicals, the American Journal of Psychiatry, Hospital and Community Psychiatry, Psychiatric Annals, Archives of General Psychiatry, and Psychiatric Quarterly.

A more complete overview of periodical literature in the mental health law field can be obtained by reading the bibliography section of the Mental Disability Law Reporter.

7. New Basic Materials

Since the publication of this casebook in mid-1974, a voluminous literature has poured out, covering many of the older issues in the field of mental health law and reaching out to new areas, previously unexplored. This literature is amply referred to throughout this Supplement.

Several basic and comprehensive discussions merit separate attention. The first of these is the Report of the Task Force on Legal and Ethical Issues contained in the Appendix to the Report of the President's Commission on Mental Health (1978). The section of the Report dealing with these issues is at pp. 42-45. The full Task Force Report is in Volume 4 of the Appendix, pp. 1359-1516 and is reprinted in full in 20 Ariz. L. Rev. 49 (1978).

A second basic document is the Report, Legal Issues in State

Mental Health Care: Proposals for Change. This valuable report is a comprehensive evaluation of mental health law issues prepared by Edward P. Scott of the Mental Health Law Project in Washington, D.C. It is published in four issues of Volume 2 of the Mental Disability Law Reporter. The sections are at 2 M.D.L.R. 55 (1977); 2 M.D.L.R. 265 (1977); and at 2 M.D.L.R. 439 (1978). The entire report contains legislative proposals and extensive analyses.

A third significant document is the Report of the Governor's Commission for Revision of the Mental Health Code of Illinois (1976). This extensive report contains legislative recommendations, most of them since enacted into law, accompanied by valuable annotations prepared by a committee chaired by Judge Joseph Schneider of Chicago.

A fourth useful study is the extensive discussion contained in Developments in the Law, Civil Commitment of the Mentally Ill, 87 Harv. L. Rev. 1190 (1974).

Chapter Two

Concepts of Mental Illness: Statements, Critiques and Defenses of the Medical Model

Pages 39-44. After (1) Psychosis, a., Schizophrenia, add:

See Goldzband, Schizophrenia in the Adversary Arena, 12 Cal. W. L. Rev. 247 (1976).

Page 53. After g., Hysterical Personality, add:

See Woolsey and Goldner, The Medical-Legal Ramifications of Hysteria, 12 Cal. W. L. Rev. 299 (1976).

Pages 69-70. After Note, The Significance of Defining Mental Illness, add:

The debate over definitions of mental illness continues. See, e.g., A. Flew, Crime or Disease? (1974); Kety, From Rationalization to Reason, 131 Am. J. Psychiat. 957 (1974); Siegler and Osmond, Models of Madness: Mental Illness is not Romantic, 8 Psych. Today 71 (November, 1974); Moore, Some Myths About "Mental Illness," 32 Arch. Gen. Psychiat. 1483 (1975); Boorse, On the Distinction Between Disease and Illness, 5 Philos. & Pub. Affairs 49 (1975); Shuman, The Right to be Unhealthy, 22 Wayne L. Rev. 61 (1975); Houlgate, Rights, Health and Mental Disease, 22 Wayne L. Rev. 87 (1975) (a response to Shuman's article); and Macklin, Mental Health and Mental Illness: Some Problems of Definition and Concept Formation, in J. Humber and R. Almeder, Biomedical Ethics and the Law (1976).

A fascinating anthropological study directed at an evaluation of labelling theory and somewhat critical of it is Murphy, Psychiatric

Labelling in Cross-Cultural Perspective, 191 Science 1019 (1976). See also Westermeyer and Wintrob, "Folk" Criteria for the Diagnosis of Mental Illness in Rural Laos: On Being Insane in Sane Places, 136 Am. J. Psychiat. 755 (1979) and Westermeyer and Wintrob, "Folk" Explanations of Mental Illness in Rural Laos, 136 Am. J. Psychiat. 901 (1979).

Pages 85-86. After Note, add:

The prolific Dr. Szasz has continued to publish extensively in the field of law and psychiatry. See, e.g., Szasz, The Theology of Therapy: The Breach of the First Amendment Through the Medicalization of Morals, 5 N.Y.U. Rev. of L. & Soc. Change 127 (1975); The Danger of Coercive Psychiatry, 61 A.B.A.J. 1246 (1975); The Myth of Psychotherapy, 28 Am. J. Psychotherapy 517 (1974); The Control of Conduct, 11 Crim. L. Bull. 617 (1975); Involuntary Psychiatry, 45 U. Cin. L. Rev. 347 (1976); and The Child as Involuntary Mental Patient: The Threat of Child Therapy to the Child's Dignity, Privacy and Self Esteem, 14 San Diego L. Rev. 1005 (1977). Dr. Szasz's newest book is Schizophrenia: The Sacred Symbol of Psychiatry (1976).

Analyses of Szasz's work are presented in Grenander, Thomas Szasz and the Right to Choose, 2 Civ. Lib. Rev. 130 (1975) and in Weinberg and Vatz, Law, Language and Forensic Psychiatry, 16 Duq. L. Rev. 583 (1977-1978). A bibliography of Szasz's major writings is Vatz and Melia, Bibliographic Essay, Q.J. Speech (1977).

Part 2
The Mentally Disabled Offender

Chapter Four

The Insanity Defense
and Related Defenses

Page 114. After 2., Selected Readings on the Insanity Defense, add:

Two significant new contributions to the insanity defense literature are H. Fingarette and A. Hasse, Mental Disabilities and Criminal Responsibility (1979), a study that further develops Professor Fingarette's earlier analysis, and G. Morris, The Insanity Defense: A Blueprint for Legislative Reform (1975).

Two recent discussions of the original M'Naghten case are D. West and A. Walk, eds., Daniel McNaughton: His Trial and Aftermath (1977), and Moran, Awaiting the Crown's Pleasure: The Case of Daniel M'Naughten, 15 Crim. 7 (1977). Recent state discussions of M'Naghten include Moore, M'Naghten is Dead—Or Is It?, 3 Hous. L. Rev. 58 (1965); Note, Texas Rejects M'Naghten, 11 Hous. L. Rev. 946 (1974); and Comment, The Insanity Defense in North Carolina, 14 Wake Forest L. Rev. 1157 (1978). See also Wingo, Squaring M'Naghten With Precedent—An Historical Note, 26 S.C.L. Rev. 81 (1974).

Other new studies include Fingarette, Disabilities of Mind and Criminal Responsibility—A Unitary Doctrine, 76 Colum. L. Rev. 236 (1976) (now included in the Fingarette-Hasse book); Gardner, Criminal Responsibility and Exculpation by Medical Category—An Instance of Not Taking Hart to Heart, 27 Ala. L. Rev. 55 (1975); Gray, The Insanity Defense: The Historical Development and Contemporary Relevance, 10 Am. Crim. L. Rev. 559 (1972); Note, Modern Insanity Tests—Alternatives, 15 Wash. L.J. 40 (1976); Ringer and McCormack, The Elusive Insanity Defense, 63 A.B.A.J. 1721 (1977); and Comment, Mens Rea and Insanity, 28 U. Maine L. Rev. 500 (1976).

A new historical study of the California insanity defense is R. Fox, So Far Disordered in Mind: Insanity in California, 1870-1930 (1978).

Page 143. After 3. *Know,* add:

See People v. Martin, 386 Mich. 407, 192 N.W.2d 215 (1971) and State v. Jones, 84 Wash. 2d 823, 529 P.2d 1040 (1974) for discussions of "knowing." For a discussion of "surface knowledge," see People v. Adams, 26 N.Y. 2d 129, 309 N.Y.S.2d 145 (1970).

C. THE "IRRESISTIBLE IMPULSE" TEST

Pages 164-165. After Note, add:

See discussions of the irresistible impulse defense in A. Goldstein, The Insanity Defense (1967) and in Note, Irresistible Impulse and the M'Naghten Rules, 23 Mod. L. Rev. 545.

Pages 165-168. After United States v. Freeman, add Note:

A powerful new recruit to the A.L.I. Model Penal Code is the California Supreme Court. See People v. Drew, 149 Cal. Rptr. 275 (1975), adopting (by a 4 to 3 vote) Section 4.01(1) of the Model Penal Code test. Footnotes 9 and 10 list the adherents, both state and federal, to one or another version of the rule. For a comment on the California change see Gunn, California Revises its Insanity Test: An Analysis of Criteria and Practical Effect, 2 Crim. Just. J. 253 (1979).

D. THE ALI MODEL PENAL CODE TEST

Page 169. After 4. *Wrongfulness,* add:

In the *Wade* case the Court followed the Freeman approach to the effect that the word "wrongfulness" applies to those who, knowing an act to be criminal, nevertheless commit it because of a delusion that the act is morally justified. For a listing of circuits that have adopted this approach, see United States v. McGraw, 515 F.2d 758 (9th Cir. 1975), reversing where the judge refused to give a proper instruction on "wrongfulness," and where the government psychiatrist testified that the defendant had capacity only if wrongfulness meant "legally wrong" rather than morally wrong.

E. THE PSYCHOPATH AND THE INSANITY DEFENSE

Pages 174-176. After Blocker v. United States, add:

NOTE: THE PSYCHOPATHIC OFFENDER

For recent writings on the psychopath see Bleechmore, Towards a Rational Theory of Criminal Responsibility: The Psychopathic Offender: Part I, 10 Melb. U.L. Rev. 19 (1975); Part II, 10 Melbourne U.L. Rev. 207 (1975). See also Slovenko, "The Psychopath": Labelling in South Africa, 5 Crime, Punishment & Correction 9 (1976) and Blair, The Medicolegal Implications of the Terms "Psychopath," "Psychopathic Personality" and "Psychopathic Disorder," 15 Med. Sci. L. 51 (1975).

F. THE DURHAM EXPERIMENT: 1954-1972, 176

Page 200. After 10., Selected Readings on the Durham Rule and the *Brawner* Case, add:

See also Commentary, United States v. Brawner: The District of Columbia Abandons the Durham Insanity Test, 25 Ala. L. Rev. 342 (1973) and Bazelon, The Morality of the Criminal Law, 49 S. Cal. L. Rev. 385 (1976). The role of Chief Justice Burger in explicating the Durham Rule at the time he sat on the District of Columbia Circuit Court of Appeals is dealt with in Lamb, Warren Burger and the Insanity Defense—Judicial Philosophy and Voting Behavior on a U.S. Court of Appeals, 24 Am. U.L. Rev. 91 (1974).

G. THE "DIMINISHED RESPONSIBILITY" TEST

Page 217. After 5., Selected Readings on Diminished Responsibility, add:

Recent writings include Arenella, The Diminished Capacity and Diminished Responsibility Defenses: Two Children of a Doomed Marriage, 77 Colum. L. Rev. 827 (1977); Comment, Oregon's Partial

Responsibility Defense: Disposition of the Defendant and Burden of Proof, 13 William L.J. 374 (1977); Lewin, Psychiatric Evidence in Criminal Cases for Purposes Other Than the Defense of Insanity, 26 Syr. L. Rev. 1051 (1975); Adleson, Diminished Capacity: The Middle Ground of Criminal Responsibility, 15 Santa Clara Law. 911 (1975); Fingarette, Diminished Mental Capacity as a Criminal Law Defense, 37 Mod. L. Rev. 264 (1974); Note, A Concept of Diminished Responsibility for Canadian Criminal Law, 33 U. Toronto Fac. L. Rev. 205 (1975); Note, Evidence of Diminished Capacity Inadmissible to Show Lack of Intent, 1976 Wis. L. Rev. 623; and Comment, Prison Conditions and Diminished Capacity—A Proposed Defense, 17 Santa Clara L. Rev. 855 (1977).

Professor Bernard Diamond, long associated with the diminished capacity defense in California, has written a provocative article, proposing a new ground for the diminished capacity defense. See Diamond, Social and Cultural Factors as a Diminished Capacity Defense in Criminal Law, 6 Bull. Am. Acad. Psychiat. & L. 195 (1978).

Recent cases include Commonwealth v. Walzack, 468 Pa. 210, 360 A.2d 914 (1976), noted, 16 Duq. L. Rev. 129 (1977-1978) and Commonwealth v. Simms, 228 Pa. Super. 85, 324 A.2d 365 (1974). Missouri has adopted the diminished responsibility test. See State v. Anderson, 515 S.W.2d 534 (Mo. 1974), noted in 40 Mo. L. Rev. 361 (1975). In People v. Wetmore, 149 Cal. Rptr. 265 (1978), the California Supreme Court ruled that the diminished capacity defense applies to all specific intent crimes, even those lacking a lesser included defense. Thus, where the defendant satisfactorily establishes his incapacity for the requisite intent, as in burglary, which the court characterized as a crime requiring a specific intent to commit a felony, he is acquitted. The influence on the diminished capacity test of the *Wetmore* and *Drew* cases is discussed in Comment, Diminished Capacity and California's New Insanity Test, 10 Pac. L.J. 751 (1979).

Page 217. After 5., Selected Readings on Diminished Responsibility, add:

NOTE: EXTREME EMOTIONAL DISTURBANCE

New York provides a defense for "extreme emotional disturbance," which reduces homicide to manslaughter. See the leading case of People v. Shelton, 385 N.Y.S.2d 708 (Sup. Ct. 1976); Comment,

Affirmative Defenses After Mullaney v. Wilbur: New York's Extreme Emotional Disturbance, 43 Brooklyn L. Rev. 171 (1976), commenting on People v. Patterson, 39 N.Y.2d 288, 347 N.E.2d 898, 383 N.Y.S.2d 573. See Patterson v. New York, 432 U.S. 197 (1977).

For a study of the Oregon situation see Comment, Proof of Extreme Emotional Disturbance in Oregon Murder Prosecutions: A Constitutional Analysis, 58 Or. L. Rev. 98 (1979). See also Note, The Burden of Proof for Extreme Emotional Disturbance and Insanity: The Deterioration of Due Process, 52 Temp. L.Q. 79 (1979).

H. ABOLISH THE INSANITY DEFENSE — YES? — NO?

Pages 217-221. After 1., Introductory Note, add:

Fascination with the notion of abolishing the insanity defense continues unabated. The prospect of abolition in New York State has been revived by the issuance of an influential report recommending abolition issued by the New York State Department of Mental Hygiene: A Report to Governor Hugh L. Carey on the Insanity Defense in New York (1978), prepared under the direction of William A. Carnahan, the department's former counsel. The report contains essays by Lawrence C. Kolb, Henry J. Steadman, John B. Wright, and William Carnahan.

The literature attacking and supporting abolitionism is vigorous. Predominant among more recent writings is Wales, An Analysis of the Proposal to "Abolish" the Insanity Defense in S. 1: Squeezing a Lemon, 124 U. Pa. L. Rev. 687 (1976). See also Shlensky, The Insanity Defense Must Go, 5 J. Legal Med. 30 (1977); Platt, The Proposal to Abolish the Federal Insanity Defense: A Critique, 10 Cal. W. L. Rev. 449 (1974); Reisner and Semmel, Abolishing the Insanity Defense: A Look at the Proposed Federal Criminal Code Reform Act in Light of Swedish Experience, 62 Calif. L. Rev. 753 (1974); Gerber, Is the Insanity Test Insane?, 20 Am. J. Juris. 111 (1975); and Halpern, The Insanity Defense: A Juridical Anachronism, 7:8 Psychiat. Annals 398 (August, 1977). An interesting collection of criticisms of the insanity defense as voiced by practicing lawyers is described and analyzed in Burton and Steadman, Legal Professionals' Perceptions of the Insanity Defense, 6 J. Psychiat. & L. 173 (1978).

Michigan has experimented recently with a "guilty but mentally ill verdict," as distinguished from the insanity defense. See Mich. Comp. Laws Ann. §768.36 (West Supp. 1977). In People v. McLeod, No. 76-01672 (Recorder's Court of Detroit), *rev'd* 77 Mich. App. 327, 258 N.W.2d 214 (1977), the trial court found that the GBMI verdict denied defendants equal protection of the laws because those found guilty under a general verdict did not face the minimum probation term provided in the statute. The trial court also found §768.36(3) to be legally "inert" because the state could not provide adequate treatment. This aspect of *McLeod* was reversed.

For discussions see Robey, Guilty But Mentally Ill, 6 Bull. Am. Acad. Psychiat. & L. 374 (1978); Note, Not Guilty But Mentally Ill: An Historical and Constitutional Analysis, 53 J. Urb. L. 471 (1976) and Note, The Constitutionality of Michigan's Guilty But Mentally Ill Verdict, 12 U. Mich. J.L. Reform 188 (1978), concluding that the GBMI statute violates the due process clause.

I. OTHER DEFENSES BASED ON MENTAL CONDITION

Pages 238-242. To Note: Defenses Based on "Involuntariness" of Behavior, add:

1. *Somnambulism.* See Casady, Costly Dysomnia: The Sleepy Murders, 9 Psychol. Today 79 (January, 1975).

2. *Hypnosis.* California has recognized a hypnosis defense in People v. Marsh, 170 Cal. App. 2d 284, 338 P.2d 495 (1959).

3. *"Automatism" based on organic physical condition.* The correct citation to the *Bratty* case is: 3 ALL E.R. 523. Add Cross, Reflections on Bratty's Case, 78 L.Q. Rev. 236 (1962).

4. *Premenstrual Syndrome.* See Horney, Menstrual Cycles and Criminal Responsibility, 2 L. & Human Behav. 25 (1978), arguing against a defense based on premenstrual tension. Says Horney: "The conclusions reached by Wallach and Rubin and the various researchers are not necessarily wrong, but they do appear to be premature."

5. *"Brainwashing" or "Coercive Persuasion."* The Patty Hearst case has emphasized the evolution of the new defense of "coercive persuasion." An argument on behalf of the new defense is presented in Delgado, Ascription of Criminal States of Mind: Toward a Defense Theory for the Coercively Persuaded ("Brainwashed") Defendant, 63 Minn. L. Rev. 1 (1978), criticized in Dressler, Professor Delgado's "Brainwashing" Defense: Courting a Determinist Legal System, 63

Minn. L. Rev. 355 (1978) and re-defended in Delgado, A Response to Professor Dressler, 63 Minn. L. Rev. 361 (1978). See also Lunde and Wilson, Brainwashing as a Defense to Criminal Liability: Patty Hearst Revisited, 13 Crim. L. Bull. 341 (1977) and David, Fact, Fiction and Criminal Defense, 44 U.M.K.C.L. Rev. 438 (1976), both of which reject the defense but suggest that evidence of brainwashing be used for purposes of mitigation. See also Reich, Brainwashing, Psychiatry and the Law, 39 Psychiat. 400 (1976). The full testimony in the Hearst case is presented in The Trial of Patty Hearst (1976). The psychiatric testimony is at pp. 76-80, 248-291, 291-314, 314-355, 399-404, 413-486, 486-491, 493-495, and 516-536.

As to defenses based on epilepsy, see Note, Epilepsy and the Alternatives for a Criminal Defense, 27 Case W.R.L. Rev. 77 (1977).

In connection with the discussion of R. v. Charlson at page 238, the correct facts are that Charlson threw his son into the river, but did not kill him.

Pages 233-242. After 1., Altered States of Consciousness, Hypnotism, Automatism and the Like, add:

See the comprehensive overview of non-insanity defense defenses presented in Lewin, Psychiatric Evidence in Criminal Cases for Purposes Other Than the Defense of Insanity, 26 Syracuse L. Rev. 1051 (1975).

Pages 247-248. After Note, add:

See Borgaonkar and Shah, the XYY Chromosome, Male-Or Syndrome?, in A. Steinberg and A. Bearn, eds., 10 Progress in Medical Genetics 135 (1974), an extraordinarily comprehensive analysis containing also a complete bibliography. See also Bartholomew and Sutherland, A Defense of Insanity and the Extra Y Chromosome: R. v. Hannell, 2 Aust. & N.Z.L.J. Crim. 29 (1969); Bartholemew, Psychopathy, Sex Chromosome Abnormalities, and the Criminal Law, 4 Adelaide L. Rev. 273 (1972); and Note, 52 N.D.L. Rev. 729 (1976). An interesting case is People v. Yukl, 83 Misc. 2d 364, 372 N.Y.S.2d 313 (1975).

Pages 252-253. After Note: Hallucinogens, add:

The *Kelley* case is discussed in Comment, People v. Kelly—The M'Naghten Rule: Should Drug-Induced Madness Constitute a Complete Defense, 6 U.W.L.A.L. Rev. 71 (1974).

Pages 253-254. After Note: The Criminal Responsibility of the Drug Addict, add new Notes:

An outstanding new contribution to the writing in this field is Fingarette, Addiction and Criminal Responsibility, 84 Yale L.J. 413 (1975). Also valuable is the discussion in Wald, Alcohol, Drugs, and Criminal Responsibility, 63 Geo. L.J. 69 (1974). A good collection of cases is Annot., Drug Addiction or Related Mental State as Defense to Criminal Charge, 73 A.L.R.3d 16; Annot., Effect of Voluntary Drug Intoxication Upon Criminal Responsibility, 73 A.L.R.3d 98. An interesting case is Gorman v. United States, 339 A.2d 401 (1975), holding that the court had no power, in light of Congressional policy, to excuse a narcotics addict from the crime of possession because of his addiction.

NOTE: CHRONIC ALCOHOLISM AS AN INSANITY DEFENSE

The subject is discussed in Comment, Public Drunkenness: An Insanity Defense, 19 St. Louis U.L.J. 530 (1975).

NOTE: SOCIAL AND CULTURAL FACTORS AS AN INSANITY DEFENSE

The defense that defendant had had a "rotten" upbringing was raised, but rejected, as an insanity defense in United States v. Alexander [Murdock], 471 F.2d 923 (D.C. Cir. 1973). See discussion in Allen, Criminal Law and the Modern Consciousness: Some Observations on Blameworthiness, 44 Tenn. L. Rev. 735, 756-760 (1977); Floud, Sociology and the Theory of Responsibility: Social Background as an Excuse for Crime, in R. Fletcher, ed., The Science of Society and the Unity of Mankind (1974) and Morse, The Twilight of Welfare Criminology: A Reply to Judge Bazelon, 49 S. Cal. L. Rev. 1247, 1251-1254 (1976).

For another use of social and cultural factors, see Diamond, Social and Cultural Factors as a Diminished Capacity Defense in Criminal Law, 6 Bull. Am. Acad. Psychiat. & L. 195 (1978).

NOTE: INSANITY DEFENSE FOR JUVENILES

For years it was thought that an insanity defense for juveniles was an anomaly inasmuch as the dispositional powers of the juvenile court have been so flexible. Recently these notions have been changing. See, e.g., Roos and Ellison, The Mentally Ill Juvenile Offender: Crisis for Law and Society, Juvenile Justice, February 1976, p. 25. A leading case is State in Interest of R.G.W., 135 N.J. Super. 125, 342 A.2d 869 (App. Div. 1975). A juvenile judge has written thoughtfully about the role of psychiatry in the juvenile system in J. Polier, The Rule of Law and the Role of Psychiatry (1968). See also Reaves, The Right to Treatment for Juvenile Offenders, 7 Cum. L. Rev. 13 (1976).

NOTE: PSYCHIATRIC EVIDENCE CONCERNING CHARACTER IN SEX OFFENSE CASES

A considerable controversy swirls around the question whether a psychiatrist should be permitted to testify where the defendant is charged with an offense involving a sexual aberration to the effect that the defendant has the character of a "normal" or non-aberrational person. The issue was first raised in People v. Jones, 42 Cal. 2d 219, 266 P.2d 38 (1954), a child-molesting case. The California court ruled such testimony admissible, analogizing to sex psychopath statutes which provide for psychiatric examinations. The *Jones* result was greeted with approbation in Curran, Expert Psychiatric Evidence of Personality Traits, 103 U. Pa. L. Rev. 999 (1955) and in Note, 42 Calif. L. Rev. 880 (1954), but denounced in Falknor and Steffen, Evidence of Character: From the "Crucible of the Community" to the "Couch of the Psychiatrist," 102 U. Pa. L. Rev. 980 (1954). The New Jersey Supreme Court in State v. Sinnott, 24 N.J. 408, 132 A.2d 298 (1957), ruled the other way. More recently, in Freeman v. State, 486 P.2d 967 (Alaska 1971) the Alaska Supreme Court has ruled admissible psychiatric testimony to show that the defendant does not have the type of personality that would lead him to commit the crime of statutory rape or of contributing to the delinquency of a minor. For a more recent general discussion of the problem, see Bates, Psychiatric Evidence of Character, 5 Anglo-Am. L. Rev. 99 (1976).

Chapter Five

The Administration of the Insanity Defense

Page 255. After A., Presenting Evidence, add:

Orland, Evidence in Psychiatric Settings, 11 Gonz. L. Rev. 665 (1976).

Pages 259-261. After Note: How to Cross-Examine a Psychiatrist, add:

See M. Blinder, Psychiatry in the Everyday Practice of Law, Ch. 13, Cross-Examination of the Psychiatric Witness (1973), and Perr, Cross-Examination of the Psychiatrist, Using Publications, 5 Bull. Amer. Acad. Psychiat. & L. 327 (1977).

B. PROCEDURES

Page 280. After 1., An Introductory Note on Procedural Issues, add:

Need an accused person be confined during the period prior to trial for purposes of a psychiatric examination? See Geller and Lister, The Process of Criminal Commitment for Pretrial Psychiatric Examination: An Evaluation, 135 Am. J. Psychiat. 53 (1978), and Stone, Comment, 135 Am. J. Psychiat. 61 (1978).

Page 283. After Note, The Diagnostic Process, add:

A good collection of cases has been brought together in Annot., Sufficiency of Psychiatric Examination to Determine Sanity of Person Charged with Federal Offense, 23 A.L.R. Fed. 710. See United States v. Smith, 436 F.2d 787 (5th Cir. 1971), *cert. denied,*

402 U.S. 976, 29 L. Ed. 2d 142, 91 S. Ct. 1680 (1971), and Lawless v. Director, Patuxent Inst., 27 Md. App. 453, 340 A.2d 756 (1975) (where the court ruled that the examination was insufficient even though the subject had been uncooperative).

For a case dealing with the sodium amytal interview see State v. Harris, 241 Or. 224, 405 P.2d 492 (1965).

See United States v. Ingman, 426 F.2d 973 (9th Cir. 1970) for a discussion of subjective history narrated by the defendant.

Consult, generally, Curnow, Legal Insanity and the Federal Courts: Does the Ninth Circuit Guide or Confuse?, 33 Fed. Bar J. 305 (1974) and Holliday, Pretrial Mental Examination Under Military Law: A Re-examination, Air Force L. Rev., Fall, 1974, p. 14. See also Orland, Evidence in Psychiatric Settings, 11 Gonz. L. Rev. 665 (1976).

For a discussion of whether the defense psychiatrist's report should be revealed to the prosecution, compare United States v. Bass, 477 F.2d 723 (9th Cir. 1973) with In Re Serra, 484 F.2d 947 (9th Cir. 1973).

Pages 293-294. After 4., The Privilege Against Self-Incrimination, add:

Is a Miranda warning required? See Note, Miranda on the Couch: An Approach to Self-Incrimination, Right to Counsel and Miranda Warnings in Pre-Trial Psychiatric Examination of Criminal Defendants, 11 Colum. J.L. & Soc. Prob. 403 (1975).

Pages 295-296. After Lee v. Erie County Court, add:

NOTE: THE PRIVILEGE AGAINST SELF-INCRIMINATION

An important new case is Blaisdell v. Commonwealth, 364 N.E.2d 191 (Mass. 1977). See also State v. Buzynski, 330 A.2d 422 (Me. 1974).

Pages 293-296. After Note: The Privilege Against Self-Incrimination, add:

4A. Lawyer-Client Privilege

See pages 1080-1096 in the Casebook for materials relating to this Section.

PRATT v. STATE

387 A.2d 779 (1978)

[Margaret Pratt shot and killed her husband. She offered an insanity defense. Two psychiatrists testified for the defense. The prosecution presented three psychiatrists, two of whom expressed their opinion that the defendant was legally responsible.]

One of the three psychiatrists presented by the State, Dr. Crowley, had originally been retained by the defense. Dr. Crowley testified that although appellant was suffering from a mental disorder at the time of the offense, she did not lack substantial capacity to conform her conduct to the requirements of the law. Appellant mounts a multi-faceted attack on the admission of this testimony arguing it should have been excluded on the grounds of: (1) the attorney-client privilege, (2) the psychiatrist-patient privilege, or (3) the work product doctrine. We conclude admission of the testimony violated the attorney-client privilege so we will not discuss the other arguments in any detail.[2]

The attorney-client privilege was defined in *Harrison v. State*, 276 Md. 122, 135, 345 A.2d 830, 838 (1975) as follows:

> "(1) Where legal advice of kind is sought (2) from a professional legal adviser in his capacity as such, (3) the communications relating to that purpose, (4) made in confidence (5) by the client, (6) are at his insistence permanently protected (7) from disclosure by himself or by the legal adviser, (8) except the protection be waived." Quoting 8 J. Wigmore, *Evidence* §2292 at 554 (McNaughton rev. 1961).

The theory behind the creation of the privilege is that a lawyer can act effectively only when he is fully advised of the facts and the client's knowledge that a lawyer cannot reveal his secrets promotes full disclosure. *Harrison v. State, supra*, 276 Md. at 133-134, 345 A.2d at 837; *Trupp v. Wolff*, 24 Md. App. 588, 608-609, 335 A.2d

---

2. We note, however, that the appellant waived any claim she might have had under the psychiatrist-patient privilege by introducing her mental condition as a defense. *Bremer v. State*, 18 Md. App. 291, 334, 307 A.2d 503, 529, *cert. denied*, 269 Md. 755 (1973), *cert. denied*, 415 U.S. 930, 94 S. Ct. 1440, 39 L. Ed. 2d 488 (1974); Md. Code, Cts. and Jud. Proc. Art. §9-109(e)(2) (1977 Supp.).

The State argues that even if the attorney-client privilege has not been waived, the privilege cannot be asserted because the work product doctrine is inapplicable. The work product doctrine, however, is separate from the attorney-client privilege and serves to protect materials from discovery that are not subject to another privilege. *See* C. McCormick, Handbook of the Law of Evidence §96 at 204-205 (2d ed. E. Cleary 1972).

171, 183-184, *cert. denied,* 275 Md. 757 (1975). The privilege is not confined in scope to communications made solely between an attorney and his client but includes communications made to agents employed by the attorney, such as a stenographer, secretary, clerk, or any employee necessary for effective operation. 8 J. Wigmore, *Evidence* §2301 at 583; C. McCormick, *Handbook of the Law of Evidence* §91 at 188-189 (2d ed. E. Cleary 1972).

In cases where a question arises concerning a client's criminal responsibility for an act, a psychiatrist is indispensable for his help in the planning and preparation of the defense as well as his testimony at trial. The attorney could hardly explore the basis of adverse testimony intelligently, without such help. *See United States v. Taylor,* 437 F.2d 371, 377 n.9 (4th Cir. 1971); *United States v. Alvarez,* 519 F.2d 1036, 1046 (3rd Cir. 1975); *United States ex rel. Edney v. Smith,* 425 F. Supp. 1038, 1047-1048 (E.D.N.Y.1976), *aff'd mem.* 556 F.2d 556 (2nd Cir. 1977); *People v. Lines,* 13 Cal. 3d 500, 119 Cal. Rptr. 225, 531 P.2d 793, 800 (1975); *United States v. Kovel,* 296 F.2d 918, 921 (2nd Cir. 1961) (Friendly J.).[3]

As the assistance of a psychiatrist is essential where the criminal responsibility of a client is in question, we hold that communications made to a psychiatrist for the purpose of seeking legal advice are within the scope of the attorney-client privilege. This position is supported by the overwhelming majority of courts and commentators that have considered the question.[4]

The State, not seriously disputing that communications made to a psychiatrist in conjunction with the preparation of an insanity defense should be afforded the protection of the attorney-client privilege, argues appellant waived any claim of privilege by placing her sanity in issue. Although there can be no question that a client may expressly or impliedly waive the attorney-client privilege, we

3. Some courts have analogized the function of a psychiatrist to that of an interpreter. *See City & County of San Francisco v. Superior Court,* 37 Cal. 2d 227, 231 P.2d 26 (1951); *Lindsay v. Lipson,* 367 Mich. 1, 116 N.W.2d 60, 63 (1962).

4. In addition to the cases cited above, *see Jones v. Superior Court,* 58 Cal. 2d 56, 22 Cal. Rptr. 879, 372 P.2d 919, 921-922 (1962); *People v. Hilliker,* 29 Mich. App. 543, 185 N.W.2d 831, 833 (1971); *State v. Kociolek,* 23 N.J. 400, 129 A.2d 417, 423-425 (1957); F. Wharton, *Criminal Evidence* §559 at 79 (13th ed. C. Torcia 1973); B. Jones, *Evidence* §21:15 at 786 (6th ed. S. Gard 1972); C. McCormick, Handbook of the Law of Evidence §91 at 188 n.82 (2d ed. E. Cleary 1972). *But see* Friedenthal, Discovery and Use of an Adverse Party's Expert Information, 14 Stan. L. Rev. 455, 463-465 (1962). The privilege, however, does not apply where the psychiatrist is retained to treat the client rather than to assist the attorney in rendering legal advice. *People v. Lines, supra,* 119 Cal. Rptr. 225, 531 P.2d at 800-801 n.12; *City & County of San Francisco v. Superior Court, supra,* 231 P.2d at 31-32.

do not think a waiver occurs when an accused places his sanity in issue. There is no precise formula for determining whether the privilege has been waived in a particular case. In deciding this question various factors such as the client's intent to waive, fairness, and consistency of conduct must be considered in view of the purpose of the privilege.

In arguing that fairness dictates that the privilege should be deemed to have been waived the State relies on the rationale of *People v. Edney,* 39 N.Y.2d 620, 385 N.Y.S.2d 23, 350 N.E.2d 400 (1976). That court concluded there was no need to protect communications made to a psychiatrist once the issue of the client's sanity was placed in issue. The court's reasoning was predicated on several factors. First, under New York law once an accused pleads insanity he is required to disclose the underlying basis of his affliction to prosecution psychiatrists.[5] Thus, the court reasoned that if an insanity plea is entered the facts in question will be available to the prosecution in any event and, as a result, the waiver rule would not deter a client from communicating with a psychiatrist hired to assist his attorney. Second, the court noted that under the work product doctrine an attorney could consult a psychiatrist without fear of future disclosure as long as the attorney, and not the client, conveyed the necessary facts to the expert.[6]

Despite *Edney* we think the better approach is that the client does not waive the attorney-client privilege by placing sanity in issue. *See* particularly, *United States v. Alvarez, supra* at 1046-1047; *People v. Lines, supra,* 119 Cal. Rptr. 225, 531 P.2d at 799-802; *State v. Kociolek, supra,* 129 A.2d at 425-426. *Cf. Pouncy v. State,* 353 So. 2d 640 (Fla. App. 1977) (accused does not waive privilege by placing sanity in issue unless trier of fact is so deprived of a valuable witness as to undermine public interest in the administration of justice). The waiver rule urged by the State would seriously undermine the purpose of the privilege by impairing effective assistance of counsel in several respects. Even though the work product doctrine serves to protect communications between the attorney and the psychiatrist, as a practical matter the advice of an expert

5. A similar provision is contained in Md. Code, Art. 59, §25(b) (1972 Repl. Vol.). Such a requirement has been upheld against attacks that it amounts to a *per se* violation of the accused's right against self-incrimination. *Bremer v. State, supra,* n.2, 18 Md. App. at 316-318, 307 A.2d at 520-521.

6. *Cf. Hall v. State,* 36 Md. App. 362, 373 A.2d 1250 (1977) (opinion of psychiatrist prepared in anticipation of litigation not discoverable under work product doctrine absent showing of exceptional circumstances).

based exclusively on an attorney's communications will be worth much less than advice given after an examination of the client. In addition, as expert testimony is essential to a defense of insanity, the attorney will eventually have to submit his client for examination before formulating a defense strategy. In so doing, he will be running the risk that the psychiatrist will later be called to testify by the State. As a result the client might be less open and candid in communicating with the psychiatrist. This in turn impairs the value of the psychiatrist's advice and lessens the effectiveness of counsel. The problem posed was convincingly stated by the Court in *United States v. Alvarez, supra* at 1046-1047.

> The issue here is whether a defense counsel in a case involving a potential defense of insanity must run the risk that a psychiatric expert whom he hires to advise him with respect to the defendant's mental condition may be forced to be an involuntary government witness. The effect of such a rule would, we think, have the inevitable effect of depriving defendants of the effective assistance of counsel in such cases. A psychiatrist will of necessity make inquiry about the facts surrounding the alleged crime, just as the attorney will. Disclosures made to the attorney cannot be used to furnish proof in the government's case. Disclosures made to the attorney's expert should be equally unavailable, at least until he is placed on the witness stand. The attorney must be free to make an informed judgment with respect to the best course for the defense without the inhibition of creating a potential government witness.

Another reason the psychiatrist's testimony should be rejected is because his employment by the other side tends to add undue weight to his testimony. In the instant case, the State emphasized this in its closing argument to the jury. This problem, however, could be eliminated by prohibiting evidence concerning the expert's original employer from being presented to the jury.

It has been suggested that application of the attorney-client privilege to psychiatrists allows the defense to suppress unfavorable experts while shopping around for an expert that supports its position. When one considers this possibility it seems that fairness would dictate that the State be granted access to all psychiatrists employed by the defense, even though it does not intend to use them at trial. A close examination of this argument, however, reveals that the State would not significantly benefit from access to these individuals. The State already has access to the underlying factual basis of the accused's mental affliction for use by its psychiatrists. Hence, the actual information disclosed would not be of any real value to the State. As long as there is a sufficient number of experts available, there is no real danger, as a practical matter, of the defense using the cloak of the privilege to remove "unfriendly" experts.

Pages 303-304. After 6., A Miscellany of Issues, add:

With respect to the right to an independent psychiatrist, see Annot., Right of Indigent Defendant in Criminal Case to Aid of State by Appointment of Investigator or Expert, 34 A.L.R.3d 1256. In United States v. Chavis, 486 F.2d 1290 (D.C. Cir. 1973), it was held error to deny the defendant an independent psychiatrist. In United States v. Hartfield, 513 F.2d 254 (9th Cir. 1975), it was held reversible error to deny defendant's motion for an E.E.G.

Pages 304-307. After Note, Burden of Proof, add:

In Patterson v. New York, 432 U.S. 197 (1977) the United States Supreme Court upheld the constitutionality of New York's second degree murder statute requiring that the defendant prove that he acted from "extreme emotional disturbance" for the purpose of reducing the offense from murder to first degree manslaughter. While the insanity defense was not at issue in Patterson, the Court relied heavily on Leland v. Oregon, 343 U.S. 790 (1952), thus reinforcing Leland's continued validity, which had been placed in question by In Re Winship, 397 U.S. 358 (1970) and Mullaney v. Wilbur, 421 U.S. 684 (1975). For an analysis of the interrelationship of these cases see Note, Due Process and the Insanity Defense: The Supreme Court's Retreat from *Winship* and *Mullaney,* 54 Ind. L.J. 95 (1978-1979).

The emergence of *Winship* and *Mullaney* and the Court's subsequent retreat from these cases have been extensively documented. See Eule, The Presumption of Sanity: Bursting the Bubble, 25 U.C.L.A.L. Rev. 637 (1978); Allen, The Restoration of In Re Winship: A Comment on Burdens of Persuasion in Criminal Cases After Patterson v. New York, 79 Mich. L. Rev. 30 (1977); and Underwood, The Thumb on the Scales of Justice: Burdens of Persuasion in Criminal Cases, 86 Yale L.J. 1299 (1977).

There has been a considerable amount of student writing on the topic. See, e.g., Note, The Constitutionality of Affirmative Defenses After Patterson v. New York, 78 Colum. L. Rev. 655 (1978); Note, Patterson v. New York, Criminal Procedure—The Burden of Proof and Affirmative Defenses, 9 U. Tol. L. Rev. 524 (1978); Note, Buzynski v. Oliver: Allocation of the Burden of Persuasion for the Insanity Defense, 63 Va. L. Rev. 147 (1977); Note, Due Process and the Insanity Defense: Examining Shifts in the Burden of Persuasion, 53 Notre Dame Law. 123 (1977); Comment, Mens Rea, Due Process and the Burden of Proving Sanity or Insanity, 5 Pepperdine L. Rev. 113 (1977); Note, The Insanity Defense in Criminal Trials—Burden of Proof, 10 Suffolk U.L. Rev. 1037 (1976); Note, The Burden of Proof for Affirmative Defenses in Homicide Cases, 12 Wake Forest L. Rev. 423 (1976); and Note, Constitutional Limitations on Allocating the Burden of Proof of Insanity to the Defendant in Murder Cases, 56 B.U.L. Rev. 499 (1976).

Earlier discussions, stressing Mullaney, include Note, The Burden of Proof and the Insanity Defense after Mullaney v. Wilbur, 28 Maine L. Rev. 435 (1976), and Note, Affirmative Defenses After Mullaney v. Wilbur: New York's Extreme Emotional Disturbance, 43 Brooklyn L. Rev. 171 (1976).

In 1978 the Indiana legislature revised its insanity defense statute to provide that the burden of proof on the issue of insanity is now on the defendant. See Ind. Code §35-41-4-1 (Supp. 1978). This is still a minority position.

In People v. Silver, 33 N.Y.2d 475, 354 N.Y.S.2d 915, 310 N.E.2d 520 (1974) the New York Court of Appeals, in a close 4 to 3 decision, with a vigorous dissent, held that the prosecution had failed, as a matter of law, to establish defendant's guilt where, in the face of ample psychiatric testimony offered on the defendant's behalf, the prosecution failed to offer expert testimony relating to defendant's sanity. See United States v. Smith, 437 F.2d 538 (6th Cir. 1970) and Annot., Proper Remedy or Disposition When It Is Held on Appeal From Federal Criminal Conviction that Government Failed to Produce Sufficient Evidence to Counter Prima Facie Defense of Insanity, 30 A.L.R. Fed. 317.

Pages 309-312. After Note: The Bifurcated Trial, add:

A bifurcated trial statute has been struck down in State ex rel. Boyd v. Green, 355 So. 2d 789 (Fla. 1978), where the court ruled that the exclusion of evidence of mental state during the "guilt" phase of the trial breached due process of law. In Hughes v. Mathews, 576 F.2d 1250 (7th Cir. 1978), the court was required to pass on a Wisconsin practice of not permitting psychiatric evidence in the "guilt" stage of a trial, limiting its use to the "insanity" stage. The Wisconsin Supreme Court had upheld this practice in Hughes v. State, 68 Wis. 2d 159, 227 N.W.2d 911 (1975); but the Seventh Circuit Court of Appeals ruled that the state, in establishing the guilt of the defendant, has the obligation of proving "all elements of the crime charged" and that the accused has the due process right of presenting relevant and competent evidence on that issue. The *Hughes* case is analyzed in Note, 1979 Wis. L. Rev. 628.

Page 312. After Note, Instruction on Commitment, add:

See Morris, Bozzetti, Rusk and Read, Whither Thou Goest? An Inquiry Into Jurors' Perceptions of the Consequences of a Successful Insanity Defense, 14 San Diego L. Rev. 1058 (1977), and State v. Hammonds, 290 N.C. 1, 224 S.E.2d 595 (1976), noted 13 Wake Forest L. Rev. 201 (1977) (jury may be instructed as to commitment procedures). In People v. Adams, 309 N.Y.S.2d 145, 26 N.Y.2d 129 (1970), *cert. denied,* 90 S. Ct. 2262, an instruction as to disposition was held improper.

Can a judge properly instruct the jury that they can recommend psychiatric treatment for the defendant if they find him guilty of second-degree murder? See United States v. Patrick, 494 F.2d 1150 (D.C. Cir. 1974).

Page 313. After Note: Can the Prosecutor Plead the Insanity Defense?, add:

The issue whether an insanity defense can be imposed on an unwilling defendant by the court, the prosecutor, or the defendant's own counsel, continues to bedevil the profession. A leading case permitting a trial judge to impose the defense, after holding a hearing on the issue, is Whalem v. United States, 346 F.2d (D.C. Cir.), *cert. denied,* 382 U.S. 862 (1965), reaffirmed in United States v. Robertson, 507 F.2d 1148 (D.C. Cir. 1974), discussed in Note, 53 Texas L. Rev. 1065 (1975). The Court changed its view somewhat in United States v. Robertson, 529 F.2d 879 (D.C. Cir. 1976). See also United States v. Wright, 511 F.2d 1311 (D.C. Cir. 1975), and consult Bruning, The Right of the Defendant to Refuse an Insanity Plea, 3 Bull. Am. Acad. Psychiat. & L. 238 (1975). Resnick, The Political Offender: Forensic Psychiatric Considerations, 6 Bull. Am. Acad. Psychiat. L. 388 (1978), urges that the choice of using an insanity defense or not should be left with the defendant in a political case.

For cases indicating that a trial judge should pay great deference to the unwillingness of a competent defendant to plead the insanity defense, see United States ex rel. Laudati v. Ternullo, 423 F. Supp. 1210 (S.D.N.Y. 1976), and Labor v. Gibson, 578 P.2d 1059 (Colo. 1978) (en banc), holding on the basis of Colorado Statutory provisions that the trial judge may not enter a plea of not guilty by reason of insanity over the objection of a competent defendant.

Even the District of Columbia Circuit Court has not been of one mind on the issue. See, e.g., Judge Bazelon's separate statement in Robertson urging a reconsideration of *Whalem*. United States v. Robertson, 507 F.2d 1148, 1161 (D.C. Cir. 1974), quoting Comment to Model Penal Code §4.03 (Tent. draft No. 4, 1955), argues that a judicial imposition of the insanity defense would be "too great an interference with the conduct of the defense." Judge Wilkey, dissenting in Robertson, suggested that the *Whalem* procedure might violate due process, the Sixth Amendment's requirement of effective assistance of counsel, and the entire adversary concept of a criminal trial. *Robertson,* at 1165.

What is the responsibility of defense counsel or of the prosecutor? Should the prosecution call to the attention of the court facts it may know about the possible non-responsibility of the defendant?

Pages 313-317. After Evans v. Kropp, add:

NOTE

See Ashley v. Texas, 319 F.2d 80 (5th Cir. 1963) (held, violation of due process where prosecutor did not inform defense counsel of information suggesting that defendant might not be competent to stand trial).

Page 317. Before Problem, add:

NOTE: THE DUTY OF THE LAWYER TO INQUIRE INTO THE FEASIBILITY OF AN INSANITY DEFENSE

The issue of the duty of a lawyer to pursue the possibility of raising an insanity or other mental illness defense in a case where preliminary facts seem to warrant it was sharply raised in People v. Corona, 145 Cal. Rptr. 894 (1978), which involved the widely publicized brutal killing of a large number of migrant workers. Defendant's lawyer, instead of asking for a fee, contracted with the defendant for exclusive rights to write about his life, especially the murder case. He later published a book entitled "Burden of Proof, The Case of Juan Corona."

There was extensive circumstantial evidence of defendant's guilt, including a "death ledger" in which the names of seven of the victims were written, substantial quantities of blood of various types in defendant's van, and several potential murder weapons. Although defense counsel in his opening statement promised to produce alibi witnesses, character witnesses, and expert witnesses, he produced none. Nor did he raise any mental illness defense. Defendant was convicted.

In reversing the conviction, the California Court of Appeals ruled that defendant had been denied effective assistance of counsel. The court carefully stated that it was not counsel's failure to raise an insanity defense that was the focus of concern, since such a decision might, in some cases, reflect carefully considered trial strategy. Rather, the problem lay in counsel's failure to provide himself with a rational basis for making such a decision. Further, there was a conflict of interest that might have precluded such a decision.

The facts concerning defendant's mental condition were strongly indicative of severe mental illness. Defendant had had a long history of schizophrenia and had been on substantial medication to keep his psychosis under control. Psychiatrists had recommended hospitalization. The crime itself was bizarre.

Corona's lawyer did not investigate these facts, and gave an entirely unpersuasive reason for failing to do so. He argued that to use an insanity type defense would have "prejudiced" the defense that the defendant had not committed the murders at all. But California's bifurcated procedure permits the issue of defendant's mental state to be resolved in a separate hearing, thus eliminating the possibility of prejudice to a defense based on not committing the act. The evidence that defendant had indeed killed the victims was overwhelming. Thus, said the Court, a failure to pursue a mental incapacity defense amounted to "a complete abandonment of the interest of the accused."

The court also pointed out that the lawyer's agreement with Corona to publish a book on his case created a conflict of interest in which the success of the book, which depended on there being a full, sensational trial crammed with gory facts concerning the murders, predominated over a successful insanity defense, which might have made such a trial unnecessary. The lawyer, in pursuit of a successful book, not only withdrew crucial mental incapacity defenses, but actually opposed a psychiatric examination of his client.

For similar cases, see United States ex rel. Lee v. Rose, 446 F. Supp. 1039 (N.D. Ill. 1978), and Wood v. Zahradnick, 578 F.2d 980 (4th Cir. 1978). In *Zahradnick* the Court affirmed the grant of habeas corpus on the basis of ineffective assistance of counsel, saying, "What Wood had done was so senseless that any lawyer should have sought available expert assistance." For a case dealing with a failure to investigate a possible intoxication defense see Commonwealth v. Bailey, 390 A.2d 1966 (Pa. 1978).

Not all claims of failure to raise an insanity defense are successful. In Wimberly v. Laird, 472 F.2d 923 (7th Cir. 1973), the appellant claimed that his conviction for premeditated murder should be reversed because his lawyer had been incompetent in not raising an insanity defense. The court held that the lawyer had in fact seriously investigated the insanity issue and had opted to claim that the petitioner was incapable of premeditated murder rather than that he was insane. Even though later psychiatric reports indicated that an insanity defense would have been meritorious, the court ruled that the lawyer's judgment had been reasonable and not incompetent.

Page 318. After Note: Feigning Insanity, add:

The case of Garrett Trapnell has been described in E. Asinof, The Fox is Crazy Too: The True Story of Garrett Trapnell, Adventurer, Skyjacker, Bank Robber, Con Man, Lover (1976). Another interesting feigning case is United States v. Makris, 398 F. Supp. 507 (D.C.S.D. Tex. 1975).

For a controversial study that asserts that most insanity acquittees play a game in order to avoid criminal responsibility, see S. Yochelson and S. Samenow, 1 The Criminal Personality 529-530 (1975).

Chapter Six

Disposition of the Mentally Ill Offender

Page 326. After Note at Top of Page, add:

The *Dixon* class patients have been followed up in T. Thornberry and J. Jacoby, The Criminally Insane: A Community Follow-up of Mentally Ill Offenders (1979).

Page 326. After Note: Impact Studies of *Baxstrom,* add:

The *Baxstrom* follow-up studies have been collected in H. Steadman and J. Cocozza, Careers of the Criminally Insane: Excessive Control of Deviance (1974).

Page 333. In Note, Competence to Plead, After First Paragraph, add:

The United States Supreme Court decision in Faretta v. California, 422 U.S. 806, 95 S. Ct. 2525, 45 L. Ed. 2d 562 (1975), providing that a competent defendant has a constitutional right to represent himself in a criminal prosecution, has reinvigorated the issue of the competence of a mentally ill defendant to do so. See, e.g., People v. Reason, 37 N.Y.2d 351, 334 N.E.2d 572 (1975), where the New York Court of Appeals, in a sharply divided decision, ruled that the standard for determining the defendant's capacity to waive counsel and act as his own attorney is the same as competence to stand trial. The defendant had been characterized (after conviction, but before sentencing) by two psychiatrists as competent to stand trial on the basis that he had had the capacity "to understand the proceedings against him" and "to assist in his own defense." The trial judge had ruled the defendant competent. The dissent argued that the two capacities are distinctly different and that no adequate finding had been made of defendant's capacity to try his own case. See also State v. Doss, 116 Ariz. 156, 568 P.2d 1054 (1977), in which the Court took the view that it was inconsistent for the trial judge to rule that the defendant was competent to make a statement to the police immediately after the homicide but incompetent to represent himself at trial.

Pages 337-349. After 3., A Psychiatrist Applies the Test, add:

See United States v. Pacelli, 521 F.2d 135 (2d Cir. 1975), for a scathing criticism of Dr. Abrahamsen's testimony concerning the capacity of a witness to testify.

Page 361. After 4., A "Scientific" Way to Measure Competence?, add:

[Brakel, Presumption, Bias, and Incompetency in the Criminal Process, 1974 Wis. L. Rev. 1105, 1124.]

I begin by taking an example from the "quality of relating to attorney" issue:

> A seventeen-year-old depressed black accused of assault and battery with a dangerous weapon is asked, "Do you have a lawyer?" and answers, "No, I have a public defender." When asked, "Do you have confidence in him?" he answered, "I don't know yet. I don't think he's very interested in my case." He received a score of 4, indicating mild incapacity and little question of adequacy on this item.

Why, however, even "mild incapacity"? Is it because of the distinction drawn by the defendant between lawyer and public defender? To me, this distinction indicates one of several possibilities, none of which have implications for competency. It may be that the defendant is not entirely clear on definitional distinctions between private lawyers and public defenders; or he may be somewhat in the dark about functional differences. Or, he may in fact be acutely aware of the distinction and by making it may be expressing a value judgment to the effect that public defenders are too much a part of the "system," not like "real" adversary private lawyers. If the response is a reflection of some lack of awareness of public versus private lawyer roles, it is a very common phenomenon, inconsequential generally and certainly neutral so far as competency is concerned. If the response is a deliberately made distinction without or even with political (politically "negative") implication, it is also common and also a reasonable insight with no negative inferences for competency.

Or is the "mild incapacity" score predicated on the mild lack of confidence expressed in response to the question specifically on this point (and perhaps implied in the earlier response)? What is wrong with some lack of confidence in the lawyer, whether public or private? Abstractly, such an attitude is perfectly reasonable and sensible. It may in this case be empirically warranted as well: the defendant may have *observed* that the lawyer wasn't very interested in his case. That perception on the part of the defendant may be an obstacle in the way the lawyer wants to play the criminal process game. It may even, because of conflict between the lawyer and his client, be detrimental to successful playing of the game. But it is not an indication that the defendant is lacking in ability to understand and/or play the game himself. It does not raise the question of his individual competency.

One can thus see here in the CAI a duplication of the problems affecting the CST. To go even further, one can see a difficulty in fact that I only posed as a possibility in the CST discussion. That is, it could be that the "mild incapacity" scoring is essentially based on the fact that the defendant was perceived as "depressed." First, one might react to this by wondering what is "abnormal" about being depressed when one is charged with assault and battery (and one is black), whether "guilty" or "innocent." Moreover, it should again be pointed out that the defendant's perceived depression is the kind of *external* indication that the tests are designed to avoid as irrelevant or too uncertain for consistent and objective interpretation. Finally, it might be worthwhile to point out that any and all of the indications presented by this example from the CAI are about as relevant to competency as the fact that the defendant is black. That fact too may raise the issue of competency as it is implicitly defined in portions of the tests. If it is believed that being black means having one or two strikes against one in the criminal justice game, then being black is equivalent to reduced competency. But is that the kind of competency the authors seek to test? Is that the kind of competency the law intends? Is that the kind of competency the law, the lawmakers or society can afford to focus on?

On the issue of "capacity to testify relevantly," the following clinical example merits examination:

> A forty-year-old, homeless male diagnosed as a simple schizophrenic breaks into a rural food store. He eats some of the food in the store and then goes to sleep. In the morning the proprietor finds him. He is arrested and charged with breaking and entering and larceny. On being interviewed there are long pauses before he can answer questions and they must be repeated gently. "I had no money . . . I was hungry . . . I was cold . . . I went to sleep." He was given a score of 2, indicating severe incapacity and a substantial question of adequacy on this item.

One wonders what assumptions are operative in this assessment. Is it that the accused is expected to play the adversary game to the hilt or else his competency is suspect? What are the rules? Judges and prosecutors must be perceived as on one side, defense counsel clearly on the other? They are each and all trustworthy and fair professionals? Maximum competency means maximum faith that in this battle of trusted professionals the truth will emerge, and society and the defendant will be vindicated, educated, edified, benefited, and so forth? Actually, there is virtually nothing in the defendant's responses that gives a clue to anything about competency. But the external (irrelevant) indicators are many. The defendant had already been classified as schizophrenic. There were long pauses in his responses. He fell asleep during the "crime." He was a homeless vagrant. These factors no doubt serve as supportive evidence of the defendant's game-perspective incompetency hinted at by the "test" responses. But what is gained in terms of neutrality or rationality by such a testing process?

A similar bias is indicated by the clinical example on the item "*self-defeating v. self-serving motivation* (legal sense)," which by its very wording comes close to explicating the bias.

> A chronic paranoid schizophrenic adult male with prior prison sentences sets a fire and turns himself in to the police. He states, "I can't make it on the outside. They won't admit me at the State Hospital. I've got to get away for a while. I'd like to get 2 or 3 years." He received a score of 4, indicating mild incapacity and little question of adequacy on this item.

But what kind of incapacity, what kind of question, what kind of competency? The startling realization is that on some items the respondent simply cannot win. An unwillingness to fight, a tacit admission of having committed the offense raises the issue of competency from the game-playing perspective. At the same time, however—as several examples in both the CST and CAI show[24] —a

---

24. On the CST, sentence item 6 makes the point explicitly. Completing "If the jury find me guilty, I . . ." with a "the only thing I can say is I'm not guilty" nets a zero, is equated with incompetency. On the CAI, the issue "capacity to disclose . . . available pertinent facts surrounding the offense . . ." has two telling "clinical examples" to the same effect:

> The alleged driver of a bank robbery getaway car is accused of armed robbery. In a high speed chase following the robbery an accident occurs and the defendant suffers a fractured skull and is unconscious for 12 hours. After emergency surgery for an epidural hematoma, the defendant complains of a retrograde amnesia from the time of the accident. He further asserts that he does not know his alleged confederate and states, "He must have made me drive at the point of a gun, but I don't remember." He was given a score of 2, indicating severely impaired functioning and a substantial question of adequacy on this item.

denial of having committed the crime is suspect from the psychiatric perspective of demonstrating the accused's inability to gain "insight" into his crime. If one admits the act, one is incompetently honest. If one denies the act, one is an incompetent recalcitrant, the question of honesty or dishonesty—truth or falsehood of the denial—not being considered.

NOTE

A study has been made of factors influencing four states (Tennessee, Ohio, North Carolina, and West Virginia) either to use or not to use the McGarry instrument. See Schreiber, Assessing Competency to Stand Trial: A Case Study of Technology Diffusion in Four States, 6 Bull. Am. Acad. Psychiat. & L. 439 (1978).

Pages 361-362. After 5., Amnesia, add:

See People v. Francabandera, 33 N.Y.2d 429, 310 N.E.2d 292 (1974); Fajeriak v. State, 520 P.2d 795 (Alaska, 1974); United States v. Sullivan, 406 F.2d 180 (2d Cir. 1969); and United States ex rel. Parson v. Anderson, 354 F. Supp. 1060 (D. Del. 1972).

Pages 362-363. After 6., Medicating the Defendant, add:

STATE v. HAYES

389 A.2d 1379 (N.H. 1978)

GRIMES, Justice.

The issues we decide in this murder case are whether a court may force a defendant to take medication during trial if he is competent to stand trial only when medicated [and] whether the defendant

---

A State police sergeant 10 years from retirement is involved in a harrowing ghetto riot. His patrol car is surrounded by a mob which overturns the car while he is in it. He is subsequently rescued unhurt. Two weeks later, while driving home after a period of duty, he has an abrupt amnestic episode. Several hours later he is arrested by fellow police officers in a suburban home with a stolen car outside the home and two neighbors hand-cuffed to a pipe. He claims an amnesia except for isolated flashbacks. "I remember a scene with two people hand-cuffed to a pipe. I don't remember how I got there. The rest is blank. I last remember being on the freeway with my car." He was diagnosed hysterical neurosis, dissociative type and given a score of 3, indicating moderate incapacity and a question of adequacy on this item.

Laboratory Report 111.

may waive his right not to be tried while incompetent by electing while competent to cease taking medication that would continue his competence. . . .

The defendant was indicted for the murder of Alan Eno on February 16, 1977. He pleaded not guilty by reason of insanity. This being a plea of confession and avoidance, the only issues to be tried are whether at the time of the offense the defendant had a mental disease and, if so, whether the crime was the product of that disease.

Before he committed the crime the defendant had been taking medication consisting of stelazine, artane, and valium, but he stopped taking them the day before the crime. After his arrest, he was put back on psychotropic medication, including lithium, stelazine, and valium.

The defendant moved that he be taken off medication seven days before his trial so that the jury could see him in his unmedicated state. The motion was granted in November 1977 over the State's objection. Thereafter the State moved for a rehearing, and an evidentiary hearing was held on January 5, 1978. The State presented evidence that at the time of the crime defendant was still under the influence of the medication. Expert evidence was also introduced that the medication the defendant had been taking since the crime increased his ability to organize his thoughts. The court reaffirmed its decision that the defendant be taken off medication and entered an order to that effect at the conclusion of the hearing. Trial was set for January 16.

On January 13, 1978, a hearing on the defendant's motion to suppress his confession was suspended to hear evidence regarding the defendant's competency to stand trial. The State offered expert testimony of a psychiatrist, the director of the forensic unit at the New Hampshire Hospital, that the defendant had deteriorated to a hypomanic state and experienced difficulty concentrating because he had discontinued his medication. The psychiatrist further testified that although the defendant could recall facts, communicate, and understand the judicial proceeding, the defendant was not as able to help his lawyer as he would be on medication, and that he would get worse if he did not start taking medication again. His opinion was that the defendant would be incompetent to stand trial on January 16. This was confirmed by another psychiatrist produced by the defendant. The defendant himself also testified. The Court concluded that the defendant was incompetent to stand trial, revoked the previous order, and transferred the following two questions:

May the Court force a defendant to be under drug medication at least four weeks prior to and during trial, against his will, where the evidence is uncontroverted that he is mentally competent to stand trial only while under the influence of said medication?

Does defendant validly waive his right to be tried while competent by electing, while medicated and competent, to be taken off drug medication before and during trial?

In *State v. Maryott,* 6 Wash. App. 96, 492 P.2d 239 (1971), the court held that compelling the defendant to take drugs at the time of his trial violated his fundamental rights. The court relied on a line of cases holding that it was impermissible to restrain a prisoner with shackles or bonds, absent a real danger of escape, because of the chance that the defendant's pain would "'take away any manner of reason.'" *Id.* at 99, 492 P.2d at 241. The court also concluded that if the State were to be allowed to drug a defendant against his will, the State could thereby control its own adversary and thus destroy the adversary process. The court in *Maryott* also feared that in cases involving the mental competency of the defendant the State's refusal to allow the defendant an opportunity to have the jury observe him in an undrugged state would deprive him of due process.

However, *Maryott* apparently was based on evidence that the drugs there involved "would affect the thought, expression, manner and content of the person using the drugs." *Id.* at 97, 492 P.2d at 240. Also, in *Maryott,* unlike in the case at bar, it does not appear that the defendant had been under the influence of drugs up until the day before the commission of the crime.

In the case before us there is no evidence that the drugs administered to the defendant affected the process or content of his thoughts. To the contrary, all the evidence indicates that the drugs used here allow the cognitive part of the defendant's brain, which has been altered by the mental disease, to come back into play. All the expert evidence supports the conclusion that the medication has a beneficial effect on the defendant's ability to function and that without the medication he is incompetent to stand trial. There is no evidence that the defendant's competence to stand trial can be maintained by less intrusive treatment techniques.

In *State v. Jojola,* 89 N.M. 489, 553 P.2d 1296 (1976), the court upheld the conviction of a defendant who had a long history of mental illness and who was kept under medication by thorazine during his trial. The expert testimony in that case was that "'Thorazine allows the mind to operate as it might were there not some organic or other type of illness affecting the mind.'" *Id.* at 492, 553 P.2d at 1299. The court held that the defendant was not denied due process when the jury viewed his demeanor while he was under medication, because he was given full opportunity to inform the jury about the medication's effect on him and also because the defendant's demeanor at trial in that case was not in issue.

We are of the opinion that the effect of the drugs on the defendant in the case before us is like the effect of drugs on the defendant in *Jojola* and unlike the effect in *Maryott,* and that the defendant has no absolute right to be tried free from the influence of the drugs administered to him in this case.

We are well aware of the dangers of allowing the State to administer drugs to a defendant against his will while he is on trial. However, we believe that the rights of defendants to be free from drugs that could control or alter their normal, disease-free thought processes will be adequately protected by the fact-finding ability of our trial courts and their sound exercise of discretion.

The defendant's demeanor in the instant case is relevant to the issue of his sanity at the time the crime was committed. He claims that he should be permitted to have the jury view him in his so-called natural state after he has ceased taking drugs for seven days. The evidence at the hearings before the trial court, however, indicated that the defendant had stopped taking his medication only the day before the crime. Expert testimony showed that he would have been under the influence of the medication at the time of the crime. The defendant would not be entitled to have the jury view him in a state as free from the effects of medication as he would be after seven days, unless there is evidence that he was in such a state at the time of the crime. The time at which the jury is to view the defendant, after he has stopped medication, is a matter for the trial court to determine on all the evidence.

Our answer to the first question is that the trial court may compel the defendant to be under medication at least four weeks prior to trial if the jury is instructed about the facts relating to the defendant's use of medication and if at some time during the trial, assuming the defendant so requests the jury views him without medication for as long as he is found to have been without it at the time of the crime. *See In re Pray,* 133 Vt. 253, 336 A.2d 174 (1975); *see generally* Winick, *Psychotropic Medication and Competence to Stand Trial,* 1977 Am. B. Foundation Research J. 769.

If the defendant by his own voluntary choice, made while competent, becomes incompetent to stand trial because he withdraws from the medication, he may be deemed to have waived his right to be tried while competent. *Illinois v. Allen,* 397 U.S. 337, 90 S. Ct. 1057, 25 L. Ed. 2d 353 (1970); *State v. Maryott,* 6 Wash. App. 96, 492 P.2d 239 (1971). Winick, *supra* at 797. The trial court should however carefully examine the defendant on the record, while competent, to establish the following: that the defendant understands that if he is taken off the psychotropic medication he may become legally incompetent to stand trial; that he understands that he has a constitutional right not to be tried while legally incompetent; that the defendant voluntarily gives up this right by requesting that he be taken off the psychotropic medication; and that he understands that the trial will continue whatever his condition may be. The answer to the second question is therefore in the affirmative.

———

The issue of medicating the criminal defendant so that he can be rendered competent to stand trial has been a controversial one, but the tide is now clearly running in favor of permitting medicated defendants to stand trial. The problem is well analyzed in Winick, Psychotropic Medication and Competence to Stand Trial, 1977 Am. Bar Found. Research J. 769. Recent significant cases are People v. Dalfonso, 24 Ill. App. 3d 748, 321 N.E.2d 379 (1st Dist. 1974), noted in 25 DePaul L. Rev. 217 (1975), holding a medicated defendant competent to stand trial; United States ex rel. Bornholdt v. Ternullo, 402 F. Supp. 374 (D.C.S.D. N.Y. 1975) (defendant fit for trial when under the influence of prolixin and artane); Govt. of Virgin Islands v. Crowe, 391 F. Supp. 987 (D. St. Croix, 1975) (fit for trial when medicated; approved); and State v. Stacy, 556 S.W.2d 552 (Tenn. Crim. App.), *cert. denied,* id. (Tenn. 1977).

In In re Pray, 133 Vt. 253, 336 A.2d 174 (1975), noted in 4 Am. J. Crim. L. 194 (1975-1976), a murder conviction was reversed because the defendant had been heavily sedated during the trial and was not his "true self."

Page 382. After 4., The *Jackson* Case, add:

In Flicker v. Florida, 352 So. 2d 165 (Fla. 1st Dist. Ct. App., 1977), a writ of prohibition which sought to prevent the prosecution of a criminal defendant earlier adjudicated incompetent to stand trial was denied. The petitioner, who had been held in jail for a total of more than fifteen months, invoked "speedy trial" grounds. The court ruled that as to the nine months during which defendant awaited trial, the adjudication of incompetency had not been removed. The court did express concern, however, about the additional six months of detention that followed the petitioner's return to jail following a hospital discharge based on the medical decision that the defendant appeared to be incompetent to stand trial.

Page 383. After 6., The *Jackson* Case, add:

The remarkable hegira of Donald Lang can be further traced in People v. Lang,—Ill.—, 391 N.E.2d 350 (1979), *aff'ing and rev'ing* People v. Lang, 62 Ill. App. 3d 688, 378 N.E.2d 1106 (1978). For a novelistic account of the *Lang* case, see E. Tidyman, Dummy (1974). A television movie based on "Dummy" has also been made. The public defender's office in Chicago asked Cook County Circuit Judge Joseph Schneider to stop the showing of the television movie on the basis that the showing would violate Lang's right to a fair trial. Judge Schneider refused. New York Times, November 24, 1978, p. A18.

Pages 384-385. After Note: Procedures, add:

In State v. Aumann, 265 N.W.2d 316 (Iowa 1978), the Iowa Supreme Court held that a statute putting the burden on a criminal defendant to prove his incompetence to stand trial does not violate due process under either the state or federal constitution. The result is criticized in Note, Should the Burden of Proving Incompetence Rest on the Incompetent?, 64 Iowa L. Rev. 984 (1979).

Pages 388-389. After 11., Selected Readings on Competence to Stand Trial, add:

An important contribution to the literature presented from a psychiatric perspective is Committee on Psychiatry and Law of the Group for the Advancement of Psychiatry, Misuse of Psychiatry in the Criminal Courts: Competency to Stand Trial (1974). New developments are traced in Slovenko, The Developing Law on Competency to Stand Trial, 5 J. Psychiat. & L. 165 (1977). See also R. Roesch and S. Golding, A Systems Analysis of Competency to Stand Trial Procedures: Implications for Forensic Services in

North Carolina (1977) and Roesch and Golding, Legal and Judicial Interpretation of Competency to Stand Trial Statutes and Procedures, 16 Criminol. 420 (1978).

Recent writings also include: Schiffer, Fitness to Stand Trial, 35 U. Toronto Fac. L. Rev. 1 (1977); and Janis, Incompetency Commitment: The Need for Procedural Safeguards and A Proposed Statutory Scheme, 23 Cath. U.L. Rev. 720 (1974). See also Steadman and Braff, Crimes of Violence and Incompetency Diversion, 66 J. Crim. L. & Criminol. 73 (1975), and Steadman and Braff, Effects of Incompetency Determinations on Subsequent Criminal Processing: Implications for Due Process, 23 Cath. U.L. Rev. 754 (1974).

A number of useful analyses of competency to stand trial law in the various states have been produced. See, e.g., Note, Competency to Stand Trial in Nebraska, 52 Neb. L. Rev. 69 (1972); Maxwell, Competency for Trial in North Dakota, 49 N. D. L. Rev. 799 (1973); and Note, Illinois Fitness for Trial: Processes, Paradoxes, Proposals, 6 Loy. U.L.J. (Chi.) 678 (1975). Florida's rules have been extensively discussed in Note, Florida's Incompetency to Stand Trial Rule: Justice in a Straitjacket, 27 U. Fla. L. Rev. 248 (1974) and in Note, Florida's Incompetency-To-Stand-Trial Rule: A Possible Life Sentence?, 4 Fla. State U.L. Rev. 523 (1976).

California's procedures have been evaluated in Parker, California's New Scheme for the Commitment of Individuals Found Incompetent to Stand Trial, 6 Pac. L.J. 484 (1975).

E. COMMITMENT FOLLOWING INSANITY ACQUITTAL.

Pages 393-396. After Note, add:

Is it necessary to hospitalize an insanity acquittee for the purpose of examining him in order to determine his committability? In People ex rel. Henig v. Commr. of Mental Hygiene, 43 N.Y.2d 334 (1977), the New York Court of Appeals ruled that it was not unconstitutional to automatically confine an NGRI for examination under a New York Statute that required it.

Outside of the District of Columbia, there is inadequate provision for the commitment of a federal defendant acquitted by reason of insanity. The federal NGRI is released with the expectation that state authorities will bring civil commitment proceedings, but there is no assurance of State action. See, e.g., United States v. Alvarez,

519 F.2d 1036 (3d Cir. 1975) and generally see Settle and Oppegard, The Pre-Trial Examination of Federal Defendants, reprinted in Oliver, Application of Psychiatry to Study, Observation, and Treatment of the Federal Offender, 35 F.R.D. 459, 475 (1964) (Appendix C).

In Kanteles v. Wheelock, 439 F. Supp 505 (D.N.H. 1977), the court ruled that both the equal protection and due process clauses were violated by the State's statutory procedure under which an untried criminal defendant could be committed upon a county grand jury's certification of insanity. See N.J. Rev. Stat. Ann. §651:8, which permits the grand jury to "omit" returning an indictment, substituting instead a certification of insanity, which triggers off a commitment proceeding.

The District of Columbia Circuit Court of Appeals has held that a retarded defendant found not guilty by reason of insanity may be indefinitely committed to a hospital for the mentally ill. See United States v. Jackson, 553 F.2d 109 (D.C. Cir. 1976), and United States v. Jackson, 553 F.2d 122 (D.C. Cir. 1977), containing a supplemental opinion.

Page 397. After 2., Selected Readings on Commitment and Release, add:

Three new additions to this literature are of particular value: D. Wexler, Criminal Commitments and Dangerous Mental Patients: Legal Issues of Confinement, Treatment, and Release (1976); German and Singer, Punishing the Not Guilty, Hospitalization of Persons Acquitted by Reasons of Insanity, 29 Rutgers L. Rev. 1011 (1976); and Burt, Of Mad Dogs and Scientists: The Perils of the "Criminal-Insane," 123 U. Pa. L. Rev. 258 (1974). See also Kaplan, the Mad and the Bad: An Inquiry Into the Disposition of the Criminally Insane, 2 J. Med. & Philos. 244 (1977) and Note, Equal Protection and Due Process for the Criminally Insane in Missouri, 43 U.M.K.C.L. Rev. 179 (1974).

The jurisdiction-oriented discussions are Note, Commitment of Persons Acquitted by Reason of Insanity: The Example of the District of Columbia, 74 Colum. L. Rev. 733 (1974), and Caulfield, Ohio Commitments of the Mentally Ill Offender, 4 Cap. U.L. Rev. 1 (1974).

The old master has written on the subject in Bazelon, Institutionalization, Deinstitutionalization and the Adversary Process, 75 Colum. L. Rev. 897 (1975).

F. THE CONDITIONS OF A CRIMINAL COMMITMENT

Page 399. After Note: Treatment for Mentally Ill Offenders, add:

An excellent discussion of the right to treatment of an NGRI is contained in German and Singer, Punishing the Not Guilty: Hospitalization of Persons Acquitted By Reason of Insanity, 29 Rutgers L. Rev. 1011, 1040-1053 (1976) and in D. Wexler, Criminal Commitments and Dangerous Mental Patients: Legal Issues of Confinement, Treatment, and Release 6-18 (1976). See also Magelby, Should the Criminally Insane Be Housed in Prisons?, 47 J. Crim. L. & Crimin. 677 (1957).

The more recent leading cases are Negron v. Preiser, 382 F. Supp. 535 (S.D.N.Y. 1974) (attacking substandard "jail wards" as seclusion cells at New York correctional hospitals and requiring that records be kept); Dunleavy v. Wilson, 397 F. Supp. 670 (D.C.S.D.N.Y. 1975) (transferred prisoners are statutorily guaranteed a right to treatment); and Scott v. Plante, 532 F.2d 939 (3d Cir. 1976) (complaints of conditions in New Jersey's maximum security institution (the Vroom Building) for the "criminally insane").

Pages 422-425. After United States ex rel. Schuster v. Herold, add:

NOTE: A FOLLOW-UP TO THE SCHUSTER CASE

On reading the *Schuster* case one might suppose that as a result of the court's remand, Schuster was thereafter released—not so. The aftermath of the *Schuster* case has been referred to by Chief Judge Kaufman as reminiscent of Solzhenitsyn's Gulag Archipelago. Although the Second Circuit Court ordered New York State to hold a sanity hearing within 60 days, the State refused for three years even to schedule a hearing, finally transferring Schuster summarily and without a hearing from Dannemora State Hospital for the Criminally Insane to Green Haven Correctional Facility, a prison. Schuster, then 70 years of age, refused to accept parole, claiming that he was entitled to unrestricted freedom. He brought a habeas corpus action. The Second Circuit Court of Appeals, invoking cruel and unusual punishment as a rationale, but not expressly holding on that basis, ordered an "absolute discharge." The fascinating post-*Schuster* tale is told in United States ex rel. Schuster v. Vincent, 524 F.2d 153 (2d Cir. 1975).

G. TRANSFERS: HOSPITAL-PRISON AND INTRAHOSPITAL

Pages 425-426. After Note: Transfers Between Prisons and Mental Hospitals, add:

The approach of the *Schuster* case has since been followed in Harmon v. McNutt, 587 P.2d 537 (Wash. 1978). In Mignone v. Vincent, 411 F. Supp. 1386 (S.D.N.Y. 1976), the court held that a brief emergency commitment from a prison to a correctional mental hospital without a hearing is acceptable, but that a 120-day delay requires explanation and justification.

The constitutionality of an involuntary transfer of an inmate from a prison to a mental hospital without benefit of a procedural due process hearing was presented in Miller v. Vitek, 437 F. Supp. 569 (D. Neb. 1977), where the federal district court held the Nebraska statute permitting such transfers unconstitutional. The district court judgment was, however, vacated by the U.S. Supreme Court in Vitek v. Jones, 436 U.S. 407 (1978) as moot, because the appellee had accepted a parole offered to him and had agreed to treatment at a veterans hospital. Justice Stevens dissented, arguing that the matter was not moot, because the appellee was still within the custody of the state. For example, if the appellee refused to take the medication prescribed for him, he could be transferred to another hospital, or possibly even returned to prison.

The courts have tended not to require judicial-type due process hearings in connection with transfers back to prison from mental hospitals. See, e.g., Cruz v. Ward, 558 F.2d 658 (2d Cir. 1977), analyzed in Note, 51 Temp. L.Q. 775 (1978), where the court held that a prisoner could be "dehospitalized" without the benefit of a judicial due process hearing. Said the court, the record did not support a showing that the existing procedures had resulted in any significant extent of erroneous deprivation of psychiatric care. Furthermore, the nature of the dehospitalization decision requires the exercise of administrative discretion.

H. RELEASING MENTALLY ILL OFFENDERS

Page 442. After Note, add:

The position of the New Jersey Psychiatric Association on the *Maik* case is stated in Perr, Problems Surrounding Release of Persons Found Not Guilty By Reason of Insanity, 20 J. For. Sci. 719 (1975).

STATE v. KROL

67 N.J. 432, 344 A.2d 289 (1975).

PASHMAN, J.

An acquittal on grounds of insanity, unlike a simple acquittal, does not automatically free the criminal defendant. The governing statute, N.J.S.A. 2A:163-3, provides that if the jury finds the defendant not guilty by reason of insanity, it must then make a special finding as to whether defendant's "insanity continues"; if it finds that defendant's "insanity" does "continue," defendant is ordered confined to the Trenton Psychiatric Hospital "until such time as he may be restored to reason." This confinement is for an indefinite period of time, and may prove permanent, for "restoration to reason" requires not merely remission of acute symptoms but complete cure of the underlying illness or personality disorder. *State v. Maik,* 60 N.J. 203, 217-18, 287 A.2d 715 (1972). A lesser degree of improvement suffices to obtain for defendant only a "conditional release" subject to summary revocation by the court. *State v. Carter,* 64 N.J. 382, 316 A.2d 449 (1974). Defendant challenges the constitutionality of this involuntary commitment procedure.

Stefan Krol stabbed his wife to death in their home. He was indicted for murder and tried in the Superior Court, Law Division in Camden County before a jury. Since he did not deny commission of the homicide, the only issue disputed at trial was whether he had been insane at the time of the act. Testimony of psychiatrists who had examined Krol before and after his wife's death indicated that he was suffering from an acute schizophrenic condition at the time of the killing, and acted under the influence of a powerful delusion that his wife was conspiring with his employer to murder him. The jury returned a verdict of not guilty by reason of insanity and found specially that defendant's insanity continued. Acting pursuant to N.J.S.A. 2A:163-3, the trial judge ordered defendant committed to the Forensic Psychiatric Unit at Trenton Psychiatric Hospital.

Defendant appealed the commitment order to the Appellate Division, which affirmed. We granted certification, 65 N.J. 561, 325 A.2d 695 (1974), to consider his contention that the standard for involuntary commitment of persons acquitted on grounds of insanity established by N.J.S.A. 2A:163-3 violates the due process and equal protection clauses of the fourteenth amendment to the federal constitution, a contention which we have not had occasion to consider in our prior decisions on this subject, *State v. Maik, supra,* and *State v. Carter, supra.*

I

Prior to considering the merits of this contention, we must first dispose of a procedural issue. On January 17, 1975, while the present matter was pending before this Court, the Camden County Court authorized the conditional release of defendant Krol, as permitted by our decision in *State v. Carter,* 64 N.J. 382, 316 A.2d 449 (1974). In granting the release, the court imposed a number of restrictive terms upon Krol: he must reside in a "Home for Sheltered Care" in close proximity to Ancora Psychiatric Hospital, continue psychiatric treatment as an outpatient, report regularly to a probation officer, and regularly inform the court of his condition; his freedom to travel is limited; and his release may be summarily revoked should he not comply with the terms of the conditional release order or should his condition change. Thus while the order released defendant from the physical custody of the State, it continues substantial restraints upon his liberty. Hence the principle, stated in *Stizza v. Essex County Juvenile & Domestic Relations Court,* 132 N.J.L. 406, 408, 40 A.2d 567 (E. & A. 1945), that commitment orders will not be reviewed after the person committed has been released and freed of all restraints upon his liberty and property does not govern this case. The present appeal is not rendered moot by the order for conditional release. Defendant still has a real and substantial interest in the validity of the original commitment order. *Cf. State v. Parmigiani,* 65 N.J. 154, 155, 320 A.2d 161 (1974); *Bower v. State,* 135 N.J.L. 564, 568-69, 53 A.2d 357 (Sup. Ct. 1947); *Sibron v. New York,* 392 U.S. 40, 50-59, 88 S. Ct. 1889, 20 L. Ed. 2d 917 (1968). Furthermore we have been informed by counsel that the defendant has not been able to obtain a satisfactory half-way house placement and has not in fact been released under the terms of this order, although he has been allowed a somewhat more limited conditional release under the terms of an order of the Camden County Court dated August 1, 1975.

II

Commitment following acquittal by reason of insanity is not intended to be punitive, for, although such a verdict implies a finding that defendant has committed the *actus reus,* it also constitutes a finding that he did so without a criminal state of mind. There is, in effect, no crime to punish. *State v. Carter, supra,* 64 N.J. at 401, 316 A.2d 449; *State v. Stern,* 40 N.J. Super. 291, 296, 123

A.2d 43 (App. Div. 1956). The rationale for involuntarily committing such persons pursuant to N.J.S.A. 2A:163-3 is, rather, to protect society against individuals who, through no culpable fault of their own, pose a threat to public safety. Chief Justice Weintraub succinctly explained the purpose of this procedure in his opinion in *State v. Maik, supra,* 60 N.J. at 213, 287 A.2d at 720:

> For present purposes it is enough to say that all the doctrines which would excuse an offender from criminal accountability because of insanity have the common characteristic of attempting to distinguish between the sick and the bad.
>
> The point to be stressed is that in drawing a line between the sick and the bad, there is no purpose to subject others to harm at the hands of the mentally ill. On the contrary, the aim of the law is to protect the innocent from injury by the sick as well as the bad.

The anomaly of the procedure established by N.J.S.A. 2A:163-3 is that although its ultimate object is to protect society against certain individuals who may pose special risk of danger, it does not at any point provide for inquiry by judge or jury into the question of whether the particular defendant involved in fact poses such a risk. The standard for commitment is simply that defendant's "insanity continues." The fact that defendant is presently suffering from some degree of mental illness and that at some point in the past mental illness caused him to commit a criminal act, while certainly sufficient to give probable cause to inquire into whether he is dangerous, does not, in and of itself, warrant the inference that he presently poses a significant threat of harm, either to himself or to others.

The consequence of this procedure is that a defendant who, despite the fact he still suffers some degree of mental illness, poses no significant danger to society, may nevertheless be deprived of his liberty for an indefinite period of time because dangerousness is, in effect, presumed from continuing insanity. The problem is most acute when the offense which defendant has committed is one which, although violating social norms, did not itself involve dangerous behavior. But even where, as in this case, the crime is a violent one, the procedure contains great potential for individual injustice.

This defect, which involves serious infringement upon personal liberty, is one of constitutional dimensions. Constitutional principles of due process require that any state action bear a reasonable relationship to some legitimate state purpose. In *Jackson v. Indiana,*

406 U.S. 715, 92 S. Ct. 1845, 32 L. Ed. 2d 435 (1972), the United States Supreme Court, applying this principle to involuntary commitment proceedings, held that the standard for commitment must bear a reasonable relationship to the ostensible purpose for which the individual is committed. That decision, which involved the commitment for incompetency to stand trial of a mentally deficient deaf-mute accused of armed robbery, did not restrict the purposes for which the state might involuntarily commit individuals accused of crime; it did require that the state tailor its standard for commitment to whatever purpose it was nominally attempting to advance. *Cf. Davy v. Sullivan,* 354 F. Supp. 1320, 1329-1330 (M.D. Ala. 1973) (holding that persons confined as sexual psychopaths must be released if their confinement is not within the nominal purposes of the statute—protection of the public and treatment). Furthermore, the state must make a meaningful factual determination as to whether defendant actually meets the standard for commitment. [Citations.]

The state may not simply presume essential adjudicatory facts. [Citations.]

Since N.J.S.A. 2A:163-3 is designed to protect the public against the risk of future dangerous behavior by persons acquitted by reason of insanity who are still suffering from mental illness, *State v. Maik, supra,* the principles of due process enunciated in *Jackson* and like cases require that the standard for commitment be cast in terms of continuing mental illness and dangerousness to self or others, not in terms of continuing insanity alone, and that some trier of fact make a meaningful determination as to whether defendant is actually within these standards.

III

This conclusion is also compelled by considerations of equal protection.

In *Baxstrom v. Herold,* 383 U.S. 107, 86 S. Ct. 760, 15 L. Ed. 2d 620 (1966), the Supreme Court held that prisoners who had allegedly developed mental illness while incarcerated and who were, as a result, being involuntarily committed to mental institutions, were entitled under the equal protection clause to substantially the same procedural protections as other persons subject to involuntary civil commitment. Among other things, *Baxstrom* held that the same standard for commitment to a particular mental institution had to be applied to prisoners and to other persons subject to involuntary civil commitment to that institution. Subsequently, in *Jackson v. Indiana,* 406 U.S. 715, 92 S. Ct. 1845, 32 L. Ed. 2d 435 (1972), the Court applied the principle of *Baxstrom* to persons determined to be incompetent to stand trial on criminal charges. It held that, except for a short observation period, a state cannot commit such a person unless it applies the same standards for commitment to him as it does to other persons involuntarily committed.

While neither of these cases deals specifically with the problem of involuntary commitment of persons acquitted by reason of insanity, the Supreme Court in these opinions has plainly attempted to enunciate a broad principle — that the fact that the person to be committed has previously engaged in criminal acts is not a constitutionally acceptable basis for imposing upon him a substantially different standard or procedure for involuntary commitment. The labels "criminal commitment" and "civil commitment" are of no constitutional significance. In *Jackson v. Indiana, supra,* 406 U.S. at 724-725, 92 S. Ct. 1845, the Supreme Court clearly indicated that it regarded this principle as one to be applied very broadly throughout the spectrum of various forms of involuntary commitment, including commitment of persons acquitted by reason of insanity.

The principles of *Baxstrom* and *Jackson* have been widely applied by the state courts and the lower federal courts to overturn procedures for involuntary commitment of persons acquitted by reason of insanity which deviate substantially from those applied to civil commitments generally. [Citations.]

In *Bolton v. Harris,* the U.S. Appeals Court struck down the District of Columbia automatic commitment statute, holding, among other things, that the standard for involuntary commitment of persons acquitted by reason of insanity must be substantially the same as that generally applied to persons civilly committed. *Id.* at 651 n.50. This holding has been followed in *People v. McQuillan, supra,* and *State ex rel. Kovach v. Schubert, supra. Cf. State ex rel. Walker v. Jenkins, supra.*

The standard for involuntary civil commitment in New Jersey is set out in N.J.S.A. 30:4-44: "If the patient shall be found not to be suffering from a mental illness, the court shall direct his discharge forthwith." "Mental illness" is defined in N.J.S.A. 30:4-23:

"Mental illness" shall mean disease to such an extent that a person so afflicted requires care and treatment for his own welfare, or the welfare of others, or of the community.

Prior to 1965, when the present statutes were enacted, New Jersey courts consistently held that a person could not be involuntarily committed unless, if permitted to remain at large, he would probably imperil his own safety or the safety or property of others. *In re Heukelekian,* 24 N.J. Super. 407, 409, 94 A.2d 501 (App. Div. 1953). *Accord, Aponic v. State,* 30 N.J. 441, 450, 153 A.2d 665 (1959); *DiGiovanni v. Pessel,* 104 N.J. Super. 550, 572, 250 A.2d 756 (App. Div. 1969), *mod. on other grounds* 55 N.J. 188, 260 A.2d 510 (1970); *In re J. W.,* 44 N.J. Super. 216, 226, 130 A.2d 64 (App. Div. 1957), *cert. den.* 24 N.J. 465, 132 A.2d 558 (1957); *In re R. R.,* 140 N.J. Eq. 371, 54 A.2d 814 (Ch. 947). Although N.J.S.A. 30:4-44 has not been construed since the 1965 amendments, N.J.S.A. 30:4-82, which incorporates the same definitions, was construed in *State v. Caralluzzo,* 49 N.J. 152, 156 n. 1, 228 A.2d 693 (1967), to continue to mean "dangerous to self or to society" and we understand that to be the proper construction of the civil commitment statute, N.J.S.A. 30:4-44. Hence, if equal protection requires the standard for involuntary commitment of persons acquitted by reason of insanity to be identical to that applicable to civil commitment proceedings generally, defendant may be committed only if he has been determined to be both mentally ill and dangerous to himself or to society.

Constitutional principles of equal protection, however, do not require that all persons be treated identically. They require only that any differences in treatment be justified by an appropriately strong state interest.

Under the so-called "two-tiered" analysis of the federal equal protection clause, the state need show only a rational basis for its classification, unless it involves "invidious" standards or infringes upon "fundamental" rights, in which case it must show a "compelling state interest." *San Antonio Independent School District v. Rodriguez,* 411 U.S. 1, 15, 93 S. Ct. 1278, 36 L. Ed. 2d 16 (1973). The Supreme Court, in deciding *Jackson v. Indiana* and *Baxstrom v. Herold,* has not clearly indicated whether differences in commitment procedure between those applicable to persons acquitted by reason of insanity and those applicable to other persons subject to civil commitment must be justified by a "compelling state interest" or whether some lesser interest will suffice. State courts considering the question have divided. *Compare State v. Kee, supra,* 510 S.W.2d at 481-82 (rational basis) *with People v. McQuillan, supra,* 221 N.W.2d at 579 n.4 (compelling state interest). It has even been suggested that *Jackson v. Indiana, supra* represents an abandonment of the "two-tiered" analysis. Nowak, "Realigning the Standards of Review Under the Equal Protection Guarantees—Prohibited, Neutral and Permissive Classifications," 62 Geo. L. Rev. 1071 (1974).

Fortunately, we need not leap into this bramble bush to decide the present case. The distinction between the standard for involuntary commitment for persons acquitted by reason of insanity and other persons lacks even a rational basis.

The State argues that persons acquitted by reason of insanity pose a special hazard to the public because they have been convicted of committing a criminal act and have proven by a preponderance of the evidence that the act resulted from mental illness, *State v. DiPaglia*, 64 N.J. 288, 315 A.2d 385 (1974), and that therefore they constitute an "exceptional class" of persons in whose confinement and treatment the State has a special interest. Accepting *arguendo* the factual assumption upon which this claim is predicated —that persons acquitted by reason of insanity pose a greater hazard to the public than other mentally ill persons—the argument does not support a claim that the State should not be required to establish that the particular defendant poses a danger to himself or society. The State does not claim that it would be more burdensome to determine whether persons such as defendant are dangerous than it is generally for persons subject to civil commitment. Its contention that, as a class, persons acquitted by reason of insanity are more likely to be dangerous than other persons, does not rationally establish that any particular individual in the class should be confined even if he is not dangerous. Cases which treat persons acquitted by reason of insanity as an "exceptional class" as urged by the State, *e.g., State v. Mills, supra; Chase v. Kearns, supra; State v. Kee, supra,* have not done so in response to a contention that persons acquitted by reason of insanity must be shown to be dangerous to be involuntarily committed but rather in response to a contention that it must be shown that such persons are mentally ill, a matter not in dispute in this case. Such cases hold that persons acquitted by reason of insanity may be committed without a fresh determination of mental illness because they have proven insanity at the time of the crime by a preponderance of the evidence and insanity is presumed to continue. Such arguments, whose soundness is doubtful at best, *see,* Note 74 Colum. L. Rev. 733, 746-750 (1974), are not pertinent to the contention that like other persons subject to involuntary commitment, persons acquitted by reasons of insanity may not be committed without a showing of dangerousness. *Johnson v. Robinson,* 509 F.2d 395, 399 n.18 (D.C. Cir. 1974) (dictum). The decisive consideration where personal liberty is involved is that each individual's fate must be adjudged on the facts of his own case, not on the general characteristics of a "class" to which he may be assigned.

IV

Having determined that the commitment provisions of N.J.S.A. 2A:163-3 (and N.J.S.A. 2A:163-2) are unconstitutional in that they authorize involuntary commitment without proof of dangerousness, the Court cannot simply stop short. Revision of the procedure for disposition of persons acquitted by reason of insanity is ultimately a matter for the Legislature. In the interim, the Court must itself formulate a constitutional and workable procedure. In doing so, we do not claim that the procedures which we adopt constitute either the only acceptable alternative or the best one. They are simply expedients to enable the machinery of justice to continue to function pending action by the Legislature.

Following acquittal by reason of insanity, the defendant may, at the request of the State, be confined in a suitable mental institution for a period of 60 days for observation and examination. Proof by defendant that his criminal conduct was the result of mental illness provides sufficient justification for holding him in custody for a reasonable period of time to determine if he in fact should be indefinitely committed. Such procedures for automatic temporary commitment, even though deviating from procedures applicable to civil commitment generally, have uniformly been upheld. *See, e.g., Bolton v. Harris,* 130 U.S. App. D.C. 1, 395 F.2d 642, 651 (D.C. Cir. 1969); *State v. Clemons,* 110 Ariz. 79, 84, 515 P.2d 324, 328 (Sup. Ct. 1973); *In re Franklin,* 7 Cal. 3d 126, 141-143, 101 Cal. Rptr. 553, 562-564, 496 P.2d 465, 474-476 (Sup. Ct. 1972); *People v. McQuillan,* 392 Mich. 511, 524-530, 221 N.W.2d 569, 575-577 (Sup. Ct. 1974). *See generally,* Hamann, "The Confinement and Release of Persons Acquitted by Reason of Insanity," 4 Harv. J. Leg. 55, 65-67 (1966); Annotation, "Validity of statutory provisions for commitment to mental institution of one acquitted on grounds of insanity without formal determination of mental condition at time of acquittal," 50 A.L.R.3d 144 (1973). While judicial decisions and scholarly commentators have differed on the most appropriate maximum to place on this period of temporary commitment, 60 days appears to be within the range of reasonableness.

Within this period, the State may move for indefinite commitment on the ground that defendant is mentally ill and, if permitted to remain at large in the general population without some restraints, is likely to pose a danger to himself or to society. If, following a hearing, the court finds that the State has shown by a preponderance of the evidence that defendant is mentally ill and is likely to pose such a danger, it should order suitable restraints placed upon defendant's liberty so as to protect the public and provide defendant with appropriate treatment. Such an order may take the form of confinement to an appropriate mental institution or other lesser restraints upon defendant's liberty—participation in a residential half-way house program, mandatory out-patient care, etc. The order should be molded so as to protect society's very strong interest in public safety but to do so in a fashion that reasonably minimizes infringements upon defendant's liberty and autonomy and gives him the best opportunity to receive appropriate care and treatment.

In establishing a standard for commitment based on dangerousness as well as mental illness, we are cognizant of the difficulties which inhere in such a standard, a problem which we discussed in some depth in our recent decision in *State v. Carter,* 64 N.J. 382, 404-405, 316 A.2d 449 (1974). Dangerousness is a concept which involves substantial elements of vagueness and ambiguity, *see e.g., Goldstein & Katz,* "Dangerousness and Mental Illness: Some Observations on the Decision to Release Persons Acquitted by Reason of Insanity," 70 Yale L.J. 224, 235-236 (1960), Rubin, "Prediction of Dangerousness in Mentally Ill Criminals," 27 Arch. Gen. Psychiat. 397, 398-399 (1972). The practical application of a dangerousness standard is further impeded by the difficulty of making valid and meaningful predictions of the likelihood of future harmful conduct, *see, e.g.,* Diamond, "The Psychiatric Prediction of Dangerousness," 23 U. Pa. L. Rev. 439 (1974); "Developments—Civil Commitment of the Mentally Ill," 87 Harv. L. Rev. 1190, 1240-1245 (1974); Rubin, *supra,* and by the subtle but strong pressures upon decision makers to overpredict dangerousness. *See, e.g.,* Diamond, *supra,* at 447; Rubin, *supra;* Dershowitz, "The Law of Dangerousness: Some Fictions about Predictions," 23 J. Legal Ed. 24 (1970). To a considerable extent, these are problems which can be dealt with only by trial judges on a case by case basis. An appellate court can only suggest guidelines for analysis.

The standard is "dangerous to self or society." Dangerous conduct is not identical with criminal conduct. Dangerous conduct involves not merely violation of social norms enforced by criminal sanctions, but significant physical or psychological injury to persons or substantial destruction of property. Persons are not to be indefinitely incarcerated because they present a risk of future conduct which is merely socially undesirable. Personal liberty and autonomy are of too great value to be sacrificed to protect society against the possibility of future behavior which some may find odd, disagreeable, or offensive, or even against the possibility of future non-dangerous acts which would be ground for criminal prosecution if actually committed. Unlike inanimate objects, people cannot be suppressed simply because they may become public nuisances. *State v. Carter, supra,* 64 N.J. at 405, 316 A.2d 449; *O'Connor v. Donaldson,* — U.S. —, —, 95 S. Ct. 2486, 45 L. Ed. 2d 396 (1975); *Cross v. Harris,* 135 U.S. App. D.C. 259, 418 F.2d 1095, 1102 (D.C. Cir. 1969); *Davy v. Sullivan,* 354 F. Supp. 1320, 1330 (M.D. Ala. 1973) (three-judge court). *Cf. Millard v. Harris,* 132 U.S. App. D.C. 146, 406 F.2d 964 (D.C. Cir. 1968).

Commitment requires that there be a substantial risk of dangerous conduct within the reasonably foreseeable future. Evaluation of the magnitude of the risk involves consideration both of the likelihood of dangerous conduct and the seriousness of the harm which may ensue if such conduct takes place. *Cross v. Harris, supra,* 1100-1101; "Developments—Civil Commitment of the Mentally Ill," 87 Harv. L. Rev. 1190, 1236-1240 (1974); Livermore, Malmquist & Meehl, "On the Justification for Civil Commitment," 115 U. Pa. L. Rev. 75, 81-83 (1968); *Goldstein & Katz, supra* at 235. It is not sufficient that the state establish a possibility that defendant might commit some dangerous acts at some time in the indefinite future. The risk of danger, a product of the likelihood of such conduct and the degree of harm which may ensue, must be substantial within the reasonably foreseeable future. On the other hand, certainty of prediction is not required and cannot reasonably be expected.

A defendant may be dangerous in only certain types of situations or in connection with relationships with certain individuals. An evaluation of dangerousness in such cases must take into account the likelihood that defendant will be exposed to such situations or come into contact with such individuals. *Cross v. Harris, supra* at 1101. *See State v. Johnson,* 8 Or. App. 263, 493 P.2d 1386 (Ct. App. 1972) (defendant potentially dangerous to her children but was unlikely to have access to them); *see generally,* Diamond, *supra* at 449.

Determination of dangerousness involves prediction of defendant's future conduct rather than mere characterization of his past conduct.

Nonetheless, defendant's past conduct is important evidence as to his probable future conduct. *Cf. In re Miller,* 73 Misc. 2d 690, 702, 342 N.Y.S.2d 315, 330 (N.Y. Cty. Ct. 1972). It is appropriate for the court to give substantial weight to the nature and seriousness of the crime committed by defendant and its relationship to his present mental condition.

It should be emphasized that while courts in determining dangerousness should take full advantage of expert testimony presented by the State and by defendant, the decision is not one that can be left wholly to the technical expertise of the psychiatrists and psychologists. The determination of dangerousness involves a delicate balancing of society's interest in protection from harmful conduct against the individual's interest in personal liberty and autonomy. This decision, while requiring the court to make use of the assistance which medical testimony may provide, is ultimately a legal one, not a medical one. *Humphrey v. Cady,* 405 U.S. 504, 509, 92 S. Ct. 1048, 31 L. Ed. 2d 394 (1972); *Dixon v. Jacobs,* 138 U.S. App. D.C. 319, 427 F.2d 589, 595 n.17 (D.C. Cir. 1970).

Once the court has determined that defendant is mentally ill and is dangerous to himself or others, it must formulate an appropriate order. As we noted in *State v. Carter, supra,* this is an exceedingly difficult task, one calling for a high degree of judicial flexibility and imagination. The object of the order is to impose that degree of restraint upon defendant necessary to reduce the risk of danger which he poses to an acceptable level. Doubts must be resolved in favor of protecting the public, but the court should not, by its order, infringe upon defendant's liberty or autonomy any more than appears reasonably necessary to accomplish this goal. Nonetheless, where the public cannot be adequately protected by any practical lesser restraint, the court is justified in ordering defendant institutionalized in an appropriate public psychiatric hospital. Court imposed restraints must, of course, always be coupled with a corresponding opportunity for care and treatment. *State v. Carter, supra,* 64 N.J. at 393-394, 316 A.2d 449; *In re D.D.,* 118 N.J. Super. 1, 6, 285 A.2d 283 (App. Div. 1966). *Cf. O'Connor v. Donaldson,* —U.S.—, 95 S. Ct. 2486, 45 L. Ed. 2d 396 (1975); *Wyatt v. Stickney,* 325 F. Supp. 781 (M.D. Ala. 1971), *aff'd sub nom. Wyatt v. Aderholt,* 503 F.2d 1305 (5th Cir. 1974).

In evaluating the possibility of imposing restraints less severe than complete institutionalization the considerations discussed in *State v. Carter, supra,* 64 N.J. at 403-404, 316 A.2d at 461 in connection with conditional release are pertinent and should be taken into account:

> The court's inquiry as to conditional release must be as broad as possible. Good patients may be bad risks. The disposition must be individualized with the focus on the offender, not the offense he committed, although such offense can serve as an indication of the harm the patient is capable of inflicting. Perhaps most important is the establishment of psychiatric out-patient care. The conditions under which the patient will live after release should certainly be conducive to his recovery, or at the very least, not aggravate his condition. His family life and friends, the area in which he lives and work that he could obtain, if it would be helpful, are all relevant. See generally, Weihofen, *supra*.

> The success of conditional release depends, to a large extent, upon the adequacy of the supervisory controls imposed by the courts to insure the public safety. The most obvious condition for safeguarding the community against a repetition of criminal behavior is a careful follow-up and required attendance for psychiatric treatment over a long period of time. Of course, the frequency of visits to the treating psychiatrist would depend upon the individualized circumstances of each case. But, in any event, the psychiatrist must continuously evaluate the patient's adjustment and be able to antic- ipate, and thus prevent psychotic episodes. Plainly, the patient must be a fit subject for out-patient treatment. Psychiatric treatment under the compul- sion of a court order without the willing cooperation of the patient would obviously be counter-productive.

Orders, either requiring institutionalization or imposing lesser restraints are subject to modification on grounds that defendant has become more or less dangerous than he was previously, or termina- tion, on the grounds that he is no longer mentally ill and dangerous, on the motion of either the State or the defendant. Where the court has probable cause to believe that a non-institutionalized defendant poses an imminent danger to himself or others, whether because the original restraints have proven inadequate, because defendant has not complied with the terms of the order, or because defendant's condition has changed, it may order defendant temporarily insti- tutionalized for further observation and evaluation pending pro- ceedings for modification of the prior order. Where defendant is temporarily institutionalized under such circumstances, a hearing on modification of the order should be conducted as promptly as is practical. Once, however, the commitment order is unconditionally terminated, the defendant must be treated thereafter like any other person for purposes of involuntary commitment. He may be com- mitted only by institution of appropriate civil commitment proceed- ings under N.J.S.A. 30:4-23 *et seq.*

We have chosen to separate determination as to whether defendant may be involuntarily committed from determination by the jury of guilt or innocence and placed the former question wholly in the hands of the trial judge, for decision after the trial, for two reasons. First, proofs pertinent to the likelihood of harmful conduct by defendant in the future are altogether different in substance and character from those pertinent to guilt or innocence or to defendant's insanity plea. Introduction of such proofs at trial creates a significant risk that the jury may be confused or may be distracted from proper consideration of guilt or innocence, the principal question before it. Second, requiring defendant to simultaneously argue to the jury both that he was insane at the time of the crime and that he is no longer mentally ill or dangerous places him in a difficult and unfair tactical position. He may reasonably fear that the jury will be very loath to reach a verdict of not guilty by reason of insanity if he successfully demonstrates that he is no longer dangerous and must be released upon such a verdict. This fear may well deter him from vigorously arguing present sanity and lack of dangerousness under such circumstances. *In re Franklin, supra,* 101 Cal. Rptr. at 558, 496 P.2d at 470; *cf.* Wiehofen, "Institutional Treatment of Persons Acquitted by Reason of Insanity," 38 Texas L. Rev. 849, 850 (1960). Separating the issues frees defendant from this potential unfairness. We re-emphase that this is merely an interim procedure adopted by the Court and is not to be understood as constitutionally compelled.

At the initial trial the jury should no longer be instructed to render a special verdict as to whether defendant's insanity continues. The trial judge should, however, instruct the jury as to the consequences of a verdict of not guilty by reason of insanity so that the jury does not act under the mistaken impression that defendant will necessarily be freed or be indefinitely committed to a mental institution.

V

In the interests of clarity, it is appropriate for us to attempt to delineate the relationship between our decision today and our prior decisions in *State v. Maik,* 60 N.J. 203, 287 A.2d 715 (1971), and *State v. Carter,* 64 N.J. 382, 316 A.2d 449 (1974). In *State v. Maik, supra,* the Court, speaking through Chief Justice Weintraub, definitively construed the commitment provisions of N.J.S.A. 2A:163-2 and 2A:163-3. *Id.,* 60 N.J. at 216-221, 287 A.2d 715. The constitutionality of these provisions was not challenged by the parties in that case and was not considered by the Court in its decision. We now conclude that the standards for commitment established in N.J.S.A. 2A:163-2 and N.J.S.A. 2A:163-3, as construed by the Court in *State v. Maik, supra,* are unconstitutional, and, to that extent, the decision in *State v. Maik* is overruled.

In *State v. Carter, supra,* the Court further elaborated the principles enunciated in *State v. Maik, supra,* and extended them to permit conditional release of persons committed under N.J.S.A. 2A:163-2 or N.J.S.A. 2A:163-3. The majority had no occasion in its opinion to consider possible challenges to the provisions of N.J.S.A. 2A:163-2 and N.J.S.A. 2A:163-3 on constitutional grounds. Since the decision in *State v. Carter* is predicated upon, and is an elaboration of, the construction of these commitment provisions set out in *State v. Maik,* the specific holdings in that case are superseded, but only to the extent inconsistent with this opinion, and particularly by our conclusion today that these provisions are unconstitutional.

VI

Defendant in the present case did not receive the type of hearing outlined above at the time of his commitment. No inquiry was made at that time into whether he was in fact dangerous to himself or others. He has since been granted a conditional release under *State v. Carter,* 64 N.J. 382, 316 A.2d 449 (1974). He is, nonetheless, entitled to a hearing within 60 days as to whether he is mentally ill and, whether, if permitted to remain at large in the general population without some restraints, he is likely to pose a danger to himself or to society.

VII

The final question to be decided is whether today's holding should be applied retroactively to other persons who are presently confined to State mental institutions following acquittal by reason of insanity. The decision to give such a holding retroactive or prospective effect is one that must depend upon a balancing of the interests of the State and the individuals affected.

Persons who have been involuntarily committed to mental institutions under an improper standard suffer continuing injury, which may extend indefinitely into the future. The effect of today's decision is not to cast doubt merely upon the adequacy of procedural safeguards surrounding the decision to commit, but upon the correctness of the very decision itself. Fairness demands that further confinement of a person presently committed be conditioned upon a showing by the State that he can in fact be committed under constitutionally proper standards. Since the number of persons involved is comparatively small, applying this holding retroactively poses little danger that the administration of justice will be impaired or excessively burdened.

We therefore conclude that today's holding should be applied retroactively to persons presently committed to State mental institutions (or conditionally released from such institutions pursuant to *State v. Carter, supra*) following acquittal by reason of insanity, and that, like the defendant, they are entitled to commitment hearings within 60 days.

Reversed and remanded.

NOTE: THE KROL CASE

The *Krol* case has been noted in 7 Seton Hall L. Rev. 412 (1976) and in 29 Rutgers L. Rev. 576 (1976). The New Jersey experience has been charted in Welaj, Commitment of the Criminally Insane: From *Maik* to *Krol*, 3 Crim. Just. Q. 197 (1975). An interesting study involving the representation of Krol patients is Singer, Insanity Acquittal in the Seventies: Observations and Empirical Analysis of One Jurisdiction, 2 M.D.L.R. 406 (1978).

In State v. Fields, 77 N.J. 282, 390 A.2d 574 (1978), the New Jersey court dealt further with release procedures for NGRIs, holding that NGRIs are entitled to automatic periodic review and the applicable standard of proof being a preponderance of the evidence. The latter holding is now cast into some doubt by the *Addington* decision.

Courts are now trending toward the requirement that commitment standards and procedures for NGRIs be roughly equivalent to those applied to purely civil patients. In addition to *Krol*, which is typical of the new approach, see, e.g., Powell v. Florida, 579 F.2d 324 (5th Cir. 1978) and Allan v. Radack, 426 F. Supp. 1052 (D.S.D. 1977). But see United States v. Ecker, 543 F.2d 178 (1976), *cert. denied*, 429 U.S. 1063 (1977), holding that the dangerousness demonstrated by a person's commission of a criminal act and subsequent acquittal by reason of insanity provides a rational basis for requiring judicial approval for the release of an NGRI where such approval is not required for a "civilly" committed person. See also United States

v. Brown, 478 F.2d 606 (D.C. Cir. 1973) and Alter v. Morris, 85 Wn. 2d 414, 536 P.2d 630 (1975) (two dissents).

An interesting case is Matter of Torsney, 47 N.Y.2d 667, 420 N.Y.S.2d 192 (1979), a New York *cause célèbre,* which involved the release, after a year of hospital confinement, of a white New York City policeman who had been acquitted by reason of insanity of the charge of unjustifiably shooting a black juvenile. Trial Judge Yoswein ordered Torsney's release from the hospital on condition that he not carry a gun, that he not be a police officer, and that he continue as an outpatient of the mental hospital for five years. This decision was unanimously reversed by the Appellate Division in Matter of Torsney, 412 N.Y.S.2d 914 (1979). A divided Court of Appeals reversed the Appellate Division and reinstated Judge Yoswein's order. All opinions are worth careful reading. Officer Torsney was subsequently dismissed from the New York City police force on the basis of his guilt of the charge of homicide, notwithstanding his acquittal in the criminal court.

For additional cases see People v. McQuillan, 392 Mich. 511 221 N.W.2d 569 (1974), discussed in Benedek and Farley, The *McQuillan* Decision: Civil Rights for the Mentally Ill Offender, 5 Bull. Am. Acad. Psychiat. & L. 438 (1977); Kovach v. Schubert, 64 Wis. 2d 612, 219 N.W.2d 341 (1975); and Reynolds v. Neill, 381 F. Supp. 1374 (N.D. Tex. 1974), *vacated and remanded sub nom.* Sheldon v. Reynolds, 422 U.S. 1050, 95 S. Ct. 2671 (1975) to the U.S. District Court (N. Tex.) for further consideration in light of O'Connor v. Donaldson. See further Reynolds v. Sheldon, 404 F. Supp. 1004 (N.D. Tex. 1975). Texas has since enacted new legislation, set forth in appendixes to this case. See reference at 1007. See also Note, 41 Mo. L. Rev. 439 (1976).

Pages 447-448. After Note: Predicting Dangerousness, add:

See Mueller and Iossi, The Placement of Long-Term "Criminally Insane" Patients in Open Settings, 26 Hosp. & Commun. Psychiat. 160 (1975) and Quinsey, Pruesse and Fernley, Oak Ridge Patients: Prerelease Characteristics and Postrelease Adjustment, 3 J. Psychiat. & L. 63 (1975).

Pages 456-459. After Note: Release of Persons . . ., add:

See generally, Note, Constitutional Standards for Release of the Civilly Committed and Not Guilty by Reason of Insanity: A Strict

Scrutiny Analysis, 20 Ariz. L. Rev. 233 (1978) and Note, Constitutional Ramifications of the Release From Confinement for Defendants Acquitted By Reason of Insanity, 40 Albany L. Rev. 391 (1976).

On revocation of conditional release, see United States ex rel. Shaban v. Essen, 386 F. Supp. 1042 (E.D.N.Y. 1974) (revocation of out-patient status of drug program person without notice and hearing held unconstitutional).

In Lublin v. Central Islip Psychiatric Center, 43 N.Y.2d 341 (1977), the New York Court of Appeals ruled that an NGRI petitioner who seeks release has to bear the burden of proof by a "fair preponderance of the credible evidence" that he is not dangerous.

In In Re Moye, 22 Cal. 3d 457, 584 P.2d 1097 (1978) the California Supreme Court ruled that an NGRI cannot constitutionally be confined in a hospital for longer than the maximum term for the offense charged. Since the legislature had placed such a limitation on confinement for sex offenders, differential treatment for NGRIs would violate equal protection.

Pages 469-471. After St. George v. State, add:

NOTE: NEGLIGENT RELEASE FROM HOSPITAL OF MENTALLY ILL OFFENDERS

An interesting case is Semler v. Psychiatric Institute of Washington, D.C., 538 F.2d 121 (4th Cir. Feb. 27, 1976), which concerned a convicted young man who had been placed on probation at a psychiatric institution. The psychiatric institution, after gradual relaxations in his in-patient status, all approved by the judge, ultimately "released" him without informing the judge. Subsequently he killed a young woman. The hospital was held liable for releasing their probationary patient without judicial approval.

The case is discussed in an excellent Note, Psychotherapists' Liability for the Release of Mentally Ill Offenders: A Proposed Expansion of the Theory of Strict Liability, 126 U. Pa. L. Rev. 204 (1977) and in Note, 2 U. Dayton L. Rev. 391 (1977).

In Grimm et al. v. Arizona Board of Pardons and Paroles, 564 P.2d 1227 (Ariz. 1977), where eight psychiatrists had characterized a convicted felon as an "extremely dangerous psychotic," the court held that it was gross negligence or recklessness for the Parole Board to parole such a person and ruled that parole board members were not immune from liability for negligence.

In Hicks v. United States, 511 F.2d 407 (D.C. Cir. 1975), hospital administrators failed adequately to inform the court of the dangerousness of an accused who had been sent to the hospital for an evaluation of his competence to stand trial. When the hospital reported to the judge that the accused was now fit for trial, he was released and later killed his wife, which he had threatened to do. The hospital was held liable for failing to give full information to the judge.

See Johnson v. United States, 409 F. Supp. 1283 (M.D. Fla. 1976), where it was held not negligence to release a psychotic patient who subsequently committed homicide, then suicide.

Pages 471-472. After 7., Other Approaches, add:

For a discussion of diversion from the criminal to the mental health system, see de Grazia, Diversion From the Criminal Process: The "Mental-Health" Experiment, 6 Conn. L. Rev. 432 (1974).

On punishment in prison after "cure" in mental hospital, see People v. Pygott, 64 Ill. App. 2d 284, 211 N.E.2d 382 (1965) and Ohio Rev. Code Ann. §2947.27 (Page Supp. 1964).

Page 472. After Note, add:

In Trivento v. Commissioner of Corrections, 135 Vt. 484, 380 A.2d 69 (1977), the Vermont Supreme Court ruled that a criminal convicted of manslaughter but not sentenced and committed instead to a state penal institution as a "psychopathic personality" is not entitled to "good time" credit to be applied against a prison sentence later imposed on him by the court after release from the treatment program on the basis that he was no longer a psychopathic personality. The Court not only ruled that the statute provided for "good time" only in the case of persons serving sentences, but also rejected an equal protection argument, holding that the purposes of "good time" are not appropriate for so-called mental health commitments, where the "punitive aspects of detention are, at least theoretically, de-emphasized. . . ." The court acknowledged that although the treatment given to the prisoner in fact was not "the ideal visualized by the legislature . . . our analysis remains unaffected."

Pages 472-474. After Note: The Briggs Law, add:

NOTE: PSYCHIATRIC CONSIDERATIONS IN SENTENCING

Generally see Dershowitz, The Role of Psychiatry in the Sentencing Process, 1 Intl. J.L. and Psychiat. 63 (1978) and Bohmer, Bad or Mad: The Psychiatrist in the Sentencing Process, 4 J. Psychiat. & L. 23 (1976). See also Campbell, Sentencing: The Use of Psychiatric Information and Presentence Reports, 60 Ky. L.J. 285 (1972).

For a discussion of the role of psychiatrists in death sentence cases see Dix, Participation by Mental Health Professionals in Capital Murder Sentencing, 1 Intl. J. L. & Psychiat. 283 (1978); Dix, The Death Penalty, "Dangerousness," Psychiatric Testimony, and Professional Ethics, 5 Am. J. Crim. L. 5 (1977); and Dix, Administration of the Texas Death Penalty Statutes: Constitutional Infirmities Related to the Prediction of Dangerousness, 55 Texas L. Rev. 1343 (1977).

NOTE: COMPETENCE TO BE EXECUTED

See Note, Insanity of the Condemned, 88 Yale L.J. 533 (1979) and Weihofen, A Question of Justice: Trial or Execution of an Insane Defendant, 37 A.B.A.J. 651 (1951). In Caritativo v. California, 357 U.S. 549 (1958) (*per curiam*), the United States Supreme Court upheld a California Supreme Court decision giving the prison warden exclusive responsibility for initiating a judicial inquiry into a prisoner's sanity. Three dissenters urged that a prisoner be permitted a better opportunity to present an insanity claim.

Chapter Seven

Indeterminate Confinement and Treatment Programs: Sex Offenders and Dangerous Offenders

Pages 489-493. After Sas v. Maryland, add:

NOTE: CHANGES IN THE PATUXENT PROGRAM

Legislation concerning the Patuxent Institution has recently been changed, following extensive criticism and examination. The major changes are the elimination of the indeterminate sentence and making Patuxent a treatment center for which inmates are permitted to volunteer for treatment, rather than being compelled. There was established a mandatory 25-year sentence for third-time violent offenders, non-parolable, except by Patuxent.

An excellent set of discussions is to be found in a symposium on Patuxent in 5 Bull. Am. Acad. Psychiat. & L. v-vii and 116-267 (1977). See Legins, The Patuxent Experiment, 5 Bull. Am. Acad. Psychiat. & L. 116 (1977); Shear, An Overview of the Contract Research Corporation Evaluation of Patuxent Institution, 5 id. at 134; Hoff, Patuxent and Discretion in the Criminal Justice System, 5 id. at 144; Singer and Bloom, A Cost-Effectiveness Analysis of Patuxent Institution, 5 id. at 161; Hoffman, Patuxent Institution From a Psychiatric Perspective, 5 id. at 171; Steadman, A New Look at Recidivism Among Patuxent Inmates, 5 id. at 200; Gordon, A Critique of the Evaluation of Patuxent Institution, with Particular Attention to the Issues of Dangerousness and Recidivism, 5 id. at 210; and Rappeport, The New Patuxent Legislation, 5 id. at 256.

See also Zenoff and Courtless, Autopsy of an Experiment: The Patuxent Experience, 5 J. Psychiat. & L. 531 (Winter 1977); Sidley,

The Evaluation of Prison Treatment and Preventive Detention Programs: Some Problems Faced by the Patuxent Institution, 2 Bull. Acad. Psychiat. & L. 73 (1974) and Rappeport, Patuxent Revisited, 3. Bull. Acad. Psychiat. & L. 10 (1975). For other discussions, consult Note, The Constitutionality of Statutes Permitting Increased Sentences for Habitual or Dangerous Criminals, 89 Harv. L. Rev. 356 (1975) and Carney, The Indeterminate Sentence at Patuxent, Crime and Delinquency, April, 1974. A new model for dealing with dangerous offenders is presented in Steele, A Model for the Imprisonment of Repetitively Violent Criminals (1974).

For the text of the new legislation see Article 31 B of the Annotated Code of Maryland (1977) (Cum. Supp.) The statute is also reprinted at 5 Bull. Am. Acad. L. & Psychiat. 260 (1977).

C. PROCEDURAL ISSUES

Pages 520-521. After Note, add:

See generally, Comment, Commitment of Sexual Psychopaths and the Requirements of Procedural Due Process, 44 Fordham L. Rev. 923 (1976). A leading Wisconsin case is State v. Torpy, 52 Wis. 2d 101,187 N.W.2d 858 (1971).

Standard of Proof. An important new question in view of the U.S. Supreme Court's ruling in Addington v. Texas is whether the constitutional standard of proof should be "clear and convincing." A pre-*Addington* discussion is Comment, Does Due Process Require Clear and Convincing Proof Before Life's Liberties are Lost?, 24 Emory L.J. 105 (1975). A leading case is People v. Burnick, 121 Cal. Rptr. 488 (1975), where the Court held that the government must establish beyond a reasonable doubt that the defendant is a "mentally disordered sex offender," defined as one who is (1) mentally disabled; (2) predisposed to commit sex crimes, to the extent that (3) he is a danger to others. The *Burnick* case is noted in 1975 Wash. U.L.Q. 1092.

Other leading cases include: United States ex rel. Stachulak v. Coughlin, 520 F.2d 931 (7th Cir. 1975), where the court held that a beyond reasonable doubt standard applied in dangerous sex offender cases. The *Stachulak* case is noted in Comment, Dangerousness, Reasonable Doubt, and Preconviction Psychopath Legislation, 1 S. Ill. U.L.J. 218 (1976). See also In Re Andrews, 368 Mass. 468, 334 N.E.2d 15 (1975), noted in 10 Suffolk U.L. Rev. 1247 (1976).

Page 533. After 5., Are Recidivist Statistics Valid?, add:

Patuxent statistics have been rigorously criticized in Wilkins, Treatment of Offenders: Patuxent Examined, 29 Rutgers L. Rev. 1102 (1976). Another version of this article is Wilkins, Putting "Treatment" on Trial, Hastings Center Report 4 (February, 1975).

Pages 534-535. After 6., Comments on Treatment, add:

People v. Feagley, 535 P.2d 373, 14 Cal. 3d 338, 121 Cal. Rptr. 509 (1975) has held that it is cruel and unusual punishment to hold sex offenders indefinitely in a sex offender treatment program if there is no treatment. The alternatives are prison or release. On adequacy of treatment see In Re Newton, 357 Mass. 346, 259 N.E.2d 190 (1970) (reversing the trial court's finding that the treatment received by the dangerous sex offender was inadequate and ruling that "more intensive treatment" would be of material benefit. Also see Irwin v. Wolff, 529 F.2d 1119 (8th Cir. 1976), holding an indeterminate confinement for a "sexual sociopath" not to be cruel and unusual punishment where the statute provides such a person should be committed to prison if not amenable to treatment.

The efficacy of treatment for sex offenders continues to be a highly controversial subject. See, e.g., H.L.P. Resnick and M. Wolfgang, Treatment of the Sex Offender (1972). A valuable bibliography of books and articles on the treatment of sex offenders is to be found at 13 Am. Crim. L. Rev. 110 (1975).

Pages 535-537. To Note, Disabilities Resulting From the Treatment Status, add:

A Texas court in Ex Parte Freeman, 486 S.W.2d 556, has ruled that "good time" may not be given for time the offender is confined in the hospital for "treatment."

Pages 557-561. After Note, The Special Review Board, add:

NOTE

For an empirical study setting forth the criteria actually used for purposes of determining the releasability of dangerous sex offenders see Dix, Determining the Continued Dangerousness of Psychologically Abnormal Sex Offenders, 3 J. Psychiat. & L. 327 (1975).

Pages 589-590. After Note: The Special Review Board, add:

NOTE: PAROLE REVOCATION

In State v. Dalonges, 128 N.J. Super. 140, 319 A.2d 257 (App. Div. 1974), the court ruled that the parole of a sex offender may not be revoked unless the offense charged is sex offense-related.

F. AN OVERVIEW AND SUGGESTIONS FOR IMPROVEMENT

Pages 596-597. To Selected Readings, add:

New general writings on sex offender programs include: Jacobs, Psychiatric Examinations in the Determination of Sexual Dangerousness in Massachusetts, 10 N.E.L. Rev. 85 (1974); The Right to Counsel and Notice in the Commitment of Sexually Dangerous Persons, 9 Suffolk U.L. Rev. 602 (1975); Hausman, Report on Sex Offenders: A Sociological, Psychiatric and Psychological Study (1972); Comment, Evolution of a Procedural Hybrid: The Sexual Sociopath Statute and Judicial Response, 13 Cal. W. L. Rev. 90 (1976-1977); and Note, California's Mentally Disordered Sex Offender Legislation: New Cases and Old Concepts, 1 Crim. Justice J. 103 (1976).

The entire concept of indeterminacy has been criticized in Dershowitz, Letting the Therapy Fit the Harm, 123 U. Pa. L. Rev. 297 (1974).

A classic study in the field is Sturup, Treating the "Untreatable": Chronic Criminals at Herstedvester (1968). Dr. Sturup has recently modified his earlier views. See Sturup, Indeterminacy as Individualization, 14 San Diego L. Rev. 1039 (1977).

Part 3
Civil Commitment

Chapter Eight

Introductory Materials

Pages 601-602. After 1., Readings on Civil Commitment, (1) General, add:

There continues to be an outpouring of books and articles dealing generally with the civil commitment process. Some are listed here; others are cited under specific subject matters.

The most comprehensive recent treatment of the civil commitment process is to be found in a series of articles, Legal Issues in State Mental Health Care: Proposals for Change, published in Volume 2 of the Mental Disability Law Reporter, Nos. 1-6. Another useful and detailed study (now somewhat dated) is the comprehensive student note, Developments in the Law: Civil Commitment of the Mentally Ill, 87 Harv. L. Rev. 1190 (1975).

A review of arguments for and against civil commitment, weighted against civil commitment, is K. Miller, Managing Madness: The Case Against Civil Commitment (1976). Two excellent historical studies are Dershowitz, The Origins of Preventive Confinement in Anglo-American Law—Part I: The English Experience, 43 U. Cin. L. Rev. 1 (1974), and Dershowitz, The Origins of Preventive Confinement in Anglo-American Law—Part II: The American Experience, 43 U. Cin. L. Rev. 781 (1974). See also Dershowitz, Preventive Confinement: A Suggested Framework for Constitutional Analysis, 51 Texas L. Rev. 1277 (1973), and Dershowitz, Indeterminate Confinement: Letting the Therapy Fit the Harm, 123 U. Pa. L. Rev. 297 (1974). Another useful historical treatment is R. Fox, the So Far Disordered in Mind: Insanity in California, 1870-1930 (1978).

A valuable study stressing international aspects of dealing with the mentally handicapped is Herr, Rights Into Action: Protecting Human Rights of the Mentally Handicapped, 26 Cath. U.L. Rev.

201 (1977). Another international study is W. Curran and T. Harding, The Law and Mental Health: Harmonizing Objectives (World Health Organization, 1977), described as a "comparative survey of existing legislation together with guidelines for its assessment and alternative approaches to its improvement." Some of the material drawn from the WHO study is presented in Curran, Comparative Analysis of Mental Health Legislation in Forty-three Countries: A Discussion of Historical Trends, 1 Intl. J.L. & Psychiat. 79 (1978).

See also Piperno, Indefinite Commitment in a Mental Hospital for the Criminally Insane: Two Models of Administration of Mental Health, 65 J. Crim. L. & Crimin. 520 (1974); Peszke, Involuntary Treatment of the Mentally Ill: Law's All or Nothing Approach, 46 Conn. B.J. 620 (1972); Arnhoff, Social Consequences of Policy Toward Mental Illness, 188 Science 1277 (June 27, 1975); and Note, A New Emancipation: Toward an End to Involuntary Civil Commitments, 48 Notre Dame Law, 1334 (1973). An account of what John Stuart Mill actually said is contained in Monahan, John Stuart Mill on the Liberty of the Mentally Ill: A Historical Note, 134 Am. J. Psychiat. 1428 (1977).

An interesting account of a Minnesota experience is D. Martindale and E. Martindale, Psychiatry and the Law: The Crusade Against Involuntary Hospitalization (1973). A useful set of materials is collected in Hearings on the Civil Rights of Institutionalized Persons, Subcomm. on the Constitution, Senate Comm. on the Judiciary, 95th Cong., 1st Sess. (June 17, 22, 23, 30, and July 1, 1977).

An important new report is A. McGarry, R. Schwitzgebel, P. Lipsitt and D. Lelos, Civil Commitment and Social Policy (1978), a careful study of the impact on the Massachusetts mental health system of the new Massachusetts Mental Health Act, which became effective on November 1, 1971.

A model commitment statute, attempting to balance the conflicting views of lawyers and psychiatrists, is offered in Roth, A Commitment Statute for Patients, Doctors, and Lawyers, 136 Am. J. Psychiat. 1121 (1979).

Page 602. After heading (2) By State, add:

Alabama: Segall, Civil Commitment in Alabama, 26 Ala. L. Rev. 215 (1973).

Arizona: Note, Protection Following Commitment: Enforcing the Rights of Persons Confined in Arizona Mental Health Facilities, 17 Ariz. L. Rev. 1090 (1975); Shuman, Hegland and Wexler, Arizona's Mental Health Services Act: An Overview and An Analysis of Proposed Amendments, 19 Ariz. L. Rev. 313 (1977).

Arkansas: Comment, Arkansas Involuntary Civil Commitment: In the Rear Guard of the Due Process Revolution, 32 Ark. L. Rev. 294 (1978).

California: Note, Civil Commitment of the Mentally Ill in California: The Lanterman-Petris-Short Act, 7 Loy. L.A.L. Rev. 93 (1974); Warren, Involuntary Commitment for Mental Disorder: The Application of California's Lanterman-Petris-Short Act, 11 L. & Society Rev. 629 (1977); Morris, Conservatorship for the "Gravely Disabled": California's Nondeclaration of Nonindependence, 15 San Diego L. Rev. 201 (1978), revised and updated in 1 Intl. J. L. & Psychiat. 395 (1978); Tieger and Kresser, Civil Commitment in California: A Defense Perspective on the Operation of the Lanterman-Petris-Short Act, 28 Hastings L.J. 1407 (1977); Note, The Lanterman-Petris-Short Act: A Review After Ten Years, 7 Golden Gate U.L. Rev. 733 (1977).

Colorado: Steingarten, Report from Colorado: The New Commitment Law, 4 J. Psychiat. and L. 105 (1976).

Connecticut: Mentally Ill in Connecticut—A Survey, 6 Conn. L. Rev. 303 (1973-1974).

Florida: Note, Involuntary Hospitalization of the Mentally Ill Under Florida's Baker Act: Procedural Due Process and the Role of the Attorney, 26 U. Fla. L. Rev. 508 (1974).

Hawaii: Comments and Questions About Mental Health Law in Hawaii, 13 Haw. B.J. 3 (1978).

Iowa: Due Process Deficiencies in Iowa's Civil Commitment Procedure, 64 Iowa L. Rev. 65 (1978).

Kentucky: Note, Civil Commitment of the Mentally Ill in Kentucky, 62 Ky. L. Rev. 769 (1973-1974).

Louisiana: Comment, The Louisiana Mental Health Law of 1977: An Analysis and a Critique, 52 Tulane L. Rev. 542 (1978).

Massachusetts: Joost and McGarry, Massachusetts Mental Health Code: Promise and Performance, 60 A.B.A.J. 95 (1974).

Michigan: Comment, Problems of Chapters 4, 5 and 8 of the New Michigan Mental Health Code, 1975 Detroit Coll. of L. Rev. 229.

Minnesota: Haydock and Orey, Involuntary Commitment in Minnesota, 28 Bench & Bar of Minn. 23 (1972); D. Martindale and E. Martindale, Psychiatry and the Law: The Crusade Against Involuntary Hospitalization (1973).

Missouri: Note, Legal Fiction, Misguided Paternalism, and Unfounded Prediction: Standards for Involuntary Civil Commitment in Missouri, 20 St. Louis U.L.J. 120 (1975); Note, Missouri's New

Mental Health Act: The Problem with Progress, 1979 Wash. U.L.Q. 209.

Montana: Troland, Involuntary Commitment of the Mentally Ill, 38 Mont. L. Rev. 307 (1977).

Nebraska: Comment, Civil Commitment: The Nebraska Substantive Standard, 7 Creighton L. Rev. 265 (1974); Peters, Teply, Wunsch and Zimmerman, Administrative Civil Commitment: The Ins and Outs of the Nebraska System, 9 Creighton L. Rev. 266 (1975); Peters, Teply, Wunsch and Zimmerman, Administrative Civil Commitment: The Nebraska Experience and Legislative Reform Under the Nebraska Mental Health Commitment Act of 1976, 10 Creighton L. Rev. 243 (1976); Hagel, Defending the Mentally Ill: A Discussion of Nebraska's Involuntary Commitment Proceedings, 57 Neb. L. Rev. 1 (1978); Committee on Mental Health, Nebraska State Bar Association, Mental Disability Law in Nebraska (1977).

North Carolina: Comment, North Carolina's New Mental Health Laws: More Due Process, 52 N.C.L. Rev. 589 (1974).

North Dakota: Lockney, Constitutional Problems with Civil Commitment of the Mentally Ill in North Dakota, 52 N.D.L. Rev. 83 (1975).

Ohio: Comment, Reforming the Mental Health Law of Ohio, 7 Akron L. Rev. 475 (1974).

Oregon: Kirkpatrick, Oregon's New Mental Commitment Statute: The Expanded Responsibilities of Courts and Counsel, 53 Or. L. Rev. 245 (1974).

Pennsylvania: Note, Civil Commitment of the Mentally Ill, 30 U. Pitt. L. Rev. 752 (1969). Note, The Gates of Cerberus: Involuntary Civil Commitment in Philadelphia, 49 Temp. L.Q. 323 (1976); Note, Pennsylvania's New Mental Health Procedures Act: Due Process of the Right to Treatment of the Mentally Ill, 81 Dick. L. Rev. 627 (1977). Note, Standard for Involuntary Civil Commitment in Pennsylvania, 38 U. Pitt. L. Rev. 535 (1977). Comment, Pennsylvania's Commitment: The Mental Health Procedures Act, 50 Temp. L.Q. 1035 (1977); Note, Pennsylvania's Mental Health Procedures Act, 15 Duquesne L. Rev. 669 (1977); Coppersmith, Deinstitutionalization in Pennsylvania, 50 State Govt. 227 (1977).

South Dakota: Note, Involuntary Civil Commitment in South Dakota: A Step Closer to Constitutional Legitimacy, 19 S.D.L. Rev. 447 (1974).

Texas: Comment, Civil Commitment in Texas—An Illusion of Due Process, 8 St. Mary's L.J. 486 (1976); G. Dix, Texas Mental Health Commitments (1978).

Washington: Comment, Striking a Balance Between Liberty and

Health: The Washington Mental Health Act, 11 Gonz. L. Rev. 720 (1976).

Wisconsin: Note, Due Process in Civil Commitment Proceedings: A Reality in Wisconsin, 3 Capital U.L. Rev. 743 (1974); Zander, Civil Commitment in Wisconsin: The Impact of Lessard v. Schmidt, 1976 Wis. L. Rev. 503.

Pages 605-607. After 2., The Functions and Objectives of Coercive Commitment, add:

NOTE: PARENS PATRIAE

The parens patriae function of the court in the civil commitment process is spelled out in State ex rel. Hawks v. Lazaro, 202 S.E.2d 109, 117-120 (W. Va. 1974). For general discussions see Development Note, 87 Harv. L. Rev. 1190 (1975); Curtis, The Checkered Career of Parens Patriae: The State as Parent or Tyrant?, 25 De Paul L. Rev. 895 (1976); Coleman and Solomon, Parens Patriae "Treatment": Legal Punishment in Disguise, 3 Hastings Con. L.Q. 345 (1976).

Page 646. Before Note: Stigma, add:

NOTE: SUBSEQUENT HISTORY OF LESSARD v. SCHMIDT AND NEW CASES

The United States Supreme Court remanded Lessard v. Schmidt, 414 U.S. 473, 38 L. Ed. 2d 661, 94 S. Ct. 713 (1974). The district court then re-decided Lessard v. Schmidt, 379 F. Supp. 1376 (E.D. Wis. 1974) (known as *Lessard II*), which was again set aside by the U.S. Supreme Court in Schmidt v. Lessard, on the basis of Huffman v. Pursue, 420 U.S. 592 (1975), discussed in 89 Harv. L. Rev. 151 (1975). It has since been reinstated in Lessard v. Schmidt (*Lessard III*), 413 F. Supp. 1318 (E.D. Wis. 1976), but it is now considered moot because of the adoption of a new civil commitment statute in Wisconsin.

For early discussions of the *Lessard* case see: Remington, Lessard v. Schmidt and Its Implications for Involuntary Civil Commitment in Wisconsin, 57 Marq. L. Rev. 65 (1973) and Note, Civil Commitment of the Mentally Ill: Lessard v. Schmidt, 23 De Paul L. Rev. 1276 (1974).

Following the decision in Lessard v. Schmidt, a number of state and federal courts were confronted with similar challenges. Some of these cases are set forth here: Bell v. Wayne County Gen. Hosp., 384 F. Supp. 1085 (E.D. Mich. 1974); Lynch v. Baxley, 386 F. Supp. 378 (M.D. Ala. 1974); In Re Fisher, 313 N.E.2d 851 (Ohio 1974); Hawks v. Lazaro, 202 S.E.2d 109 (W. Va. 1974); People v. Sansone, 18 Ill. App. 3d 315, 309 N.E.2d 733 (1974), discussed in Beis, Rights of the Mentally Disabled—The Conflicting Steps Taken in Illinois, 24 De Paul L. Rev. 545 (1975); Kendall v. True, 391 F. Supp. 413 (W.D. Ky. 1975); Lausche v. Commr., 225 N.W. 2d 366 (Minn. 1974); Doremus v. Farrell, 407 F. Supp. 509 (D. Neb. 1975); Coll v. Hyland, 411 F. Supp. 905 (D. N.J. 1976); Stamus v. Leonhardt, 414 F. Supp. 439 (S.D. Iowa, 1976); French v. Blackburn, 428 F. Supp. 1351 (M.D. N.C. 1977); Suzuki v. Quisenberry, 411 F. Supp. 1113 (D.C.D. Hawaii, 1976); Wessel v. Pryor, 461 F. Supp. 1144 (D. Ark. 1978); Colyar v. Third Judicial District Court for Salt Lake County,—F. Supp.—(D. Utah, 1979); Kyles v. Klein,—F. Supp.—(D. Idaho, 1978).

Page 646. After Note: Stigma, add:

See Segal, Attitudes Toward the Mentally Ill: A Review, 23 Social Work 211 (1978); Rabkin, Public Attitudes Toward Mental Illness: A Review of the Literature, 10 Schizophrenia Bull. 9 (1974); and Kreisman and Joy, Family Response to the Mental Illness of a Relative: A Review of the Literature, 10 Schizophrenia Bull. 34 (1974). Cited in the *Parham* case by Chief Justice Burger for the proposition that it is the "symptomatology of a mental or emotional illness" that is "truly" stigmatizing, is Schwartz, Myers and Astrachan, Psychiatric Labelling and the Rehabilitation of the Mental Patient, 32 Archives of Gen. Psychiat. 329 (1974), who conclude "that the stigma of mental hospitalization is not a major problem for the ex-patient." At 333. See also Phillips, Rejection of the Mentally Ill: The Influence of Behavior and Sex, 29 Am. Soc. Rev. 679, 686-687 (1964), also cited by Chief Justice Burger.

Chapter Nine

Standards for Commitment

Page 676. After first full paragraph, add:

The mental illness standard has been analyzed in Note, Standards of Mental Illness in the Insanity Defense and Police Power Commitments: A Proposal for a Uniform Standard, 60 Minn. L. Rev. 1289 (1976) (arguing that the definition of mental illness used in the insanity defense should apply to civil commitments). The equal protection clause has been invoked in Note, Mental Illness: A Suspect Classification?, 83 Yale L.J. 1237 (1974).

For a sophisticated discussion of mental illness in the context of civil commitment, see Morse, Crazy Behavior, Morals and Science: An Analysis of Mental Health Law, 51 S. Cal. L. Rev. 527, 542-560 (1978).

Pages 676-677. After 4., Disablement, add:

Wisconsin's statute defines a "gravely disabled" person as one who "evidences a very substantial risk of physical impairment or injury to the subject individual, as manifested by evidence that his or her judgment is so affected that he or she is unable to protect himself or herself in the community and that reasonable provision for his or her protection is not available in the community and the individual is not appropriate for placement under §55.06. (Wis. Stat. §51.20(1) (a) (3).)"

In In the Matter of Gary Seefeld, No. 454-225 (Wis. Cir. Ct. Milwaukee County, October 31, 1977) a Wisconsin Circuit Court affirmed a probate court ruling that this section is unconstitutional under the applicable *Lessard* case. A lower court had ruled the "gravely disabled" portion of the statute unconstitutional because it lacked an "overt act" requirement. The Appellate Court held that the statute was deficient because it did not require a finding of "dangerousness" beyond a reasonable doubt. The court also found the statute to be unconstitutionally vague. The court said although the statute did not require an "overt act," that requirement could be read in. As long as the judge commits on the basis of an overt act, the statute is constitutional.

For a fascinating study of the use of the "gravely disabled" standard in California, see Morris, Conservatorship for the "Gravely Disabled": California's Nondeclaration of Nonindependence, 15 San Diego L. Rev. 201 (1978), revised and updated as Morris, Conservatorship for the "Gravely Disabled": California's Nondeclaration of Nonindependence, 1 Intl. J.L. & Psychiat. 395 (1978). Professor Morris establishes that the public policy objectives of the California legislation have been subverted by the use of the conservatorship as a means of achieving involuntary commitment without the stringent procedural due process safeguards required for involuntary civil commitment generally. Further, the conservatee in California is in the anomalous position of being both voluntary and involuntary, competent and incompetent. More recently the California Supreme Court has tightened up conservatorship procedures in Heap v. Roulet, 23 Cal. 3d 219 152 Cal. Rptr, 425, 590 P.2d 1 (1979).

Page 678. Before 2., Dangerousness, add:

An intriguing study of how the standards of California's Lanterman-Petris-Short Act are applied in practice is Warren, Involuntary Commitment for Mental Disorder: The Application of California's Lanterman-Petris-Short Act, 11 L. & Socy. 629 (1977).

O'CONNOR v. DONALDSON

422 U.S. 563, 45 L. Ed. 2d 396, 95 S. Ct. 2488 (1975)

MR. JUSTICE STEWART delivered the opinion of the Court.

The respondent, Kenneth Donaldson, was civilly committed to confinement as a mental patient in the Florida State Hospital at Chattahoochee in January 1957. He was kept in custody there against his will for nearly 15 years. The petitioner, Dr. J. B. O'Connor, was the hospital's superintendent during most of this period. Throughout his confinement Donaldson repeatedly, but unsuccessfully, demanded his release, claiming that he was not mentally ill, and that, at any rate, the hospital was not providing treatment for his supposed illness. Finally, in February 1971, Donaldson brought this lawsuit under 42 U.S.C. §1983, in the United States District Court for the Northern District of Florida, alleging that O'Connor, and other members of the hospital staff named as defendants, had intentionally and maliciously deprived him of his constitutional right to liberty.[1] After a four-day trial, the jury returned a verdict assessing both compensatory and punitive damages against O'Connor and a codefendant. The Court of Appeals for the Fifth Circuit affirmed the judgment, 493 F.2d 507. We granted O'Connor's petition for certiorari, 419 U.S. 894, 95 S. Ct. 171, 42 L. Ed.2d 138 because of the important constitutional questions seemingly presented.

I

Donaldson's commitment was initiated by his father, who thought that his son was suffering from "delusions." After hearings before a county judge of Pinellas County, Fla., Donaldson was found to be suffering from "paranoid schizophrenia" and was committed for "care, maintenance, and treatment" pursuant to Florida statutory provisions that have since been repealed.[2] The state law was

1. Donaldson's original complaint was filed as a class action on behalf of himself and all of his fellow patients in an entire department of the Florida State Hospital at Chattahoochee. In addition to a damages claim, Donaldson's complaint also asked for habeas corpus relief ordering his release, as well as the release of all members of the class. Donaldson further sought declaratory and injunctive relief requiring the hospital to provide adequate psychiatric treatment.

After Donaldson's release and after the District Court dismissed the action as a class suit, Donaldson filed an amended complaint, repeating his claim for compensatory and punitive damages. Although the amended complaint retained the prayer for declaratory and injunctive relief, that request was eliminated from the case prior to trial. See 493 F.2d 507, 512-513.

2. The judicial commitment proceedings were pursuant to §394.22(11) of the State Public Health Code, which provided:

"Whenever any person who has been adjudged mentally incompetent requires confinement or restraint to prevent self-injury or violence to others, the said judge shall direct that such person be forthwith delivered to a superintendent of a Florida state hospital, for the mentally ill, after admission has been authorized under regulations approved by the board of commissioners of state institutions, for care, maintenance, and treatment, as provided in sections 394.09, 394.24, 394.25, 394.26 and 394.27, or make such other disposition of him as he may be permitted by law. . . ." Fla. Laws 1955-1958 Extra. Sess., c. 31403, §1, p. 62.

Donaldson had been adjudged "incompetent" several days earlier under §394.22(1), which provided for such a finding as to any person who was "incompetent by reason of mental illness, sickness, drunkenness, excessive use of drugs, insanity, or other mental or physical condition, so that he is incapable of caring for himself or managing his property, or is likely to dissipate or lose his property or become the victim of designing persons, or inflict harm on himself or others. . . ." Fla. Gen. Laws 1955, c. 29909, §3, p. 831.

less than clear in specifying the grounds necessary for commitment, and the record is scanty as to Donaldson's condition at the time of the judicial hearing. These matters are, however, irrelevant, for this case involves no challenge to the initial commitment, but is focused, instead, upon the nearly 15 years of confinement that followed.

The evidence at the trial showed that the hospital staff had the power to release a patient, not dangerous to himself or others, even if he remained mentally ill and had been lawfully committed.[3] Despite many requests, O'Connor refused to allow that power to be exercised in Donaldson's case. At the trial, O'Connor indicated that he had believed that Donaldson would have been unable to make a "successful adjustment outside the institution," but could not recall the basis for that conclusion. O'Connor retired as superintendent shortly before this suit was filed. A few months thereafter, and before the trial, Donaldson secured his release and a judicial restoration of competency, with the support of the hospital staff.

The testimony at the trial demonstrated, without contradiction,

---

It would appear that §394.22(11) (a) contemplated that involuntary commitment would be imposed only on those "incompetent" persons who "require[d] confinement or restraint to prevent self-injury or violence to others." But this is not certain, for §394.22(11) (c) provided that the judge could adjudicate the person a "harmless incompetent" and release him to a guardian upon a finding that he did "not require confinement or restraint to prevent self-injury or violence to others and that treatment in the Florida State Hospital is unnecessary or would be without benefit to such person. . . ." Fla. Gen. Laws 1955, c.29909, §3, p. 835 (emphasis added). In this regard, it is noteworthy that Donaldson's "Order for Delivery of Mentally Incompetent" to the Florida State Hospital provided that he required "confinement or restraint to prevent self-injury or violence to others, or to insure proper treatment." (Emphasis added.) At any rate, the Florida commitment statute provided no judicial procedure whereby one still incompetent could secure his release on the ground that he was no longer dangerous to himself or others.

Whether the Florida statute provided a "right to treatment" for involuntarily committed patients is also open to dispute. Under §394.22(11) (a), commitment "to prevent self-injury or violence to others" was "for care, maintenance, and treatment." Recently Florida has totally revamped its civil commitment law and now provides a statutory right to receive individual medical treatment. Fla. Stat. Ann. §394.459 (1973).

3. The sole *statutory* procedure for release required a judicial reinstatement of a patient's "mental competency." Public Health Code §§394.22(15) and (16), Fla. Gen. Laws 1955, c.29909, §3, pp. 838-841. But this procedure could be initiated by the hospital staff. Indeed, it was at the staff's initiative that Donaldson was finally restored to competency, and liberty, almost immediately after O'Connor retired from the superintendency.

In addition, witnesses testified that the hospital had always had its own procedure for releasing patients—for "trial visits," "home visits," "furloughs," or "out of state discharges" —even though the patients had not been judicially restored to competency. Those conditional releases often became permanent, and the hospital merely closed its books on the patient. O'Connor did not deny at trial that he had the power to release patients; he conceded that it was his "duty" as superintendent of the hospital "to determine whether that patient having once reached the hospital was in such condition as to request that he be considered for release from the hospital."

that Donaldson had posed no danger to others during his long confinement, or indeed at any point in his life. O'Connor himself conceded that he had no personal or secondhand knowledge that Donaldson had ever committed a dangerous act. There was no evidence that Donaldson had ever been suicidal or been thought likely to inflict injury upon himself. One of O'Connor's codefendants acknowledged that Donaldson could have earned his own living outside the hospital. He had done so for some 14 years before his commitment, and immediately upon his release he secured a responsible job in hotel administration.

Furthermore, Donaldson's frequent requests for release had been supported by responsible persons willing to provide him any care he might need on release. In 1963, for example, a representative of Helping Hands, Inc., a halfway house for mental patients, wrote O'Connor asking him to release Donaldson to its care. The request was accompanied by a supporting letter from the Minneapolis Clinic of Psychiatry and Neurology, which a codefendant conceded was a "good clinic." O'Connor rejected the offer, replying that Donaldson could be released only to his parents. That rule was apparently of O'Connor's own making. At the time, Donaldson was 55 years old, and, as O'Connor knew, Donaldson's parents were too elderly and infirm to take responsibility for him. Moreover, in his continuing correspondence with Donaldson's parents, O'Connor never informed them of the Helping Hands offer. In addition, on four separate occasions between 1964 and 1968, John Lembcke, a college classmate of Donaldson's and a longtime family friend, asked O'Connor to release Donaldson to his care. On each occasion O'Connor refused. The record shows that Lembcke was a serious and responsible person, who was willing and able to assume responsibility for Donaldson's welfare.

The evidence showed that Donaldson's confinement was a simple regime of enforced custodial care, not a program designed to alleviate or cure his supposed illness. Numerous witnesses, including one of O'Connor's codefendants, testified that Donaldson had received nothing but custodial care while at the hospital. O'Connor described Donaldson's treatment as "milieu therapy." But witnesses from the hospital staff conceded that, in the context of this case, "milieu therapy" was a euphemism for confinement in the "milieu" of a mental hospital.[4] For substantial periods, Donaldson was simply

4. There was some evidence that Donaldson, who is a Christian Scientist, on occasion refused to take medication. The trial judge instructed the jury not to award damages for any period of confinement during which Donaldson had declined treatment.

kept in a large room that housed 60 patients, many of whom were under criminal commitment. Donaldson's requests for ground privileges, occupational training, and an opportunity to discuss his case with O'Connor or other staff members were repeatedly denied.

At the trial, O'Connor's principal defense was that he had acted in good faith and was therefore immune from any liability for monetary damages. His position, in short, was that state law, which he had believed valid, had authorized indefinite custodial confinement of the "sick," even if they were not given treatment and their release could harm no one.[5]

The trial judge instructed the members of the jury that they should find that O'Connor had violated Donaldson's constitutional right to liberty if they found that he had

> confined [Donaldson] against his will, knowing that he was not mentally ill or dangerous or knowing that if mentally ill he was not receiving treatment for his alleged mental illness. . . .

> Now, the purpose of involuntary hospitalization is treatment and not mere custodial care or punishment if a patient is not a danger to himself or others. Without such treatment there is no justification from a constitutional standpoint for continued confinement unless you should also find that [Donaldson] was dangerous to either himself or others.[6]

5. At the close of Donaldson's case in chief, O'Connor moved for a directed verdict on the ground that state law at the time of Donaldson's confinement authorized institutionalization of the mentally ill even if they posed no danger to themselves or others. This motion was denied. At the close of all the evidence, O'Connor asked that the jury be instructed that "if defendants acted pursuant to a statute which was not declared unconstitutional at the time, they cannot be held accountable for such action." The District Court declined to give this requested instruction.

6. The District Court defined treatment as follows:

> You are instructed that a person who is involuntarily civilly committed to a mental hospital does have a constitutional right to receive such treatment *as will give him a realistic opportunity to be cured or to improve his mental condition.*" (Emphasis added.) O'Connor argues that this statement suggests that a mental patient has a right to treatment even if confined by reason of dangerousness to himself or others. But this is to take the above paragraph out of context, for it is bracketed by paragraphs making clear the trial judge's theory that treatment is constitutionally required only if mental illness alone, rather than danger to self or others, is the reason for confinement. If O'Connor had thought the instructions ambiguous on this point, he could have objected to them and requested a clarification. He did not do so. We accordingly have no occasion here to decide whether persons committed on grounds of dangerousness enjoy a "right to treatment."

In pertinent part, the instructions read as follows:

> The Plaintiff claims in brief that throughout the period of his hospitalization he was not mentally ill or dangerous to himself or others, and claims further that if he was mentally ill, or if Defendants believed he was mentally ill, Defendants withheld from him the treatment necessary to improve his mental condition.

The trial judge further instructed the jury that O'Connor was immune from damages if he

> reasonably believed in good faith that detention of [Donaldson] was proper for the length of time he was so confined. . . .

> However, mere good intentions which do not give rise to a reasonable belief that detention is lawfully required cannot justify [Donaldson's] confinement in the Florida State Hospital.

The jury returned a verdict for Donaldson against O'Connor and a codefendant, and awarded damages of $38,500, including $10,000 in punitive damages.[7]

The Court of Appeals affirmed the judgment of the District Court in a broad opinion dealing with "the far-reaching question whether the Fourteenth Amendment guarantees a right to treatment to persons involuntarily civilly committed to state mental hospitals," 493 F.2d, at 509. The appellate court held that when, as in Donaldson's case, the rationale for confinement is that the patient is in need of treatment, the Constitution requires that minimally adequate treatment in fact be provided. *Id.*, at 521. The court further expressed the view that, regardless of the grounds for involuntary civil commitment, a person confined against his will at a state mental institution has "a constitutional right to receive such individual treatment as will give him a reasonable opportunity to be cured or to improve his mental condition." *Id.*, at 520. Conversely, the

---

The Defendants claim, in brief, that Plaintiff's detention was legal and proper, or if his detention was not legal and proper, it was the result of mistake, without malicious intent. . . .

In order to prove his claim under the Civil Rights Act, the burden is upon the Plaintiff in this case to establish by a preponderance of the evidence in this case the following facts:

That the Defendants confined Plaintiff against his will, knowing that he was not mentally ill or dangerous or knowing that if mentally ill he was not receiving treatment for his alleged mental illness. . . .

[T]hat the Defendants' acts and conduct deprived the Plaintiff of his Federal Constitutional right not to be denied or deprived of his liberty without due process of law as that phrase is defined and explained in these instructions. . . .

You are instructed that a person who is involuntarily civilly committed to a mental hospital does have a constitutional right to receive such treatment as will give him a realistic opportunity to be cured or to improve his mental condition.

Now, the purpose of involuntary hospitalization is treatment and not mere custodial care or punishment if a patient is not a danger to himself or others. Without such treatment there is no justification from a constitutional stand-point for continued confinement unless you should also find that the Plaintiff was dangerous either to himself or others.

7. The trial judge had instructed that punitive damages should be awarded only if "the act or omission of the Defendant or Defendants which proximately caused injury to the Plaintiff was maliciously or wantonly or oppressively done."

court's opinion implied that it is constitutionally permissible for a State to confine a mentally ill person against his will in order to treat his illness, regardless of whether his illness renders him dangerous to himself or others. See *id.,* at 522-527.

II

We have concluded that the difficult issues of constitutional law dealt with by the Court of Appeals are not presented by this case in its present posture. Specifically, there is no reason now to decide whether mentally ill persons dangerous to themselves or to others have a right to treatment upon compulsory confinement by the State, or whether the State may compulsorily confine a non-dangerous, mentally ill individual for the purpose of treatment. As we view it, this case raises a single, relatively simple, but nonetheless important question concerning every man's constitutional right to liberty.

The jury found that Donaldson was neither dangerous to himself nor dangerous to others, and also found that, if mentally ill, Donaldson had not received treatment.[8] That verdict, based on abundant evidence, makes the issue before the Court a narrow one. We need not decide whether, when, or by what procedures, a mentally ill person may be confined by the State on any of the grounds which, under contemporary statutes, are generally advanced to justify involuntary confinement of such a person—to prevent injury to the public, to ensure his own survival or safety,[9] or to alleviate or cure his illness. See Jackson v. Indiana, 406 U.S. 715, 736-737, 92 S. Ct. 1845, 1857-1858, 32 L. Ed. 2d 435; Humphrey v. Cady, 405 U.S.

8. Given the jury instructions, see n.6 *supra,* it is possible that the jury went so far as to find that O'Connor knew not only that Donaldson was harmless to himself and others but also that he was not mentally ill at all. If it so found, the jury was permitted by the instructions to rule against O'Connor regardless of the nature of the "treatment" provided. If we were to construe the jury's verdict in that fashion, there would remain no substantial issue in this case: That a wholly sane and innocent person has a constitutional right not to be physically confined by the State when his freedom will pose a danger neither to himself nor to others cannot be seriously doubted.

9. The judge's instructions used the phrase "dangerous to himself." Of course, even if there is no foreseeable risk of self-injury or suicide, a person is literally "dangerous to himself" if for physical or other reasons he is helpless to avoid the hazards of freedom either through his own efforts or with the aid of willing family members or friends. While it might be argued that the judge's instructions could have been more detailed on this point, O'Connor raised no objection to them, presumably because the evidence clearly showed that Donaldson was not "dangerous to himself" however broadly that phrase might be defined.

504, 509, 92 S. Ct. 1048, 1052, 31 L. Ed. 2d 394. For the jury found that none of the above grounds for continued confinement was present in Donaldson's case.[10]

Given the jury's findings, what was left as justification for keeping Donaldson in continued confinement? The fact that state law may have authorized confinement of the harmless mentally ill does not itself establish a constitutionally adequate purpose for the confinement. See Jackson v. Indiana, *supra,* 406 U.S., at 720-723, 92 S. Ct., at 1849-1851; McNeil v. Director, Patuxent Institution, 407 U.S. 245, 248-250, 92 S. Ct. 2083, 2086-2087, 32 L. Ed. 2d 719. Nor is it enough that Donaldson's original confinement was founded upon a constitutionally adequate basis, if in fact it was, because even if his involuntary confinement was initially permissible, it could not constitutionally continue after that basis no longer existed. Jackson v. Indiana, *supra,* 406 U.S., at 738, 92 S. Ct., at 1858; McNeil v. Director, Patuxent Institution, *supra.*

A finding of "mental illness" alone cannot justify a State's locking a person up against his will and keeping him indefinitely in simple custodial confinement. Assuming that that term can be given a reasonably precise content and that the "mentally ill" can be identified with reasonable accuracy, there is still no constitutional basis for confining such persons involuntarily if they are dangerous to no one and can live safely in freedom.

May the State confine the mentally ill merely to ensure them a living standard superior to that they enjoy in the private community? That the State has a proper interest in providing care and assistance to the unfortunate goes without saying. But the mere presence of mental illness does not disqualify a person from preferring his home to the comforts of an institution. Moreover, while the State may arguably confine a person to save him from harm, incarceration is rarely if ever a necessary condition for raising the living standards

10. O'Connor argues that, despite the jury's verdict, the Court must assume that Donaldson was receiving treatment sufficient to justify his confinement, because the adequacy of treatment is a "nonjusticiable" question that must be left to the discretion of the psychiatric profession. That argument is unpersuasive. Where "treatment" is the sole asserted ground for depriving a person of liberty, it is plainly unacceptable to suggest that the courts are powerless to determine whether the asserted ground is present. See Jackson v. Indiana, 406 U.S. 715, 92 S. Ct. 1845, 32 L. Ed. 2d 435. Neither party objected to the jury instruction defining treatment. There is, accordingly, no occasion in this case to decide whether the provision of treatment, standing alone, can ever constitutionally justify involuntary confinement or, if it can, how much or what kind of treatment would suffice for that purpose. In its present posture this case involves not involuntary treatment but simply involuntary custodial confinement.

of those capable of surviving safely in freedom, on their own or with the help of family or friends. See Shelton v. Tucker, 364 U.S. 479, 488-490, 81 S. Ct. 247, 252-253, 5 L. Ed. 2d 231.

May the State fence in the harmless mentally ill solely to save its citizens from exposure to those whose ways are different? One might as well ask if the State, to avoid public unease, could incarcerate all who are physically unattractive or socially eccentric. Mere public intolerance or animosity cannot constitutionally justify the deprivation of a person's physical liberty. See, *e.g.*, Cohen v. California, 403 U.S. 15, 24-26, 91 S. Ct. 1780, 1787-1789, 29 L. Ed. 2d 284; Coates v. City of Cincinnati, 402 U.S. 611, 615, 91 S. Ct. 1686, 1689, 29 L. Ed. 2d 214; Street v. New York, 394 U.S. 576, 592, 89 S. Ct. 1354, 1365-1366, 22 L. Ed. 2d 572; cf. U.S. Dept. of Agriculture v. Moreno, 413 U.S. 528, 534, 93 S. Ct. 2821, 2825-2826, 37 L. Ed. 2d 782.

In short, a State cannot constitutionally confine without more a nondangerous individual who is capable of surviving safely in freedom by himself or with the help of willing and responsible family members or friends. Since the jury found, upon ample evidence, that O'Connor, as an agent of the State, knowingly did so confine Donaldson, it properly concluded that O'Connor violated Donaldson's constitutional right to freedom.

III

O'Connor contends that in any event he should not be held personally liable for monetary damages because his decisions were made in "good faith." Specifically, O'Connor argues that he was acting pursuant to state law which, he believed, authorized confinement of the mentally ill even when their release would not compromise their safety or constitute a danger to others, and that he could not reasonably have been expected to know that the state law as he understood it was constitutionally invalid. A proposed instruction to this effect was rejected by the District Court.

The District Court did instruct the jury, without objection, that monetary damages could not be assessed against O'Connor if he had believed reasonably and in good faith that Donaldson's continued confinement was "proper," and that punitive damages could be awarded only if O'Connor had acted "maliciously or wantonly or oppressively." The Court of Appeals approved those instructions. But that court did not consider whether it was error for the trial judge to refuse the additional instruction concerning O'Connor's claimed reliance on state law as authorization for Donaldson's continued confinement. Further, neither the District Court nor the Court of Appeals acted with the benefit of this Court's most recent decision on the scope of the qualified immunity possessed by state officials under 42 U.S.C. §1983. Wood v. Strickland, 420 U.S. 308, 95 S. Ct. 992, 43 L. Ed. 2d 214.

Under that decision, the relevant question for the jury is whether O'Connor "knew or reasonably should have known that the action he took within his sphere of official responsibility would violate the constitutional rights of [Donaldson], or if he took the action with the malicious intention to cause a deprivation of constitutional rights or other injury to [Donaldson]." *Id.,* at 322, 95 S. Ct. at 1001. See also Scheuer v. Rhodes, 416 U.S. 232, 247-248, 94 S. Ct. 1683, 1692, 40 L. Ed. 2d 90; Wood v. Strickland, *supra,* 420 U.S., at 330, 95 S. Ct., at 1005 (opinion of Powell, J.). For purposes of this question, an official has, of course, no duty to anticipate unforeseeable constitutional developments. Wood v. Strickland, *supra,* at 322, 95 S. Ct., at 1004.

Accordingly, we vacate the judgment of the Court of Appeals and remand the case to enable that court to consider, in light of Wood v. Strickland, whether the District Judge's failure to instruct with regard to the effect of O'Connor's claimed reliance on state law rendered inadequate the instructions as to O'Connor's liability for compensatory and punitive damages.

Vacated and remanded.

[For the Concurring Opinion of Chief Justice Burger, dealing with the right to treatment issue, see p. 187.]

NOTE: THE DONALDSON CASE

The *Donaldson* case has generated a great amount of legal literature, much of it dealing with the "standards" issue, some of it dealing with its right to treatment aspect. A highly useful discussion of Donaldson from the psychiatric perspective is Kopolow, A Review of Major Implications of the O'Connor v. Donaldson Decision, 133 Am. J. Psychiat. 379 (1976). See also Grant, *Donaldson,* Dangerousness, and The Right to Treatment, 3 Hastings Con. L.Q. 599 (1976). Student notes include: 89 Harv. L. Rev. 70 (1975); 7 N.C. Cent. L.J. 174 (1975); 9 Akron L. Rev. 374 (1975); 51 Wash. L. Rev. 764 (1976); 43 Tenn. L. Rev. 366 (1976); 47 Colo. L. Rev. 299 (1976); 10 U. Rich. L. Rev. 402 (1976); 4 Hofstra L. Rev. 511 (1976); 29 Okla. L. Rev. 117 (1976); 11 U. Tulsa L.J. 604 (1976); and 13 Cal. W. L. Rev. 168 (1976-1977).

Kenneth Donaldson has written an absorbing book about his experience. See K. Donaldson, Insanity Inside Out (1976). A case similar to Donaldson's is Bartlett v. State, 52 A.D.2d 318, 383 N.Y.S.2d 763 (1976) (damages upheld for patient held without treatment for 37 years in state mental hospital).

An interesting collection of articles is contained in V. Bradley and G. Clarke, Paper Victories and Hard Realities: The Implementation of the Legal and Constitutional Rights of the Mentally Disabled — Selected Papers on the Supreme Court Decision, O'Connor v. Donaldson (1976).

Page 678. After 2. Dangerousness: Generally, before Note, add:

MATHEW v. NELSON

461 F. Supp. 707 (N.D. Ill. 1978).

TONE, Circuit Judge.

[The plaintiff challenged the constitutionality of Ill. Rev. Stat. ch. 91-½ §1-11 (1975), which permitted the involuntary civil commitment of a mentally ill dangerous person without requiring the showing of a recent overt act. The court held an evidentiary hearing, at which two experts for each of the two parties testified, and received learned articles and treatises on the issue of proving dangerousness from the parties.[2] The applicable section of the statute has since been repealed and an overt act requirement enacted.]

---

2. The order defined the issues as follows:

(a) the degree of accuracy or reliability with which a diagnosis or prediction of "dangerousness"* can be made by those trained in psychiatry, psychology, or medicine in the absence of a recent overt act or threat,

(b) the degree of such accuracy or reliability when there has been a recent

(i) threat, or

(ii) overt act

(c) whether, assuming that a prediction of acceptable reliability is ordinarily impossible without such an act or threat, there are exceptional cases in which such a prediction can be made in the absence of such an act or threat (*e.g.*, a person who begins to behave in the same depressed and withdrawn manner he did prior to a suicide attempt some years earlier, but who has made no recent attempt or threat).

(d) questions (a), (b), and (c) when the condition to be determined is "inability to care for one's self."**

*Used herein as meaning the condition of a "person in need of mental treatment," who "is reasonably expected at the time the determination is being made or within a reasonable time thereafter to intentionally or unintentionally physically injure himself or other persons," as defined in Ill. Rev. Stat., ch. 91½, §1-11 (1975).

**Used herein as meaning the condition of a "person in need of mental treatment" who

[W]e hold that plaintiffs are not entitled to injunctive or declaratory relief for reasons we proceed to state.

The Illinois statute,[3] as interpreted by the Illinois Appellate Court in *People v. Sansone,* 18 Ill. App. 3d 315, 324, 309 N.E.2d 733, 739 (1st Dist. 1974), *leave to appeal denied,* 56 Ill. 2d 584 (1974),[4] must be read as not requiring proof of a recent overt act.[5] It is the absence of such a requirement that in plaintiffs' view makes the statute unconstitutional.

Plaintiffs ask us to find that the reasonable expectation of injury described in the statute (to which we sometimes refer, for convenience, as "dangerousness," despite the general antipathy toward that term among the experts) cannot be determined in the absence of a recent overt act, and to hold that therefore civil commitment when there has not been such an act violates due process. We cannot make the requested finding.

The evidence relied on by plaintiffs in support of their position indicates that there is a high degree of error in predicting dangerous-

---

is "unable to care for himself so as to guard himself from physical injury or to provide for his physical needs," as defined in the challenged statute.

3. Plaintiffs challenge as violative of due process the provision of the Illinois Mental Health Code of 1967, Ill. Rev. Stat. ch. 91½, §§1-1, et seq. (1975), which permits involuntary commitment of a person in need of mental treatment, who is defined as follows:

. . . any person afflicted with a mental disorder, not including a person who is mentally retarded, as defined in this Act, if that person, as a result of such mental disorder, is reasonably expected at the time the determination is being made or within a reasonable time thereafter to intentionally or unintentionally physically injure himself or other persons, or is unable to care for himself so as to guard himself from physical injury or to provide for his own physical needs. This term does not include a person whose mental processes have merely been weakened or impaired by reason of advanced years.

Ill. Rev. Stat. ch. 91½, 1-11 (1973).

4. The *Sansone* decision also stated that the state was required to prove the facts upon which commitment was based by clear and convincing evidence. More recently the Illinois Supreme Court has confirmed that this is the applicable standard. *In re Stephenson,* 67 Ill. 2d 544, 10 Ill. Dec. 507, 367 N.E.2d 1273 (1977). Plaintiffs do not challenge the clear-and-convincing standard in this action. Compare *In re Stephenson, supra,* with *United States ex rel. Stachulak v. Couglin,* 520 F.2d 931 (7th Cir. 1975).

5. During the course of this proceeding plaintiffs have defined "recent" as meaning within the past year. In their most recent brief they suggest that we not set "an absolute time limit" but "merely employ the term 'recent' and indicate that the term would not encompass acts which occur at a point where the lapse of time has been so great that the probative value of the prior conduct has substantially diminished."

The term "overt act" is defined by plaintiffs for purposes of this proceeding as follows:

(1) An act or an omission which physically injures the actor or another, or which constitutes a failure to care for one's self so as to guard against physical injury or provide for one's own physical needs.

(2) an attempt to commit such an act or omission, or

(3) a threat to commit such an act or omission.

ness, regardless of whether the subjects are mentally ill and regardless of whether the patient's history includes a recent overt act.[6] Plaintiffs, in view of their position as to the predictive or diagnostic capacity of psychiatrists, might be expected to argue that no commitment based on dangerousness is permissible, but they do not go so far. They limit their attack to the absence of an overt act requirement, and the issue before us is therefore a narrow one.

The learned articles to which plaintiffs refer us,[7] and plaintiffs' expert witnesses as well, rely heavily on a number of statistical studies, the shortcomings of which were pointed out in expert testimony offered by the defendants: the studies used as a measure only subsequent violent acts that resulted in legal proceedings; they did not take into account any treatment the subjects may have received prior to release; most used sample populations comprised of persons convicted of crimes, many of whom were not mentally ill.

No study has attempted to measure the extent to which the predictability of dangerousness is enhanced by a history of a recent overt act. (See note 6, *supra*.) There has of course been no study based on sample populations of mentally ill persons who have not been confined despite a finding of dangerousness. No study called to our attention attempts to measure the incidence of violent behavior in a sample population of persons civilly committed for dangerousness; and in any event the failure of a person actually to harm himself or another after a finding of dangerousness has led to his civil commitment to prevent such a result would not mean

6. As defendants' expert Dr. Robert L. Sadoff testified, "[T]he studies uniformly criticize the ability of psychiatrists to predict dangerousness and they did not differentiate whether that low predictability was based on prior act or not." [Tr. 132.] As a recent law review note points out, no study has attempted to determine the extent to which a recent overt act requirement would reduce the incidents of incorrect predictions of dangerousness. Note, *Overt Dangerous Behavior as a Constitutional Requirement for Involuntary Commitment of the Mentally Ill*, 44 U. Chi. L. Rev. 562, 584 (1977).

7. Representative studies can be found documented in Cocozza and Steadman, *The Failure of Psychiatric Predictions of Dangerousness: Clear and Convincing Evidence*, 29 Rutgers L. Rev. 1084 (1976); Steadman, *Some Evidence on the Inadequacy of the Concept and Determination of Dangerousness in Law and Psychiatry*, 1 J. Psychiatry and Law 409 (1973); Rubin, *Prediction of Dangerousness in Mentally Ill Criminals*, 27 Archives of Genl. Psychiatry 397 (1972); Wenk, *et al., Can Violence be Predicted?*, 18 Crime & Delinquency 393 (1972). Among the articles referring to the studies are Albers, *et al., Involuntary Hospitalization and Psychiatric Testimony: The Fallibility of the Doctrine of Immaculate Perception*, 6 Cap. L. Rev. 11 (1976); Ennis and Litwack, *Psychiatry and the Presumption of Expertise: Flipping Coins in the Courtroom*, 62 Cal. L. Rev. 693 (1974); von Hirsch, *Prediction of Criminal Conduct and Preventive Confinement of Convicted Persons*, 21 Buff. L. Rev. 717 (1972).

that he was not "reasonably likely" to do so had the commitment not occurred. Hence the limited value of statistical studies in this area. As Dr. Irwin N. Perr, an expert called by the defendants, testified in referring to the testimony given by plaintiffs' experts, "[T]he discussion this morning has dealt with statistics but has lost sight of people and what you really deal with clinically."

Dr. Perr and the other expert called by defendants, Robert L. Sadoff, were practicing psychiatrists and teachers, Dr. Perr being a Professor of Psychiatry at Rutgers Medical School and Dr. Sadoff an Associate Professor of Clinical Psychiatry at the University of Pennsylvania. Both had had extensive experience in forensic psychiatry and both were members of a task force of the American Psychiatric Association working on the problem of involuntary hospitalization. Their qualifications were unimpeachable, and both were credible witnesses.

Both testified in substance that there are cases in which a psychiatrist can determine in a clinical examination that the subject is reasonably expected to injure himself or another within a reasonable time after the examination is made, even though there is no history of an overt act, as defined for purposes of this case. Examples were given of instances in which such a diagnosis could be made in the absence of a recent overt act. According to Dr. Perr, these instances are not "insignificant" by which, we take it, he meant not insignificant in number. The testimony indicated that these views were held by most psychiatrists. Thus Dr. Perr testified,

> I think that the opinions that I have expressed in this matter would reflect the vast majority, or at least 90 per cent of psychiatrists on this matter. I think I would represent the general view.

From the evidence, we find that there are instances in which a psychiatrist can determine from a psychiatric clinical examination that a mentally ill person is reasonably likely to injure himself or another even though the person's history does not include a recent overt act, as defined for purposes of this proceeding. (See note 5, *supra.*) These cases may be relatively few, but they are not so insignificant that they can be discarded in our evaluation. If we were to adopt plaintiffs' position, we would be holding that Illinois is powerless to protect the mentally ill person and society in these cases. We are unwilling to reach such a conclusion even though in most cases a somewhat more reliable prediction can be made if there is a history of a recent overt act.

The weakness in plaintiffs' attack is that it is aimed at the statute, as interpreted, in the abstract rather than at an unlawful commitment in a particular case or an unlawful practice carried on by state officers. It may well be that in most cases the psychiatric determination necessary to support the finding of reasonable expectation that the statute requires could not be made in the absence of an overt act, just as it could not be made in the absence of other facts found in the patient's history or discovered in examining him. In those cases, the evidence will not justify a determination of dangerousness.

Implicit in plaintiffs' constitutional theory is the assumption that many commitments are made without sufficient evidence of dangerousness. If this is true, the remedy lies in the protection of the individual's right in each commitment proceeding, or a challenge to a pervasive practice of state officers if one exists, not in striking down the statute.

In considering how conclusive the showing of risk must be in order to satisfy the due process requirement in civil commitments of the mentally ill, the nature and purpose of such a commitment is relevant. The person committed, by definition, lacks the capacity to exercise his own volition in favor of or against commitment. The issue is whether to commit him temporarily for treatment and, not only in society's interest but in his own interest, to protect against physical injury to himself or others while he is unable himself to exercise the necessary judgment to protect himself.

Plaintiffs also argue, alternatively, that without an overt act requirement the statute is unconstitutionally vague. We find no basis for this argument in the Supreme Court decisions cited by plaintiffs, *Papachristou v. City of Jacksonville,* 405 U.S. 156, 92 S. Ct. 839, 31 L. Ed. 2d 110 (1972); *Giaccio v. Pennsylvania,* 382 U.S. 399, 86 S. Ct. 518, 15 L. Ed. 2d 447 (1966); and *Louisiana v. United States,* 380 U.S. 145, 85 S. Ct. 817, 13 L. Ed. 2d 709 (1965). The statute does not give the trier of fact an unstructured discretion to commit the mentally ill person. It requires a specific finding by the trier of fact that the person is expected, at the time of the determination or within a reasonable time thereafter, intentionally to inflict physical injury on himself or another person. This standard is as precise as the circumstances permit and, in our opinion, satisfies due process. The legislature was not required to attempt to detail the evidence that would be required to support the finding. Even with respect to a criminal statute, that is unnecessary.

We have considered the opinions of the district courts that have viewed an overt act requirement as constitutionally required. *Lessard v. Schmidt,* 349 F. Supp. 1078 (E.D. Wis. 1972) (three-judge court), *vacated on other grounds,* 414 U.S. 433, 94 S. Ct. 713, 38 L. Ed. 2d 661 (1974), *on remand,* 379 F. Supp. 1376 (1974), *vacated on other grounds,* 421 U.S. 957, 95 S. Ct. 1943, 44 L. Ed. 2d 445 (1975), *on remand,* 413 F. Supp. 1318 (1976) (reinstating prior judgment); *Stamus v. Leonhardt,* 414 F. Supp. 439, 451 (S.D. Iowa 1976); *Doremus v. Farrell,* 407 F. Supp. 509, 514-515 (D. Neb. 1975) (three-judge court); *Lynch v. Baxley,* 386 F. Supp. 378, 391 (M.D. Ala. 1974) (three-judge court); *Suzuki v. Quisenberry,* 411 F. Supp. 1113 (D. Haw. 1977). In none of these cases, so far as can be determined from the opinions, did the court have before it expert evidence of the kind received in this case.

The problem of inability to care for one's self has been largely ignored in the offers of evidence. We should think that in most, if not all, cases in which commitment is sought on this ground, evidence of some prior act or omission which demonstrates the alleged inability will be necessary, but in the absence of evidence we cannot make a finding to that effect. The *Sansone* decision was addressed to the problem of reasonable expectation of injury to one's self or another rather than inability to care for one's self, and the clause of the statute allowing commitment on the latter ground appears not to have been authoritatively interpreted. We do not know whether this clause is currently being interpreted by Illinois commitment courts as requiring a previous history of recent inability to care for one's self or whether commitments are being made without such a history. Under the foregoing circumstances we cannot determine the clause to be unconstitutional.

McMILLEN, District Judge, concurring.

Although I concur in the merits of the foregoing decision, I feel it appropriate to add a few comments of my own, particularly since I dissented in the decision by this same three-judge court on August 18, 1975.

A review of the evidence, taken both at the hearing on September 28, 1977 and in the agreed record when we entered our decision of August 18, 1975, convinces me that the plaintiffs have misapprehended their remedy. They seek to declare the pertinent provision of the Illinois Mental Health Code unconstitutional on the ground that it does not contain a requirement that dangerousness be proved by a recent overt act or statement. In short, plaintiffs seek to have this element of proof inserted into the Illinois statute by judicial amendment. As Judge Tone points out above, however, the remedy must properly be pursued on a case-by-case basis by individuals who seek a review of their incarceration on specific constitutional grounds.

The expert witnesses agree that dangerousness cannot be accurately predicted either on the basis of recent overt acts or by psychiatric evaluation. The evidence shows that certain types of psychotic individuals can be dangerous without any prior history of overt acts, and others with such prior history are not predictably dangerous. Therefore, the criteria selected by the plaintiffs are not medically reliable and are not as dependable or precise as the statute itself. Since the profession of psychiatry has not been able to devise a method of reliably predicting dangerousness, neither the plaintiffs nor the courts have been able to find a formula which will fill this existing void. This does not render §1-11 invalid, however.

A substantial constitutional question could be raised concerning whether any statute providing for involuntary commitment of deranged persons is valid unless it affords the same safeguards for personal liberty as in criminal cases. If a person has committed an overt act in Illinois sufficiently dangerous to constitute a crime, but is found not guilty by reason of insanity, then he can be incarcerated for treatment for the same period of time as though he had been found guilty. *Ill. Rev. Stat.*, Ch. 38, §1005-2-4, as amended by P.A. 80-164 (1977). On the other hand, if he has not committed a crime and does not want to be deprived of his liberty, it is difficult to comprehend exactly what public need is being served by incarcerating him except the *parens patriae* objective of doing something for his own good.

Whether or not this laudable objective overcomes an individual's right to liberty is highly questionable, in my mind. It is not the objective of §1-11 of the Illinois Mental Health Code which attempts to balance the interest of the general public against the individual's right to freedom. The Special Joint Committee on Revision of the Mental Health Code is now considering a revision of §1-11 which will specifically require proof of a recent overt act or significant threat before involuntary commitment is permitted, but this is quite different from invalidating the present section because of the absence of such requirement.

The foregoing perhaps leads to the conclusion that deranged persons should be confined against their wills only on the same grounds as other persons, specifically criminals. This may also lead to the requirement that previous dangerous acts must be proven beyond a reasonable doubt, with all of the other due process safeguards afforded to a person charged with a crime. This extreme departure from the stipulated issue remaining in this case has not been presented by either party, and therefore we are not called upon to decide it. I advert to it merely because the evidence indicates that this may be the alternative before the final solution is found to the problem of involuntary commitment without conviction for a crime. Cf. *In re Stephenson,* 67 Ill. 2d 544, 10 Ill. Dec. 507, 367 N.E.2d 1273 (1977).

NOTE: THE "OVERT ACT" REQUIREMENT

Following its appearance in the *Lessard* case, the constitutional requirement that dangerousness be established by evidence of a recent overt act, attempt or threat to do substantial harm has spread rapidly. See Note, Overt Dangerous Behavior as a Constitutional Requirement for Involuntary Civil Commitment of the Mentally Ill, 44 U. Chi. L. Rev. 562 (1977) and Note, 7 Loy. Chi. L. Rev. 507 (1976). A new adoption of the test is Suzuki v. Alba, 438 F. Supp. 1106, 1110 (D. Haw. 1977).

Page 682. At end of page, add:

See Brooks, Notes on Defining the "Dangerousness" of the Mentally Ill, in C. Frederick, ed., Dangerous Behavior, A Problem in Law and Mental Health (1978), and Shah, Dangerousness: Some Definitional, Conceptual, and Public Policy Issues in B. Sales, ed., Perspectives in Law and Psychology (Vol. I) (1977). How judges and psychiatrists define dangerousness is discussed in Simon and Cockerham, Civil Commitment, Burden of Proof, and Dangerous Acts: A Comparison of the Perspectives of Judges and Psychiatrists, 5 J. Psychiat. & L. 571 (1977).

Page 686. At end of first full paragraph, add:

FURTHER NOTES ON PREDICTION

The issue of predictability of dangerousness has loomed as one of the most controversial issues in mental health law. Much of the important research in this area has been done by Henry Steadman and his colleague, Joseph Cocozza. See, e.g., references at p. 326 of this Casebook. The Steadman-Cocozza Baxstrom studies are summarized in H. Steadman and J. Cocozza, Careers of the Criminally Insane (1974). See also Steadman and Braff, Effects of Incompetency Determinations on Subsequent Criminal Processing: Implications for Due Process, 23 Cath. U.L. Rev. 754 (1974) and Steadman and Braff, Crimes of Violence and Incompetency Diversion, 66 J. Crim. L. & Criminol. 73 (1975).

The methodology of the Steadman-Cocozza Baxstrom studies was acutely criticized in Allen, Book Review, N. Morris, The Future of Imprisonment, 73 Mich. L. Rev. 1516, 1524-1528 (1975). Cocozza and Steadman have themselves acknowledged weaknesses in these studies in a later article, Cocozza and Steadman, The Failure of Psychiatric Predictions of Dangerousness: Clear and Convincing Evidence, 29 Rutgers L. Rev. 1084 (1976), in which they report the findings of another study of dangerous and non-dangerous defendants found incompetent to stand trial.

A leading article attacking the validity of psychiatric testimony on dangerousness is Ennis and Litwack, Psychiatry and the Presumption of Expertise: Flipping Coins in the Courtroom, 62 Calif. L. Rev. 693 (1974).

A psychiatrically-oriented discussion taking the same position, from the psychiatric perspective, is Diamond, The Psychiatric Prediction of Dangerousness, 123 U. Pa. L. Rev. 439 (1974). See also Cohen, Groth and Siegel, The Clinical Prediction of Dangerousness, 24 Crime & Delinq. 28 (1978); Schlesinger, The Prediction of Dangerousness in Juveniles, 24 Crime & Delinq. 40 (1978); Fagin, The Policy Implications of Predictive Decision-Making: "Likelihood" and "Dangerousness" in Civil Commitment Proceedings, 24 Public Policy 491 (1976); and Greenland, The Prediction and Management of Dangerous Behavior: Social Policy Issues, 1 Intl. J.L. & Psychiat. 205 (1978).

Prediction research has been criticized in Monahan, Prediction Research and the Emergency Commitment of Dangerous Mentally Ill Persons: A Reconsideration, 135 Am. J. Psychiat. 198 (1978).

For a study of the use of dangerousness predictions in connection with the Texas death penalty statute, see Dix, Administration of the Texas Death Penalty Statutes: Constitutional Infirmities Related to the Prediction of Dangerousness, 55 Texas L. Rev. 1343 (1977).

For additional prediction discussions, see Laves, The Prediction of "Dangerousness" as a Criterion for Involuntary Commitment: Constitutional Considerations, 3 J. Psychiat. & L. 291 (1975), and Megargee, The Prediction of Dangerous Behavior, 3 Crim. Justice & Behavior 3 (1976). See also Mesnikoff and Lauterbach, The Association of Violent Dangerous Behavior with Psychiatric Disorders: A Review of the Research Literature, 3 J. Psychiat. & L. 415 (1975) and Peszke, Is Dangerousness an Issue for Physicians in Emergency Commitment?, 132 Am. J. Psychiat. 825 (1975). Dr. Peszke's discussion is commented upon by Stone, Comment on Peszke Article, 132 Am. J. Psychiat. 829 (1975); Hartman and Allison, Predicting Dangerousness, 25 Med. Trial Tech. Q. 131 (1978).

Professor George Dix has proposed that a "true experiment" be conducted to assess the validity of predictions of imminent violence, in which a random sample of persons presented for civil commitment on the basis of imminent violence would be denied commitment, in order to find out what proportion of them behave as predicted. Dix, "Civil" Commitment of the Mentally Ill and the Need for Data on the Prediction of Dangerousness, 19 Amer. Behav. Scient. 318 (1976). Professor Monahan has criticized the proposal as presenting an unacceptable level of risk to the community and proposes four alternative methodologies of his own. Monahan, Strategies for an Empirical Analysis of the Prediction of Violence in Emergency Civil Commitment, 1 L. & Human Behav. 363 (1977).

The question of crime among ex-mental patients has stimulated a great deal of research. The first of the major studies was Brill and Malzberg, Statistical Report on the Arrest Record of Male Ex-Patients, Age 16 or Over, released from New York State Mental Hospitals during the period 1946-1948, New York State Department of Mental Hygiene (August 1962). This study was followed by Rappeport and Lassen, Dangerousness Arrest Rate Comparisons of Discharged Patients and the General Population, 121 Am. J. Psychiat. 776 (1965). A more recent, and controversial study is Zitrin, Hardesty, Burdock and Drosaman, Crime and Violence Among Mental Patients, 133 Am. J. Psychiat. 142 (1976). An even more recent study concludes that "the public has little to fear from the mentally ill." See Cocozza, Melick and Steadman, Trends in Violent Crime Among Ex-Mental Patients, 16 Criminology 317 (1978).

A new sociological study is S. Pfohl, Predicting Dangerousness: The Social Construction of Psychiatric Reality (1978).

Page 689. After 4., Involuntary Commitment Defended, add:

See generally, M. Peszke, Involuntary Treatment of the Mentally Ill: The Problem of Autonomy (1975), a vigorous defense of hospitalization. Also, Chodoff, The Case for Involuntary Hospitalization of the Mentally Ill, 133 Am. J. Psychiat. 496 (1976); Rachlin, Pam and Milton, Civil Liberties versus Involuntary Hospitalization, 132 Am. J. Psychiat. 758-759 (1975); and Peszke, Involuntary Treatment of the Mentally Ill: Law's All or Nothing Approach, 46 Conn. B.J. 620 (1972).

Pages 690-691. After Treffert, Dying With Their Rights On, add:

NOTE

The expression "dying with their rights on" has caught fire, especially among members of the psychiatric profession. Another version of Dr. Treffert's views is presented in Treffert, Dying With Their Rights On, 2 Prism 49 (an AMA publication), February, 1974. See also Treffert, The Practical Limits of Patients' Rights, 5.4 Psychiat. Annals 91 (1975), and Treffert and Krajeck, In Search of a Sane Commitment Statute, 6 Psychiat. Annals 56 (1976).

Pages 700-702. After Note: Should Suicidal Persons Be Committed, add:

For a careful analysis of the validity of committing persons perceived as suicidal see Greenberg, Involuntary Psychiatric Commitment to Prevent Suicide, 49 N.Y.U.L. Rev. 227 (1974). See also Schwartz, Flinn and Slawson, Suicide in the Psychiatric Hospital, 132 Am. J. Psychiat. 150 (1975).

Page 712. After Note, add:

On the issue of a constitutional right to commit suicide, see Note, Suicide and the Compulsion of Lifesaving Medical Procedures: An Analysis of the Refusal of Treatment Cases, 44 Brooklyn L. Rev. 285 (1978); Paris, Compulsory Medical Treatment and Religious Freedom: Whose Law Shall Prevail? 10 U.S.F.L. Rev. 1 (1975) (both containing discussions of the Heston case); and Bryn, Compulsory Life-Saving Treatment for the Competent Adult, 44 Fordham L. Rev. 1 (1975).

Page 717. After Note, add:

Another effort on the part of Mayock to be released is reported in Mayock v. Martin, Civ. No. 13074, July 25, 1969, U.S. District Court, Conn. Unreported.

Pages 725-726. After The Aged and Infirm Cases, add:

See also Regan, Protective Services for the Elderly: Commitment, Guardianship and Alternatives, 13 Wm. & Mary L. Rev. 569 (1972), and Alexander, On Being Imposed Upon by Artful or Designing Persons—The California Experience With the Involuntary Placement of the Aged, 14 San Diego L. Rev. 1083 (1977). Also consult Report of the Special Committee on Aging, U.S. Senate, Mental Health Care and The Elderly: Shortcomings in Public Policy (November, 1971).

Chapter Ten

Alternatives to Involuntary Commitment

A. THE "LEAST DRASTIC ALTERNATIVE" APPROACH

Page 734. After first full paragraph, add:

See also Lipsius, Judgments of Alternatives to Hospitalization, 130 Am. J. Psychiat. 892 (1973), and Hoffman and Foust, Least Drastic Treatment of the Mentally Ill: A Doctrine in Search of its Senses, 14 San Diego L. Rev. 1100 (1977).

B. ABOLISHING INVOLUNTARY CIVIL COMMITMENT

Page 736. After second paragraph, add:

A well-stated psychiatric position in favor of hospitalization is presented in Rachlin, Pam, and Milton, Civil Liberties Versus Involuntary Hospitalization, 132 Am. J. Psychiat. 189 (1975) (opposing abolition). K. Miller, Managing Madness: The Case Against Civil Commitment (1976) marshalls strong and persuasive arguments against hospitalization.

C. VOLUNTARY HOSPITALIZATION

Pages 736-739. After 1., Introductory Note, add:

In Appeal of Niccoli, 472 Pa. 389, 372 A.2d 749 (Pa. 1977), the Pennsylvania Supreme Court vacated an involuntary commitment and remanded, on the basis that there was sufficient evidence to establish that the appellant had already voluntarily hospitalized himself because of his recognition that he needed treatment, and that the civil commitment had substituted an involuntary proceeding for a voluntary one, so that the patient ended up in the same hospital as an involuntary rather than voluntary patient. The court invoked the "least restrictive alternative" approach.

Pages 748-749. After Note, add:

See also Olin v. Olin, Informed Consent in Voluntary Mental Hospital Admissions, 132 Am. J. Psychiat. 938 (1975); Farmers, The "Voluntary" Psychiatric Patient, 45 J. Kans. Bar Assoc. 37 (1976); Applebaum, The Voluntary Patient—A Psychiatrist's Perspective, 45 J. Kan. Bar A. 45 (1976); Palmer and Wohl, Voluntary Admission Forms: Does the Patient Know What He's Signing?, 23 Hosp. & Commun. Psychiat. 250 (1972); Gilboy, Informal Admission of Patients to State Psychiatric Institutions, 47 Am. J. Orthopsychiat. 321 (1977); Szasz, Voluntary Hospitalization: An Unacknowledged Practice of Medical Fraud, 287 New Eng. J. Med. 277 (1972). In Emery v. State, 26 Utah 2d 1, 4, 483 P.2d 1296, 1298 (1971) the court said: "A voluntary patient at the [mental] hospital is as much 'confined' and has as little freedom as a mentally alert trusty in a jail or prison."

Chapter Twelve

Procedural Issues

Page 777. Before A., Emergency Hospitalization, add:

In the last few years, due process procedural protections in the civil commitment process have developed rapidly. For general discussions see, e.g., Note, Procedural Safeguards for the Involuntary Commitment of the Mentally Ill in the District of Columbia, 28 Cath. U.L. Rev. 855 (1979); Slovenko, Criminal Justice Procedures in Civil Commitment, 24 Wayne L. Rev. 1 (1977); Comment, The "Crime" of Mental Illness: Extension of "Criminal" Procedural Safeguards to Involuntary Civil Commitments, 66 J. Crim. L. & Crimin. 255 (1975); Comment, Progress in Involuntary Commitment, 49 Wash. L. Rev. 617 (1974); Note, Due Process and the Development of "Criminal" Safeguards in Civil Commitment Adjudications, 42 Fordham L. Rev. 613 (1974).

Page 793. After first full paragraph, add:

IN THE MATTER OF SHIRLEY PASBRIG

Circuit Court in Probate, Milwaukee County, Wis. December 19, 1978

SHAUGHNESSY, J.

Motion was brought on behalf of Shirley Pasbrig to dismiss the involuntary commitment petition on the ground that the pleadings were insufficient to confer jurisdiction on the court to allow the holding of a probable cause hearing and on the further grounds that there was insufficient evidence of dangerousness elicited at the probable cause hearing to justify a bindover. Briefs were submitted by the attorneys for Shirley Pasbrig and also by the Corporation Counsel of Milwaukee County.

Section 51.15(4) (a), Wis. Stats., requires that the law enforcement officer shall sign a statement of emergency detention which shall provide detailed specific information concerning the recent overt acts, attempts or threats to act or the pattern of recent acts or omissions on which the belief under subsection (1) is based and the names of the persons observing or reporting such overt acts, attempts or threats to act, or pattern of recent acts or omissions.

Section 51.15(4) (b), Wis. Stats., provides that if the Treatment Director determines to detain the subject individual, the Treatment Director may supplement in writing the statement filed by the law enforcement officer and may include therein other specific information concerning his belief that the individual meets the standard for commitment. The filing of the original statement, together with the supplemental statement, with the court has the same effect as petition for commitment under §51.20, Wis. Stats.

Section 51.20(1) (c), Wis. Stats., provides in part that the petition shall contain a clear and concise statement of the facts which constitute probable cause to believe the allegations of the petition.

The officer's statement contains information on which his belief for detention was based: "Subject was in showroom of Metropolitan Cadillac climbing on new cars and swearing. Subject refused to leave and became combative." The statement does not state whether the officer personally observed the conduct or whether information regarding this conduct was obtained from others. The statement does not contain dates as to when the conduct took place. The only dates mentioned in the pleadings are the dates on which Shirley was taken into custody. These dates are stated as November 13, 1978, in the law enforcement officer's statement of emergency detention, and November 13, 1971, in the Treatment Director's supplement.

The Treatment Director's supplement states at Paragraph 6 that Shirley Pasbrig is mentally ill and at Paragraph 7 lists the specific diagnosis as manic depressive illness, manic phase.

The Treatment Director's supplement meets the requirements of §51.15(4) (b), Wis. Stats.

The statement of emergency detention by the police officer and the supplement by the Treatment Director do not contain a clear and concise statement of facts which constitute probable cause to believe that Shirley Pasbrig is dangerous per §51.20(1) (a)2. a., b. or c., Wis. Stats. In State ex rel. Pflanz v. County Court, 36 Wis. 2d 550, which was a criminal case involving a tax evasion, the court, on page 562, stated:

> . . . [T]he present practice requires a complaint to state the facts evidencing probable cause. This may be done either directly in the complaint or indirectly by an affidavit setting forth the basis for the probable cause and made a part of the complaint by incorporation. In either event, the facts will be in the complaint and available on review if their sufficiency is challenged. . . .

The motion to dismiss is granted.

D. OTHER PROCEDURAL PROTECTIONS

Page 795. After 3., The Right to a Jury Trial, add:

For a discussion of the appropriateness of a jury trial in civil commitment proceedings, see Note, 87 Harv. L. Rev. 1190, 1291-1295 (1974).

Page 805. Before 5, add:

THE ATTORNEY'S ROLE AT THE COMMITMENT HEARING: GUIDELINES AND PRACTICAL CONSIDERATIONS GUIDELINES FOR DEFENSE COUNSEL IN COMMITMENT CASES

2 Mental Disability Law Reporter 427 (1978)

In October, 1977, the Michigan Supreme Court promulgated new Probate Court Rules 730 to 746. The Probate Court Rules (PCRs) govern civil admission and discharge proceedings under Michigan's Mental Health Code. One provision of these innovative new rules is particularly significant to attorneys who represent persons subject to probate court proceedings under the Mental Health Code. PC Rule 732 *Attorneys* provides:

1. Continuing Appointment of an Attorney. The attorney of record must represent the respondent in all probate court proceedings under the Mental Health Code until he is discharged by court order or another attorney has filed an appearance on the respondent's behalf.

2. Duties.

The attorney must

(1) consult with the respondent about alternatives to hospitalization, and

(2) serve as an advocate for the respondent's preferred disposition.

To help define an attorney's role under this Rule in a civil commitment proceeding, the Michigan State Bar Committee on Mentally Disabled adopted the following Guidelines and published them for comment in December, 1977. The Committee has submitted these guidelines to the Committee on Professional and Judicial Ethics for review, and anticipates submission of the guidelines to the Commissioners of the State Bar.

GUIDELINES

1. *The attorney should be familiar with the facts of the case and learn the client's objectives.* This is done by conducting an initial client interview, at the hospital if necessary, promptly after appointment. The initial interview should, at a minimum, have the following goals: explanation of commitment law and procedures, including the consequences of commitment; discussion of the alternatives available to the client, especially possibility of placement in a less restricted setting in the community (See PCR 732.2(1)); determination of the client's version of the facts; and determination of the client's wishes.

After the client interview, a thorough investigation of the case should be made, starting with the legal sufficiency of the petition and two physician's certificates. This would include interviews with the committing and/or treating doctors, the family members and the petitioners and other witnesses. Factual issues are often open to dispute. Hospital records should be examined and an independent expert examination sought. A full psychiatric evaluation should be obtained, at state expense if the client is indigent, with a view toward determining three separate items. First, the current mental state of the client. Second, the feasibility of less restrictive alternatives to commitment. Third, assistance to the attorney in understanding the client, the hospital reports, and the ways to most effectively cross-examine the committing physicians.

2. *The attorney should determine the range of alternatives open to the client.* This determination is based first on a thorough knowledge and investigation of the law and the facts of the case, and

second, on the practical alternatives available to the client. For example, are there any open beds in half-way houses that could be utilized as an alternative to commitment? This can best be explored by talking to the community mental health workers involved in the case and the social workers at the hospital, and to the doctor who conducts the independent expert examination at counsel's request. Is the client an alcoholic who can get treatment for this condition elsewhere? (See MCLA 330.1402.)

3. *The attorney should advise the client about possible dispositions of the case.* The attorney's advice can indicate whether or not the attorney feels the client's objectives are unwise or unrealistic. If this is so, the client should be informed why the objectives are felt to be unwise or not realistic. At the same time, it should be made clear to the client that the client has a right to have his own views advocated. It is certainly one of the attorney's jobs to provide accurate and perceptive legal advice. This should be done in a non-paternalistic fashion, recognizing the client's right to choose among the various options available. Once the attorney has advised the client and has determined the client's objectives, the attorney must advocate the client's position zealously within the bounds of the law. If an attorney does not believe he can represent the client's chosen course, he should withdraw from the case except in circumstances where the client would be left fully unrepresented. In such cases, the attorney should leave the question of further participation to the client. (See PCR 732.4)

Once the attorney and the client have come to an understanding of objectives and have agreed on the best means of going after the objectives, the attorney and client have, in effect, made a contract which the attorney is bound to honor.

4. *Prior to the hearing, the attorney should enter into negotiations with relevant persons concerning the case.*

Often, discussions with hospital staff, the petitioner, the client's family and the prosecuting attorney will indicate formal or informal alternatives to a hearing. Frequently, the case can be settled through these negotiations and a resolution found which is viewed as appropriate by the client.

5. *Prior to the trial, the attorney should effectively protect the client's procedural rights if that will further the client's wishes.*

Defense counsel should carefully examine the procedure followed in the initial commitment process to see if it is in compliance with the Mental Health Act. Any irregularities should be challenged.

Careful examination should be given to decisions whether to file preliminary motions, whether to demand preliminary hearings and whether to waive or assert the right to jury trial.

6. *The client should be afforded effective advocacy at the hearing.*

This requires traditional advocate skills. The lawyer should object to inadmissible evidence and cross-examine witnesses who favor commitment, including hospital psychiatrists. The basis of the expert testimony should be vigorously examined and questioned. This requires developing a level of expertise in defense counsel about the profession of psychiatry. Questions of accuracy of diagnosis, accuracy of future prediction of dangerousness, biases of the psychiatric profession, and other such issues must be examined. This requires detailed study in the psychiatric literature and familiarization with psychiatric terminology and testing. Just as an attorney in a personal injury case must be familiar with engineering terminology and testing for metal fatigue and coefficient of friction, so must an attorney in the mental health area be familiar with psychiatry. If an attorney is not familiar, then in addition to independent study it may also be necessary to petition the court to appoint an expert witness, an independent medical examiner, to assist counsel in the trial (MCLA 330.1463; PCR 733).

7. *Commitment is not the sole issue.*

Treatment must be adequate and its lack precludes commitment: Will the client receive more than medication and "milieu" therapy? How often is he seen by a psychiatrist? Is there group therapy, activity or recreational therapy? What is it? What are the plans for placement? (See PCR 741.)

8. *The client should be represented throughout each phase of the commitment process including the periodic review phases and including any subsequent petitions which are filed.*

See PCR 732.1. If a client is released and then re-petitioned in the future, the attorney originally representing the client should be reappointed to the case. If this is not done, this provision should be brought to the attention of the court.

COMMENTARY

One result of the 1974 Michigan Mental Health Code has been the involvement of many attorneys in an area of practice which was somewhat unfamiliar territory: representation of the mentally different in the arcane world of psychiatry. These attorneys encountered a debate within the legal profession over the role of the attorney who represents the subject of a petition for civil commitment: should the attorney be an advocate for the client's wishes, or guardian of the attorney's perception of the client's best interest?

The recent decision in *State of Wisconsin ex rel. Memmel and Pagels v. Mundy,* No. 441-417 (Wisc. Cir. Ct., Milwaukee County, 1976), 1 MDLR 183, *aff'd* 249 N.W.2d 573 (1977) held that the legal representation of defendants in mental commitment cases, provided by a closed panel of six court-appointed attorneys over a period of more than one year, systematically violated the defendants' rights to due process of law, trial by jury and the effective assistance of counsel. The Wisconsin Supreme Court stated that it is a constitutional requirement that legal representation be provided by attorneys occupying a truly adversary position.

There is no tradition in mental health law equivalent to the tradition that has grown up in criminal law which can guide attorneys to effective representation. It is settled in criminal law that even a "guilty" defendant has a right to trial by jury, a right not to incriminate himself, and the other substantive and procedural due process rights allowed by the Constitution. Our legal system is prepared to let the guilty go free to protect the rights of the innocent. The presumption of innocence is honored by vigorous representation of clients. In mental health law, however, the presumption of sanity does not appear to be nearly as well-honored as the presumption of innocence. Further, there are societal pressures, feelings of paternalism, and in some cases, feelings of dislike or even fear for or of the client, that exert strong forces on defense counsel to apply pressures on the client to agree to commitment.

A starting place for guidelines for defense counsel would be the American Bar Association's Canons of Professional Responsibility. Canon 7 indicates "a lawyer should represent a client zealously within the bounds of the law." Canon 5 indicates "a lawyer should exercise independent professional judgment on behalf of a client." In an informal ethical opinion rendered by the Honorable Michael G. Harrison for the Committee on Professional and Judicial Ethics (C1-184), on May 22, 1975, Judge Harrison points out that within the parameters of these two Canons, the obligation to best represent the client's interest exists. Harrison indicates that counsel must assure that the procedural and substantive safeguards which are set forth in the Mental Health Code are afforded the client, unless the attorney, in his or her best judgment, deems such to be unnecessary to the strategy decided upon by the attorney to achieve the client's goal in any individual case.

Harrison further states that each avenue should be explored and exhausted, including alternatives to institutionalization. Harrison's further point is that counsel also has a right and obligation to make recommendations to the client after making a detailed factual investigation of the case and, in the event a client is not inclined to accept the advice, the attorney must make a determination as to whether to go to hearing or trial in accordance with the client's direction, or to withdraw under Canon 2.

The Wisconsin case suggests that if the client wishes a safeguard to be asserted, the attorney has some obligation to assert it. There, the attorneys waived the right to subpoena witnesses in 99% of the cases, failed to cross-examine witnesses, failed to request a transcript of the preliminary hearing, and waived the right to jury trial in all but one of 1,238 cases. Further, the attorneys waived the right to file written motions in 100% of the cases. The court held that this went far beyond attorneys exercising their best judgment and, in fact, constituted ineffective representation by counsel.

The Mental Health Code, Mich. Comp. Laws Ann. §§330.1400 *et seq.*, which sets forth the rights of any person prior to commitment to a hospital at §§330.1453-1465, affords some guidance. These rights make it clear, as Judge Harrison points out in his opinion, that the appointment of an attorney under the Code is as legal representative, not as guardian. As the Wisconsin Supreme Court points out in footnote 3 of its Opinion, the right to counsel is satisfied by an attorney only if the attorney occupies a truly adversary position. See: *State ex rel. Memmel* v. *Mundy,* 249 N.W.2d at 577, citing *Lessard* v. *Schmidt,* 349 F. Supp. 1078 (E.D. Wis. 1972), *judgment re-entered,* 413 F. Supp. 1318 (1976); *Quesnell* v. *State,* 83 Wash. 2d 222, 238, 517 P.2d 568, 577 (1974); *Denton* v. *Commonwealth,* 383 S.W.2d, 681, 682 (Ky. Ct. App. 1964); *Suzuki* v. *Quisenberry,* 411 F. Supp. 1113, 1129 (D. Hawaii 1976), 1 MDLR 10, 46; *Lynch* v. *Baxley,* 386 F. Supp. 378, 379 (M.D. Ala. 1974). *Accord, Bell* v. *Wayne County General Hospital,* 384 F. Supp. 1085 (E.D. Mich. 1974).

One further problem should be mentioned. Generally, in litigation, a preliminary issue is the ability of the client to understand and assist the attorney. In civil commitment cases, it is assumed that effective assistance by the client will occur and the issue is whether or not to commit, without any preliminary inquiry into "competency to stand trial."

In some cases, however, defense counsel is presented with a client with whom communication is so difficult, that the client's objectives cannot be ascertained. In these cases, counsel must first exhaust every reasonable effort to establish rapport with the client. Counsel must recognize that such factors as psychotropic medication, the effects of forced institutionalization, a mistrust of the legal system, and unusual thought patterns may make communication between the attorney and the client more difficult than usual. If the client's objectives still cannot be ascertained, or his assistance in the preparation of the case cannot be obtained after these special efforts are made, counsel must then proceed even without the assistance of the client. In these cases, the attorney, acting as an advocate, must determine what disposition would be perceived by the client as most satisfactory to him and then advocate zealously for that disposition. See ABA Ethical Consideration 7-12.

In performing in civil commitment cases, an attorney should not allow outside influence to color the nature of the service rendered to the client. There are often tremendous pressures placed upon defense counsel by the court, mental health professionals, family members, or other members of the community to allow the state to "help" the respondent by institutionalization. Such persons are often motivated by sincere and honest desires to assist the respondent through a difficult time. However, to be an effective advocate, these pressures should be resisted and the attorney should focus on the client's own perception of his needs and desires. See Disciplinary Rule 5-101 A, 5-107, ABA Ethical Considerations 5-1, 5-21.

It should never be forgotten that the attorney is the only person among all the various people involved in a commitment case whose role it is to advocate on behalf of the respondent's own perception of his or her interests. Regardless of the attorney's own feelings about the client's state of mind, the attorney must continue to be a vigorous advocate throughout the case. See Disciplinary Rule 7-101 A, ABA Ethical Considerations 7-7, 7-8, 7-9, 7-17, 7-19, 7-20. Only in this way can the integrity of the system be preserved and a just result for all concerned be obtained.

The literature on the role of the lawyer in the civil commitment process has grown considerably as the function of the mental health lawyer has proliferated. One of the most thoughtful defenses of the pure advocacy role is Note, The Role of Counsel in the Civil Commitment Process: A Theoretical Framework, 84 Yale L.J. 1540 (1975), a role questioned in Galie, An Essay on the Civil Commitment Lawyer: Or How I Learned to Hate the Adversary System,

6 J. Psychiat. & L. 71 (1978). See also Cyr, The Role and Functions of the Attorney in the Civil Commitment Process: The District of Columbia's Approach, 6 J. Psychiat. & L. 107 (1978) and Dix, The Role of the Lawyer in Proceedings Under the Texas Mental Health Code, 39 Texas B.J. 982 (1976).

Also of value are the following: Chernoff and Schaffer, Defending the Mentally Ill: Ethical Quicksand, 10 Am. Crim. L. Rev. 505 (1972); Litwack, The Role of Counsel in Civil Commitment Proceedings: Emerging Problems, 62 Calif. L. Rev. 816 (1974); Mutnick and Lazar, A Practical Guide to Involuntary Commitment Proceedings, 11 Willamette L.J. 315 (1975); Dickey and Remington, Legal Assistance for Institutionalized Persons—An Overlooked Need, 1 So. Ill. U.L.J. 175 (1976); Brakel, The Role of the Lawyer in the Mental Health Field, 1977 Am. B. Found. Research J. 467, commented upon by Woody, Comment, The Lawyer in the Mental Health Field: Beyond Brakel, 1979 Am. B. Found. Research J. 211; and Note, Role of Attorney in Civil Commitment Proceedings, 61 Marq. L. Rev. 187 (1977); and Brunetti, The Right to Counsel, Waiver Thereof, and Effective Assistance of Counsel in Civil Commitment Proceedings, 29 Sw. L.J. 684 (1975). See also discussion in Note, 87 Harv. L. Rev. 1190, 1283-1291 (1974).

See also Epstein and Lowinger, Do Mental Patients Want Legal Counsel?, 45 Am. J. Orthopsychiat. 88 (1975), and Page, Toward Evaluating the Meaningfulness of Legal Counsel for Psychiatric Patients, 24 Canada's Mental Health 6 (Sept. 1976).

The role of the guardian ad litem is discussed in Levin, Guardian Ad Litem in a Family Court, 34 Md. L. Rev. 341 (1974); Hodmann and Dwyer, Guardians ad Litem in Wisconsin, 48 Marq. L. Rev. 445 (1965); Note, Guardians Ad Litem, 45 Iowa L. Rev. 376 (1960); Note, A Current Misunderstanding as to Guardians Ad Litem, 28 Mass. L.Q. 52 (1943).

A collection of articles on legal and non-legal advocacy on behalf of the mentally disabled is L. Kopolow and H. Bloom, Mental Health Advocacy: An Emerging Force in Consumers' Rights (1977). Of particular interest in this group are: Scott, The Mental Health Advocacy Service: A Legal Perspective (at 42) and Van Ness and Perlin, Mental Health Advocacy—The New Jersey Experience (at 62). The collection contains a model advocacy statute at 87.

An interesting but unreported case is Wisconsin ex rel. Memmel v. Mundy, decided in the Circuit Court, Civil Division, Milwaukee County, Wis., August 18, 1976; and discussed in Scallet, The Realities of Mental Health Advocacy: State ex rel. Memmel v. Mundy,

L. Kopolow and H. Bloom, Mental Health Advocacy: An Emerging Force in Consumers' Rights 79 (1977).

The Circuit Court ruled on a system then in effect in Milwaukee whereby the probate judge handpicked a small number of lawyers to represent respondents in involuntary civil commitment hearings. Plaintiffs' claim, upheld by the Circuit Court, was that there was denial of due process of law, specifically of right to counsel. The record showed a systematic failure of the court-appointed lawyers to provide adequate representation for their clients.

The Circuit Court characterized the practices of the Milwaukee probate court as presenting "as bleak a picture as has probably ever been presented of justice in Milwaukee County. A massive and systematic deprivation of the constitutional rights of people who are unable to voice their protests has been accomplished by the cooperation of the bench and bar of Milwaukee County."

Said the Court, "It is unconscionable that lawyers and judges, who are trained in the law and who have a special duty to protect the constitutional rights of those who are unable to protect themselves, could participate in such a scheme to bilk citizens of their constitutional rights. Although this suit names the Director of Milwaukee County Institutions, the onus of this debacle lies squarely with the lawyers and judges who operated this 'greased runway to the County Mental Health Center,' as the Milwaukee Journal recently characterized the commitment system. Despite frequent and continued criticism of the system by the newspapers, bar associations, mental health groups and others, the Probate Court judges continued to operate a system which they must have known was illegal in every facet of its operation."

The Court concluded with a quotation:

> Lord Bolingbroke accurately described the present situation many years ago when he said: "The profession of the law, in its nature the noblest and most beneficial to mankind, is in its abuse and abasement the most sordid and pernicious." (Quoted in People v. Salomon, 184 Ill. 490, 1900).

The order in State ex rel. Memmel v. Mundy was modified by the Wisconsin Supreme Court in State ex rel. Memmel v. Mundy, 75 Wis. 2d 276, 249 N.W.2d 573 (1977), but the main holding of the decision below dealing with constitutionality was not altered.

The picture in Milwaukee today is remarkably different because commitment respondents are now represented by a vigorous and sophisticated public defender who is chief of the Mental Health Division, Tom Zander. In his latest report of August, 1979 Zander reports that in nine months 254 cases were handled. Only 2 percent (4) were involuntarily committed, although during the same period 25 percent of cases handled by members of the private bar were committed. Of Zander's clients, 17 percent became voluntary patients, 9 percent became patients in the community, and 72 percent of the cases were dismissed. The dismissals resulted from (a) insufficient evidence of mental illness (12 percent); insufficient evidence of dangerousness (6 percent); or because of technical irregularities (21 percent). See Zander, The Mental Commitment Law as Scapegoat (Milwaukee, Wis. August, 1979).

The adequacy of legal services for institutionalized persons is discussed in Dickey, The Lawyer and the Quality of Service to the Poor and Disadvantaged Client: Legal Services to the Institutionalized, 27 De Paul L. Rev. 407 (1978). A general treatment of the problem is contained in Bellow and Kettleson, From Ethics to Politics: Confronting Scarcity and Fairness in Public Interest Practice, 58 B.U.L. Rev. 337 (1978). An excellent discussion of clinical practices in the mental health law area is Lowry and Kennedy, Clinical Law in the Area of Mental Health, 1979 Wis. L. Rev. 373.

Page 806. After 5., The Right to an Independent Psychiatrist, add:

NOTE

See Farrell, The Right of an Indigent Civil Commitment Defendant to Psychiatric Assistance of His Own Choice at State Expense, 11 Idaho L. Rev. 141 (1975).

Pages 806-808. After 6., The Use of Hearsay in Commitment Hearings, add:

Note, Hearsay Bases of Psychiatric Opinion Testimony: A Critique of Federal Rule of Evidence 703, 51 S. Cal. L. Rev. 129 (1977).

Pages 808-809. After 7., The Privilege Against Self-Incrimination, add:

See Note, Application of the Fifth Amendment Privilege Against Self-Incrimination to the Civil Commitment Proceeding, 1973 Duke L.J. 729 and Note, 87 Harv. L. Rev. 1190, 1303-1313 (1974).

The Texas Court of Civil Appeals in McGuffin v. State, 571 S.W.2d 56 (Tex. 1978) has held that a constitutional privilege against self-incrimination does not apply in an involuntary civil commitment case, distinguishing such cases from criminal and juvenile cases. Citing Middendorf v. Henry, 425 U.S. 25, 96 S. Ct. 1281, 47 L. Ed. 2d 556 (1976), where the Supreme Court refused to grant the right to a lawyer in a court martial proceeding, the Texas court said, "We are concerned with the State's right under our statutes to have a jury observe the patient to determine her mental health to consider the possibility of treatment and/or the prevention of harm to herself or others."

Page 809. After 8, The Burden of Proof, add:

ADDINGTON v. TEXAS

99 S. Ct. 1804 (1979)

MR. CHIEF JUSTICE BURGER delivered the opinion of the Court.

The question in this case is what standard of proof is required by the Fourteenth Amendment to the Constitution in a civil proceeding brought under state law to commit an individual involuntarily for an indefinite period to a state mental hospital.

I

On seven occasions between 1969 and 1975 appellant was committed temporarily, Texas Mental Health Code Ann., Art. 5547-31-39 (Vernon), to various Texas state mental hospitals and was committed for indefinite periods, *id.*, at 5547-40-57, to Austin State Hospital on three different occasions. On December 18, 1975, when appellant was arrested on a misdemeanor charge of "assault by threat" against his mother, the county and state mental health authorities therefore were well aware of his history of mental and emotional difficulties.

Appellant's mother filed a petition for his indefinite commitment in accordance with Texas law. The county psychiatric examiner interviewed appellant while in custody and after the interview issued a Certificate of Medical Examination for Mental Illness. In the Certificate, the examiner stated his opinion that appellant was "mentally ill and require[d] hospitalization in a mental hospital." Art. 5547-42.

Appellant retained counsel and a trial was held before a jury to determine in accord with the statute:

(1) whether the proposed patient is mentally ill, and if so

(2) whether he requires hospitalization in a mental hospital for his own welfare and protection or the protection of others, and if so

(3) whether he is mentally incompetent. [Art. 5547-51.]

The trial on these issues extended over six days.

The State offered evidence that appellant suffered from serious delusions, that he often had threatened to injure both of his parents and others, that he had been involved in several assaultive episodes while hospitalized and that he had caused substantial property damage both at his own apartment and at his parents' home. From these undisputed facts, two psychiatrists, who qualified as experts, expressed opinions that appellant suffered from psychotic schizophrenia and that he had paranoid tendencies. They also expressed medical opinions that appellant was probably dangerous both to himself and to others. They explained that appellant required hospitalization in a closed area to treat his condition because in the past he had refused to attend out-patient treatment programs and had escaped several times from mental hospitals.

Appellant did not contest the factual assertions made by the State's witnesses; indeed, he conceded that he suffered from a mental illness. What appellant attempted to show was that there was no substantial basis for concluding that he was probably dangerous to himself or others.

The trial jury submitted the case to the jury with the instructions in the form of two questions:

1) Based on clear, unequivocal and convincing evidence, is Frank O'Neal Addington mentally ill?

2) Based on clear, unequivocal and convincing evidence, does Frank O'Neal Addington require hospitalization in a mental hospital for his own welfare and protection or the protection of others?

Appellant objected to these instructions on several grounds, including the trial court's refusal to employ the "beyond a reasonable doubt" standard of proof.

The jury found that appellant was mentally ill and that he required hospitalization for his own or others' welfare. The trial court then entered an order committing appellant as a patient to Austin State Hospital for an indefinite period.

Appellant appealed that order to the Texas Court of Civil Appeals, arguing, among other things, that the standards for commitment violated his substantive due process rights and that any standard of proof for commitment less than that required for criminal convictions, *i.e.*, beyond a reasonable doubt, violated his procedural due process rights. The Court of Civil Appeals agreed with appellant on the standard of proof issue and reversed the judgment of the trial court. Because of its treatment of the standard of proof, that court did not consider any of the other issues raised in the appeal.

On appeal, the Texas Supreme Court reversed the Court of Civil Appeals' decision. In so holding the supreme court relied primarily upon its previous decision in *State* v. *Turner,* 556 S.W.2d 563 (Tex.), *cert. denied,* 435 U.S. 929 (1977).

In *Turner,* the Texas Supreme Court held that a "preponderance of the evidence" standard of proof in a civil commitment proceeding satisfied due process. The court declined to adopt the criminal law standard of "beyond a reasonable doubt" primarily because it questioned whether the State could prove by that exacting standard that a particular person would or would not be dangerous in the future. It also distinguished a civil commitment from a criminal conviction by noting that under Texas law the mentally ill patient has the right to treatment, periodic review of his condition and immediate release when no longer deemed to be a danger to himself or others. Finally, the *Turner* court rejected the "clear and convincing" evidence standard because under Texas rules of procedure juries could be instructed only under a beyond a reasonable doubt or a preponderance standard of proof.

Reaffirming *Turner,* the Texas Supreme Court in this case concluded that the trial court's instruction to the jury, although not in conformity with the legal requirements, had benefited appellant, and hence the error was harmless. Accordingly, the court reinstated the judgment of the trial court.

We noted probable jurisdiction, 435 U.S. 967. After oral argument it became clear that no challenge to the constitutionality of any Texas statute was presented. Under 28 U.S.C. §1257 (2) no appeal is authorized; accordingly, construing the papers filed as a petition for a writ of certiorari, we now grant the petition.

II

The function of a standard of proof, as that concept is embodied in the Due Process Clause and in the realm of factfinding, is to "instruct the fact finder concerning the degree of confidence our society thinks he should have in the correctness of factual conclusions for a particular type of adjudication." *In re Winship*, 397 U.S. 358, 370 (1970) (Harlan, J., concurring). The standard serves to allocate the risk of error between the litigants and to indicate the relative importance attached to the ultimate decision.

Generally speaking, the evolution of this area of the law has produced across a continuum three standards or levels of proof for different types of cases. At one end of the spectrum is the typical civil case involving a monetary dispute between private parties. Since society has a minimal concern with the outcome of such private suits, plaintiff's burden of proof is a mere preponderance of the evidence. The litigants thus share the risk of error in roughly equal fashion.

In a criminal case, on the other hand, the interests of the defendant are of such magnitude that historically and without any explicit constitutional requirement they have been protected by standards of proof designed to exclude as nearly as possible the likelihood of an erroneous judgment.[2] In the administration of criminal justice our society imposes almost the entire risk of error upon itself. This is accomplished by requiring under the Due Process Clause that the state prove the guilt of an accused beyond a reasonable doubt. *In re Winship*, 397 U.S. 358 (1970).

The intermediate standard, which usually employs some combination of the words "clear," "cogent," "unequivocal" and "convincing," is less commonly used, but nonetheless "is no stranger to the civil law." *Woodby* v. *INS*, 385 U.S. 276, 285 (1967). See also McCormick, Evidence §320 (1954); 9 Wigmore, Evidence §2498 (3d ed. 1940). One typical use of the standard is in civil cases involving allegations of fraud or some other quasi-criminal wrongdoing by the defendant. The interests at stake in those cases are deemed to be more substantial than mere loss of money and some jurisdictions accordingly reduce the risk to the defendant of having his reputation tarnished erroneously by increasing the plaintiff's burden of proof. Similarly, this Court has used the "clear, unequivocal and convincing" standard of proof to protect particularly important individual interests in various civil cases. See, *e.g., Woodby* v. *INS, supra,* at 285 (deportation); *Chaunt* v. *United States,* 364 U.S. 350, 353

2. Compare Morano, A Reexamination of the Development of the Reasonable Doubt Rule, 55 B.U.L. Rev. 507 (1975) (reasonable doubt represented a less strict standard than previous common-law rules) with May, Some Rules of Evidence, 10 Am. L. Rev. 642 (1875) (reasonable doubt constituted a stricter rule than previous ones). See generally Underwood, The Thumb on the Scales of Justice: Burdens of Persuasion in Criminal Cases, 86 Yale L. J. 1299 (1977).

(1960) (denaturalization); *Schneiderman* v. *United States,* 320 U.S. 118, 125, 159 (1943) (denaturalization).

Candor suggests that, to a degree, efforts to analyze what lay jurors understand concerning the differences among these three tests or the nuances of a judge's instructions on the law may well be largely an academic exercise; there are no directly relevant empirical studies.[3] Indeed, the ultimate truth as to how the standards of proof affect decisionmaking may well be unknowable, given that factfinding is a process shared by countless thousands of individuals throughout the country. We probably can assume no more than that the difference between a preponderance of the evidence and proof beyond a reasonable doubt probably is better understood than either of them in relation to the intermediate standard of clear and convincing evidence. Nonetheless, even if the particular standard-of-proof catch-words do not always make a great difference in a particular case, adopting a "standard of proof is more than an empty semantic exercise." *Tippett* v. *Maryland,* 436 F.2d 1153, 1166 (4th Cir. 1971) (Sobeloff, J., concurring and dissenting), *cert. dismissed* sub nom. *Murel* v. *Baltimore City Criminal Court,* 407 U.S. 355 (1972). In cases involving individual rights, whether criminal or civil, "the standard of proof at a minimum reflects the value society places on individual liberty." *Ibid.*

III

In considering what standard should govern in a civil commitment proceeding, we must assess both the extent of the individual's interest in not being involuntarily confined indefinitely and the state's interest in committing the emotionally disturbed under a particular standard of proof. Moreover, we must be mindful that the function of legal process is to minimize the risk of erroneous decisions. See *Mathews* v. *Eldridge,* 424 U.S. 319, 335 (1976); *Speiser* v. *Randall,* 357 U.S. 513, 525-526 (1958).

A

This Court repeatedly has recognized that civil commitment for any purpose constitutes a significant deprivation of liberty that

3. There have been some efforts to evaluate the effect of varying standards of proof on jury factfinding, see, *e.g.,* L.S.E. Jury Project, Juries and the Rules of Evidence, 1973 Crim. L. Rev. 208, but we have found no study comparing all three standards of proof to determine how juries, real or mock, apply them.

requires due process protection. See, *e.g., Jackson* v. *Indiana,* 406 U.S. 715 (1972); *Humphrey* v. *Cady,* 405 U.S. 504 (1972); *In re Gault,* 387 U.S. 1 (1967); *Specht* v. *Patterson,* 386 U.S. 605 (1967). Moreover, it is indisputable that involuntary commitment to a mental hospital after a finding of probable dangerousness to self or others can engender adverse social consequences to the individual. Whether we label this phenomena "stigma" or choose to call it something else is less important than that we recognize that it can occur and that it can have a very significant impact on the individual.

The state has a legitimate interest under its *parens patriae* powers in providing care to its citizens who are unable because of emotional disorders to care for themselves; the state also has authority under its police power to protect the community from the dangerous tendencies of some who are mentally ill. Under the Texas Mental Health Code, however, the State has no interest in confining individuals involuntarily if they are not mentally ill or if they do not pose some danger to themselves or others. Since the preponderance standard creates the risk of increasing the number of individuals erroneously committed, it is at least unclear to what extent, if any, the state's interests are furthered by using a preponderance standard in such commitment proceedings.

The expanding concern of society with problems of mental disorders is reflected in the fact that in recent years many states have enacted statutes designed to protect the rights of the mentally ill. However, only one state by statute permits involuntary commitment by a mere preponderance of the evidence, Miss. Code Ann. §41-21-75, and Texas is the only state where a court has concluded that the preponderance of the evidence standard satisfies due process. We attribute this not to any lack of concern in those states, but rather to a belief that the varying standards tend to produce comparable results. As we noted earlier, however, standards of proof are important for their symbolic meaning as well as for their practical effect.

At one time or another every person exhibits some abnormal behavior which might be perceived by some as symptomatic of a mental or emotional disorder, but which is in fact within a range of conduct that is generally acceptable. Obviously such behavior is no basis for compelled treatment and surely none for confinement. However, there is the possible risk that a factfinder might decide to commit an individual based solely on a few isolated instances of unusual conduct. Loss of liberty calls for a showing that the individual suffers from something more serious than is demonstrated by idiosyncratic behavior. Increasing the burden of proof is one way to impress the factfinder with the importance of the decision and thereby perhaps to reduce the chances that inappropriate commitments will be ordered.

The individual should not be asked to share equally with society the risk of error when the possible injury to the individual is significantly greater than any possible harm to the state. We conclude that the individual's interest in the outcome of a civil commitment proceeding is of such weight and gravity that due process requires the state to justify confinement by proof more substantial than a mere preponderance of the evidence.

B

Appellant urges the Court to hold that due process requires use of the criminal law's standard of proof—"beyond a reasonable doubt." He argues that the rationale of the *Winship* holding that the criminal law standard of proof was required in a delinquency proceeding applies with equal force to a civil commitment proceeding.

In *Winship*, against the background of a gradual assimilation of juvenile proceedings into traditional criminal prosecutions, we declined to allow the state's "civil labels and good intentions" to "obviate the need for criminal due process safeguards in juvenile courts." 397 U.S., at 365-366. The Court saw no controlling difference in loss of liberty and stigma between a conviction for an adult and a delinquency adjudication for a juvenile. *Winship* recognized that the basic issue—whether the individual in fact committed a criminal act—was the same in both proceedings. There being no meaningful distinctions between the two proceedings, we required the state to prove the juvenile's act and intent beyond a reasonable doubt.

There are significant reasons why different standards of proof are called for in civil commitment proceedings as opposed to criminal prosecutions. In a civil commitment state power is not exercised in a punitive sense.[4] Unlike the delinquency proceeding in *Winship*, a

---

4. The State of Texas confines only for the purpose of providing care designed to treat the individual. As the Texas Supreme Court said in *State* v. *Turner*, 556 S.W.2d 563, 566 (1977): "The involuntary mental patient is entitled to treatment, to periodic and recurrent review of his mental condition, and to release at such time as he no longer presents a danger to himself and others."

civil commitment proceeding can in no sense be equated to a criminal prosecution. Cf. *Woodby* v. *INS, supra,* at 284-285.

In addition, the "beyond a reasonable doubt" standard historically has been reserved for criminal cases. This unique standard of proof, not prescribed or defined in the Constitution, is regarded as a critical part of the "moral force of the criminal law," 397 U.S., at 364, and we should hesitate to apply it too broadly or casually in noncriminal cases. Cf. *ibid.*

The heavy standard applied in criminal cases manifests our concern that the risk of error to the individual must be minimized even at the risk that some who are guilty might go free. *Patterson* v. *New York,* 432 U.S. 198, 208 (1977). The full force of that idea does not apply to a civil commitment. It may be true that an erroneous commitment is sometimes as undesirable as an erroneous conviction, 5 Wigmore §1400. However, even though an erroneous confinement should be avoided in the first instance, the layers of professional review and observation of the patient's condition, and the concern of family and friends generally will provide continuous opportunities for an erroneous commitment to be corrected. Moreover, it is not true that the release of a genuinely mentally ill person is no worse for the individual than the failure to convict the guilty. One who is suffering from a debilitating mental illness and in need of treatment is neither wholly at liberty nor free of stigma. See Chodoff, The Case for Involuntary Hospitalization of the Mentally Ill, 133 Am. J. Psychiatry 496, 498 (1976); Schwartz, et al., Psychiatric Labeling and the Rehabilitation of the Mental Patient, 31 Arch. Gen. Psychiatry 329, 335 (1974). It cannot be said, therefore, that it is much better for a mentally ill person to "go free" than for a mentally normal person to be committed.

Finally, the initial inquiry in a civil commitment proceeding is very different from the central issue in either a delinquency proceeding or a criminal prosecution. In the latter cases the basic issue is a straightforward factual question—did the accused commit the act alleged. There may be factual issues to resolve in a commitment proceeding, but the factual aspects represent only the beginning of the inquiry. Whether the individual is mentally ill and dangerous to either himself or others and is in need of confined therapy turns on the *meaning* of the facts which must be interpreted by expert psychiatrists and psychologists. Given the lack of certainty and the fallibility of psychiatric diagnosis, there is a serious question as to whether a state could ever prove beyond a reasonable doubt that an individual is both mentally ill and likely to be dangerous. See *O'Connor* v. *Donaldson,* 422 U.S. 563, 584 (1976) (concurring opinion); *Blocker* v. *United States,* 110 U.S. App. D.C. 41, 288 F.2d 853, 860-861 (1961) (concurring opinion). See also *Tippett* v. *Maryland,* 436 F.2d 1153, 1165 (4th Cir. 1973) (Sobeloff, J., concurring and dissenting), *cert. dismissed* sub nom. *Murel* v. *Baltimore City Criminal Court,* 407 U.S. 355 (1974); Note, Civil Commitment of the Mentally Ill.: Theories and Procedures, 79 Harv. L. Rev. 1288, 1291 (1968); Note, Due Process and the Development of "Criminal" Safeguards in Civil Commitment Adjudications, 42 Ford. L. Rev. 611, 624 (1974).

The subtleties and nuances of psychiatric diagnosis render certainties virtually beyond reach in most situations. The reasonable doubt standard of criminal law functions in its realm because there the standard is addressed to specific, knowable facts. Psychiatric diagnosis, in contrast, is to a large extent based on medical "impressions" drawn from subjective analysis and filtered through the experience of the diagnostician. This process often makes it very difficult for the expert physician to offer definite conclusions about any particular patient. Within the medical discipline, the traditional standard for "factfinding" is a "reasonable medical certainty." If a trained psychiatrist has difficulty with the categorical "beyond a reasonable doubt" standard, the untrained lay juror—or indeed even a trained judge—who is required to rely upon expert opinion could be forced by the criminal law standard of proof to reject commitment for many patients desperately in need of institutionalized psychiatric care. See Note, 42 Ford. L. Rev., at 624. Such "freedom" for a mentally ill person would be purchased at a high price.

That practical considerations may limit a constitutionally based burden of proof is demonstrated by the reasonable doubt standard, which is a compromise between what is possible to prove and what protects the rights of the individual. If the state was required to guarantee error-free convictions, it would be required to prove guilt beyond all doubt. However, "[d]ue process does not require that every conceivable step be taken, at whatever cost, to eliminate the possibility of convicting an innocent person." *Patterson* v. *New York,* 432 U.S. 197, 208 (1977). Nor should the state be required to employ a standard of proof that may completely undercut its efforts to further the legitimate interests of both the state and the patient that are served by civil commitments.

That some states have chosen—either legislatively or judicially—to adopt the criminal law standard[5] gives no assurance that the more stringent standard of proof is needed or is even adaptable to the needs of all states. The essence of federalism is that states must be free to develop a variety of solutions to problems and not be forced into a common, uniform mold. As the substantive standards for civil commitment may vary from state to state, procedures must be allowed to vary so long as they meet the constitutional minimum. See Monahan and Wexler, A Definite Maybe: Proof and Probability in Civil Commitment, 2 Law & Human Behavior 49, 53-54 (1978); Share, The Standard of Proof in Involuntary Civil Commitment Proceedings, 1977 Det. Coll. L. Rev. 209, 210. We conclude that it is unnecessary to require states to apply the strict, criminal standard.

C

Having concluded that the preponderance standard falls short of meeting the demands of due process and that the reasonable doubt standard is not required, we turn to a middle level of burden of proof that strikes a fair balance between the rights of the individual and the legitimate concerns of the state. We note that 20 states, most by statute, employ the standard of "clear and convincing" evidence;[6] three states use "clear, *cogent,* and convincing" evidence;[7] and two states require "clear, *unequivocal* and convincing" evidence.[8]

In *Woodby* v. *INS,* 385 U.S. 276 (1967), dealing with deportation

5. Haw. Rev. Stat. §334-60 (4) (I); Idaho Code §66-329 (i); Kan. Stat. Ann. §59-2917; Mont. Rev. Codes Ann. §38-1305 (7); Okla. Stat., Tit. 43A, §54.1 (C); Ore. Rev. Stat. §426.130; Utah Code Ann. §64-7-36(6); Wis. Stat. §51.20 (14) (e); *Superintendent of Worcester State Hospital* v. *Hagberg.* —Mass.—,372 N.E.2d 242 (1978); *Proctor* v. *Butler,* 380 A.2d 673 (N.H. 1977); *In re Hodges,* 325 A.2d 605 (D.C. 1974); *Lausche* v. *Commr. of Public Welfare,* 302 Minn. 65, 225 N.W.2d 366 (1974), *cert. denied,* 420 U.S. 993 (1975). See also *In re J. W.,* 44 N.J. Super. 216, 130 A.2d 64 (App. Div.), *cert. denied,* 24 N.J. 465, 132 A.2d 558 (1957); *Danton* v. *Commonwealth,* 383 S.W.2d 681 (Ky. 1964) (dicta).

6. Ariz. Rev. Stat. Ann. §36-540; Colo. Rev. Stat. §27-10-111 (1); Conn. Gen. Stat. §17-178 (c); Del. Code, Tit. 16, §5010 (2); Ga. Code §88-501 (a); Ill. Rev. Stat., ch. 91½, §3-808; Iowa Code §299.12; La. Rev. Stat. Ann., Tit. 28, §55E (West); Me. Rev. Stat. Ann. Tit. 34, §2334 (5) (A) (1); Mich. Stat. Ann., §14.800 (465); Neb. Rev. Stat. §83-1035; N. M. Stat. Ann. §34-2A-11C; N. D. Cent. Code §25-03.1-19; Ohio Rev. Code Ann. §5122.15 (B); Pa. Cons. Stat. Tit. 50, §7304 (f); S.C. Code §44-17-580; S. D. Comp. Laws Ann. §27A-9-18; Vt. Stat. Ann. Tit. 18, §7616 (b); Md. Dept. of Health & Mental Hygiene Reg. 10.04.03G; *In re Beverly,* 342 So. 2d 481 (Fla. 1977).

7. N.C. Gen. Stat. §122-58.7 (i); Wash. Rev. Code §71.05.310; *State ex rel. Hawks* v. *Lazaro,* 202 S.E.2d 109 (W. Va. 1974).

8. Ala. Code, Tit. 22, §52-10 (a); Tenn. Code Ann. §33-604 (d).

and *Schneiderman* v. *United States,* 320 U.S. 118, 125, 159 (1943), dealing with denaturalization, the Court held that "clear, unequivocal and convincing" evidence was the appropriate standard of proof. The term "unequivocal," taken by itself, means proof that admits of no doubt,[9] a burden approximating, if not exceeding, that used in criminal cases. The issues in *Schneiderman* and *Woodby* were basically factual and therefore susceptible of objective proof and the consequences to the individual were unusually drastic—loss of citizenship and expulsion from the United States.

We have concluded that the reasonable doubt standard is inappropriate in civil commitment proceedings because, given the uncertainties of psychiatric diagnosis, it may impose a burden the state cannot meet and thereby erect an unreasonable barrier to needed medical treatment. Similarly, we conclude that use of the term "unequivocal" is not constitutionally required, although the states are free to use that standard. To meet due process demands, the standard has to inform the factfinder that the proof must be greater than the preponderance of the evidence standard applicable to other categories of civil cases.

We noted earlier that the trial court employed the standard of "clear, unequivocal and convincing" evidence in appellant's commitment hearing before a jury. That instruction was constitutionally adequate. However, determination of the precise burden equal to or greater than the "clear and convincing" standard which we hold is required to meet due process guarantees is a matter of state law which we leave to the Texas Supreme Court.[10] Accordingly, we remand the case for further proceedings not inconsistent with this opinion.

Vacated and remanded.

Mr. Justice Powell took no part in the consideration or decision of this case.

Page 809. After 8., add:

NOTE: THE ADDINGTON CASE

The Supreme Court decision in *Addington* leaves open a significant question. What is it that is to be proved by "clear and convincing evidence"? The concept of "dangerousness," however described in a

9. See Webster's Third New International Dictionary 2494 (1969).
10. We noted earlier the court's holding on harmless error. See p. 4, *ante.*

statute, is subject to a large variety of definitions. See, e.g., Brooks, Notes on Defining the "Dangerousness" of the Mentally Ill, in C. Frederick, Dangerous Behavior: A Problem in Law and Mental Health (1978).

There are at least three models involved in applying a standard of proof to dangerousness. The first was adopted in *Lessard*, where the court required only that "all *facts* necessary to show that an individual is mentally ill and dangerous" required proof beyond a reasonable doubt. (Italics added). See Casebook, page 636.

The second model requires a prediction that the mentally ill candidate for commitment will engage in the future in behavior that is labelled dangerous behavior. This is often, but not always, physically violent behavior. Many studies tend to show that such predictions cannot be made with a sufficient degree of accuracy to meet any traditional standard of proof. See, e.g., Cocozza and Steadman, The Failure of Psychiatric Predictions of Dangerousness: Clear and Convincing Evidence, 29 Rutgers L. Rev. 1048 (1976). The lowest standard, preponderance of evidence, requires at the very least an increment of accuracy a mite over 50 percent. "Clear and convincing" has frequently been quantified as requiring approximately 60 to 75 percent of accuracy. "Beyond a reasonable doubt" has often been quantified as requiring approximately 90 percent of accuracy. For a fuller discussion of quantification of burdens of proof see Simon and Cockerham, Civil Commitment, Burden of Proof, and Dangerous Acts: A Comparison of the Perspective of Judges and Psychiatrists, 5 J. Psychiat. and L. 57, (1977).

Prediction studies persuasively show that predictions of dangerousness tend to fall well below 50 percent in the extent of their accuracy. Where this second model is followed (and there is reason to believe that many judges do follow it), a paradox is presented. How can you prove by a standard requiring well over 50 percent of accuracy that which research tells you cannot be proved by 50 percent of accuracy?

The third model avoids the paradox by presenting a definition of dangerousness in which the prediction element is but one factor. Depending on the gravity of the projected behavior and on other factors, the court can determine that even a 20 percent likelihood that violent behavior will occur is enough to justify a finding that the person presented for civil commitment is "dangerous." This approach was first spelled out in Note, 87 Harv. L. Rev. 1190, 1295-1503 (1974) and more contemporaneously discussed in Monahan and Wexler, A Definite Maybe: Proof and Probability in Civil Commitment, 2 L. and Human Behav. 37 (1978).

For other pre-*Addington* writings see Share, The Standard of Proof in Involuntary Civil Commitment Proceedings, 1977 Detroit Coll. L. Rev. 209 (1977); Note, Standard and Burden of Proof in Mental Commitment and Release Proceedings, 3 Wm. Mitchell L. Rev. 193 (1977); Comment, Does Due Process Require Clear and Convincing Proof Before Life's Liberties May be Lost?, 24 Emory L.J. 105 (1975); Note, Civil Commitment: Due Process and the Standard of Proof, 23 De Paul L. Rev. 1500 (1974); Note, Involuntary Civil Commitments—How Heavy the Burden, 29 Baylor L. Rev. 187 (1977).

An analysis geared to a Massachusetts case, Superintendent of Worcester State Hospital v. Hagberg, 1978 Mass. Adv. Sh. 187, is Comment, The Standard of Proof in Civil Commitment Proceedings in Massachusetts, 1 W. N.E.L. Rev. 71 (1978). The Massachusetts standard is beyond a reasonable doubt. The California Supreme Court has held that the standard of proof for "gravely disabled" is beyond a reasonable doubt. See Estate of Roulet, 152 Cal. Rptr. 425 (1979).

9. Due Process Procedures for Minors

PARHAM v. J.L. AND J.R.

99 S. Ct. 2493 (1979)

Mr. Chief Justice Burger delivered the opinion of the Court.

The question presented in this appeal is what process is constitutionally due a minor child whose parents or guardian seek state administered institutional mental health care for the child and specifically whether an adversary proceeding is required prior to or after the commitment.

(a) Appellee,[1] J. R., a child being treated in a Georgia state mental hospital, was a plaintiff in this class-action[2] suit based on 42

---

1. Pending our review one of the named plaintiffs before the District Court, J. L., died. Although the individual claim of J. L. is moot, we discuss the facts of this claim because, in part, they form the basis for the District Court's holding.

2. The class certified by the District Court, without objection by appellants, consisted "of all persons younger than 18 years of age now or hereafter received by any defendant for observation and diagnosis and/or detained for care and treatment at any 'facility' within the State of Georgia pursuant to" Ga. Code §88-503.1. Although one witness testified that on any given day there may be 200 children in the class, in December 1975 there were only 140.

U.S.C. §1983, in the District Court for the Middle District of Georgia. Appellants are the State's Commissioner of the Department of Human Resources, the Director of the Mental Health Division of the Department of Human Resources and the Chief Medical Officer at the hospital where appellee was being treated. Appellee sought a declaratory judgment that Georgia's voluntary commitment procedures for children under the age of 18, Ga. Code, §§88-503.1, 88-503.2,[3] violated the Due Process Clause of the Fourteenth Amendment and requested an injunction against its future enforcement.

A three-judge District Court was convened pursuant to 28 U.S.C. §§2281 and 2284. After considering expert and lay testimony and extensive exhibits and after visiting two of the State's regional mental health hospitals, the District Court held that Georgia's statutory scheme was unconstitutional because it failed to protect adequately the appellees' due process rights, *J. L.* v. *Parham,* 412 F. Supp. 112, 139 (M.D. Ga. 1976).

To remedy this violation the court enjoined future commitments based on the procedures in the Georgia statute. It also commanded Georgia to appropriate and expend whatever amount was "reasonably necessary" to provide nonhospital facilities deemed by the appellant state officials to be the most appropriate for the treatment of those members of plaintiffs' class, n.2, *supra,* who could be treated in a less drastic, nonhospital environment. *Id.,* at 139.

Appellants challenged all aspects of the District Court's judgment. We noted probable jurisdiction, 431 U.S. 936, and heard argument during the 1977 Term. The case was then consolidated with *Secretary of Public Welfare* v. *Institutionalized Juveniles,* No. 77-1715, and reargued this Term.

(b) J. L., a plaintiff before the District Court who is now deceased, was admitted in 1970 at the age of six years to Central State Regional Hospital in Milledgeville, Ga. Prior to his admission, J. L. had received out-patient treatment at the hospital for over two months. J. L.'s mother then requested the hospital to admit him indefinitely.

The admitting physician interviewed J. L. and his parents. He

3. Section 88-503.1 provides:

"The superintendent of any facility may receive for observation and diagnosis . . . any individual under 18 years of age for whom such application is made by his parent or guardian. . . . If found to show evidence of mental illness and to be suitable for treatment, such person may be detained by such facility for such period and under such conditions as may be authorized by law."

Section 88-503.2 provides:

"The superintendent of the facility shall discharge any voluntary patient who has recovered from his mental illness or who has sufficiently improved that the superintendent determines that hospitalization of the patient is no longer desirable."

learned that J. L.'s natural parents had divorced and his mother had remarried. He also learned that J. L. had been expelled from school because he was uncontrollable. He accepted the parents' representation that the boy had been extremely aggressive and diagnosed the child as having a "hyperkinetic reaction to childhood."

J. L.'s mother and stepfather agreed to participate in family therapy during the time their son was hospitalized. Under this program J. L. was permitted to go home for short stays. Apparently his behavior during these visits was erratic. After several months the parents requested discontinuance of the program.

In 1972, the child was returned to his mother and stepfather on a furlough basis, *i.e.*, he would live at home but go to school at the hospital. The parents found they were unable to control J. L. to their satisfaction which created family stress. Within two months they requested his readmission to Central State. J. L.'s parents relinquished their parental rights to the county in 1974.

Although several hospital employees recommended that J. L. should be placed in a special foster home with "a warm, supported, truly involved couple," the Department of Family and Children Services was unable to place him in such a setting. On October 24, 1975, J. L. filed this suit requesting an order of the court placing him in a less drastic environment suitable to his needs.

(c) Appellee, J. R., was declared a neglected child by the county and removed from his natural parents when he was three months old. He was placed in seven different foster homes in succession prior to his admission to Central State Hospital at the age of seven.

Immediately preceeding his hospitalization, J. R. received outpatient treatment at a county mental health center for several months. He then began attending school where he was so disruptive and incorrigible that he could not conform to normal behavior patterns. Because of his abnormal behavior J. R.'s seventh set of foster parents requested his removal from their home. The Department of Family and Children Services then sought his admission at Central State. The agency provided the hospital with a complete socio-medical history at the time of his admission. In addition, three separate interviews were conducted with J. R. by the admission team of the hospital.

It was determined that he was borderline retarded, and suffered an "unsocialized, aggressive reaction to childhood." It was recommended unanimously that he would "benefit from the structured environment" of the hospital and would "enjoy living and playing with boys of the same age."

J. R.'s progress was re-examined periodically. In addition, unsuccessful efforts were made by the Department of Family and Children Services during his stay at the hospital to place J. R. in various foster homes. On October 24, 1975, J. R. filed this suit requesting an order of the court placing him in a less drastic environment suitable to his needs.

(d) Georgia Code, §88-503.1 provides for the voluntary admission to a state regional hospital of children such as J. L. and J. R. Under that provision admission begins with an application for hospitalization signed by a "parent or guardian." Upon application the superintendent of each hospital is given the power to admit temporarily any child for "observation and diagnosis." If, after observation, the superintendent finds "evidence of mental illness" and that the child is "suitable for treatment" in the hospital, then the child may be admitted "for such period and under such conditions as may be authorized by law."

Georgia's mental health statute also provides for the discharge of voluntary patients. Any child who has been hospitalized for more than five days may be discharged at the request of a parent or guardian. §88-503.3 (a). Even without a request for discharge, however, the superintendent of each regional hospital has an affirmative duty to release any child "who has recovered from his mental illness or who has sufficiently improved that the superintendent determines that hospitalization of the patient is no longer desirable." §88-503.2.

Georgia's Mental Health Director has not published any statewide regulations defining what specific procedures each superintendent must employ when admitting a child under 18. Instead, each regional hospital's superintendent is responsible for the procedures in his or her facility. There is substantial variation among the institutions with regard to their admission procedures and their procedures for review of patients after they have been admitted. A brief description of the different hospitals' procedures[4] will demonstrate the variety of approaches taken by the regional hospitals throughout the State.

Southwestern Hospital in Thomasville, Ga. was built in 1966. Its children and adolescent program was instituted in 1974. The children and adolescent unit in the hospital has a maximum capacity of 20

4. Although the State has eight regional hospitals, superintendents from only seven of them were deposed. In addition, the District Court included only seven hospitals in its list of members of the plaintiff class. Apparently, the eighth hospital, Northwest Regional in Rome, Ga., had no children being treated there. The District Court's order was issued against the State Commissioner of the Department of Human Resources, who is responsible for the activities of all eight hospitals, including Northwest Regional.

beds, but at the time of suit only 10 children were being treated there.

The Southwestern superintendent testified that the hospital has never admitted a voluntary child patient who was not treated previously by a community mental health clinic. If a mental health professional at the community clinic determines that hospital treatment may be helpful for a child, then clinic staff and hospital staff jointly evaluate the need for hospitalization, the proper treatment during hospitalization and a likely release date. The initial admission decision thus is not made at the hospital.

After a child is admitted, the hospital has weekly reviews of his condition performed by its internal medical and professional staff. There also are monthly reviews of each child by a group composed of hospital staff not involved in the weekly reviews and by community clinic staff people. The average stay for each child who was being treated at Southwestern in 1975 was 100 days.

Atlanta Regional Hospital was opened in 1968. At the time of the hearing before the District Court, 17 children and 21 adolescents were being treated in the hospital's children and adolescent unit.

The hospital is affiliated with nine community mental health centers and has an agreement with them that "persons will be treated in the comprehensive community mental health centers in every possible instance, rather than being hospitalized." The admission criteria at Atlanta Regional for voluntary and involuntary patients are the same. It has a formal policy not to admit a voluntary patient unless the patient is found to be a threat to himself or others. The record discloses that approximately 25 percent of all referrals from the community centers are rejected by the hospital admissions staff.

After admission the staff reviews the condition of each child every week. In addition, there are monthly utilization reviews by nonstaff mental health professionals; this review considers a random sample of children's cases. The average length of each child's stay in 1975 was 161 days.

The Georgia Mental Health Institute (GMHI) in Decatur, Ga. was built in 1965. Its children and adolescent unit housed 26 children at the time this suit was brought.

The hospital has a formal affiliation with four community mental health centers. Those centers may refer patients to the hospital only if they certify that "no appropriate alternative resources are available within the client's geographic area." For the year prior to the trial in this case, no child was admitted except through a referral from a clinic. Although the hospital has a policy of generally accepting for 24 hours all referrals from a community clinic, it has a team of staff members who review each admission. If the team finds "no reason not to treat in the community" and the Deputy Superintendent of the hospital agrees, then it will release the applicant to his home.

After a child is admitted, there must be a review of the admission decision within 30 days. There is also an unspecified periodic review of each child's need for hospitalization by a team of staff members. The average stay for the children who were at GMHI in 1975 was 346 days.

Augusta Regional Hospital was opened in 1969 and is affiliated with 10 community mental health clinics. Its children and adolescent unit housed 14 children in December 1975.

Approximately 90 percent of the children admitted to the hospital have first received treatment in the community, but not all of them were admitted based on a specific referral from a clinic. The admission criterion is whether "the child needs hospitalization" and that decision must be approved by two psychiatrists. There is also an informal practice of not admitting a child if his parents refuse to participate in a family therapy program.

The admission decision is reviewed within 10 days by a team of staff physicians and mental health professionals; thereafter, each child is reviewed every week. In addition, every child's condition is reviewed by a team of clinic staff members every 100 days. The average stay for the children at Augusta in December 1975 was 92 days.

Savannah Regional Hospital was built in 1970 and it housed 16 children at the time of this suit. The hospital staff members are also directors of the community mental health clinics.

It is the policy of the hospital that any child seeking admission on a nonemergency basis must be referred by a community clinic. The admission decision must be made by a staff psychiatrist and it is based on the materials provided by the community clinic, an interview with the applicant and an interview with the parents, if any, of the child.

Within three weeks after admission of a child, there is review by a group composed of hospital and clinic staff members and people from the community, such as juvenile court judges. Thereafter, the hospital staff reviews each child weekly. If the staff concludes that a child is ready to be released, then the community committee reviews the child's case to assist in placement. The average stay of the children being treated at Savannah in December 1975 was 127 days.

West Central Hospital in Columbus, Ga. was opened in December 1974 and it was organized for budgetary purposes with several community mental health clinics. The hospital itself has only 20 beds for children and adolescents, 16 of which were occupied at the time this suit was filed.

There is a formal policy that all children seeking admission to the hospital must be referred by a community clinic. The hospital is regarded by the staff as "the last resort in treating a child;" 50 percent of the children referred are turned away by the admissions team at the hospital.

After admission, there are staff meetings daily to discuss problem cases. The hospital has a practicing child psychiatrist who reviews cases once a week. Depending on the nature of the problems, the consultant reviews between 1 and 20 cases. The average stay of the children who were at West Central in December 1975 was 71 days.

The children's unit at Central State Regional Hospital in Milledgeville, Ga. was added to the existing structure during the 1970s. It can accommodate 40 children. The hospital also can house 40 adolescents. At the time of suit, the hospital housed 37 children under 18, including both named plaintiffs.

Although Central State is affiliated with community clinics, it seems to have a higher percentage of nonreferral admissions than any of the other hospitals. The admissions decision is made by an "admissions evaluator" and the "admitting physician." The evaluator is a Ph.D. in psychology, a social worker or a mental health-trained nurse. The admitting physician is a psychiatrist. The standard for admission is "whether or not hospitalization is the more appropriate treatment" for the child. From April 1974 to November 1975, 9 of 29 children applicants screened for admission were referred to noninstitutional settings.

All children who are temporarily admitted are sent to the children and adolescent unit for testing and development of a treatment plan. Generally, seven days after the admission, members of the hospital staff review all of the information compiled about a patient "to determine the need for continued hospitalization." Thereafter, there is an informal review of the patient approximately every 60 days. The patients who were at Central State in December 1975 had been there on the average 456 days. There is no explanation in the record for this large variation from the average length of hospitalization at the other institutions.

Although most of the focus of the District Court was on the State's mental hospitals, it is relevant to note that Georgia presently funds over 50 community mental health clinics and 13 specialized foster care homes. The State has built seven new regional hospitals within the past 15 years and it has added a new children's unit to its oldest hospital. The State budget in fiscal year 1976 was almost $150 million for mental health care. Georgia ranks 22d among the States in per capita expenditures for mental health and 15th in total expenditures.[5]

The District Court nonetheless rejected the State's entire system of providing mental health care on both procedural and substantive grounds. The District Court found that 46 children could be "optimally cared for in another, less restrictive, non-hospital setting if it were available." 412 F. Supp., at 124. These "optimal" settings included group homes, therapeutic camps and home care services. The Governor of Georgia and the Chairmen of the two Appropriations Committees of its legislature, testifying in the District Court, expressed confidence in the Georgia program and informed the court that the State could not justify enlarging its budget during fiscal year 1977 to provide the specialized treatment settings urged by appellees in addition to those then available.

Having described the factual background of Georgia's mental health program and its treatment of the named plaintiffs, we turn now to examine the legal bases for the District Court's judgment.

II

In holding unconstitutional Georgia's statutory procedure for voluntary commitment of juveniles, the District Court first determined that commitment to any of the eight regional hospitals[6] constitutes a severe deprivation of a child's liberty. The court defined this liberty interest both in terms of a freedom from bodily restraint and freedom from the "emotional and psychic harm" caused by the institutionalization.[7] Having determined that a liberty interest is implicated by a child's admission to a mental hospital,

5. The source for these data is National Assn. of State Mental Health Prog. Directors, State Report: State Mental Health Agency Expenditures (Aug. 1, 1978).

6. The record is very sparse with regard to the physical facilities and daily routines at the various regional hospitals. The only hospital discussed by appellees' expert witness was Central State. The District Court visited Central State and one other hospital, but did not discuss the visits in its opinion.

7. In both respects the District Court found strong support for its holding in this Court's decision in *In re Gault,* 387 U.S. 1 (1967). In that decision we held that a state cannot institutionalize a juvenile delinquent without first providing certain due process protections.

the court considered what process is required to protect that interest. It held that the process due "includes at least the right after notice to be heard before an impartial tribunal." 412 F. Supp., at 139.

In requiring the prescribed hearing, the court rejected Georgia's argument that no adversary-type hearing was required since the State was merely assisting parents who could not afford private care by making available treatment similar to that offered in private hospitals and by private physicians. The court acknowledged that most parents who seek to have their children admitted to a state mental hospital do so in good faith. It, however, relied on one of appellees' witnesses who expressed an opinion that "some still look upon mental hospitals as a 'dumping ground.'" *Id.*, at 138.[8] No specific evidence of such "dumping," however, can be found in the record.

The District Court also rejected the argument that review by the superintendents of the hospitals and their staffs was sufficient to protect the child's liberty interest. The court held that the inexactness of psychiatry, coupled with the possibility that the sources of information used to make the commitment decision may not always be reliable, made the superintendent's decision too arbitrary to satisfy due process. The court then shifted its focus drastically from what was clearly a procedural due process analysis to what appears to be a substantive due process analysis and condemned Georgia's "officialdom" for its failure, in the face of a state-funded 1973 report[9] outlining the "need" for additional resources to be spent on nonhospital treatment, to provide more resources for noninstitutional mental health care. The court concluded that there was a causal relationship between this intransigence and the State's ability to provide any "flexible due process" to the appellees. The District Court therefore ordered the State to appropriate and expend such resources as would be necessary to provide non-hospital treatment to those members of appellees' class who would benefit from it.

---

8. In light of the District Court's holding that a judicial or quasi-judicial body should review voluntary commitment decisions, it is at least interesting to note that the witness who made the statement quoted in the text was not referring to parents as the people who "dump" children into hospitals. This witness opined that some juvenile court judges and child welfare agencies misused the hospitals. App. to Juris. Statement 768. See also Rolfe and MacClintock, The Due Process Rights of Minors "Voluntarily Admitted" to Mental Institutions, 4 J. Psych. & L. 333, 351 (1976) (hereinafter Rolfe and MacClintock).

9. This report was conducted by the Study Commission on Mental Health Services for Children and Youth and was financed by the State of Georgia. The Commission was made up of eight distinguished scholars in the field of mental health. They spent six months studying the five regional hospitals that were in existence at that time.

III

In an earlier day, the problems inherent in coping with children afflicted with mental or emotional abnormalities were dealt with largely within the family. See S. Brakel and R. Rock, The Mentally Disabled and the Law 4 (1971). Sometimes parents were aided by teachers or a family doctor. While some parents no doubt were able to deal with their disturbed children without specialized assistance, others, especially those of limited means and education, were not. Increasingly, they turned for assistance to local, public sources or private charities. Until recently most of the states did little more than provide custodial institutions for the confinement of persons who were considered dangerous. *Id.*, at 5-6; Slovenko, Criminal Justice Procedures in Civil Commitment, 24 Wayne L. Rev. 1, 3 (1977) (hereinafter Slovenko).

As medical knowledge about the mentally ill and public concern for their condition expanded, the states, aided substantially by federal grants,[10] have sought to ameliorate the human tragedies of seriously disturbed children. Ironically, as most states have expanded their efforts to assist the mentally ill, their actions have been subjected to increasing litigation and heightened constitutional scrutiny. Courts have been required to resolve the thorny constitutional attacks on state programs and procedures with limited precedential guidance. In this case appellees have challenged Georgia's procedural and substantive balance of the individual, family and social interests at stake in the voluntary commitment of a child to one of its regional mental hospitals.

The parties agree that our prior holdings have set out a general approach for testing challenged state procedures under a due process claim. Assuming the existence of a protectible property or liberty interest, the Court has required a balancing of a number of factors:

> First, the private interest that will be affected by the official action; second, the risk of an erroneous deprivation of such interest through the procedures used, and the probable value, if any, of additional or substitute procedural safeguards; and finally, the Government's interest, including the function involved and the fiscal and administrative burdens that the additional or substitute procedural requirement would entail. [*Mathews* v. *Eldridge*, 424 U.S. 319, 335 (1976); *Smith* v. *OFFER*, 431 U.S. 816, 847-848 (1977).]

In applying these criteria, we must consider first the child's interest

10. See, *e.g.*, Community Health Centers Act, 77 Stat. 290, as amended, 42 U.S.C. §2681 *et seq.*

in not being committed. Normally, however, since this interest is inextricably linked with the parents' interest in and obligation for the welfare and health of the child, the private interest at stake is a combination of the child's and parents' concerns.[11] Next we must examine the State's interest in the procedures it has adopted for commitment and treatment of children. Finally, we must consider how well Georgia's procedures protect against arbitrariness in the decision to commit a child to a state mental hospital.

(a) It is not disputed that a child, in common with adults, has a substantial liberty interest in not being confined unnecessarily for medical treatment and that the State's involvement in the commitment decision constitutes state action under the Fourteenth Amendment. See *Addington* v. *Texas,* No. 77-5992, at 7 (Apr. 30, 1979); *In re Gault,* 387 U.S. 1, 27 (1967); *Specht* v. *Patterson,* 386 U.S. 605 (1967). We also recognize that commitment sometimes produces adverse social consequences for the child because of the reaction of some to the discovery that the child has received psychiatric care. Cf. *Addington* v. *Texas, supra,* at 7.

This reaction, however, need not be equated with the community response resulting from being labeled by the state as delinquent, criminal, or mentally ill and possibly dangerous. See *ibid; In re Gault, supra,* at 23; *Paul* v. *Davis,* 424 U.S. 693, 711-712 (1976). The state through its voluntary commitment procedures does not "label" the child; it provides a diagnosis and treatment that medical specialists conclude the child requires. In terms of public reaction, the child who exhibits abnormal behavior may be seriously injured by an erroneous decision not to commit. Appellees overlook a significant source of the public reaction to the mentally ill, for what is truly "stigmatizing" is the symptomatology of a mental or emotional illness. *Addington* v. *Texas, supra,* at 10. See also Schwartz, Myers and Astrachan, Psychiatric Labeling and the Rehabilitation of the Mental Patient, 31 Archives of General Psychiatry 329 (1974).[12] The pattern of untreated, abnormal behavior—even if

11. In this part of the opinion we will deal with the issues arising when the natural parents of the child seek commitment to a state hospital. In Part IV we will deal with the situation presented when the child is a ward of the state.

12. See also Gove and Fain, The Stigma of Mental Hospitalization, 28 Archives of General Psychiatry 494, 500 (1973); Phillips, Rejection of the Mentally Ill: The Influence of Behavior and Sex, 29 Am. Soc. Rev. 679, 686-687 (1964). Research by Schwartz, Myers and Astrachan and that of Gove and Fain found "that the stigma of mental hospitalization is not a major problem for the ex-patient." Schwartz, Myers and Astrachan, Psychiatric Labeling and the Rehabilitation of the Mental Patient, 31 Archives of General Psychiatry 329, 333 (1974).

nondangerous—arouses at least as much negative reaction as treatment that becomes public knowledge. A person needing, but not receiving, appropriate medical care may well face even greater social ostracism resulting from the observable symptoms of an untreated disorder.[13]

However, we need not decide what effect these factors might have in a different case. For purposes of this decision, we assume that a child has a protectible interest not only in being free of unnecessary bodily restraints but also in not being labeled erroneously by some because of an improper decision by the state hospital superintendent.

(b) We next deal with the interests of the parents who have decided, on the basis of their observations and independent professional recommendations, that their child needs institutional care. Appellees argue that the constitutional rights of the child are of such magnitude and the likelihood of parental abuse is so great that the parents' traditional interests in and responsibility for the upbringing of their child must be subordinated at least to the extent of providing a formal adversary hearing prior to a voluntary commitment.

Our jurisprudence historically has reflected Western Civilization concepts of the family as a unit with broad parental authority over minor children. Our cases have consistently followed that course; our constitutional system long ago rejected any notion that a child is "the mere creature of the State" and, on the contrary, asserted that parents generally "have the right, coupled with the high duty, to recognize and prepare [their children] for additional obligations." *Pierce* v. *Society of Sisters,* 268 U.S. 510, 535 (1924). See also *Wisconsin* v. *Yoder,* 406 U.S. 205, 213 (1972); *Prince* v. *Massachusetts,* 321 U.S. 158, 166 (1944); *Meyer* v. *Nebraska,* 262 U.S. 390, 400 (1923). Surely, this includes a "high duty" to recognize symptoms of illness and to seek and follow medical advice. The law's concept of the family rests on a presumption that parents possess what a child lacks in maturity, experience, and capacity for judgment required for making life's difficult decisions. More important, historically it has recognized that natural bonds of affection lead parents to act in the best interests of their children. 1 W. Blackstone, Commentaries* 447; 2 Kent, Commentaries on American Law* 190.

---

13. As Schwartz, Myers and Astrachan concluded:

"Discharge [from a mental hospital] before disturbed behavior is well controlled may advance the patient into an inhospitable world that can incubate the chronicity that was to be avoided in the first place." 31 Archives of General Psychiatry 335.

As with so many other legal presumptions, experience and reality may rebut what the law accepts as a starting point; the incidence of child neglect and abuse cases attests to this. That some parents "may at times be acting against the interests of their child" as was stated in *Bartley* v. *Kremens,* 402 F. Supp. 1039, 1047-1048 (E.D. Pa. 1975), vacated, 431 U.S. 119 (1977), creates a basis for caution, but is hardly a reason to discard wholesale those pages of human experience that teach that parents generally do act in the child's best interests. See Rolfe and MacClintock 348-349. The statist notion that governmental power should supersede parental authority in *all* cases because *some* parents abuse and neglect children is repugnant to American tradition.

Nonetheless, we have recognized that a state is not without constitutional control over parental discretion in dealing with children when their physical or mental health is jeopardized. See *Wisconsin* v. *Yoder, supra,* at 230; *Prince* v. *Massachusetts, supra,* at 166. Moreover, the Court recently declared unconstitutional a state statute that granted parents an absolute veto over a minor child's decision to have an abortion. *Planned Parenthood of Missouri* v. *Danforth,* 428 U.S. 52 (1976). Appellees urge that these precedents limiting the traditional rights of parents, if viewed in the context of the liberty interest of the child and the likelihood of parental abuse, require us to hold that the parents' decision to have a child admitted to a mental hospital must be subjected to an exacting constitutional scrutiny, including a formal, adversary, pre-admission hearing.[14]

Appellees' argument, however, sweeps too broadly. Simply because the decision of a parent is not agreeable to a child or because it involves risks does not automatically transfer the power to make that decision from the parents to some agency or officer of the state. The same characterizations can be made for a tonsillectomy, appendectomy or other medical procedure. Most children, even in adolescence, simply are not able to make sound judgments concerning many decisions, including their need for medical care or treatment. Parents can and must make those judgments. Here there is no finding by the District Court of even a single instance of bad

14. Judge Friendly has cogently pointed out:
"It should be realized that procedural requirements entail the expenditure of limited resources, that at some point the benefit to individuals from an additional safeguard is substantially outweighed by the cost of providing such protection, and that the expense in protecting those likely to be found undeserving will probably come out of the pockets of the deserving." Friendly, Some Kind of Hearing, 123 U. Pa. L. Rev. 1267, 1276 (1975). See also *Wheeler* v. *Montgomery,* 397 U.S. 280, 282 (1970) (dissenting opinion).

faith by any parent of any member of appellees' class. We cannot assume that the result in *Meyer* v. *Nebraska, supra,* and *Pierce* v. *Society of Sisters, supra,* would have been different if the children there had announced a preference to learn only English or a preference to go to a public, rather than a church, school. The fact that a child may balk at hospitalization or complain about a parental refusal to provide cosmetic surgery does not diminish the parents' authority to decide what is best for the child. See generally Goldstein, Medical Case for the Child at Risk: On State Supervention of Parental Autonomy, 86 Yale L.J. 645, 664-668 (1977). Bennett, Allocation of Child Medical Care Decision-making Authority: A Suggested Interest Analysis, 62 Va. L. Rev. 285, 308 (1976). Neither state officials nor federal courts are equipped to review such parental decisions.

Appellees place particular reliance on *Planned Parenthood,* arguing that its holding indicates how little deference to parents is appropriate when the child is exercising a constitutional right. The basic situation in that case, however, was very different; *Planned Parenthood* involved an absolute parental veto over the child's ability to obtain an abortion. Parents in Georgia in no sense have an absolute right to commit their children to state mental hospitals; the statute requires the superintendent of each regional hospital to exercise independent judgment as to the child's need for confinement. See p. 5, *supra.*

In defining the respective rights and prerogatives of the child and parent in the voluntary commitment setting, we conclude that our precedents permit the parents to retain a substantial, if not the dominant, role in the decision, absent a finding of neglect or abuse, and that the traditional presumption that the parents act in the best interests of their child should apply. We also conclude, however, that the child's rights and the nature of the commitment decision are such that parents cannot always have absolute and unreviewable discretion to decide whether to have a child institutionalized. They, of course, retain plenary authority to seek such care for their children, subject to a physician's independent examination and medical judgment.

(c) The State obviously has a significant interest in confining the use of its costly mental health facilities to cases of genuine need. The Georgia program seeks first to determine whether the patient seeking admission has an illness that calls for in-patient treatment. To accomplish this purpose, the State has charged the superintendents of each regional hospital with the responsibility for determining, before authorizing an admission, whether a prospective patient is mentally ill and whether the patient will likely benefit from hospital care. In addition, the State has imposed a continuing duty on hospital superintendents to release any patient who has recovered to the point where hospitalization is no longer needed.

The State in performing its voluntarily assumed mission also has a significant interest in not imposing unnecessary procedural obstacles that may discourage the mentally ill or their families from seeking needed psychiatric assistance. The *parens patriae* interest in helping parents care for the mental health of their children cannot be fulfilled if the parents are unwilling to take advantage of the opportunities because the admission process is too onerous, too embarrassing or too contentious. It is surely not idle to speculate as to how many parents who believe they are acting in good faith would forego state-provided hospital care if such care is contingent on participation in an adversary proceeding designed to probe their motives and other private family matters in seeking the voluntary admission.

The State also has a genuine interest in allocating priority to the diagnosis and treatment of patients as soon as they are admitted to a hospital rather than to time-consuming procedural minuets before the admission.[14] One factor that must be considered is the utilization of the time of psychiatrists, psychologists and other behavioral specialists in preparing for and participating in hearings rather than performing the task for which their special training has fitted them. Behavioral experts in courtrooms and hearings are of little help to patients.

The *amicus* brief of the American Psychiatric Association points out at page 20 that the average staff psychiatrist in a hospital presently is able to devote only 47 percent of his time to direct patient care. One consequence of increasing the procedures the state must provide prior to a child's voluntary admission will be that mental health professionals will be diverted even more from the treatment of patients in order to travel to and participate in—and wait for—what could be hundreds—or even thousands—of hearings each year. Obviously the cost of these procedures would come from the public monies the legislature intended for mental health care. See Slovenko 34-35.

(d) We now turn to consideration of what process protects adequately the child's constitutional rights by reducing risks of error without unduly trenching on traditional parental authority and without undercutting "efforts to further the legitimate interests of both the state and the patient that are served by" voluntary commitments. *Addington* v. *Texas*, No. 77-5992, at 12. See also *Mathews* v. *Eldridge*, 424 U.S. 319, 335 (1976). We conclude that the risk of error inherent in the parental decision to have a child institutionalized for mental health care is sufficiently great that some kind of inquiry should be made by a "neutral factfinder" to determine whether the statutory requirements for admission are satisfied. See *Goldberg* v. *Kelly*, 397 U.S. 254, 271 (1970); *Morrissey* v. *Brewer*, 408 U.S. 471, 489 (1972). That inquiry must carefully probe the child's background using all available sources, including, but not limited to, parents, schools and other social agencies. Of course, the review must also include an interview with the child. It is necessary that the decisionmaker have the authority to refuse to admit any child who does not satisfy the medical standards for admission. Finally, it is necessary that the child's continuing need for commitment be reviewed periodically by a similarly independent procedure.[15]

We are satisfied that such procedures will protect the child from an erroneous admission decision in a way that neither unduly burdens the states nor inhibits parental decisions to seek state help.

Due process has never been thought to require that the neutral and detached trier of fact be law-trained or a judicial or administrative officer. See *Goldberg* v. *Kelly, supra,* at 271; *Morrissey* v. *Brewer, supra,* at 489. Surely, this is the case as to medical decisions for "neither judges nor administrative hearing officers are better qualified than psychiatrists to render psychiatric judgments." *In re Roger S.,* 19 Cal. 3d 921, 941, 569 P.2d 1286, 1299 (1977) (Clark, J., dissenting). Thus, a staff physician will suffice, so long as he or she is free to evaluate independently the child's mental and emotional condition and need for treatment.

It is not necessary that the deciding physician conduct a formal or quasi-formal hearing. A state is free to require such a hearing, but due process is not violated by use of informal, traditional medical investigative techniques. Since well-established medical procedures already exist, we do not undertake to outline with specificity precisely what this investigation must involve. The mode and procedure of medical diagnostic procedures is not the business of judges. What is best for a child is an individual medical decision that must be left

15. As we discuss more fully later, p. 31, *infra,* the District Court did not decide and we therefore have no reason to consider at this time what procedures for review are independently necessary to justify continuing a child's confinement. We merely hold that a subsequent, independent review of the patient's condition provides a necessary check against possible arbitrariness in the *initial* admission decision.

to the judgment of physicians in each case. We do no more than emphasize that the decision should represent an independent judgment of what the child requires and that all sources of information that are traditionally relied on by physicians and behavioral specialists should be consulted.

What process is constitutionally due cannot be divorced from the nature of the ultimate decision that is being made. Not every determination by state officers can be made most effectively by use of "the procedural tools of judicial and administrative decisionmaking." *Board of Curators of the U. of Missouri* v. *Horowitz*, 435 U.S. 78, 90 (1978). See also *Greenholtz* v. *Nebraska Penal & Correctional Complex*, No. 78-201, at 11 (May 29, 1979); *Cafeteria & Restaurant Workers Local 473* v. *McElroy*, 367 U.S. 886, 895 (1961).[16]

Here the questions are essentially medical in character: whether the child is mentally or emotionally ill and whether he can benefit from the treatment that is provided by the state. While facts are plainly necessary for a proper resolution of those questions, they are only a first step in the process. In an opinion for a unanimous Court, we recently stated in *Addington* v. *Texas, supra,* at 10-11, "whether a person is mentally ill . . . turns on the *meaning* of the facts which must be interpreted by expert psychiatrists and psychologists."

Although we acknowledge the fallibility of medical and psychiatric diagnosis, see *O'Connor* v. *Donaldson*, 422 U.S. 563, 584 (1975) (concurring opinion), we do not accept the notion that the shortcomings of specialists can always be avoided by shifting the decision from a trained specialist using the traditional tools of medical science to an untrained judge or administrative hearing officer after a judicial-

---

16. Relying on general statements from past decisions dealing with governmental actions not even remotely similar to those involved here, the dissent concludes that if a protectible interest is involved then there must be some form of traditional, adversary, judicial or administrative hearing either before or after its deprivation. That result is mandated, in their view, regardless of what process the state has designed to protect the individual and regardless of what the record demonstrates as to the fairness of the state's approach.

The dissenting approach is inconsistent with our repeated assertion that "due process is *flexible* and calls for such procedural protections as the particular situation demands." *Morrissey* v. *Brewer*, 408 U.S. 471, 481 (1972). Just as there is no requirement as to exactly what procedures to employ whenever a traditional judicial-type hearing is mandated, compare *Goss* v. *Lopez*, 419 U.S. 565 (1975); *Wolff* v. *McDonnell*, 418 U.S. 539 (1973); *Morrissey* v. *Brewer, supra,* with *Goldberg* v. *Kelly*, 397 U.S. 254 (1970), there is no reason to require a judicial-type hearing in all circumstances. As the scope of governmental action expands into new areas creating new controversies for judicial review, it is incumbent on courts to design procedures that protect the rights of the individual without unduly burdening the legitimate efforts of the states to deal with difficult social problems. The judicial model for factfinding for all constitutionally protected interests, regardless of their nature, can turn rational decisionmaking into an unmanageable enterprise.

type hearing. Even after a hearing, the nonspecialist decisionmaker must make a medical-psychiatric decision. Common human experience and scholarly opinions suggest that the supposed protections of an adversary proceeding to determine the appropriateness of medical decisions for the commitment and treatment of mental and emotional illness may well be more illusory than real. See Albers, Pasewark and Meyer, Involuntary Hospitalization and Psychiatric Testimony: The Fallibility of the Doctrine of Immaculate Perception, 6 Cap. U.L. Rev. 11, 15 (1976).[17]

Another problem with requiring a formalized, factfinding hearing lies in the danger it poses for significant intrusion into the parent-child relationship. Pitting the parents and child as adversaries often will be at odds with the presumption that parents act in the best interests of their child. It is one thing to require a neutral physician to make a careful review of the parents' decision in order to make sure it is proper from a medical standpoint; it is a wholly different matter to employ an adversary contest to ascertain whether the parents' motivation is consistent with the child's interests.

Moreover, it is appropriate to inquire into how such a hearing would contribute to the long range successful treatment of the patient. Surely, there is a risk that it would exacerbate whatever tensions already existed between the child and the parents. Since the parents can and usually do play a significant role in the treatment while the child is hospitalized and even more so after release, there is a serious risk that an adversary confrontation will adversely affect the ability of the parents to assist the child while in the hospital. Moreover, it will make his subsequent return home more difficult. These unfortunate results are especially critical with an emotionally disturbed child; they seem likely to occur in the context of an adversary hearing in which the parents testify. A confrontation over such intimate family relationships would distress the normal adult parents and the impact on a disturbed child almost certainly would be significantly greater.[18]

17. See Albers and Pasewark, Involuntary Hospitalization: Surrender at the Courthouse, 2 Am. J. Comm. Psych. 288 (1974) (mean hearing time for 300 consecutive commitment cases was 9.2 minutes): Miller and Schwartz, County Lunacy Commission Hearings: Some Observations of Commitment to a State Mental Hospital, 14 Soc. Prob. 26 (1966) (mean time for hearings was 3.8 minutes); Scheff, The Societal Reaction to Deviance: Ascriptive Elements in the Psychiatric Screening of Mental Patients in a Midwestern State, 11 Soc. Prob. 401 (1964) (average hearing lasted 9.2 minutes). See also Cohen, The Function of the Attorney and the Commitment of the Mentally Ill, 44 U. Texas L. Rev. 424 (1966).

18. While not altogether clear, the District Court opinion apparently contemplated a hearing preceded by a written notice of the proposed commitment. At the hearing the child

It has been suggested that a hearing conducted by someone other than the admitting physician is necessary in order to detect instances where parents are "guilty of railroading their children into asylums" or are using "voluntary commitment procedures in order to sanction behavior of which they disapprove." Ellis, Volunteering Children: Parental Commitment of Minors to Mental Institutions, 62 Calif. L. Rev. 840, 850-851 (1974). See also *J. L. v. Parham,* 412 F. Supp. 112, 133 (M. D. Ga. 1976); Brief for Appellee 38. Curiously it seems to be taken for granted that parents who seek to "dump" their children on the state will inevitably be able to conceal their motives and thus deceive the admitting psychiatrists and the other mental health professionals who make and review the admission decision. It is elementary that one early diagnostic inquiry into the cause of an emotional disturbance of a child is an examination into the environment of the child. It is unlikely if not inconceivable that a decision to abandon an emotionally normal, healthy child and thrust him into an institution will be a discrete act leaving no trail of circumstances. Evidence of such conflicts will emerge either in the interviews or from secondary sources. It is unrealistic to believe that trained psychiatrists, skilled in eliciting responses, sorting medically relevant facts and sensitive to motivational nuances will often be deceived about the family situation surrounding a child's emotional disturbance.[19] Surely a lay, or even law-trained factfinder, would be no more skilled in this process than the professional.

By expressing some confidence in the medical decision-making process, we are by no means suggesting it is error free. On occasion

---

presumably would be given an opportunity to be heard and present evidence, and the right to cross-examine witnesses, including, of course, the parents. The court also required an impartial trier of fact who would render a written decision reciting the reasons for accepting or rejecting the parental application.

Since the parents in this situation are seeking the child's admission to the state institution, the procedure contemplated by the District Court presumably would call for some other person to be designated as a guardian *ad litem* to act for the child. The guardian, in turn, if not a lawyer, would be empowered to retain counsel to act as an advocate of the child's interest.

Of course, a state may elect to provide such adversary hearings in situations where it perceives that parents and a child may be at odds, but nothing in the Constitution compels such procedures.

19. In evaluating the problem of detecting "dumping" by parents, it is important to keep in mind that each of the regional hospitals has a continuing relationship with the Department of Family and Children Services. The staffs at those hospitals refer cases to the Department when they suspect a child is being mistreated and thus are sensitive to this problem. In fact, J. L.'s situation is in point. The family conflicts and problems were well documented in the hospital records. Equally well documented, however, were the child's severe emotional disturbances and his need for treatment.

parents may initially mislead an admitting physician or a physician may erroneously diagnose the child as needing institutional care either because of negligence or an overabundance of caution. That there may be risks of error in the process affords no rational predicate for holding unconstitutional an entire statutory and administrative scheme that is generally followed in more than 30 states.[20] "[P]rocedural due process rules are shaped by the risk of error inherent in the truthfinding process as applied to the generality of cases, not the rare exceptions." *Mathews* v. *Eldridge,* 424 U.S. 319, 344 (1976). In general, we are satisfied that an independent medical decisionmaking process, which includes the thorough psychiatric investigation described earlier followed by additional periodic review of a child's condition, will protect children who should not be admitted; we do not believe the risks of error in that process would be significantly reduced by a more formal, judicial-type hearing. The issue remains whether the Georgia practices, as described in the record before us, comport with these minimum due process requirements.

(e) Georgia's statute envisions a careful diagnostic medical inquiry to be conducted by the admitting physician at each regional hospital. The *amicus* brief of the Solicitor General explains, at pp. 7-8:

[I]n every instance the decision whether or not to accept the child for treatment is made by a physician employed by the State. . . .

20. Alaska Stat. Ann. §47.30.020 (1962); Ariz. Rev. Stat. Ann. §36-518, 519 (1974 rev.); Ark. Stat. Ann. §59-405B (1971); Cal. Hosp. & Inst. Code Ann. §6000 (West 1972 rev.); D.C. Code §21-511, 512 (1973); Fla. Stat. §394.465 (1) (a) (1973); Ga. Code §88-503.1, 503.2 (1969 rev.); Haw. Rev. Stat. §334-60 (a) (2) (1976 rev.) (only for child less than 15), Idaho Code §66-318, 320 (1973 rev.) (parent may admit child under 14, but child over 16 may obtain release); Ill. Rev. Stat. ch. 91½, §5-2, 6-2 (1978 Supp.); Ind. Code §16-14-9.1-2 (1973 rev.); Kan. Stat. Ann. §59-2905, 2907 (1976); Ky. Rev. Stat. §202A.020 (1978); La. Rev. Stat. Ann. §28:57C (West 1975); Md. Ann. Code, Art. 59, §11 (g) (1972 rev.) (parental consent permissible only to some facilities), Mass. Gen. Laws Ann., ch. 123, §10 (a) (1969); Mich. Stat. Ann. §14.800 (415) (2) (1976 rev.) (child may object within 30 days and receive a hearing); Miss. Code Ann. §41-21-103 (c) (1972) (certificate of need for treatment for two physicians required); Mo. Rev. Stat. §202.1151 (2), 1152 (2) (1977); Nev. Rev. Stat. §422A.540, 560 (1978); N.Y. Mental Hyg. Law §31.13 (1976) (parent may admit, but child may obtain own release); N.D. Cent. Code §25-03.1-04 (1978); Ohio Rev. Code Ann. §5122.02 (B) (1970); Okla. Stat., Tit. 43A, §184 (1978); Ore. Rev. Stat. §426. 220 (1) (1977); Pa. Stat. Ann., Tit. 50, §7201 (Purdon 1973) (only for child less than 14); R.I. Gen. Laws §26-2-8 (1978 Cum. Supp.) (requires certificate of two physicians that child is insane); S.C. Code §44-17-310 (2) (1976); S.D. Comp. Laws Ann. §27A-8-2 (1976); Tenn. Code Ann. §33-601 (a) (1) (1977); Utah Code Ann. §64-7-29, 31 (2) (1953); Wash. Rev. Code §72.23.070 (2) (1978) (child over 13 also must consent); W. Va. Code §27-4-1 (b) (1976 rep.) (consent of child over 12 required); Wyo. Stat. §25-3-106 (a) (1) (i) (1977 rep.).

That decision is based on interviews and recommendations by hospital or community health center staff. The staff interviews the child and the parent or guardian who brings the child to the facility . . . [and] attempts are made to communicate with other possible sources of information about the child. . . .

Focusing primarily on what it saw as the absence of any formal mechanism for review of the physician's initial decision, the District Court unaccountably saw the medical decision as an exercise of "unbridled discretion." 412 F. Supp., at 136. But extravagant characterizations are no substitute for careful analysis and we must examine the Georgia process in its setting to determine if, indeed, any one person exercises such discretion.

In the typical case the parents of a child initially conclude from the child's behavior that there is some emotional problem—in short, that "something is wrong." They may respond to the problem in various ways, but generally the first contact with the State occurs when they bring the child to be examined by a psychologist or psychiatrist at a community mental health clinic.

Most often, the examination is followed by outpatient treatment at the community clinic. In addition, the child's parents are encouraged, and sometimes required, to participate in a family therapy program to obtain a better insight into the problem. In most instances, this is all the care a child requires. However, if, after a period of outpatient care, the child's abnormal emotional condition persists, he may be referred by the local clinic staff to an affiliated regional mental hospital.

At the regional hospital an admissions team composed of a psychiatrist and at least one other mental health professional examines and interviews the child—privately in most instances. This team then examines the medical records provided by the clinic staff and interviews the parents. Based on this information, and any additional background that can be obtained, the admissions team makes a diagnosis and determines whether the child will likely benefit from institutionalized care. If the team finds either condition not met, admission is refused.

If the team admits a child as suited for hospitalization, the child's condition and continuing need for hospital care are reviewed periodically by at least one independent, medical review group. For the most part, the reviews are as frequent as weekly, but none are less often than once every two months. Moreover, as we noted earlier the superintendent of each hospital is charged with an affirmative statutory duty to discharge any child who is no longer mentally ill or in need of therapy.[21]

As with most medical procedures, Georgia's are not totally free from risk of error in the sense that they give total or absolute assurance that every child admitted to a hospital has a mental illness optimally suitable for institutionalized treatment. But it bears repeating that "procedural due process rules are shaped by the risk of error inherent in the truthfinding process as applied to the generality of cases, not the rare exceptions." *Mathews* v. *Eldridge, supra,* at 344.

Georgia's procedures are not "arbitrary" in the sense that a single physician or other professional has the "unbridled discretion" the District Court saw to commit a child to a regional hospital. To so find on this record would require us to assume that the physicians, psychologists and mental health professionals who participate in the admission decision and who review each others' conclusions as to the continuing validity of the initial decision are either oblivious or indifferent to the child's welfare—or that they are incompetent. We note, however, the District Court found to the contrary; it was "impressed by the conscientious, dedicated state employed psychiatrists who, with the help of equally conscientious dedicated state employed psychologists and social workers, faithfully care for the plaintiff children. . . ." 412 F. Supp., at 138.

This finding of the District Court also effectively rebuts the suggestion made in some of the briefs *amici* that hospital administrators may not actually be "neutral and detached" because of institutional pressure to admit a child who has no need for hospital care. That such a practice may take place in some institutions in some places affords no basis for a finding as to Georgia's program; the evidence in the record provides no support whatever for that charge against the staffs at any of the State's eight regional hospitals. Such cases, if they are found, can be dealt with individually;[22] they do not lend themselves to class-action remedies.

We are satisfied that the voluminous record as a whole supports the

21. While the record does demonstrate that the procedures may vary from case to case, it also reflects that no child in Georgia was admitted for indefinite hospitalization without being interviewed personally and without the admitting physician checking with secondary sources, such as school or work records.

22. One important means of obtaining individual relief for these children is the availability of habeas corpus. As the appellants' brief explains, "Ga. Code §88-502.11 provides that at any time and without notice a person detained in a facility, or a relative or friend of such person, may petition for a writ of habeas corpus to question the cause and legality of the detention of the person." Brief for Appellants 36-37.

conclusion that the admissions' staffs of the hospitals have acted in a neutral and detached fashion in making medical judgments in the best interests of the children. The State, through its mental health programs, provides the authority for trained professionals to assist parents in examining, diagnosing and treating emotionally disturbed children, through its hiring practices it provides well staffed and equipped hospitals and—as the District Court found—conscientious public employees to implement the State's beneficent purposes.

Although our review of the record in this case satisfies us that Georgia's general administrative and statutory scheme for the voluntary commitment of children is not *per se* unconstitutional, we cannot decide on this record whether every child in appellees' class received an adequate, independent diagnosis of his emotional condition and need for confinement under the standards announced earlier in this opinion. On remand, the District Court is free to and should consider any individual claims that initial admissions did not meet the standards we have described in this opinion.

In addition, we note that appellees' original complaint alleged that the State had failed to provide adequate periodic review of their need for institutional care and claimed that this was an additional due process violation. Since the District Court held that the appellees' original confinement was unconstitutional, it had no reason to consider this separate claim. Similarly, we have no basis for determining whether the review procedures of the various hospitals are adequate to provide the process called for or what process might be required if a child contests his confinement by requesting a release. These matters require factual findings not present in the District Court's opinion. We have held that the periodic reviews described in the record reduce the risk of error in the initial admission and thus they are necessary. Whether they are sufficient to justify continuing a voluntary commitment is an issue for the District Court on remand. The District Court is free to require additional evidence on this issue.

IV

(a) Our discussion in Part III was directed at the situation where a child's natural parents request his admission to a state mental hospital. Some members of appellees' class, including J. R., were wards of the State of Georgia at the time of their admission. Obviously their situation differs from those members of the class who have natural parents. While the determination of what process is due varies somewhat when the state, rather than a natural parent, makes the request for commitment, we conclude that the differences in the two situations do not justify requiring different procedures at the time of the child's initial admission to the hospital.

For a ward of the State, there may well be no adult who knows him thoroughly and who cares for him deeply. Unlike with natural parents where there is a presumed natural affection to guide their action, Blackstone* 447; Kent* 190, the presumption that the state will protect a child's general welfare stems from a specific state statute. Ga. Code Ann. §24A-101. Contrary to the suggestion of the dissent, however, we cannot assume that when the State of Georgia has custody of a child it acts so differently from a natural parent in seeking medical assistance for the child. As Mr. Justice Stewart's concurring opinion points out, *post,* at p. 3, no one has questioned the validity of the statutory presumption that the State acts in the child's best interest. Nor could such a challenge be mounted on the record before us. There is no evidence that the State, acting as guardian, attempted to admit any child for reasons unrelated to the child's need for treatment. Indeed, neither the District Court nor the appellees has suggested that wards of the State should receive any constitutional treatment different from children with natural parents.

Once we accept that the State's application of a child for admission to a hospital is made in good faith, then the question is whether the medical decisionmaking approach of the admitting physician is adequate to satisfy due process. We have already recognized that an independent medical judgment made from the perspective of the best interests of the child after a careful investigation is an acceptable means of justifying a voluntary commitment. We do not believe that the soundness of this decisionmaking is any the less reasonable in this setting.

Indeed, if anything, the decision with regard to wards of the State may well be even more reasonable in light of the extensive written records that are compiled about each child while in the State's custody. In J. R.'s case, the admitting physician had a complete social and medical history of the child before even beginning the diagnosis. After carefully interviewing him and reviewing his extensive files, three physicians independently concluded that institutional care was in his best interests. See p. 4, *supra.*

Since the state agency having custody and control of the child *in loco parentis* has a duty to consider the best interests of the child with respect to a decision on commitment to a mental hospital, the State may constitutionally allow that custodial agency to speak for the child, subject, of course, to the restrictions governing natural parents. On this record we cannot declare unconstitutional Georgia's admission procedures for wards of the State.

(b) It is possible that the procedures required in reviewing a ward's need for continuing care should be different from those used to review a child with natural parents. As we have suggested earlier, the issue of what process is due to justify continuing a voluntary commitment must be considered by the District Court on remand. In making that inquiry the District Court might well consider whether wards of the State should be treated with respect to continuing therapy differently from children with natural parents.

The absence of an adult who cares deeply for a child has little effect on the reliability of the initial admission decision, but it may have some effect on how long a child will remain in the hospital. We noted in *Addington* v. *Texas, supra,* at 10, "the concern of family and friends will provide continuous opportunities for an erroneous commitment to be corrected." For a child without natural parents, we must acknowledge the risk of being "lost in the shuffle." Moreover, there is at least some indication that J. R.'s commitment was prolonged because the Department of Family and Children Services had difficulty finding a foster home for him. Whether wards of the State generally have received less protection than children with natural parents, and, if so, what should be done about it, however, are matters that must be decided in the first instance by the District Court on remand,[23] if the Court concludes the issue is still alive.

V

It is important that we remember the purpose of Georgia's comprehensive mental health program. It seeks substantively and at great cost to provide care for those who cannot afford to obtain private treatment and procedurally to screen carefully all applicants to assure that institutional care is suited to the particular patient. The State resists the complex of procedures ordered by the District

---

23. To remedy the constitutional violation, the District Court ordered hearings to be held for each member of the plaintiff class, see n. 2, *supra.* For 46 members of the class found to be treatable in "less drastic" settings, the District Court also ordered the State to expend such monies as was necessary to provide alternative treatment facilities and programs. While the order is more appropriate as a remedy for a substantive due process violation, the court made no findings on that issue. The order apparently was intended to remedy the procedural due process violation it found. Since that judgment is reversed, there is no basis for us to consider the correctness of the remedy.

Court because in its view they are unnecessary to protect the child's rights, they divert public resources from the central objective of administering health care, they risk aggravating the tensions inherent in the family situation and they erect barriers that may discourage parents from seeking medical aid for a disturbed child.

On this record we are satisfied that Georgia's medical factfinding processes are reasonable and consistent with constitutional guarantees. Accordingly, it was error to hold unconstitutional the State's procedures for admitting a child for treament to a state mental hospital. The judgment is therefore reversed and the case is remanded to the District Court for further proceedings consistent with this opinion.

Reversed and remanded.

MR. JUSTICE STEWART, concurring in the judgment.

For centuries it has been a canon of the common law that parents speak for their minor children.[1] So deeply imbedded in our traditions is this principle of law that the Constitution itself may compel a State to respect it. *Meyer* v. *Nebraska,* 262 U.S. 390; *Pierce* v. *Society of Sisters,* 268 U.S. 510.[2] In ironic contrast, the District Court in this case has said that the Constitution *requires* the State of Georgia to *disregard* this established principle. I cannot agree.

There can be no doubt that commitment to a mental institution results in a "massive curtailment of liberty," *Humphrey* v. *Cady,* 405 U.S. 504, 509. In addition to the physical confinement involved, *O'Connor* v. *Donaldson,* 422 U.S. 563, a person's liberty is also substantially affected by the stigma attached to treatment

---

1. See W. Blackstone, Commentaries* 452-453; J. Kent, 2 Commentaries 203-206 (3d ed. 1832); J. Schouler, A Treatise on the Law of Domestic Relations, 335-353 (3d ed. 1882); G. W. Field, The Legal Relations of Infants 63-80 (1888).

"It is cardinal with us that the custody, care and nurture of the child reside first in the parents, whose primary function and freedom include preparation for obligations the state can neither supply nor hinder." *Prince* v. *Massachusetts,* 321 U.S. 158, at 166.

"The history and culture of Western civilization reflect a strong tradition of parental concern for the nurture and upbringing of their children. This primary role of the parents in the upbringing of their children is now established beyond debate as an enduring American tradition." *Wisconsin* v. *Yoder,* 406 U.S. 205, at 232.

"Because he may not foresee the consequences of his decision, a minor may not make an enforceable bargain. He may not lawfully work or travel where he pleases, or even attend exhibitions of constitutionally protected adult motion pictures. Persons below a certain age may not marry without parental consent." *Planned Parenthood of Missouri* v. *Danforth,* 428 U.S. 52, 102 (Stevens, J., concurring in part and dissenting in part).

Cf. *Stump* v. *Sparkman,* 435 U.S. 349, 366 (dissenting opinion).

2. "The child is not the mere creature of the State; those who nurture him and direct his destiny have the right, coupled with the high duty, to recognize and prepare him for additional obligations." *Pierce* v. *Society of Sisters,* 268 U.S. 510, 535.

in a mental hospital.[3] But not every loss of liberty is governmental deprivation of liberty, and it is only the latter that invokes the Due Process Clause of the Fourteenth Amendment.

The appellees were committed under the following section of the Georgia Code:

> Authority to receive voluntary patients—
>
> (a) The superintendent of any facility may receive for observation and diagnosis any individual 18 years of age, or older, making application therefor, any individual under 18 years of age for whom such application is made by his parent or guardian and any person legally adjudged to be incompetent for whom such application is made by his guardian. If found to show evidence of mental illness and to be suitable for treatment, such person may be given care and treatment at such facility and such person may be detained by such facility for such period and under such conditions as may be authorized by law. [Ga. Code Ann. §88-503.1.]

Clearly, if the appellees in this case were adults who had voluntarily chosen to commit themselves to a state mental hospital, they could not claim that the State had thereby deprived them of liberty in violation of the Fourteenth Amendment. Just as clearly, I think, children on whose behalf their parents have invoked these voluntary procedures can make no such claim.

The Georgia statute recognizes the power of a party to act on behalf of another person under the voluntary commitment procedures in two situations: when the other person is a minor not over 17 years of age and the party is that person's parent or guardian, and when the other person has been "legally adjudged incompetent" and the party is that person's guardian. In both instances two conditions are present. First, the person being committed is presumptively incapable of making the voluntary commitment decision for himself. And second, the parent or guardian is presumed to be acting in that person's best interests.[4] In the case of guardians, these presumptions are grounded in statutes whose validity nobody has questioned in this case. Ga. Code Ann. §49-201 (1978 Supp.).[5] In the case of

---

3. The fact that such a stigma may be unjustified does not mean it does not exist. Nor does the fact that public reaction to past commitment may be less than the reaction to aberrant behavior detract from this assessment. The aberrant behavior may disappear, while the fact of past institutionalization lasts forever.

4. This is also true of a child removed from the control of his parents. For the juvenile court then has a duty to "secure for him care as nearly as possible equivalent to that which [his parents] should have given him." Ga. Code Ann. §24A-101.

5. "The power of the guardian over the person of his or her ward shall be the same as that of the parent over his or her child, the guardian standing in his or her place; and in like manner it shall be the duty of the guardian to protect and maintain, and, according to the circumstances of the ward, to educate him or her."

parents, the presumptions are grounded in a statutory embodiment of long-established principles of the common law.

Thus the basic question in this case is whether the Constitution requires Georgia to ignore basic principles so long accepted by our society. For only if the State in this setting is constitutionally compelled always to intervene between parent and child can there be any question as to the constitutionally required extent of that intervention. I believe this basic question must be answered in the negative.[6]

Under our law parents constantly make decisions for their minor children that deprive the children of liberty, and sometimes even of life itself. Yet surely the Fourteenth Amendment is not invoked when an informed parent decides upon major surgery for his child, even in a state hospital. I can perceive no basic constitutional differences between commitment to a mental hospital and other parental decisions that result in a child's loss of liberty.

I realize, of course, that a parent's decision to commit his child to a state mental institution results in a far greater loss of liberty than does his decision to have an appendectomy performed upon the child in a state hospital. But if, contrary to my belief, this factual difference rises to the level of a constitutional difference, then I believe that the objective checks upon the parents' commitment decision, embodied in Georgia law and thoroughly discussed, at pp. 21-24 of the Court's opinion, are more than constitutionally sufficient.

To be sure, the presumption that a parent is acting in the best interests of his child must be a rebuttable one, since certainly not all parents are actuated by the unselfish motive the law presumes. Some parents are simply unfit parents. But Georgia clearly provides that an unfit parent can be stripped of his parental authority under laws dealing with neglect and abuse of children.[7]

This is not an easy case. Issues involving the family and issues concerning mental illness are among the most difficult that courts have to face, involving as they often do serious problems of policy disguised as questions of constitutional law. But when a state legis-

6. *Planned Parenthood of Mo.* v. *Danforth,* 428 U.S. 52, was an entirely different case. The Court's opinion today discusses some of these differences, *ante,* at 18, but I think there is a more fundamental one. The *Danforth* case involved an expectant mother's right to decide upon an abortion—a personal substantive constitutional right. *Roe* v. *Wade,* 410 U.S. 113; *Doe* v. *Bolton,* 410 U.S. 179. By contrast the appellees in this case had no substantive constitutional right not to be hospitalized for psychiatric treatment.

7. See Mr. Justice Brennan's dissenting opinion, p. 6, and no. 16, *post.*

lature makes a reasonable definition of the age of minority, and creates a rebuttable presumption that in invoking the statutory procedures for voluntary commitment a parent is acting in the best interests of his minor child, I cannot believe that the Fourteenth Amendment is violated. This is not to say that in this area the Constitution compels a State to respect the traditional authority of a parent, as in the *Meyer* and *Pierce* cases. I believe, as in *Prince* v. *Massachusetts*, 321 U.S. 158, that the Constitution would tolerate intervention by the State.[8] But that is a far cry from holding that such intervention is constitutionally compelled.

For these reasons I concur in the judgment.

MR. JUSTICE BRENNAN, with whom MR. JUSTICE MARSHALL and MR. JUSTICE STEVENS join, concurring in part and dissenting in part.

I agree with the Court that the commitment of juveniles to state mental hospitals by their parents or by state officials acting *in loco parentis* involves state action that impacts upon constitutionally protected interests and therefore must be accomplished through procedures consistent with the constitutional mandate of due process of law. I agree also that the District Court erred in interpreting the Due Process Clause to require preconfinement commitment hearings in all cases in which parents wish to hospitalize their children. I disagree, however, with the Court's decision to pretermit questions concerning the post-admission procedures due Georgia's institutionalized juveniles. While the question of the frequency of post-admission review hearings may properly be deferred, the right to at least one post-admission hearing, can and should be affirmed now. I also disagree with the Court's conclusion concerning the procedures due juvenile wards of the State of Georgia. I believe that the Georgia statute is unconstitutional in that it fails to accord pre-confinement hearings to juvenile wards of the State committed by the State acting *in loco parentis*.

I

RIGHTS OF CHILDREN COMMITTED TO MENTAL INSTITUTIONS

Commitment to a mental institution necessarily entails a "massive curtailment of liberty," *Humphrey* v. *Cady*, 405 U.S. 504, 509

---

8. The *Prince* case held that the State may constitutionally intervene in the parent-child relationship for the purpose of enforcing its child labor law.

If the State intervened, its procedures would, of course, be subject to the limitations imposed by the Fourteenth Amendment.

(1972), and inevitably affects "fundamental rights." *Baxstrom* v. *Herold*, 383 U.S. 107, 113. Persons incarcerated in mental hospitals are not only deprived of their physical liberty. They are also deprived of friends, family, and community. Institutionalized mental patients must live in unnatural surroundings under the continuous and detailed control by strangers. They are subject to intrusive treatment which, especially if unwarranted, may violate their right to bodily integrity. Such treatment modalities may include forced administration of psychotropic medication,[1] aversive conditioning,[2] convulsive therapy,[3] and even psychosurgery.[4] Furthermore, as the Court recognizes, see maj. op., at 15, persons confined in mental institutions are stigmatized as sick and abnormal during confinement and, in some cases, even after release.[5]

Because of these considerations our cases have made clear that commitment to a mental hospital "is a deprivation of liberty which the State cannot accomplish without due process of law." *O'Connor* v. *Donaldson*, 422 U.S. 563, 580 (1975) (Burger, C. J., concurring). See, *e.g.*, *McNeil* v. *Director*, 407 U.S. 245 (1972) (defective delinquent commitment following expiration of prison term); *Sprecht* v. *Patterson*, 386 U.S. 605 (1967) (sex offender commitment following criminal conviction); *Chaloner* v. *Sherman*, 242 U.S. 455, 461 (1917) (incompetence inquiry). In the absence of a voluntary, knowing and intelligent waiver, adults facing commitment to mental institutions are entitled to full and fair adversarial hearings in which the necessity for their commitment is established to the satisfaction of a neutral tribunal. At such hearings they must be accorded the right to "be present with counsel, have an opportunity to be heard, be confronted with witnesses against [them], have the right to cross-examine, and to offer evidence of [their] own." *Specht* v. *Patterson*, 386 U.S. 605, 610 (1967).

These principles also govern the commitment of children. "Con-

1. See Winters v. Miller, 446 F.2d 65 (2nd Cir. 1971), *cert. denied*, 404 U.S. 985 (1971); Scott v. Plante, 532 F.2d 939 (3rd Cir. 1976); Souder v. McGuire, 423 F. Supp. 830 (M.D. Pa. 1976).

2. See Knecht v. Gillman, 488 F.2d 1136 (8th Cir. 1973); Mackey v. Procunier, 477 F.2d 877 (9th Cir. 1973).

3. See *Wyatt* v. *Hardin*, No. 3195-N (M.D. Ala., Feb. 28, 1975, June 26, 1975, and July 1, 1975); *Price* v. *Shepard*, 239 N.W.2d 905 (Minn. 1976), 1 M.D.L.R. 120; *Nelson* v. *Hudspeth*, C.A. No. J75-40 (R) (S.D. Miss., May 16, 1977).

4. See *Kaimowitz* v. *Michigan Department of Mental Health*, No. 73-19434-AW (Cir. Ct. Wayne County, Mich., July 10, 1973), 1 M.D.L.R. 147.

5. See generally Note, Civil Commitment of the Mentally Ill, 87 Harv. L. Rev. 1190, 1200 (1974).

stitutional rights do not mature and come into being magically only when one attains the state-defined age of majority. Minors, as well as adults, are protected by the Constitution and possess constitutional rights." See, *e.g., Breed* v. *Jones,* 421 U.S. 519 (1975); *Goss* v. *Lopez,* 419 U.S. 565 (1975); *Tinker* v. *Des Moines School Dist.,* 393 U.S. 1 (1967)." *Planned Parenthood* v. *Danforth,* 428 U.S. 52, 74 (1976).

Indeed, it may well be argued that children are entitled to more protection than are adults. The consequences of an erroneous commitment decision are more tragic where children are involved. Children, on the average, are confined for longer periods than are adults.[6] Moreover, childhood is a particularly vulnerable time of life[7] and children erroneously institutionalized during their formative years may bear the scars for the rest of their lives.[8] Furthermore, the provision of satisfactory institutionalized mental care for children generally requires a substantial financial commitment[9] that too often has not been forthcoming.[10] Decisions of the lower courts have chronicled the inadequacies of existing mental health facilities for children. See, *e.g., N.Y. State Assoc. Retarded Children* v. *Rockefeller,* 357 F. Supp. 752, 756 (E.D.N.Y. 1973) (Conditions at Willowbrook School for the Mentally Retarded are "inhumane," involving "failure to protect the physical safety of the children," substantial personnel shortage, and "poor" and "hazardous" conditions); *Wyatt* v. *Stickney,* 344 F. Supp. 387, 391 (MD Ala. 1972), *aff'd* sub nom. *Wyatt* v. *Aderholt,* 503 F.2d 1305 (5th Cir. 1974) ("grossly substandard" conditions at Partlow School for the Mentally Retarded lead to "hazardous and deplorable inadequacies in the institution's operations.")[11]

In addition, the chances of an erroneous commitment decision are particularly great where children are involved. Even under the best of

6. See National Institute of Mental Health, Division of Biometry, Statistical Note 90, at 14 table 8 (Public Health Service, July 1973).

7. See J. Bowlby, Child Care and the Growth of Love 80 (1965); J. Horocks, The Psychology of Adolescence 156 (1970); Elkin, Agents of Socialization in Children's Behavior 360 (Bergman ed. 1968).

8. See B. Flint, The Child and the Institution 14-15 (1966); H. Leland and D. Smith, Mental Retardation; Present and Future Perspectives 86 (1974); N. Hobbs, The Futures of Children 142-143 (1975).

9. See Joint Commission on the Mental Health of Children, Crisis in Child Mental Health: Challenges for the 1970s, at 271 (1969).

10. See R. Kugel and W. Walfensberger, Changing Patterns in Residential Services for the Mentally Retarded 22 (1969).

11. See also *Wheeler* v. *Glass,* 473 F. 983 (7th Cir. 1973); *Davis* v. *Watkins,* 384 F. Supp. 1196 (ND Ohio 1974); *Welsch* v. *Likins,* 373 F. Supp. 487 (Minn. 1974).

circumstances psychiatric diagnosis and therapy decisions are fraught with uncertainties. See *O'Connor* v. *Donaldson,* 422 U.S. 563, 584 (1975) (Burger, C. J., concurring). These uncertainties are aggravated when, as under the Georgia practice, the psychiatrist interviews the child during a period of abnormal stress in connection with the commitment, and without adequate time or opportunity to become acquainted with the patient.[12] These uncertainties may be further aggravated when economic and social class separate doctor and child, thereby frustrating the accurate diagnosis of pathology.[13]

These compounded uncertainties often lead to erroneous commitments since psychiatrists tend to err on the side of medical caution and therefore hospitalize patients for whom other dispositions would be more beneficial.[14] The National Institute of Mental Health recently found that only 36 percent of patients below age 20 who were confined at St. Elizabeths Hospital actually required such hospitalization.[15] Of particular relevance to this case, a Georgia study Commission on Mental Health Services for Children and Youth concluded that more than half of the State's institutionalized children were not in need of confinement if other forms of care were made available or used. Cited in *J. L.* v. *Parham,* 412 F. Supp. 112, 122 (MD Ga. 1976).

II

RIGHTS OF CHILDREN COMMITTED BY THEIR PARENTS

A

Notwithstanding all this Georgia denies hearings to juveniles institutionalized at the behest of their parents. Georgia rationalizes this practice on the theory that parents act in their children's best interests and therefore may waive their children's due process rights. Children incarcerated because their parents wish them confined, Georgia contends, are really voluntary patients. I cannot accept this argument.

12. See J. Simons, Psychiatric Examination of Children 1, 6 (1974); Laurie and Rieger, Psychiatric and Psychological Examination of Children, in 2 American Handbook of Psychiatry 19 (S. Arieti ed. 1974).

13. See Joint Commission on the Mental Health of Children, *supra,* n.9, at 267.

14. See T. Scheff, Being Mentally Ill: A Sociological Theory (1966); Ennis & Witwack, Psychiatry and the Presumption of Expertise: Flipping Coins in the Courtroom, 62 Calif. L. Rev. 693 (1974).

15. See National Institute of Mental Health, Statistical Note 115, Children and State Mental Hospitals 4 (Apr. 1975).

In our society, parental rights are limited by the legitimate rights and interests of their children. "Parents may be free to become martyrs themselves. But it does not follow they are free, in identical circumstances, to make martyrs of their children before they have reached the age of full and legal discretion when they can make that choice for themselves." *Prince* v. *Massachusetts,* 321 U.S. 158, 170 (1944). This principle is reflected in the variety of statutes and cases that authorize state intervention on behalf of neglected or abused children[16] and that, *inter alia,* curtail parental authority to alienate their children's property,[17] to withhold necessary medical treatment,[18] and to deny children exposure to ideas and experiences they may later need as independent and autonomous adults.[19]

This principle is also reflected in constitutional jurisprudence. Notions of parental authority and family autonomy cannot stand as absolute and invariable barriers to the assertion of constitutional rights by children. States, for example, may not condition a minor's right to secure an abortion on attaining her parents' consent since the right to an abortion is an important personal right and since disputes between parents and children on this question would fracture family autonomy. See *Planned Parenthood of Missouri* v. *Danforth,* 428 U.S. 52, 75 (1976).

This case is governed by the rule of *Danforth.* The right to be free from wrongful incarceration, physical intrusion and stigmatization has significance for the individual surely as great as the right to an abortion. Moreover, as in *Danforth,* the parent-child dispute at issue here cannot be characterized as involving only a routine child-rearing

16. See generally S. Katz, When Parents Fail (1971); M. Midonick and D. Bersharov, Children, Parents and the Courts: Juvenile Delinquency, Ungovernability and Neglect (1972); Wald, State Intervention on Behalf of "Neglected" Children. A Search for Realistic Standards, 27 Stan. L. Rev. 985 (1975).

17. See, *e.g., Martorell* v. *Ochoa,* 276 F. 99 (1st Cir. 1921).

18. See, *e.g., Jehovah's Witnesses* v. *Kings County Hosp.,* 278 F. Supp. 488 (W.D. Wash. 1967), *Aff'd,* 390 U.S. 598 (1968); *In re Sampson,* 65 Misc. 2d 658, 317 N.Y.S.2d 641 (Fam. Ct.), *aff'd,* 37 App. Div. 2d 668, 323 N.Y.S.2d 253, *aff'd,* 29 N.Y. 900, 278 N.C. 918, 328 N.Y.S. 2d 686 (1972); *State* v. *Perricone,* 37 N.J. 463, 181 A.2d 751 (1962). Similarly, more recent legal disputes involving the sterilization of children have led to the conclusion that parents are not permitted to authorize operations with such far-reaching consequences. See, *e.g., A. L.* v. *G. R. H.,* 325 N.S.2d 501 (Ct. App. Ind. 1975); *In re N. K. R.,* 515 S.W.2d 470 (Mo. 1974); *Frazier v. Love,* 440 S.W.2d 33 (Civ. App. Tex. 1969).

19. See *Commonwealth* v. *Renfrew,* 332 Mass. 492, 126 N.E.2d 109 (1955); *Meyerkorth* v. *State,* 173 Neb. 889, 115 N.W.2d 585 (1962), *appeal dismissed,* 372 U.S. 705 (1963); *Application of Auster,* 198 Misc. 1055, 100 N.Y.S.2d 60 (Sup. Ct. 1950), *aff'd,* 278 App. Div. 656, 104 N.Y.S.2d 65 (2d Dept.), *aff'd,* 302 N.Y. 855, 100 N.E.2d 47, *appeal dismissed,* 342 U.S. 884 (1951).

decision made within the context of an ongoing family relationship. Indeed, *Danforth* involved only a potential dispute between parent and child, whereas here a break in family autonomy has actually resulted in the parents' decision to surrender custody of their child to a state mental institution. In my view, a child who has been ousted from his family has even greater need for an independent advocate.

Additional considerations counsel against allowing parents unfettered power to institutionalize their children without cause or without any hearing to ascertain that cause. The presumption that parents act in their children's best interests, while applicable to most child-rearing decisions, is not applicable in the commitment context. Numerous studies reveal that parental decisions to institutionalize their children often are the results of dislocation in the family unrelated to the children's mental condition.[20] Moreover, even well-meaning parents lack the expertise necessary to evaluate the relative advantages and disadvantages of in-patient as opposed to out-patient psychiatric treatment. Parental decisions to waive hearings in which such questions could be explored, therefore, cannot be conclusively deemed either informed or intelligent. In these circumstances, I respectfully suggest, it ignores reality to assume blindly that parents act in their children's best interests when making commitment decisions and when waiving their children's due process rights.

B

This does not mean States are obliged to treat children who are committed at the behest of their parents in precisely the same manner as other persons who are involuntarily committed. The demands of due process are flexible and the parental commitment decision carries with it practical implications that States may legitimately take into account. While as a general rule due process requires that commitment hearings precede involuntary hospitalization, when parents seek to hospitalize their children special considerations militate in favor of postponement of formal commitment proceedings and against mandatory adversarial preconfinement commitment hearings.

20. Murdock, Civil Rights of the Mentally Retarded: Some Critical Issues, 48 Notre Dame Lay. 138 (1972); Vogel & Bell, The Emotionally Disturbed Child as the Family Scapegoat, in a Modern Introduction to the Family 412 (1968).

First, the prospect of an adversarial hearing prior to admission might deter parents from seeking needed medical attention for their children. Second, the hearings themselves might delay treatment of children whose home life has become impossible and who require some form of immediate state care. Furthermore, because adversarial hearings at this juncture would necessarily involve direct challenges to parental authority, judgment or veracity, preadmission hearings may well result in pitting the child and his advocate against the parents. This, in turn, might traumatize both parent and child and make the child's eventual return to his family more difficult.

Because of these special considerations I believe that States may legitimately postpone formal commitment proceedings when parents seek in-patient psychiatric treatment for their children. Such children may be admitted, for a limited period, without prior hearing, so long as the admitting psychiatrist first interviews parent and child and concludes that short term in-patient treatment would be appropriate.

Georgia's present admission procedures are reasonably consistent with these principles. See maj. op., at 21. To the extent the District Court invalidated this aspect of the Georgia juvenile commitment scheme and mandated preconfinement hearings in all cases, I agree with the Court that the District Court was in error.

C

I do not believe, however, that the present Georgia juvenile commitment scheme is constitutional in its entirety. Although Georgia may postpone formal commitment hearings, when parents seek to commit their children, the State cannot dispense with such hearings altogether. Our cases make clear that, when protected interests are at stake, the "fundamental requirement of due process is the opportunity to be heard at a meaningful time and in a meaningful manner." *Matthews* v. *Eldridge,* 424 U.S. 319, 333 (1976), quoting in part from *Armstrong* v. *Manzo,* 380 U.S. 545, 552 (1965). Whenever prior hearings are impracticable, States must provide reasonably prompt postdeprivation hearings. Compare *North Georgia Finishing Inc.* v. *Di-Chem Inc.,* 419 U.S. 601 (1975), with *Mitchell* v. *W. T. Grant Co.,* 416 U.S. 600 (1974).

The informal postadmission procedures that Georgia now follows are simply not enough to qualify as hearings—let alone reasonably prompt hearings. The procedures lack all the traditional due process safeguards. Commitment decisions are made *ex parte.* Georgia's institutionalized juveniles are not informed of the reasons for their commitment; nor do they enjoy the right to be present at the commitment determination, nor the right to representation, the right to be heard, the right to be confronted with adverse witnesses, the right to cross-examine, or the right to offer evidence of their own. By any standard of due process, these procedures are deficient. See *Wolff* v. *McDonnell,* 418 U.S. 539 (1974), *Morrissey* v. *Brewer,* 408 U.S. 471 (1972), *McNeil* v. *Director,* 407 U.S. 245 (1972), *Sprecht* v. *Patterson,* 386 U.S. 605, 610 (1967). See also *Goldberg* v. *Kelly,* 397 U.S. 254, 269-271 (1970). I cannot understand why the Court pretermits condemnation of these *ex parte* procedures which operate to deny Georgia's institutionalized juveniles even "some form of hearing," *Matthews* v. *Eldridge, supra,* at 333, before they are condemned to suffer the rigors of long term institutional confinement.[21]

The special considerations that militate against preadmission commitment hearings when parents seek to hospitalize their children do not militate against reasonably prompt postadmission commitment hearings. In the first place, postadmission hearings would not delay the commencement of needed treatment. Children could be cared for by the State pending the disposition decision.

Second, the interest in avoiding family discord would be less significant at this stage since the family autonomy already will have been fractured by the institutionalization of the child. In any event, postadmission hearings are unlikely to disrupt family relationships. At later hearings the case for and against commitment would be based upon the observations of the hospital staff and the judgments of the staff psychiatrists, rather than upon parental observations and recommendations. The doctors urging commitment, and not the parents, would stand as the child's adversaries. As a consequence, postadmission commitment hearings are unlikely to involve direct challenges to parental authority, judgment or veracity. To defend the child, the child's advocate need not dispute the parents' original decision to seek medical treatment for their child, or even, for that matter, their observations concerning the child's behavior. The advocate need only argue, for example, that the child had sufficiently improved during his hospital stay to warrant out-patient

---

21. The National Institute of Mental Health has reported: "that thousands upon thousands of elderly patients now confined on the back wards of . . . state (mental) institutions were first admitted as children thirty, forty, and even fifty years ago. A recent report from one state estimates that one in every four children admitted to its mental hospitals 'can anticipate being permanently hospitalized for the next 50 years of their lives.'" Joint Commission on the Mental Health of Children, *supra* n. 9, at 5-6.

treatment or outright discharge. Conflict between doctor and advocate on this question is unlikely to lead to family discord.

As a consequence, the prospect of a postadmission hearing is unlikely to deter parents from seeking medical attention for their children and the hearing itself is unlikely to so traumatize parent and child as to make the child's eventual return to the family impracticable.

Nor would postadmission hearings defeat the primary purpose of the state juvenile mental health enterprise. Under the present juvenile commitment scheme, Georgia parents do not enjoy absolute discretion to commit their children to public mental hospitals. See maj. op., at 28. Superintendents of state facilities may not accept children for long term treatment unless they first determine that the children are mentally ill and will likely benefit from long term hospital care. See *id.*, at 29. If the Superintendent determines either condition is unmet, the child must be released, or refused admission, regardless of the parents' desires. See *id.*, at 29. No legitimate state interest would suffer if the Superintendent's determinations were reached through fair proceedings with due consideration of fairly presented opposing viewpoints rather than through the present practice of secret, *ex parte* deliberations.[22]

Nor can the good faith and good intentions of Georgia's psychiatrists and social workers, adverted to by the Court, see maj. op., at 30, excuse Georgia's *ex parte* procedures. Georgia's admitting psychiatrists, like the school disciplinarians described in *Goss* v. *Lopez,* 419 U.S. 565 (1975), "although proceeding in utmost good faith, frequently act on the reports and advice of others; and the controlling facts and the nature of the conduct under challenge are often disputed." *Id.,* at 580. See A-36-40, Testimony of Dr. Messinger. Here as in *Goss* the "risk of error is not at all trivial, and it should be guarded against if that may be done without prohibitive cost or interference with the . . . process." "'Fairness can rarely be obtained by secret, one-sided determination of facts decisive of rights. . . .' 'Secrecy is not congenial to truthseeking and self-righteousness gives

22. Indeed, post-admission hearings may well advance the purposes of the state enterprise. First, hearings will promote accuracy and ensure that the Superintendent diverts children who do not require hospitalization to more appropriate programs. Second, the hearings themselves may prove therapeutic. Children who feel that they have received a fair hearing may be more likely to accept the legitimacy of their confinement, acknowledge their illness and cooperate with those attempting to give treatment. This, in turn, would remove a significant impediment to successful therapy. See Katz, The Right to Treatment — An Enchanting Legal Fiction?, 36 U. Chi. L. Rev. 755, 768-769 (1969); *O'Connor* v. *Donaldson, supra,* 422 U.S., at 579 (Burger, C. J., concurring).

too slender an assurance of rightness. No better instrument has been devised for arriving at truth than to give a person in jeopardy of serious loss notice of the case against him and opportunity to meet it.'" *Goss* v. *Lopez, supra,* at 580, quoting in part from *Anti-Fascist Committee* v. *McGrath,* 341 U.S. 123, 171-172 (1951) (Frankfurter, J., concurring).

III

RIGHTS OF CHILDREN COMMITTED BY
THEIR STATE GUARDIANS

Georgia does not accord prior hearings to juvenile wards of the State of Georgia committed by state social workers acting *in loco parentis.* The Court dismisses a challenge to this practice on the grounds that state social workers are obliged by statute to act in the children's best interest. See maj. op., at 31.

I find this reasoning particularly unpersuasive. With equal logic it could be argued that criminal trials are unnecessary since prosecutors are not supposed to prosecute innocent persons.

To my mind, there is no justification for denying children committed by their social workers the prior hearings that the Constitution typically requires. In the first place, such children cannot be said to have waived their rights to a prior hearing simply because their social workers wished them to be confined. The rule that parents speak for their children, even if it were applicable in the commitment context, cannot be transmuted into a rule that state social workers speak for their minor clients. The rule in favor of deference to parental authority is designed to shield parental control of childrearing from state interference. See *Pierce* v. *Society of Sisters,* 268 U.S. 510, 535 (1925). The rule cannot be invoked in defense of unfettered state control of child-rearing or to immunize from review the decisions of state social workers. The social worker-child relationship is not deserving of the special protection and deference accorded to the parent-child relationship and state officials acting *in loco parentis* cannot be equated with parents. See *O'Connor* v. *Donaldson,* 422 U.S. 563 (1975); *Wisconsin* v. *Yoder,* 406 U.S. 205 (1972).

Second, the special considerations that justify postponement of formal commitment proceedings whenever parents seek to hospitalize their children are absent when the children are wards of the State and are being committed upon the recommendations of their social workers. The prospect of pre-admission hearings is not likely to deter state social workers from discharging their duties and securing psychiatric attention for their disturbed clients. Moreover, since the children will already be in some form of state custody as wards of the State, prehospitalization hearings will not prevent needy children from receiving state care during the pendency of the commitment proceedings. Finally, hearings in which the decisions of state social workers are reviewed by other state officials are not likely to traumatize the children or to hinder their eventual recovery.

For these reasons I believe that, in the absence of exigent circumstances, juveniles committed upon the recommendation of their social workers are entitled to preadmission commitment hearings. As a consequence, I would hold Georgia's present practice of denying these juveniles prior hearings unconstitutional.

IV

Children incarcerated in public mental institutions are constitutionally entitled to a fair opportunity to contest the legitimacy of their confinement. They are entitled to some champion who can speak on their behalf and who stands ready to oppose a wrongful commitment. Georgia should not be permitted to deny that opportunity and that champion simply because the children's parents or guardians wish them to be confined without a hearing. The risk of erroneous commitment is simply too great unless there is some form of adversarial review. And fairness demands that children abandoned by their supposed protectors to the rigors of institutional confinement be given the help of some separate voice.

SECRETARY OF PUBLIC WELFARE OF PENNSYLVANIA v. INSTITUTIONALIZED JUVENILES

99 S. Ct. 2523 (1979)

Mr. Chief Justice Burger delivered the opinion of the Court.

This appeal raises issues similar to those decided in *Parham* v. *J. R.,* No. 75-1690, *ante,* as to what process is due when the parents or guardian of a child seek state institutional mental health care.

This is the second time we have reviewed a district court's judgment that Pennsylvania's procedures for the voluntary admission of mentally ill and mentally retarded children to a state hospital are unconstitutional. In the earlier suit five children who were between the ages of 15 and 18 challenged the 1966 statute pursuant to which they had been admitted to Haverford State Hospital. Pa. Stat. Ann., tit. 50, §§4402, 4403 (Purdon). After a three-judge District Court, with one judge dissenting, declared the statute unconstitutional, *Bartley* v. *Kremens,* 402 F. Supp. 1039 (E.D. Pa. 1975), the Pennsylvania Legislature amended its mental health code with regard to the mentally ill. The amendments placed adolescents over the age of 14 in essentially the same position as an adult for purposes of a voluntary admission. Mental Health Procedures Act of 1976, §201, Pa. Stat. Ann., tit. 50, §7201 (Purdon). Under the new statute, the named plaintiffs could obtain their requested releases from the State hospitals independent of the constitutionality of the 1966 statute and we therefore held that the claims of the named plaintiffs were moot. *Kremens* v. *Bartley,* 431 U.S. 119, 129 (1975). We then remanded the case to the District Court for "reconsideration of the class definition, exclusion of those whose claims are moot and substitution of class representatives with live claims." *Id.,* at 135.

On remand, 12 new plaintiffs, appellees here, were named to represent classes of mentally ill and mentally retarded children. Nine of the children were younger than 14 and constituted all of those who had been admitted to the State's hospitals for the mentally ill in accordance with the 1976 Act at the time the suit was brought; three other children represented a class of patients who were 18 and younger and who had been or would be admitted to a state hospital for the mentally retarded under the 1966 Act and 1973 regulations implementing that Act. All 12 children had been admitted on the application of parents or someone standing *in loco parentis* with State approval after an independent medical examination.

The suit was filed against several named defendants, the Pennsylvania Secretary of Public Welfare and the directors of three state owned and operated facilities. The District Court, however, certified a defendant class that consisted of "directors of all mental health and mental retardation facilities in Pennsylvania which are subject to regulation by the defendant Secretary of Public Welfare." *Institutionalized Juveniles* v. *Secretary of Public Welfare,* 459 F. Supp. 30, 40 n.37 (E.D. Pa. 1977).[1]

---

1. Appellants argue that the State's regulation of admission to private hospitals is insufficient to constitute state action for purposes of the Due Process Clause of the Fourteenth Amendment. They, however, did not contest the District Court's definition of the

Representatives of the nine mentally ill children sought a declaration that the admission procedures embodied in §201[2] of the Pennsylvania Mental Health Procedures Act of 1976, Pa. Stat. Ann., tit. 50, §7201 (Purdon), which subsequently have been expanded by regulations promulgated by the Secretary of Public Welfare, 8 Pennsylvania Bulletin 2433 (1978), violated their procedural due process rights and requested the court to issue an injunction against the statute's future enforcement. The three mentally retarded children presented the same claims as to §§402[3] and 403[4] of the Mental Health and Mental Retardation Act of 1966, Pa. Stat. Ann., tit. 50, §§4402, 4403 (Purdon), and the regulations promulgated thereunder.[5]

---

defendant class, which included directors of both public and private facilities. In light of our holding that Pennsylvania's procedures comport with due process, we do not decide whether the District Court correctly found state action.

2. Section 201 provides, "A parent, guardian or person standing in loco parentis to a child less than 14 years of age may subject such child to examination and treatment under this act, and in so doing shall be deemed to be acting for the child."

3. Section 402 provides:

"(a) Application for voluntary admission to a facility for examination, treatment and care may be made by:

"(2) A parent, guardian or individual standing in loco parentis to the person to be admitted, if such person is eighteen years of age or younger.

"(b) When an application is made, the director of the facility shall cause an examination to be made. If it is determined that the person named in the application is in need of care or observation, he may be admitted."

4. Section 403 provides:

"(a) Application for voluntary commitment to a facility for examination, treatment and care may be made by:

"(2) A parent, guardian or individual standing in loco parentis to the person to be admitted, if such person is eighteen years of age or younger.

"(b) The application shall be in writing, signed by the applicant in the presence of at least one witness. When application is made, the director of the facility shall cause an examination to be made. If it is determined that the person named in the application is in need of care or observation, he shall be committed for a period not to exceed thirty days."

5. The 1973 regulations provide in part:

"1. [M]entally retarded juveniles may be referred by either a pediatrician, or general physician or psychologist;

"2. This referral must be accomplished by a psychiatric evaluation and that report must indicate with specificity the reasons that the person requires institutional care; however, a medical or psychological evaluation may accompany the referral of a mentally retarded juvenile;

"3. The Director of the Institution . . . shall have conducted an independent examination of the proposed juvenile, and if his results disagree with the professional's opinion, the Director . . . shall discharge the juvenile;

"5. Within 24 hours after the juvenile's admission, every youth who is at least 13 years of age must receive written notification (which he signs) explaining his rights indicating that

The District Court certified two subclasses of plaintiffs[6] under Fed. Rule Civ. Proc. 23 and held that the statutes challenged by each subclass were unconstitutional. It held that the State's procedures were insufficient to satisfy the Due Process Clause of the Fourteenth Amendment.

The District Court's analysis in this case was similar to that used by the District Court in *J. L.* v. *Parham,* 412 F. Supp. 138 (M.D. Ga. 1973), *reversed and remanded* sub nom. *Parham* v. *J. R.,* No. 75-1690, *ante.* The court in this case concluded that these children had a constitutionally protected liberty interest that could not be "waived" by their parents. This conclusion, coupled with the perceived fallibility of psychiatric diagnosis, led the court to hold that only a formal adversary hearing could suffice to protect the children in appellees' class from being needlessly confined in mental hospitals.

To further protect the children's interests, the court concluded that the following procedures were required before any child could be admitted voluntarily to a mental hospital:

1) 48-hour notice prior to any hearing;

2) legal counsel "during all significant stages of the commitment process;"

3) the child's presence at all commitment hearings;

4) a finding by an impartial tribunal based on clear and convincing evidence that the child required institutional treatment;

5) a probable cause determination within 72 hours after admission to a hospital;

6) a full hearing, including the right to confront and cross-examine

---

he will be given a status report periodically of his condition; that he can contact by telephone or by mail his parents or the person who requested his admission; and that he will be furnished with the number of counsel . . . that he can call for representation . . .;

"6. In the event that a juvenile whose chronological age is 13 or older objects (either orally or in writing) to remaining in the Institution, the Director . . . *if he feels it is necessary for the youth to remain,* may continue the institutionalization for two business days during which time he shall notify the applicant and the referral unit so that either party may institute a 406 [involuntary commitment] proceeding. . . ." 3 Pennsylvania Bulletin 1840 (1973).

6. One subclass consisted of "all juveniles under the age of fourteen who are subject to inpatient treatment under Article II of the 1976 Act." *Institutionalized Juveniles* v. *Secretary of Public Welfare, supra,* at 41. The other subclass was "mentally retarded juveniles age eighteen or younger." *Id.,* at 42. Appellants argue that the District Court failed to heed our admonition in remanding this case previously that it should "'stop, look, and listen' before certifying a class in order to adjudicate constitutional claims." 431 U.S., at 125. Given our disposition of the merits of this appeal, we need not decide whether these subclasses satisfy the requirements of Fed. Rule Civ. Proc. 23.

witnesses, within two weeks from the date of the initial admission. App. to Juris. Statement 1097a-1098a.[7]

Appellants, all of the defendants before the District Court, appealed the judgment. We noted probable jurisdiction, and consolidated the case with *Parham* v. *J. R.*, No. 75-1690. 437 U.S. 902.

II

(a) Much of what we said in *Parham* v. *J. R.* applies with equal force to this case. The liberty rights and interests of the appellee children, the prerogatives, responsibilities and interests of the parents and the obligations and interests of the State are the same. Our holding as to what process is due in *Parham* controls here, particularly:

> We conclude that the risk of error inherent in the parental decision to have a child institutionalized for mental health care is sufficiently great that some kind of inquiry should be made by a "neutral factfinder" to determine whether the statutory requirements for admission are satisfied. . . . That inquiry must carefully probe the child's background using all available sources, including, but not limited to, parents, schools and other social agencies. Of course, the review must also include an interview with the child. It is necessary that the decisionmaker have the authority to refuse to admit any child who does not satisfy the medical standards for admission. Finally, it is necessary that the child's continuing need for commitment be reviewed periodically by a similarly independent procedure. [*Parham* v. *J. R., supra,* at 20-21.]

The only issue is whether Pennsylvania's procedures for the voluntary commitment of children comply with these requirements.

(b) Unlike in *Parham* v. *J. R.*, where the statute being challenged was general and thus the procedures for admission were evaluated hospital-by-hospital, the statute and regulations in Pennsylvania are specific. Our focus here is on the codified procedures declared unconstitutional by the District Court.

The Mental Health Procedures Act of 1976 and regulations promulgated by the Secretary describe the procedures for the voluntary admission for inpatient treatment of mentally ill children. Section 201 of the Act provides that "a parent, guardian, or person standing in loco parentis to a child less than 14 years of age" may apply for a voluntary examination and treatment for the child. After the child

---

7. Judge Broderick dissented from the judgment of the majority. In his view the majority "has prescribed 'an overdose' of due process." *Institutionalized Juveniles* v. *Secretary of Public Welfare, supra,* at 53 (Broderick, J., dissenting).

receives an examination and is provided with temporary treatment, the hospital must formulate "an individual treatment plan . . . by a treatment team." Within 72 hours the treatment team is required to determine whether in-patient treatment is "necessary" and why. Pa. Stat. Ann., tit. 50, §7205. The hospital must inform the child and his parents both of the necessity for institutional treatment and of the nature of the proposed treatment. *Ibid.*

Regulations promulgated under the 1976 Act provide that each child shall be re-examined and his or her treatment plan reviewed not less than once every 30 days. See §7100.108 (a), 8 Pennsylvania Bulletin 2436 (1978). The regulations also permit a child to object to the treatment plan and thereby obtain a review by a mental health professional independent of the treatment team. The findings of this person are reported directly to the director of the hospital who has the power and the obligation to release any child who no longer needs institutional treatment.

The statute indeed provides three methods for release of a child under the age of 14 from a mental hospital. First the child's parents or guardian may effect his release at will. Pa. Stat. Ann., tit. 50, §7206 (b) (Purdon). Second, "any responsible party" may petition the juvenile court if the person believes that treatment in a less restrictive setting would be in the best interests of the child. *Ibid.* If such a petition is filed, an attorney is appointed to represent the child's interests and a hearing is held within 10 days to determine "what inpatient treatment, if any, is in the minor's best interest." *Ibid.* Finally, the director of the hospital may release any child whenever institutional treatment is no longer medically indicated. §7206 (c).

The Mental Health and Mental Retardation Act of 1966 regulates the voluntary admission for in-patient hospital habilitation of the mentally retarded. The admission process has been expanded significantly by regulations promulgated in 1973 by Pennsylvania's Secretary of Public Welfare. 3 Pennsylvania Bulletin 1840 (1973). Unlike the procedure for the mentally ill, a hospital is not permitted to admit a mentally retarded child based solely on the application of a parent or guardian. All children must be referred by a physician and each referral must be accompanied by a medical or psychological evaluation. In addition, the director of the institution must make an independent examination of each child and if he disagrees with the recommendation of the referring physician as to whether hospital care is "required," the child must be discharged. Mentally retarded children or anyone acting on their behalf may petition for a writ of habeas corpus to challenge the sufficiency or legality of the "proceedings leading to such person's commitment." Pa. Stat. Ann., tit. 50, §4426 (Purdon).

Any child older than 13 who is admitted to a hospital must have his rights explained to him and must be informed that a status report on his condition will be provided periodically. The older child is also permitted to object, either orally or in writing, to his hospitalization. After such objection, the director of the facility, if he feels that hospitalization is still necessary, must institute an involuntary commitment proceeding under §406 of the Act, Pa. Stat. Ann., tit. 50, §4406 (Purdon).

What the statute and regulations do not make clear is how the hospital staff decides that in-patient care is required for a child. The Director of Haverford State Hospital for the mentally ill was the sole witness called by either side to testify about the decisionmaking process at a state hospital. She described the process as follows:

> [T]here is an initial examination made by the psychiatrist, and is so designated as an admission note on the hospital record. Subsequently, for all adolescents on the Adolescent Service at Haverford State Hospital, there are routine studies done, such as an electroencephalograph, a neurological examination, a medical examination, and a complete battery of psychological tests and school evaluation, as well as a psychiatric evaluation. When all their data has been compiled, an entire staff conference is held, which is called a new case conference, at which point the complete case is re-examined and it is decided whether or not the child needs hospitalization, and at the same time, as well, an adequate treatment course is planned." App. to Juris. Statement 112a.

In addition to the physical and mental examinations that are conducted for each child within the institutions, the staff compiles a substantial "pre-admission background information" file on each child.[8] After the child is admitted, there is a periodic review of the child's condition by the staff. His status is reviewed by a different

---

8. Appellees argue that not much weight should be accorded to these files because the record does not make clear whether they were used in making the admission decision. The District Court, however, found that "virtually all of the information was received by the admitting facilities prior to admission." *Institutionalized Juveniles* v. *Secretary of Public Welfare,* 451 F. Supp. 30, 36 n.15 (F.D. Pa. 1978). The court did acknowledge that it was not clear to what extent the information was used, but nonetheless admitted all of the records into evidence. Since it was available, we, like the District Court, assume the information served as a factual basis for some portions of the diagnoses of the children at the time of their admission to the hospitals.

social worker at least every 30 days. Since the State places a great deal of emphasis on family therapy, the parents or guardians are met with weekly to discuss the child's case. *Id.*, at 113a.

We are satisfied that these procedures comport with the due process requirements set out earlier. No child is admitted without at least one and often more psychiatric examinations by an independent team of mental health professionals whose sole concern under the statute is whether the child needs and can benefit from institutional care. The treatment team not only interviews the child and parents but also compiles a full background history from all available sources. If the treatment team concludes that institutional care is not in the child's best interest, it must refuse the child's admission. Finally, every child's condition is reviewed at least every 30 days. This program meets the criteria of our holding in *Parham*.[9] Accordingly, the judgment of the District Court that Pennsylvania's statutes and regulations are unconstitutional is reversed and the case is remanded for further proceedings consistent with this opinion.

Reversed and remanded.

For the reasons stated in his concurring opinion in *Parham* v. *J. R.,* ante, Mr. Justice Stewart concurs in the judgment.

MR. JUSTICE BRENNAN, with whom MR. JUSTICE MARSHALL and MR. JUSTICE STEVENS join, concurring in part and dissenting in part.

I agree with the Court that the commitment of juveniles to public or private mental institutions by their parents involves state action that impacts upon constitutionally protected interests and therefore must be accomplished through procedures consistent with the constitutional mandate of due process of law. For the reasons stated in my opinion in *Parham* v. *J.R.,*—U.S.—,—(1979) (Brennan, J., concurring in part and dissenting in part) I also agree that Pennsyl-

---

9. Although the District Court briefly described the situation of each of the children in appellees' class, it did not indicate the process for each of their admissions. We cannot determine on the record before us whether each child's admission conformed to our due process standards. Just as in *Parham,* individual members of appellees' class are free to argue on remand that their particular commitments violated those standards.

Also, we note that as in *Parham* we are faced only with the issue of what process is due at the initial admission and thus we are not deciding what post-admission procedures are constitutionally adequate to continue a voluntary commitment. The District Court had no reason to consider that issue and indeed from our reading of appellees' complaint there does not appear to be any specific challenge to the State's review procedures. However, we leave it to the District Court on remand to determine what further proceedings are necessary.

vania's preadmission psychiatric interview procedures pass constitutional muster. I cannot agree, however, with the Court's decision to pretermit questions concerning Pennsylvania's post-admission procedures. See Ct. op., at 10 n.9. In my view these procedures should be condemned now.

Pennsylvania provides neither representation nor reasonably prompt post admission hearings to mentally retarded children 13 years of age and younger. For the reasons stated in my opinion in *Parham* v. *J. R., supra,* I believe that this is unconstitutional.

As a practical matter, mentally retarded children over 13 and children confined as mentally ill fare little better. While under current regulations these children must be informed of their right to a hearing and must be given the telephone number of an attorney within 24 hours of admission, see 459 F. Supp. 30, 49, 51 (Broderick, J., dissenting),* the burden of contacting counsel and the burden of initiating proceedings is placed upon the child. In my view this placement of the burden vitiates Pennsylvania's procedures. Many of the institutionalized children are unable to read, write, comprehend the formal explanation of their rights or use the telephone. See App., at 1019 (testimony of L. Glenn). Few, as a consequence, will be able to take the initiative necessary for them to secure the advice and assistance of a trained representative. Few will be able to trigger the procedural safeguards and hearing rights that Pennsylvania formally provides. Indeed, for most of Pennsylvania's institutionalized children the recitation of rights required by current regulations will amount to no more than a hollow ritual. If the children's constitutional rights to representation and to a fair hearing are to be guaranteed in substance as well as in form and if the commands of the Fourteenth Amendment are to be satisfied, then waiver of those constitutional rights cannot be inferred from mere silence or inaction on the part of the institutionalized child. Cf. *Johnson* v. *Zerbst,* 304 U.S. 458, 464 (1938). Pennsylvania must assign each institutionalized child a representative obliged to initiate contact with the child and ensure that the child's constitutional rights are fully protected. Otherwise it is inevitable that the children's due process rights will be lost through inadvertence, inaction, or incapacity. See 459 F. Supp. 30, 44 n.47; 402 F .Supp. 1039, 1050-1051.

---

*See also 16 Pa. Stat. Ann. §9960.6 (c) (1974) (Pennsylvania Public Defender obliged to represent institutionalized children in commitment and related proceedings).

NOTE: PROCEDURES FOR THE COMMITMENT OF MINORS

The issue of procedural due process in connection with the involuntary civil commitment of minors has received much attention in the law review and other literature, almost all of which is now pre-Parham as decided by the United States Supreme Court. It should be kept in mind that interpretations of state constitutional law may provide procedural due process protections more protective than those enunciated in *Parham*. See, e.g., In re Roger S., 139 Cal. Rptr. 861, 566 P.2d 997 (1977), in which the California Supreme Court held that minors confronted with commitment are entitled to procedural due process of law along the traditional lines of an adversarial hearing. The *Roger S.* case is extensively discussed at 66 Calif. L. Rev. 180, 344-373 (1978). See also Hoffman, The "Due Process" Rights of Minors in Mental Hospitals, 13 U.S.F.L. Rev. 63 (1978).

For discussions of the issue of hospitalizing minors see Note, The Mental Hospitalization of Children and the Limits of Parental Authority, 88 Yale L.J. 186 (1978). A particularly balanced and useful analysis of the rights of minors in connection with commitment is Bezanson, Toward Revision of Iowa's Juvenile Commitment Laws: Thoughts on the Limits of Effective Governmental Intervention, 63 Iowa L. Rev. 561 (1978). An earlier but still valuable treatment of the issue is Ellis, Volunteering Children: Parental Commitment of Minors to Mental Institutions, 62 Calif. L. Rev. 840 (1974). See also Note, On the Voluntary Admission of Minors, 8 J.L. Reform 189 (1974); Note, "Voluntary" Admission of Children to Mental Hospitals: A Conflict of Interest Between Parent and Child, 36 Md. L. Rev. 153 (1976); Note, Minors' Right to Due Process: Does it Extend to Commitment to Mental Institutions, 52 Notre Dame Lawyer 136 (1976); Note, Due Process Limitations on Parental Rights to Commit Children to Mental Institutions, 48 U. Colo. L. Rev. 235 (1977); and Comment, Voluntary Commitment of Minors, 23 N.Y.L.S.L. Rev. 339 (1977). See also Szasz, The Child as Involuntary Mental Patient: The Threat of Child Therapy to the Child's Dignity, Privacy and Self-Esteem, 14 San Diego L. Rev. 1005 (1977).

A general analysis is contained in Bennett, Allocation of Child Medical Care Decision-Making Authority: A Suggested Interest Analysis, 62 Va. L. Rev. 285 (1976). See also Miller and Burt, Children's Rights on Entering Therapeutic Institutions, 134 Am. J. Psychiat. 153 (1977).

NOTE: PSYCHIATRIC SERVICES FOR MINORS: PARENTAL CONSENT AND KNOWLEDGE

The development of a certain extent of legal independence of minors has given rise to a growing body of law and legal literature dealing with the right of minors to receive medical treatment, in this case psychiatric treatment, without the knowledge or consent of parents. Some of the more useful discussions are Note, Counseling the Counselors: Legal Implications of Counseling Minors Without Parental Consent, 31 Md. L. Rev. 332 (1971); Note, Children: Health Services for Minors in Oklahoma: Capacity to Give Self-Consent to Medical Care and Treatment, 30 Okla. L. Rev. 385 (1977); Wadlington, Minors and Health Care: The Age of Consent, 11 Osgoode Hall L.J. 115 (1973); Dunn, The Availability of Abortion, Sterilization, and Other Medical Treatment for Minor Patients, 44 U.M.K.C.L. Rev. 1 (1975); Pilpel, Minors' Rights to Medical Care, 36 Albany L. Rev. 462 (1972); Robitscher, "Child Psychiatry and the Law" in S. Copel, ed., Behavior Pathology of Childhood and Adolescence, 422 (1973); Rosenberg and Katz, Legal Issues of Consent in the Psychiatric Treatment of Minors, 8 Psychiat. Opinion 32 (1971); and Shlensky, Minors' Rights to Psychiatric Outpatient Treatment Without Parental Consent in Illinois, 61 Ill. B.J. 650 (1973); Rosenberg and Katz, Legal Issues of Consent in the Psychiatric Treatment of Minors, 8 Psychiat. Opin. 32 (1971). A good general discussion is Chapter 9, The Minor and the Psychiatrist, in A. Holder, Legal Issues in Pediatrics and Adolescent Medicine (1977). See also J. Wilson, The Rights of Adolescents in the Mental Health System (1978).

ILLINOIS MENTAL HEALTH AND DEVELOPMENTAL DISABILITIES CODE (1978)

ARTICLE V. ADMISSION OF MINORS
Sec. 3-500.
A minor may be admitted to a mental health facility for treatment of a mental illness or emotional disturbance only as provided in this Article or as provided in Section 3-10-5 of the Unified Code of Corrections, as now or hereafter amended.
Sec. 3-501.
(a) Any minor 14 years of age or older may request and receive counseling services or psychotherapy on an outpatient basis. The

consent of his parent, guardian or person in loco parentis shall not be necessary to authorize outpatient counseling or psychotherapy. The minor's parent, guardian or person in loco parentis shall not be informed of such counseling or psychotherapy without the consent of the minor unless the facility director believes such disclosure is necessary. If the facility director intends to disclose the fact of counseling or psychotherapy, the minor shall be so informed. However, until the consent of the minor's parent, guardian or person in loco parentis has been obtained, outpatient counseling or psychotherapy shall be limited to not more than 5 sessions, a session lasting not more than 45 minutes.

(b) The minor's parent, guardian or person in loco parentis shall not be liable for the costs of outpatient counseling or psychotherapy which is received by the minor without the consent of the minor's parent, guardian or person in loco parentis.

Sec. 3-502.

Any minor 16 years of age or older may be admitted to a mental health facility as a voluntary patient under Article IV of this Chapter if the minor himself executes the application. A minor so admitted shall be treated as an adult under Article IV and shall be subject to all of the provisions of that Article. The minor's parent, guardian, or person in loco parentis shall be immediately informed of the admission.

Sec. 3-503.

(a) Any minor may be admitted to a mental health facility for inpatient treatment upon application to the facility director of the facility, if the facility director finds that the minor has a mental illness or emotional disturbance of such severity that hospitalization is necessary and that the minor is likely to benefit from inpatient treatment. Prior to admission, a psychiatrist or clinical psychologist who has personally examined the minor shall state in writing that the minor meets the standard for admission. The statement shall set forth in detail the reasons for such conclusion and shall indicate what alternatives to hospitalization have been explored.

(b) The application may be executed by a parent or guardian or, in the absence of a parent or guardian, by a person in loco parentis. Application may be made for a minor who is a ward of the State by the Department of Children and Family Services or by the Department of Corrections.

Sec. 3-504.

(a) A minor who is eligible for admission under Section 3-503 and who is in such a condition that immediate hospitalization is necessary may be admitted upon the application of an interested person 18 years of age or older when, after diligent effort, the minor's parent, guardian or person in loco parentis cannot be located. Following admission of the minor, the facility director of the mental health facility shall continue efforts to locate the minor's parent, guardian or person in loco parentis. If such person is located and consents in writing to the admission, the minor may continue to be hospitalized. However, upon notification of the admission, the parent, guardian or person in loco parentis may request the minor's discharge subject to the provisions of Section 3-508.

(b) If no parent, guardian or person in loco parentis can be found within 3 days, excluding Saturdays, Sundays or holidays, after the admission of a minor, or if such person refuses either to consent to admission of the minor or to request his discharge, a petition shall be filed under the Juvenile Court Act to ensure that appropriate guardianship is provided.

Sec. 3-505.

The application for admission under Section 3-503 or 3-504 shall contain in large, bold-face type a statement in simple nontechnical terms of the minor's objection and hearing rights under this Article. A minor 12 years of age or older shall be given a copy of the application and his right to object shall be explained to him in an understandable manner. A copy of the application shall also be given to the person who executed it, to the minor's parent, guardian or person in loco parentis, and attorney, if any, and to 2 other persons whom the minor may designate.

Sec. 3-506.

Twenty days after the admission of a minor under Section 3-503 or 3-504, the facility director shall review the minor's record and assess the need for continuing hospitalization. The facility director shall consult with the person who executed the application for admission if continuing hospitalization is indicated and request authorization for continued treatment of the minor. The request and authorization shall be noted in the minor's record. Every 60 days thereafter a review shall be conducted and a new authorization shall be secured from the person who executed the application for as long as the hospitalization continues. Failure or refusal to authorize continued treatment shall constitute a request for the minor's discharge.

Sec. 3-507.

(a) Objection may be made to the admission of a minor under Section 3-503 or 3-504. When an objection is made, the minor shall be discharged at the earliest appropriate time, not to exceed 5 days, excluding Saturdays, Sundays and holidays, unless the objection is withdrawn in writing or unless, within that time, a petition for review of the admission and 2 certificates are filed with the court.

(b) The written objection shall be submitted to the facility director of the facility by an interested person 18 years of age or older on the minor's behalf or by the minor himself if he is 12 years of age or older. Each objection shall be noted in the minor's record.

(c) The 2 certificates which accompany the petition shall be executed pursuant to Section 3-703. Each certificate shall be based upon a personal examination and shall specify that the minor has a mental illness or an emotional disturbance of such severity that hospitalization is necessary, that he can benefit from inpatient treatment, and that a less restrictive alternative is not appropriate. If the minor is 12 years of age or older the certificate shall state whether the minor was advised of his rights under Section 3-208.
Sec. 3-508.

Whenever a parent, guardian, or person in loco parentis requests the discharge of a minor admitted under Section 3-503 or 3-504, the minor shall be discharged at the earliest appropriate time, not to exceed 5 days to the custody of such person unless within that time the minor, if he is 12 years of age or older, or the facility director objects to the discharge in which event he shall file with the court a petition for review of the admission accompanied by 2 certificates prepared pursuant to paragraph (c) of Section 3-507.
Sec. 3-509.

Upon receipt of a petition filed pursuant to Section 3-507 or 3-508, the court shall appoint counsel for the minor and shall set a hearing to be held within 5 days, excluding Saturdays, Sundays and holidays. The court shall direct that notice of the time and place of the hearing be served upon the minor, his attorney, the person who executed the application, the objector, and the facility director. The hearing shall be conducted pursuant to Article VIII of this Chapter. Hospitalization of the minor may continue pending further order from the court.
Sec. 3-510.

The court shall disapprove the admission and order the minor discharged if it determines that the minor does not have a mental illness or an emotional disturbance of such a severity that hospitalization is necessary, that he cannot benefit from inpatient treatment, or that a less restrictive alternative is appropriate. Unless the court orders the discharge of the minor, the court shall authorize the

continued hospitalization of the minor for the remainder of the admission period or may make such orders as it deems appropriate pursuant to Section 3-815. When the court has authorized continued hospitalization, no new objection to the hospitalization of the minor may be heard for 20 days without leave of the court.
Sec. 3-511.

Unwillingness or inability of the minor's parent, guardian, or person in loco parentis to provide for his care or residence shall not be grounds for the court's refusing to order the discharge of the minor. In that case, a petition may be filed under the Juvenile Court Act to ensure that appropriate care or residence is provided.

10. Evidence Generally

See Orland, Evidence in Psychiatric Settings, 11 Gonz. L. Rev. 665 (1976).

11. Appeals

In Shuman v. Florida, 358 So. 2d 1333 (Fla. 1978) the Florida Supreme Court ruled that the cost of a transcript for an indigent person's appeal from an order of continued involuntary hospitalization should be taxed against the county in which the hearing is held.

E. REMEDIES FOR IMPROPER COMMITMENT

Page 817. After Note, add:

See Note, Abuse of Process Defined, 28 Ark. L. Rev. 388 (1974).

Chapter Thirteen

The Civil Rights and Liberties of Patients Confined in Mental Hospitals

Page 819. Before 1., Competence, add:

General readings. See, generally, Ferleger, Loosing the Chains: In-Hospital Civil Liberties of Mental Patients, 13 Santa Clara Lawyer 447 (1973) and Note, Protection Following Commitment: Enforcing the Rights of Persons Confined in Arizona Mental Health Facilities, 17 Ariz. L. Rev. 1090 (1976).

Also consult, generally, G. Annas, The Rights of Hospital Patients (1975).

A valuable collection of in-hospital patient problems is presented in Brakel, Legal Problems of People in Mental and Penal Institutions: An Exploratory Study, 1978 Am. Bar Found. Research J. 565.

Page 825. Before 3., The Right to Privacy, add:

See Gostin, Freedom of Expression and the Mentally Disordered: Philosophical and Constitutional Perspectives, 50 Notre Dame Law. 419 (1975).

Pages 841-842. After Note, add:

The Rosenhan article has continued to stir up controversy. See, e.g., Weiner, "On Being Insane in Insane Places": A Process (Attributional) Analysis and Critique, 84 J. Abn. Psych. 442 (1975); Spitzer, On Pseudoscience in Science, Logic in Remission, and Psychiatric Diagnosis: A Critique of Rosenhan's "On Being Sane in Insane

Places," 84 J. Abn. Psych. 442 (1975); Crown, "On Being Sane in Insane Places": A Comment from England, 84 J. Abn. Psych. 453 (1975); and Million, Reflections on Rosenhan's "On Being Sane in Insane Places," 84 J. Abn. Psych. 456 (1975). Rosenhan has responded to these critiques in Rosenhan, The Contextual Nature of Psychiatric Diagnosis, 84 J. Abn. Psych. 462 (1975).

Chapter Fourteen

The Right to Treatment

Pages 845-846. After 2., Selected Readings, add:

Problems of implementation of the right to treatment are discussed in Note, The *Wyatt* Case: Implementation of a Judicial Decree Ordering Institutional Change, 84 Yale L.J. 1338 (1975) and in Note, Implementation Problems in Institutional Reform Litigation 91 Harv. L. Rev. 428 (1977). A broad discussion of institutional reform litigation, with references to right to treatment cases, is Special Project, The Remedial Process in Institutional Reform Litigation, 78 Colum. L. Rev. 784 (1978). A model for implementation is presented in Hoffman and Dunn, Beyond *Rouse* and *Wyatt:* An Administrative Law Model for Expanding the Implementing the Mental Patient's Right to Treatment, 61 Va. L. Rev. 297 (1975). See also Lottman, Enforcement of Judicial Decrees: Now Comes the Hard Part, 1 M.D.L.R. 69 (1976) and V. Bradley and G. Clarke, eds., Paper Victories and Hard Realities: The Implementation of the Legal and Constitutional Rights of the Mentally Disabled (1976).

A comprehensive survey of right to treatment law is provided in National Association of Attorneys General, The Right to Treatment in Mental Health Law (1976). A collection of early papers on right to treatment issues is S. Golann and W. Fremouw, eds., The Right to Treatment for Mental Patients (1976). See also Schwitzgebel, The Right to Effective Mental Treatment, 62 Calif. L. Rev. 936 (1974) and La Rue, Justiciability and Mental Health, 32 Wash. & Lee L. Rev. 347 (1975). The role of the courts in right to treatment litigation is challenged in Miller, The "Right to Treatment": Can the

Courts Rehabilitate and Cure?, 46 The Public Interest 96 (1977).

The consequences of the *Wyatt* litigation are explored in Leaf, Alabama After *Wyatt:* PIL (Public Interest Law) Intervention Into a Mental Health Services Delivery System, in B. Weisbrod, et al., eds., Public Interest Law: An Economic and Institutional Analysis 374 (1978).

A new constitutional approach to the right to treatment based on the cruel and unusual punishment clause is presented in Note, Right to Treatment for the Civilly Committed: A New Eighth Amendment Basis, 45 U. Chi. L. Rev. 731 (1978). An approach based on the least restrictive alternative right is presented in Spece, Preserving the Right to Treatment: A Critical Assessment and Constructive Development of Constitutional Right to Treatment Theories, 20 Ariz. L. Rev. 1 (1978).

The right to treatment has been treated to extensive student comment. See, e.g., 20 Vill. L. Rev. 214 (1974); 27 U. Fla. L. Rev. 295 (1974); 46 Miss. L.J. 345 (1975); 1974 Wash. U.L.Q. 787; and 27 Okla. L. Rev. 238 (1974); 14 Wash. L. Rev. 291 (1975); 35 La. L. Rev. 563 (1975); 24 Clev. St. L. Rev. 557 (1975); 3 Ohio Northern U.L. Rev. 550 (1975); 22 Loy. L. Rev. 373 (1975-1976).

Page 852. Before 5., add:

In 1976 the American Psychiatric Association reconsidered its 1967 position on the right to care and treatment and issued a new position statement emphasizing that it "now joins and endorses efforts toward this goal by stating its explicit support of this right." The A.P.A. statement urged that the right to treatment apply to voluntary as well as to involuntary patients and to those in the community as well as in the hospital. See American Psychiatric Association Position Statement on the Right to Adequate Care and Treatment for the Mentally Ill and Mentally Retarded, (December 1976), 134 Am. J. Psychiat. 354 (1977).

For further psychiatric reactions, see Stone, The Right to Treatment and the Psychiatric Establishment, 4 Psychiatric Annals 21 (1974); Stone, Overview: The Right to Treatment—Comments on the Law and its Impact, 132 Am. J. Psychiat. 1125 (1975); Cohen, Cohen and Sadoff, Right to Treatment, 3 Bull. Amer. Acad. Psychiat. and L. 59 (1975); and Sadoff, Risks for State and Private Hospital Psychiatrists In Re Right to Treatment, 3 Bull. Acad. Psychiat. and L. 32 (1975).

Page 871. After Note: Reactions to the *Wyatt* Case, add:

O'CONNOR v. DONALDSON

422 U.S. 563, 45 L. Ed. 2d 396, 95 S. Ct. 2486 (1975)

Mr. Chief Justice BURGER, concurring.

Although I join the Court's opinion and judgment in this case, it seems to me that several factors merit more emphasis than it gives them. I therefore add the following remarks.

I

With respect to the remand to the Court of Appeals on the issue of official immunity from liability for monetary damages,[1] it seems to me not entirely irrelevant that there was substantial evidence that Donaldson consistently refused treatment that was offered to him, claiming that he was not mentally ill and needed no treatment.[2] The Court appropriately takes notice of the uncertainties of psychiatric diagnosis and therapy, and the reported cases are replete with evidence of the divergence of medical opinion in this vexing area. *E.g.,* Greenwood v. United States, 350 U.S. 366, 375, 76 S. Ct. 410, 415, 100 L. Ed. 412 (1956). See also Drope v. Missouri, 420 U.S. 162, 95 S. Ct. 896, 43 L. Ed. 2d 103 (1975). Nonetheless, one of the few areas of agreement among behavioral specialists is that an uncooperative patient cannot benefit from therapy and that the first step in effective treatment is acknowledgment by the patient that he is suffering from an abnormal condition. See *e.g.,* Katz, The Right to Treatment—An Enchanting Legal Fiction? 36 U. Chi. L. Rev. 755, 768-769 (1969). Donaldson's adamant refusal to do so should be taken into account in considering petitioner's good-faith defense.

Perhaps more important to the issue of immunity is a factor re-

1. I have difficulty understanding how the issue of immunity can be resolved on this record and hence it is very likely a new trial on this issue may be required: if that is the case I would hope these sensitive and important issues would have the benefit of more effective presentation and articulation on behalf of petitioner.

2. The Court's reference to "milieu therapy," *ante,* at 2490 may be construed as disparaging that concept. True, it is capable of being used simply to cloak official indifference, but the reality is that some mental abnormalities respond to no known treatment. Also, some mental patients respond, as do persons suffering from a variety of physiological ailments, to what is loosely called "milieu treatment," *i.e.,* keeping them comfortable, well nourished, and in a protected environment. It is not for us to say in the baffling field of psychiatry that "milieu therapy" is always a pretense.

ferred to only obliquely in the Court's opinion. On numerous occasions during the period of his confinement Donaldson unsuccessfully sought release in the Florida courts; indeed, the last of these proceedings was terminated only a few months prior to the bringing of this action. See 234 So. 2d 114 (1969), *cert. denied,* 400 U.S. 869, 91 S. Ct. 104, 27 L. Ed. 2d 109 (1970). Whatever the reasons for the state courts' repeated denials of relief, and regardless of whether they correctly resolved the issue tendered to them, petitioner and the other members of the medical staff at Florida State Hospital would surely have been justified in considering each such judicial decision as an approval of continued confinement and an independent intervening reason for continuing Donaldson's custody. Thus, this fact is inescapably related to the issue of immunity and must be considered by the Court of Appeals on remand and, if a new trial on this issue is ordered, by the District Court.[3]

II

As the Court points out, *ante,* at 2491 n.6, the District Court instructed the jury in part that "a person who is involuntarily civilly committed to a mental hospital does have a *constitutional* right to receive such treatment *as will give him a realistic opportunity to be cured,*" (emphasis added), and the Court of Appeals unequivocally approved this phrase, standing alone, as a correct statement of the law. 493 F.2d 507, 520 (5th Cir. 1974). The Court's opinion plainly gives no approval to that holding and makes clear that it binds neither the parties to this case nor the courts of the Fifth Circuit. See *ante,* at 2495 n.12. Moreover, in light of its importance for future litigation in this area, it should be emphasized that the Court of Appeals' analysis has no basis in the decisions of this Court.

A

There can be no doubt that involuntary commitment to a mental hospital, like involuntary confinement of an individual for any reason, is a deprivation of liberty which the State cannot accomplish without due process of law. Specht v. Patterson, 386 U.S. 605, 608, 87 S. Ct. 1209, 1211, 18 L. Ed. 2d 326 (1967). Cf. In re Gault, 387

---

3. That petitioner's counsel failed to raise this issue is not a reason why it should not be considered with respect to immunity in light of the Court's holding that the defense was preserved for appellate review.

U.S. 1, 12-13, 87 S. Ct. 1428, 1435-1436, 18 L. Ed. 2d 527 (1967). Commitment must be justified on the basis of a legitimate state interest, and the reasons for committing a particular individual must be established in an appropriate proceeding. Equally important, confinement must cease when those reasons no longer exist. See McNeil v. Director, Patuxent Institution, 407 U.S. 245, 249-250, 92 S. Ct. 2083, 2086-2087, 32 L. Ed. 2d 719 (1972); Jackson v. Indiana, 406 U.S. 715, 738, 92 S. Ct. 1845, 1858, 32 L. Ed. 2d 435 (1972).

The Court of Appeals purported to be applying these principles in developing the first of its theories supporting a constitutional right to treatment. It first identified what it perceived to be the traditional bases for civil commitment—physical dangerousness to oneself or others, or a need for treatment—and stated:

> [W]here, as in Donaldson's case, the rationale for confinement is the *"parens patriae"* rationale that the patient is in need of treatment, the due process clause requires that minimally adequate treatment be in fact provided. . . . "To deprive any citizen of his or her liberty upon the altruistic theory that the confinement is for humane therapeutic reasons and then fail to provide adequate treatment violates the very fundamentals of due process." [493 F.2d, at 521.]

The Court of Appeals did not explain its conclusion that the rationale for respondent's commitment was that he needed treatment. The Florida statutes in effect during the period of his confinement did not require that a person who had been adjudicated incompetent and ordered committed either be provided with psychiatric treatment or released, and there was no such condition in respondent's order of commitment. Cf. Rouse v. Cameron, 125 U.S. App. D.C. 366, 373 F.2d 451 (1967). More important, the instructions which the Court of Appeals read as establishing an absolute constitutional right to treatment did not require the jury to make any findings regarding the specific reasons for respondent's confinement or to focus upon any rights he may have had under state law. Thus, the premise of the Court of Appeals' first theory must have been that, at least with respect to persons who are not physically dangerous, a State has no power to confine the mentally ill except for the purpose of providing them with treatment.

That proposition is surely not descriptive of the power traditionally exercised by the States in this area. Historically, and for a considerable period of time, subsidized custodial care in private foster homes or boarding houses was the most benign form of care provided incompetent or mentally ill persons for whom the States assumed responsibility. Until well into the 19th century the vast majority of such persons were simply restrained in poorhouses, almshouses, or jails. See A. Deutsch, The Mentally Ill in America 38-54, 114-131 (2d ed. 1949). The few States that established institutions for the mentally ill during this early period were concerned primarily with providing a more humane place of confinement and only secondarily with "curing" the persons sent there. See *id.,* at 98-113.

As the trend toward state care of the mentally ill expanded, eventually leading to the present statutory schemes for protecting such persons, the dual functions of institutionalization continued to be recognized. While one of the goals of this movement was to provide medical treatment to those who could benefit from it, it was acknowledged that this could not be done in all cases and that there was a large range of mental illness for which no known "cure" existed. In time, providing places for the custodial confinement of the so-called "dependent insane" again emerged as the major goal of the States' programs in this area and remained so well into this century. See *id.,* at 228-271; D. Rothman, The Discovery of the Asylum 264-295 (1971).

In short, the idea that States may not confine the mentally ill except for the purpose of providing them with treatment is of very recent origin, and there is no historical basis for imposing such a limitation on state power. Analysis of the sources of the civil commitment power likewise lends no support to that notion. There can be little doubt that in the exercise of its police power a State may confine individuals solely to protect society from the dangers of significant antisocial acts or communicable disease. Cf. Minnesota ex rel. Pearson v. Probate Court of Ramsey County, 309 U.S. 270, 60 S. Ct. 523, 84 L. Ed. 744 (1940); Jacobson v. Massachusetts, 197 U.S. 11, 25-29, 25 S. Ct. 358, 360-362, 49 L. Ed. 643 (1905). Additionally, the States are vested with the historic *parens patriae* power, including the duty to protect "persons under legal disabilities to act for themselves." Hawaii v. Standard Oil Co., 405 U.S. 251, 257, 92 S. Ct. 885, 888, 31 L. Ed. 2d 184 (1972). See also Mormon Church v. United States, 136 U.S. 1, 56-58, 10 S. Ct. 792, 807-808, 34 L. Ed. 481 (1890). The classic example of this role is when a State undertakes to act as "'the general guardian of all infants, idiots, and lunatics.'" Hawaii v. Standard Oil Co., *supra,* 405 U.S., at 257, 92 S. Ct., at 888, quoting 3 W. Blackstone, Commentaries *47.

Of course, an inevitable consequence of exercising the *parens patriae* power is that the ward's personal freedom will be substantially restrained, whether a guardian is appointed to control his property, he is placed in the custody of a private third party, or committed to an institution. Thus, however the power is implemented, due process requires that it not be invoked indiscriminately. At a minimum, a particular scheme for protection of the mentally ill must rest upon a legislative determination that it is compatible with the best interests of the affected class and that its members are unable to act for themselves. Cf. Mormon Church v. United States, *supra*. Moreover, the use of alternative forms of protection may be motivated by different considerations, and the justifications for one may not be invoked to rationalize another. Cf. Jackson v. Indiana, 406 U.S., at 737-738, 92 S. Ct., at 1857-1858. See also American Bar Foundation, The Mentally Disabled and the Law 254-255 (S. Brakel and R. Rock ed. 1971).

However, the existence of some due process limitations on the *parens patriae* power does not justify the further conclusion that it may be exercised to confine a mentally ill person only if the purpose of the confinement is treatment. Despite many recent advances in medical knowledge, it remains a stubborn fact that there are many forms of mental illness which are not understood, some which are untreatable in the sense that no effective therapy has yet been discovered for them, and that rates of "cure" are generally low. See Schwitzgebel, The Right to Effective Mental Treatment, 62 Calif. L. Rev. 936, 941-948 (1974). There can be little responsible debate regarding "the uncertainty of diagnosis in this field and the tentativeness of professional judgment." Greenwood v. United States, 350 U.S., at 375, 76 S. Ct., at 415. See also Ennis and Litwack, Psychiatry and the Presumption of Expertise: Flipping Coins in the Courtroom, 62 Calif. L. Rev. 693, 697-719 (1974).[5] Similarly, as previously observed, it is universally recognized as fundamental to effective therapy that the patient acknowledge his illness and cooperate with those attempting to give treatment; yet the failure of a large proportion of mentally ill persons to do so is a common phenomenon. See Katz, *supra*, 36 U. Chi. L. Rev., at 768-769. It may be that some persons in either of these categories,[6] and there may be others, are unable to function in society and will suffer real harm to

5. Indeed, there is considerable debate concerning the threshold questions of what constitutes "mental disease" and "treatment." See Szasz, The Right to Health, 57 Geo. L.J. 734 (1969).

6. Indeed, respondent may have shared both of these characteristics. His illness, paranoid schizophrenia, is notoriously unsusceptible to treatment, see Livermore, Malmquist, and Meehl, On the Justifications for Civil Commitment, 117 U. Pa. L. Rev. 75, 93, and n.52 (1968), and the reports of the Florida State Hospital staff which were introduced into evidence expressed the view that he was unwilling to acknowledge his illness and was generally uncooperative.

themselves unless provided with care in a sheltered environment. See, *e.g.,* Lake v. Cameron, 124 U.S. App. D.C. 264, 270-271, 364 F.2d 657, 663-664 (1966) (dissenting opinion). At the very least, I am not able to say that a state legislature is powerless to make that kind of judgment. See Greenwood v. United States, *supra.*

B

Alternatively, it has been argued that a Fourteenth Amendment right to treatment for involuntarily confined mental patients derives from the fact that many of the safeguards of the criminal process are not present in civil commitment. The Court of Appeals described this theory as follows:

> [A] due process right to treatment is based on the principle that when the three central limitations on the government's power to detain—that detention be in retribution for a specific offense; that it be limited to a fixed term; and that it be permitted after a proceeding where the fundamental procedural safeguards are observed—are absent, there must be a *quid pro quo* extended by the government to justify confinement. And the *quid pro quo* most commonly recognized is the provision of rehabilitative treatment. [493 F.2d, at 522.]

To the extent that this theory may be read to permit a State to confine an individual simply because it is willing to provide treatment, regardless of the subject's ability to function in society, it raises the gravest of constitutional problems, and I have no doubt the Court of Appeals would agree on this score. As a justification for a constitutional right to such treatment, the *quid pro quo* theory suffers from equally serious defects.

It is too well established to require extended discussion that due process is not an inflexible concept. Rather, its requirements are determined in particular instances by identifying and accommodating the interests of the individual and society. See, *e.g.,* Morrissey v. Brewer, 408 U.S. 471, 480-484, 92 S. Ct. 2593, 2599-2602, 33 L. Ed. 2d 484 (1972); McNeil v. Director, Patuxent Institution, 407 U.S., at 249-250, 92 S. Ct., at 2086-2087; McKeiver v. Pennsylvania, 403 U.S. 528, 545-555, 91 S. Ct. 1976, 1986-1991, 29 L. Ed. 2d 647 (1971) (plurality opinion). Where claims that the State is acting in the best interests of an individual are said to justify reduced procedural and substantive safeguards, this Court's decisions require that they be "candidly appraised." In re Gault, 387 U.S., at 21, 27-29, 87 S. Ct., at 1440, 1443-1445. However, in so doing judges are not free to read their private notions of public policy or public health into the Constitution. Olsen v. Nebraska ex rel. Western Reference & Bond Assn., 313 U.S. 236, 246-247, 61 S. Ct. 862, 865-866, 85 L. Ed. 1305 (1941).

The *quid pro quo* theory is a sharp departure from, and cannot co-exist with, due process principles. As an initial matter, the theory presupposes that essentially the same interests are involved in every situation where a State seeks to confine an individual; that assumption, however, is incorrect. It is elementary that the justification for the criminal process and the unique deprivation of liberty which it can impose requires that it be invoked only for commission of a specific offense prohibited by legislative enactment. See Powell v. Texas, 392 U.S. 514, 541-544, 88 S. Ct. 2145, 2158-2160, 20 L. Ed. 2d 1254 (1968) (opinion of Black, J.).[7] But it would be incongruous, for example, to apply the same limitation when quarantine is imposed by the State to protect the public from a highly communicable disease. See Jacobson v. Massachusetts, 197 U.S., at 29-30, 25 S. Ct., at 362-363.

A more troublesome feature of the *quid pro quo* theory is that it would elevate a concern for essentially procedural safeguards into a new substantive constitutional right.[8] Rather than inquiring whether strict standards of proof or periodic redetermination of a patient's condition are required in civil confinement, the theory accepts the absence of such safeguards but insists that the State provide benefits which, in the view of a court, are adequate "compensation" for confinement. In light of the wide divergence of medical opinion regarding the diagnosis of and proper therapy for mental abnormalities, that prospect is especially troubling in this area and cannot be squared with the principle that "courts may not substitute for the judgments of legislators their own understanding of the public welfare, but must instead concern themselves with the validity under the Constitution of the methods which the legislature has selected." In re Gault, 387 U.S., at 71, 87 S. Ct., at 1466 (Harlan, J., concurring and dissenting). Of course, questions regarding the adequacy of

7. This is not to imply that I accept all of the Court of Appeals' conclusions regarding the limitations upon the States' power to detain persons who commit crimes. For example, the notion that confinement must be "for a fixed term" is difficult to square with the widespread practice of indeterminate sentencing, at least where the upper limit is a life sentence.

8. Even advocates of a right to treatment have criticized the *quid pro quo* theory on this ground. *E.g.*, Developments in the Law—Civil Commitment of the Mentally Ill, 87 Harv. L. Rev. 1190, 1325 n.39 (1974).

procedure and the power of a State to continue particular confinements are ultimately for the courts, aided by expert opinion to the extent that is found helpful. But I am not persuaded that we should abandon the traditional limitations on the scope of judicial review.

C

In sum, I cannot accept the reasoning of the Court of Appeals and can discern no basis for equating an involuntarily committed mental patient's unquestioned constitutional right not to be confined without due process of law with a constitutional right to *treatment*.[9] Given the present state of medical knowledge regarding abnormal human behavior and its treatment, few things would be more fraught with peril than to irrevocably condition a State's power to protect the mentally ill upon the providing of "such treatment as will give [them] a realistic opportunity to be cured." Nor can I accept the theory that a State may lawfully confine an individual thought to need treatment and justify that deprivation of liberty solely by

9. It should be pointed out that several issues which the Court has touched upon in other contexts are not involved here. As the Court's opinion makes plain, this is not a case of a person's seeking release because he has been confined "without ever obtaining a judicial determination that such confinement is warranted." McNeil v. Director, Patuxent Institution, 407 U.S. 245, 249, 92 S. Ct. 2083, 2086, 32 L. Ed. 2d 719 (1972). Although respondent's amended complaint alleged that his 1956 hearing before the Pinellas County Court was procedurally defective and ignored various factors relating to the necessity for commitment, the persons to whom those allegations applied were either not served with process or dismissed by the District Court prior to trial. Respondent has not sought review of the latter rulings, and this case does not involve the rights of a person in an initial competency or commitment proceeding. Cf. Jackson v. Indiana, 406 U.S. 715, 738, 92 S. Ct. 1845, 1858, 32 L. Ed. 2d 435 (1972); Specht v. Patterson, 386 U.S. 605, 87 S. Ct. 1209, 18 L. Ed. 2d 326 (1967); Minnesota ex rel. Pearson v. Probate Court of Ramsey County, 309 U.S. 270, 60 S. Ct. 523, 84 L. Ed. 744 (1940).

Further, it was not alleged that respondent was singled out for discriminatory treatment by the staff of Florida State Hospital or that patients at that institution were denied privileges generally available to other persons under commitment in Florida. Thus, the question whether different bases for commitment justify differences in conditions of confinement is not involved in this litigation. Cf. Jackson v. Indiana, supra 406 U.S., at 723-730, 92 S. Ct., at 1850-1854; Baxstrom v. Herold, 383 U.S. 107, 86 S. Ct. 760, 15 L. Ed. 2d 620 (1966).

Finally, there was no evidence whatever that respondent was abused or mistreated at Florida State Hospital or that the failure to provide him with treatment aggravated his condition. There was testimony regarding the general quality of life at the hospital, but the jury was not asked to consider whether respondent's confinement was in effect "punishment" for being mentally ill. The record provides no basis for concluding, therefore, that respondent was denied rights secured by the Eighth and Fourteenth Amendments. Cf. Robinson v. California, 370 U.S. 660, 82 S. Ct. 1417, 8 L. Ed. 2d 758 (1962).

providing some treatment. Our concepts of due process would not tolerate such a "trade-off." Because the Court of Appeals' analysis could be read as authorizing those results, it should not be followed.

NOTE: MORALES v. TURMAN

A significant aftermath to the *Donaldson* case is Morales v. Turman, 562 F.2d 933 (5th Cir. 1977), in which the Fifth Circuit Court of Appeals, relying on the Supreme Court's decision in Donaldson, in effect repudiated the spirit of the earlier Fifth Circuit decision, Donaldson v. O'Connor, 493 F.2d 507 (5th Cir. 1974), Casebook at 1123.

A Texas federal district court in Morales v. Turman, 383 F. Supp. 53 (E.D. Tex. 1974) had [in a 70-page decision and order] articulated a constitutional right to treatment for confined juvenile delinquents. The Fifth Circuit remanded for a three-judge court, a decision subsequently reversed by the U.S. Supreme Court. On reconsideration, the Fifth Circuit, remanding for a further evidentiary hearing to consider changes in juvenile facilities later made by the State of Texas, took the occasion to question not only the validity of a constitutional right to treatment for juvenile offenders, but also a right to treatment for the mentally ill.

NOTE: PROTECTION FROM HARM

In cases dealing with the mentally retarded the courts have been reluctant to hold that there is a federal constitutional right to treatment, but have instead articulated a constitutional right to "protection from harm" based in part on the ban against cruel and unusual punishment of the Eighth Amendment. The most significant cases in this area are the so-called *"Willowbrook"* cases (named after the well-known institution), New York State Association for Retarded Children, Inc. v. Carey, 393 F. Supp. 715 (E.D.N.Y. 1975) and New York State Association for Retarded Children v. Rockefeller, 357 F. Supp. 752 (E.D.N.Y. 1973). The rejection of a right to treatment in Rockefeller is at 758-765, the assertion of a right to protection from harm at 764-765. The consent decree emanating from Carey, which goes well beyond what was contemplated in Rockefeller, is reprinted in 1 Mental Disability L. Rep. 58 (1976). The protection from harm rationale was approvingly referred to in Halderman v. Pennhurst State School, 446 F. Supp. 1295, 1321 (E.D. Pa. 1977) as well as in Woe v. Mathews, 408 F. Supp. 419, 428-429 (E.D.N.Y. 1976). For a fuller explication see Note, Voluntarily Confined Mental Retardates: The Right to Treatment v. the Right to Protection from Harm, 23 Cath. U.L. Rev. 787 (1974) and Mason and Menolascino, The Right to Treatment for Mentally Retarded Citizens: An Evolving Legal and Scientific Interface, 10 Creighton L. Rev. 124 (1976).

For a case dealing with a statutory right see Welsch v. Likins, 373 F. Supp. 487 (D. Minn. 1974).

Page 876. After Note, add:

Controversy surrounds the issue of the responsibility of the hospital for the safety of patients who are "absent without authorization." Two recent federal cases deal with the apparent suicides of such VA hospital patients. In one case the court found liability; in the other, not. Both cases were brought under the Federal Tort Claims Act, 28 U.S.C. §1346(b) and 2671. The decisions in both cases depend on an evaluation of foreseeability of harm.

In Smith v. United States, 437 F. Supp. 1004 (E.D. Pa. 1977), the decedent, diagnosed as paranoid schizophrenic, had had a long history of violence and suicide attempts, one less than a month before his death. He also had exhibited impulsive behavior one week before the fateful and negligent transfer.

Smith was transferred, without a psychiatric evaluation, to open facilities. That very same day Smith left the hospital, jumped in front of a train, and was killed.

The court cited a parallel case, Dinnerstein v. United States, 486 F.2d 34 (2d Cir. 1973), where the patient had been negligently assigned to an unsupervised and unrestricted floor, from which he jumped. In Smith, evidence of the patient's previous behavior which indicated greater security, and a failure to provide a pre-transfer psychiatric evaluation, as locally accepted standards of medical practice required, led to a finding of negligence.

In Castillo v. United States, 552 F.2d 1385 (10th Cir. 1977), the patient (Montoya), though bizarre and diagnosed as chronic undifferentiated schizophrenic, had not been perceived as dangerous. Montoya had a history of elopement. On the day he was run over by a train and killed, Montoya's absence went unnoticed for over three hours. Although in permitting Montoya to elope, hospital personnel had in effect violated a provision in a 1953 VA administrative procedures manual calling for "close observation of patients who have known or suspected suicidal, assaultive, convulsive or elopement tendencies," the court decided that this was not negligence per se. Furthermore, said the court, there was no causal link between the hazard regulated against and the patient's death.

See Cooper, Medical Treatment Facility Liability for Patient Suicide and Other Self-Injury, 3 J. Legal Med. 20 (January, 1975); Perr, Suicide and Civil Litigation, 19 J. Forensic 261 (1974); and Comment, Civil Liability for Suicide: An Analysis of the Causation Issue, 1978 Ariz. St. L.J. 573.

Chapter Fifteen

The Right to Refuse Treatment

Pages 877-879. After 1., Introductory Note, add:

General Readings

See Brooks, the Right to Refuse Treatment, 4 Admin. in Mental Health 90 (1977); Note, 87 Harv. L. Rev. 1190, 1344-1358 (1974); Halleck, Legal and Ethical Aspects of Behavior Control, 131 Am. J. Psychiat. 381 (1974); Note, Advances in Mental Health: A Case for the Right to Refuse Treatment, 43 Temp. L.Q. 354 (1975); Shapiro, Legislating the Control of Behavior Control: Autonomy and the Coercive Use of Organic Therapies, 47 S. Cal. L. Rev. 237 (1974); Jacob, The Right of the Mental Patient to His Psychosis, 39 Mod. L. Rev. 17 (1976); and Schwartz, In the Name of Treatment: Autonomy, Civil Commitment, and the Right to Refuse Treatment, 50 Notre Dame Law. 808 (1975).

Pages 897-898. After Note, add:

RENNIE v. KLEIN
462 F. Supp. 1131 (D. N.J. 1978)

BROTMAN, District Judge.

This matter is before the court on the motion of plaintiff, John E. Rennie, for a preliminary injunction pursuant to Fed. R. Civ. P. 65. Plaintiff is an involuntary patient of Ancora Psychiatric Hospital, a state institution. He seeks to enjoin the defendant psychiatrists and officials at Ancora from forcibly administering drugs to him in the absence of an emergency situation. The complaint is grounded on 42 U.S.C. §1983, with jurisdiction pursuant to 28 U.S.C. §1343. The following are the court's findings of fact and conclusions of law, Fed. R. Civ. P. 52.

FINDINGS OF FACT

I. Procedural History

[By agreement between counsel for the Division of Mental Health Advocacy of the Public Advocate and the Deputy Attorney General, the issue in this case was narrowed to whether the plaintiff had "the right to refuse medication in non-emergent circumstances." At the outset, the court issued a restraining order that plaintiff not be medicated against his will beyond a maintenance dose of 15 mg. of prolixin hydrochloride per day, except for emergencies.

The court held fourteen days of hearings. Testimony was taken from hospital officials and employees, including three hospital psychiatrists and the director of the State Division of Mental Health and Hospitals; from three outside psychiatrists for the plaintiff and two outside psychiatrists for the defendant.

During the hearings, plaintiff attempted suicide by swallowing an overdose of pills. Defendants promptly moved to remove the restraining order. The court convened all the doctors to consider future treatment for the plaintiff. It was agreed that plaintiff should be treated with an anti-depressant medication, followed by lithium carbonate when the depression lifted. There was disagreement about when an antipsychotic drug should be used. Plaintiff consented to the proposed treatment and the temporary restraining order was dissolved.

The hospital director stated that, if an antipsychotic drug were used later, it would not be prolixin, because of plaintiff's aversion to it. The court devoted a great deal of attention to examining studies concerning prolixin. Defendant argued that since prolixin would not be used, plaintiff's attempt to enjoin its use was moot.

Later, the hospital used thorazine, because the plaintiff had become "dangerous to himself, other patients, and the staff." The hospital placed the plaintiff in restraint for three days, then used thorazine.

The court decided that "[s]ince the testimony indicates that the benefits of and detrimental side effects of all psychotropic drugs are similar, the case as a whole is not moot."]

II. The Plaintiff's Personal History

John Rennie is a highly intelligent 38-year-old white divorced male. Before his psychiatric difficulties began, he worked as a pilot and a flight instructor. His first symptoms of mental illness appeared in December 1971. Serious problems commenced early in 1973, in the wake of his twin brother's death in an airplane accident.

His medical history is lengthy and can only be highlighted here. His first admission to Ancora Psychiatric Hospital was on April 1, 1973. He was depressed and suicidal, and diagnosed as a paranoid schizophrenic. Mellaril, an antipsychotic drug, was given, and plaintiff was released on April 5 to the Fairmont Farms Hospital, a private facility.

There followed a revolving door series of readmissions and releases. His second admission was from May 2, 1973 to June 1, 1973, with plaintiff exhibiting similar suicidal ideas and religious delusions. By his third admission, from February 18 to February 26, 1974, he began to exhibit some aggressive and abusive symptoms. Thorazine, another antipsychotic drug, was used. Delusions that he was Christ continued in the fourth admission in March 1974.

Subsequent admissions showed further trials of different medicines. During the sixth admission, from April 9 to May 7, 1974 on a voluntary commitment, there is the first indication of a refusal to take medication. He was discharged against medical advice. His eighth admission, on a voluntary commitment from August 26 to September 10, 1974, was initiated when the Secret Service brought him to state authorities after he threatened to kill President Ford. His behavior again was abusive and assaultive. This type of assaultive behavior continued during his ninth admission from September 18 to October 12, 1974, so that the hospital placed him on homicidal precautions. He was also on homicidal precautions during his tenth admission in January 1975. His eleventh admission was involuntary and lengthy, from November 16, 1975 to June 9, 1976. His behavior was erratic, alternating between being depressed and suicidal to manic and homicidal. There was a suicide attempt on December 14 by an overdose of mellaril. Both psychotropic drugs, such as haldol, mellaril and prolixin decanoate, as well as lithium, were utilized. During this hospitalization, his diagnosis for a time was changed to manic depressive illness.

Throughout this period, plaintiff was inconsistent in his attitude toward the various medications, refusing at times and cooperating at others. One of many causes of his repeated discharges and readmissions is his failure to continue taking medications after he has left the hospital's custody.

Plaintiff's twelfth and present admission to Ancora began on August 10, 1976, pursuant to an involuntary commitment. Although committed, he has never been declared incompetent. The admitting diagnosis was manic depressive illness, circular type. He was placed on lithium and on suicidal and homicidal precautions. Later psychotropic drugs were added. Again, at various times, medication was refused. In December 1976, the Public Advocate's Office became involved in Mr. Rennie's case. After conversation with Mr. Gelman, the hospital agreed that medication would not be forced against the patient's will. Following an injection of prolixin decanoate on January 5, 1977, plaintiff became extremely psychotic and threatened suicide. During 1977, plaintiff was shifted between a number of medications, including thorazine, prolixin, etrafon, haldol, elavil, and lithium. Frequent incidents of fights with other patients and attendants were reported. Suicidal and delusional periods were also reported.

One particular incident prior to the commencement of this lawsuit should be noted. On November 17, 1977, plaintiff reported that evening shift attendants beat him with sticks while he was tied to a bed. The next day he pointed out the sticks, which were hidden at the nurses' station. The investigation that followed resulted in the suspension of one employee for three days. Plaintiff and the attendant remained together in the same ward.

In brief fashion, this summarizes plaintiff's history to December 1977, when this suit was commenced. The events of that month will be discussed further, *infra*.

III. Ancora Psychiatric Hospital

Ancora Psychiatric Hospital is a state facility for the mentally ill in Hammonton, New Jersey. It has been accredited by the Joint Commission on Accreditation of Hospitals. Dr. Ortanez and Dr. Bugaoan were the patient's treating psychiatrists during the time relevant to this litigation.

During most of his current admission, plaintiff has been housed in a barren, bleak ward; it has been described as more like a prison than a hospital. Plaintiff sometimes has difficulty obtaining a pillow for his bed. His days contain long blocks of unproductive and unstructured time. In general, doctors at Ancora do not have sufficient time for each patient. However, as a result of this lawsuit, the doctors are spending more time with Mr. Rennie.

IV. The Medication

A. BENEFITS OF PSYCHOTROPIC DRUGS

Prolixin or Fluphenazine belongs to a group of chemicals variously described as antipsychotic or psychotropic drugs. It comes in long-acting (prolixin decanoate) and short-acting (prolixin hydrochloride) form. Prolixin Decanoate is the only psychotropic drug to come in a form that will last approximately two weeks. Zander, *Prolixin Decanoate: A Review of the Research,* in 2 Mental Disability L. Rep. 37 (1977).

Many other major tranquilizers exist which are very similar to prolixin hydrochloride, both in therapeutic action and side effect. Plotkin, *Limiting the Therapeutic Orgy: Mental Patients' Right to Refuse Treatment,* 72 Nw. U.L. Rev. 461, 475 (1977). These include thorazine, mellaril, haldol and trilafon. There is no evidence supporting the superiority of any one of these drugs. Bozzuto, *Use of Antipsychotic Agents for Schizophrenia,* 1977 Drug Therapy 40.

In the past twenty years, psychotropic drugs have played an increasingly important role in the treatment of mental illness, and are now widely used. Psychotropic drugs tend to shorten hospital stays and allow patients to function in the community. Many consider use of these drugs necessary in any treatment program, especially for schizophrenics. Winick, *Psychotropic Medication and Competence to Stand Trial,* 1977 Am. B. Found. Res. J. 769, 773-774; Zander, *supra.* Dr. Stinnett went so far as to testify that the failure to treat an acutely psychotic patient with drugs would be malpractice, *Whitree v. State,* 56 Misc. 2d 693, 290 N.Y.S.2d 486, 501 (1968); *Nason v. Superintendent of the Bridgewater State Hospital,* 353 Mass. 604, 233 N.E.2d 908, 910 (1968).

More studies exist demonstrating the efficacy of the psychotropic drugs in the treatment of schizophrenia than for any other mode of treatment. DuBose, *Of the Parens Patriae Commitment Power and Drug Treatment of Schizophrenia: Do the Benefits to the Patient Justify Involuntary Treatment?,* 60 Minn. L. Rev. 1149, 1167 (1976). Defendants offered a number of studies establishing the efficacy of prolixin in the treatment of schizophrenics. May, et al., *Schizophrenia—A Follow-up Study of Results of Treatment,* 33 Arch. Genl. Psychiatry, 474, 474-478, 481-486 (1976); *Bozzuto, supra* at 44; E. Spohn, et al., *Phenothiazine Effects on Psychological and Psychophysiological Dysfunction in Chronic Schizophrenics,* 34 Arch. Genl. Psychiatry 633 (1977). *See also* Zander, *supra.*

Of course, the research is not conclusive. Double blind testing is difficult because a placebo group will not experience the usual side effects. Thus the patient and the testers may know that he is unmedicated. Also no studies can conclusively compare the pain of schizophrenic mental states and physical side effects of medication simply because both are subjective experiences. Furthermore, new studies raise questions about recidivism and the efficacy of using psychotropic medication in every case. Gunderson, *Drugs and Psychosocial Treatment of Schizophrenia Revisited*, Dec. 1977 Psychiatry Digest 25; Simpson, et al., *Psychotic Exacerbation Produced by Neuroleptics*, 37 Diseases of the Nervous System 367 (1976). Patients do react idiosyncratically to any particular psychotropic drug.

However, the court can appropriately make certain generalizations even at this stage of scientific knowledge. Psychotropic drugs are effective in reducing thought disorder in a majority of schizophrenics. With first admission patients, success rates of as high as 95 percent have been obtained. Success rates are less impressive with chronic patients. DuBose, *supra* at 1173. However, no other treatment modality has achieved equal success in the treatment of schizophrenics. Hollister, *Choice of Antipsychotic Drugs*, 127 Amer. J. Psychiatry 104, 104 (1970).

Furthermore, psychotropic drugs are required in order for some patients to effectively participate in and benefit from other types of therapy, such as individual or group psychotherapy and occupational therapy. Comment, *Forced Drug Medication of Involuntarily Committed Mental Patients*, 20 St. Louis U.L.J. 100, 112 (1975); Winick, *supra* at 781.

In sum, psychotropic drugs are widely accepted in present psychiatric practice. A. Brooks, *Law, Psychiatry and the Mental Health System* 878 (1974). They are the treatment of choice for schizophrenics today.

B. SIDE EFFECTS OF PSYCHOTROPIC DRUGS

Unfortunately, all of the psychotropic drugs cause dysfunctions of the central nervous system called extrapyramidal symptoms, as well as other side effects. All these vary among individuals. Zander, *supra* at 39. On the average, among all patients, no one drug is much worse than the others at any given therapeutic dosage.[3]

A number of short term autonomic side effects have commonly been reported. These include blurred vision, dry mouth and throat, constipation or diarrhea, palpitations, skin rashes, low blood pressure, faintness and fatigue. Winick, *supra* at 782 n. 66; Plotkin, *supra* at 476; DuBose, *supra* at 1203. These side effects tend to

---

3. Long-acting prolixin may be worse than the short-acting medications. Zander, *supra* at 39. However, as prolixin has been eliminated as the drug of choice, the court will not focus on the distinction.

diminish after a few weeks. Sudden death may also be a side effect in rare cases.

Among the extrapyramidal side effects, the two most common are akinesia and akathesia. Akinesia refers to a state of diminished spontaneity, and feeling of weakness and muscle fatigue. Zander, supra; Rifkin, et al., *Fluphenazine Decanoate, Oral Fluphenazine, and Placebo in Treatment of Remitted Schizophrenics,* 34 Arch. Genl. Psychiatry 1215, 1216 (1977). Patients with severe cases of akinesia had to be dropped from the Rifkin study of prolixin. Akathesia is a subjective state and refers to an inability to be still; a motor restlessness which may provide a shaking of the hands or arms or feet or an irresistable desire to keep walking or tapping the feet. Both of these side effects are temporary and terminate either during or after the drug regime; the effects can also be treated with antocholinergic or antiparkinsonian drugs such as cogentin. However cogentin has side effects of its own, including blurred vision and salivation.

A potential permanent side effect of prolixin and other anti-psychotic medication is tardive dyskinesia. Tardive dyskinesia is characterized by rhythmical, repetitive, involuntary movements of the tongue, face, mouth, or jaw, sometimes accompanied by other bizarre muscular activity. Winick, *supra;* Zander, *supra;* DuBose, *supra.* The risk of this disorder is greatest in elderly patients, especially women, and is associated with prolonged use. Zander, *supra* at 40.

Finally, it should be mentioned that British researchers have suggested a link between prolixin and suicidal depression. Zander, *supra.* It is too early for scientists, much less the court, to draw any firm conclusions from this research.

C. LITHIUM CARBONATE

As lithium is another drug previously used and presently recommended by some doctors in Mr. Rennie's case, a short discussion is appropriate. Lithium carbonate is now established as the most effective treatment available for mania, an affective disorder marked by extreme elation, hyperactivity, grandiosity, and accelerated thinking and speaking. It also prevents the recurrence of both the manic and depressive episodes which alternatively afflict patients with bipolar manic-depression. However, in a bipolar case, an anti-depressant such as tofranil, amitriptylene or imipramine must be added to prevent depression.

V. The Appropriate Treatment for Mr. Rennie

A. PLAINTIFF'S CONDITION AS OF DECEMBER 1977

It is at this juncture appropriate to resume the history of Mr. Rennie and the events which raised the forced medication issue. In early December 1977, the staff of Ancora felt that plaintiff was highly homicidal, and that his general condition was deteriorating. On December 5, a meeting was convened attended by Dr. Bugaoan, Dr. Pepernik, Dr. Ortanez, and the members of plaintiff's treatment team to discuss the situation. The next day, Dr. Pepernik sought and received permission from the Attorney General's office to administer medication without consent. At a hospital treatment team meeting on December 7, a multi-modal treatment plan for plaintiff was formulated, including the administration of prolixin hydrochloride. The decision to compel medication was made to prevent plaintiff from harming other patients, staff, and himself and to ameliorate his delusional thinking pattern. Prolixin was chosen because, in the decanoate form, it is the only injectable long-acting drug. It was thought that in the post-hospitalization period, it would be easiest to maintain Mr. Rennie on prolixin decanoate, with one injection every two weeks, since he had a history of failing to continue his medication once released. In the month following the initiation of the prolixin regime, Mr. Rennie's condition improved markedly. After his dosage was lowered to 15 mg/day by the court order of December 30, it was reported that his behavior was controllable. However the staff psychiatrists felt the dosage to be insufficient to treat his thought disorder.

B. PLAINTIFF'S DIAGNOSIS

Obviously, before drugs can be prescribed, plaintiff's condition must be known. Perhaps the question most contested during the hearings was plaintiff's proper diagnosis. While psychotropic drugs are generally regarded as the treatment of choice for schizophrenia, lithium, with an antidepressant, is the treatment of choice for manic depression. As plaintiff is presently willing to take lithium,[4] this case would be moot if manic depression were the consensus diagnosis.

As noted earlier, at various times during plaintiff's prior hos-

---

4. In the past, Mr. Rennie has refused lithium, stating it made him too depressed. His assessment of the drug was correct. At the time, the hospital apparently would not give him an antidepressant in addition to the lithium. Perhaps as a result of these hearings, all now agree that lithium is best at curbing the manic side of manic depression, and that in a bipolar case such as plaintiff's, an antidepressant such as tofranil is also necessary.

pitalizations, diagnoses of both schizophrenia and manic depression were offered. There is a thin line between these two illnesses. No expert indicated any medical agreement as to whether the two disorders arise from different environmental causes, or represent different physiological states within the brain. Instead, the testimony concentrated on symptomatology. Furthermore, there was little testimony on how the psychopharmacological substances work in the brain. This emphasis on symptoms and lack of certainty about causation and physiopathology demonstrates the tentativeness of much psychiatric diagnosis as compared to the usual physical diagnosis. The experts who testified concerning Mr. Rennie's disorder are in great disagreement. Drs. Heller and Bugaoan believe plaintiff is schizophrenic. Drs. Ortanez and Pepernik give a diagnosis of schizophrenia, affective type. But Ortanez agrees that plaintiff has also shown a manic depression symptoms at times. Dr. Stinnett diagnoses plaintiff as manic depressive, but offers schizo-affective disorder as a possible alternative diagnosis. Finally, Drs. Limoges and Pepper feel that plaintiff suffers only from manic depression.

There is much overlap between the two diagnoses and disagreement among experts. Manic depression is basically a mood disorder, while schizophrenia is primarily a thought disorder, characterized by delusions, hallucinations, and faulty logic. However, manic depressives can also show thought disorders at the manic end of the mood swing. But, true schizophrenia is characterized by sustained rather than episodic periods of thought disorder. Further, a manic depressive's periods of thought disorder will be tied to his mood swings, unlike a schizophrenic's cognitive dysfunctions. In addition, schizophrenics can show mood disorder as a secondary symptom. This is called schizophrenia, affective type, or schizo-affective disorder.

The problem facing the doctors diagnosing Mr. Rennie is obviously complex. Simplified for the lawyer's mind, one of the key inquiries is whether Rennie's assertions that he is the "alpha omega," or Christ, are firm and fixed schizophrenic delusions or mere grandiosity characteristic of his manic euphoria. Dr. Limoges believes the latter and thus would only prescribe lithium and an antidepressant to combat plaintiff's manic depression.

Dr. Stinnett however testified that while his diagnosis was manic depression, the distinction is largely academic. He found the symptoms to warrant both antipsychotic medication and lithium. An antipsychotic was deemed necessary both to curb the patient's perceived delusions and to control the destructive aspects of his behavior. While Dr. Ortanez lacks Dr. Stinnett's experience and expertise,[5] as the treating physician Dr. Ortanez also believed that both antipsychotics and lithium would be appropriate based on his perception of combined symptoms.

A little knowledge can be dangerous, and this court is hesitant to diagnose mental illness and prescribe medication. But it is possible to draw these conclusions. Plaintiff is acutely psychotic at times. Aside from his adverse reaction to psychotropics, the best course of treatment for Mr. Rennie would combine psychotropic medication with lithium and an antidepressant. However, the position that he has no fixed delusions, thus making use of a psychotropic unnecessary, is, at the least, a reasonable proposition.

C. USE OF PHARMACO-THERAPY AS THE SOLE THERAPY

Defendants have produced at least one study, May, *supra,* demonstrating that drugs alone are an effective means of curing schizophrenia. Testimony has also indicated that drugs must be used initially to bring Mr. Rennie into contact with reality before any other therapy may be usefully employed.

However, the court rejects any solution to the problems of this case which would allow Mr. Rennie to be treated with an antipsychotropic drug alone. Dr. Stinnett expressed in the strongest possible terms that both pharmacotherapy and psychotherapy would have to be used to improve Mr. Rennie's conditions and not one without the other. The court fully accepts Dr. Stinnett's recommendation. Dr. Pepper concurred in stating that medicine cannot be successful outside of a good total treatment plan. Only in the context of a trusting relationship achieved through psychotherapy can medicine be employed in a rational way.

D. PLAINTIFF'S REACTION TO PSYCHOTROPICS

John Rennie suffers from many of the side effects described above. He experiences blurred vision and a dry mouth. On thorazine, his blood pressure has dropped. He also suffers from akathesia on prolixin, getting uncontrollable tremors. This, and the fact that he feels his senses are dulled, are his two principal reasons for refusal of prolixin. Despite the hospital's assertion that Mr. Rennie has faked akathesia, this court is convinced that the akathesia is real and extremely unpleasant. The hospital doctors are to be faulted

5. In this case, opportunity to observe Mr. Rennie's everchanging symptoms may be the best way to arrive at an appropriate diagnosis. None of the outside experts besides Dr. Greenberg had this luxury.

for ignoring plaintiff's subjective reports of akathesia while on prolixin.

Mr. Rennie also has shown wormlike movements of the tongue. This is a preliminary symptom which is possibly indicative that tardive dyskinesia may develop if medication is continued. Thus, there is a risk of permanent damage from psychotropic medication in Mr. Rennie's case, and Mr. Rennie requires extremely close monitoring if these drugs are to be continued.

E. THE EFFICACY OF FORCED MEDICATION

As noted above, a trusting relationship or therapeutic alliance between psychiatrist and patient is essential for a drug regimen to succeed. Plaintiff has demonstrated that psychotropic drugs are less efficacious in a hostile or negative environment. As a corollary to this, even if the best drug is prescribed, if the patient is unwilling to accept it, the positive effects are greatly lessened, especially in terms of long range benefits. *O'Connor v. Donaldson,* 422 U.S. 563, 579, 95 S. Ct. 2486, 45 L. Ed. 2d 396 (1975) (Burger, C.J., concurring).

F. PLAINTIFF'S COMPETENCY TO MAKE MEDICATION DECISIONS

John Rennie's psychiatric problems are of a cyclical nature, so that on some days he is psychotic. Dr. Pepper testified that plaintiff's refusal of prolixin is not a product of his mental disorder. However, Dr. Stinnett found that during his examination on February 25, 1978, Mr. Rennie was not capable of making a decision on treatment in his best interests. The court feels that Dr. Pepernik's assessment is most accurate, and that Mr. Rennie's wishes should be taken into account on any treatment decision. But the court finds that his capacity to participate in the refusal of medicine or the choice of medicine is somewhat limited, depending on the day. Shwed, *Protecting the Rights of the Mentally Ill,* 64 A.B.A.J. 564, 566 (1978); Comment, *Forced Drug Medication, supra* at 113. The court does believe that Mr. Rennie's reports of his subjective reactions to particular drugs are generally accurate.

CONCLUSIONS OF LAW

I. Introduction—New Jersey Law

A New Jersey state court has recently been faced with a factual situation very similar to this case. *In re Hospitalization of B,* 156

N.J. Super. 231, 383 A.2d 760 (Law Div. 1977) involved an involuntarily committed patient who was refusing prolixin. B had not responded to all conventional therapies, and the treating physician sought the court's permission to administer a psychotropic drug. B had not been declared incompetent. N.J. Ct. R. 4:83.

Looking to the New Jersey statutes, the court quoted N.J.S.A. 30:4-24.2(d)(1), which states that:

> No medication shall be administered unless at the written order of a physician. Notation of each patient's medication shall be kept in his treatment records. At least weekly, the attending physician shall review the drug regimen of each patient under his care. All physician's orders or prescriptions shall be written with a termination date, which shall not exceed 30 days. Medication shall not be used as punishment, for the convenience of staff, as a substitute for a treatment program, or in quantities that interfere with the patient's treatment program. Voluntarily committed patients shall have the right to refuse medication.

Based on this statute the court held that involuntarily committed patients do not have the right to refuse medication. Involuntary patients "are protected by nothing more than the court's review, the occasional consultation of an independent expert and the promised administrative procedure." 156 N.J. Super. at 238, 383 A.2d at 764. Thus, plaintiff is proceeding under §1983 to determine if the state scheme is constitutionally defective.

New Jersey does recognize the emerging right to treatment of mental patients. N.J. S.A. 30:4-24.1; *State v. Carter,* 64 N.J. 382, 393-304, 316 A.2d 449 (1974); *see also Wyatt v. Aderholt,* 503 F.2d 1305 (5th Cir. 1974).

II. Standards on a Preliminary Injunction

Generally, four factors are to be considered on an application for a preliminary injunction: (1) whether the moving party has shown that it is likely to prevail on the merits, (2) whether the movant has demonstrated that he would be irreparably harmed if the preliminary injunction is denied, (3) whether the grant of the injunction would harm other interested parties to a greater extent than it would benefit movant, and (4) whether the public interest would be served. *A. O. Smith Corp. v. F.T.C.,* 530 F.2d 515, 525 (3rd Cir. 1976). Defendants argue that there can be no showing of probability of success on the merits where novel legal issues are raised.

Certainly the issue of a federal right to refuse medication is novel and complex. However, the case has not followed the usual course of a preliminary injunction hearing. Hearings have been held on fourteen dates over a period of four months. The court has heard testimony from nine psychiatrists. Counsel have aided the court with excellent briefs. Thus, while more information is always desirable, the court feels that it should not avoid a consideration of the merits in this instance merely because the issues are novel.

III. Abstention

[Here the Court considers the abstention issue and decides that it would be inequitable to abstain at this stage of the proceedings.]

IV. The Federal Constitutional Issues

The plaintiff alleges numerous constitutional grounds in support of his position. These claims generally track the course charted in *Scott v. Plante,* 532 F.2d 939 (3rd Cir. 1976). *See also Souder v. McGuire,* 423 F. Supp. 830 (M.D. Pa. 1976). Scott, a patient of Trenton State Hospital, had five pro se complaints dismissed by the district court. One claim challenged the involuntary administration of medications, including thorazine, mellaril, and trilafon. The Third Circuit, in reversing the motion to dismiss, outlined in dictum how such a claim could establish a constitutional deprivation.

. . . [E]xisting case law points to at least three[9] conceivable deprivations that may accompany the involuntary administration of such substances by state officers acting under color of state law to inmates confined in a state institution. . . . [T]he involuntary administration of drugs which affect mental processes . . . could amount, under an appropriate set of facts, to an interference with Scott's rights under the first amendment. *See Mackey v. Procunier,* 477 F.2d 877 (9th Cir. 1973); *Kaimowitz v. Dept. of Mental Health,* Civ. No. 73-19434-AW (Mich. Cir. Ct., Wayne County, July 10, 1973). Moreover, on this record we must assume that Scott, though perhaps properly committable, has never been adjudicated an incompetent who is incapable of giving an informed consent to medical treatment. Under these circumstances due process would require, in the absence of an emergency, that some form of notice and opportunity to be heard

9. A possible fourth constitutional deprivation might include invasion of the inmate's right to bodily privacy. . . . See, e.g., Roe v. Wade, 410 U.S. 113, 93 S. Ct. 705, 35 L. Ed. 2d 147 . . . (1973).

be given to Scott or to someone standing *in loco parentis* to him before he could be subjected to such treatment. Finally, under certain conditions, Scott's claim may raise an eighth amendment issue respecting cruel and unusual punishment. *See Knecht v. Gillman,* 488 F.2d 1136 (8th Cir. 1973); *Mackey v. Procunier, supra* at 878. 532 F.2d at 946-947. The court will consider each of these four claims in relation to the facts of this case.

A. CRUEL AND UNUSUAL PUNISHMENT

As Dr. Rotov testified, there is great potential for the abuse of psychotropic medication, and careful scrutiny is required when they are involuntarily administered. Comment, *Advances in Mental Health: A Case for the Right to Refuse Treatment,* 48 Temp. L.Q. 354, 364 (1975). The court will assume that the eighth amendment prohibition on cruel and unusual punishment does apply to protect persons confined in mental institutions. *See Ingraham v. Wright,* 430 U.S. 651, 669 n.37, 97 S. Ct. 1401, 51 L. Ed. 2d 711 (1977).

The question is whether use of antipsychotic drugs in plaintiff's case is justified as treatment or whether it can be classified as punishment by the court. *Knecht v. Gillman,* 488 F.2d 1136, 1138 (8th Cir. 1973). A number of cases have found eighth amendment violations despite claims of therapeutic value. *Knecht, supra; Mackey v. Procunier,* 477 F.2d 877 (9th Cir. 1973); *Pena v. New York State Division for Youth,* 419 F. Supp. 203, 207 (S.D.N.Y. 1976); *Nelson v. Heyne,* 355 F. Supp. 451, 455 (N.D. Ill. 1972). However, each case is clearly distinguishable from the one at bar. In *Knecht,* the drug apomorphine was found to have no proven therapeutic value and its use was not recognized as acceptable medical practice. 488 F.2d at 1138, 1140; *see* Plotkin, *supra* at 494. Furthermore, while the behavior modification program was believed to have long-term benefits, the adverse effects seemed *unnecessarily* harsh. Comment, *The Right Against Treatment: Behavior Modification and the Involuntarily Committed,* 23 Cath. U.L. Rev. 774, 782 (1974). In *Nelson, Pena,* and *Mackey,* the courts found that the drugs were used improperly and for punishment rather than as part of an ongoing psychotherapeutic program. *Cf. Welsh v. Likins,* 373 F. Supp. 487, 503 (D. Minn. 1974).

In contrast, psychotropic drugs have been proven effective. Furthermore, the Ancora staff has established that they were trying to use prolixin as an integral component of an overall treatment program. While the side effects of prolixin are serious, they are not *unnecessarily* harsh in light of the potential benefits. Accordingly, the court finds no eighth amendment violation. Prolixin was justifiably administered as treatment, not punishment.

B. First Amendment

Another constitutional argument advanced in support of a right to refuse treatment is a first amendment right to freedom of expression, including both the right to communicate and the right to think. Plotkin, *supra* at 494. Plaintiff argues in this case that drugs may be used to punish or suppress truthful expression critical of the institution. Certainly plaintiff has a history of justifiably criticizing hospital procedure. However, there is no evidence that the hospital administered the medications in this case in an attempt to suppress those statements.

Plaintiff also argues that the use of drugs interferes with his mental processes and thus deprives him of his right to mentation. *Kaimowitz v. Dept. of Mental Health,* Civ. No. 73-19434 (Cir. Ct. Wayne County, Michigan July 10, 1973), *reprinted in* A. Brooks, *Law, Psychiatry and the Mental Health System, supra* at 902; *Scott, supra* at 946; Comment, *Advances in Mental Health, supra* at 366. In *Kaimowitz,* the court held that an adult may not give legally adequate consent to experimental psychosurgery, in part because of first amendment protection of the freedom to generate ideas. Any court must be deeply concerned with potential state control of individual thought and carefully scrutinize instances of forced psychiatric treatment.

In the case at bar, the court does not believe that first amendment analysis requires the use of drugs to be enjoined. First, Dr. Greenberg indicated that plaintiff's ability to perform on intelligence tests has not been impaired. Most importantly, plaintiff has indicated a desire to be cured of his mental illness. In his action, he is asserting a right to be treated, and has testified that he *wants* to be cured, not warehoused. Thus, the hospital's efforts to alter his thinking disorder cannot be seen as a first amendment violation. The court need not reach the question of whether insane or disordered thought is within the scope of first amendment protection. Comment, *Advances in Mental Health, supra* at 366-367.

However, plaintiff also claims that a side effect of prolixin is that it dulls his senses and makes it difficult for him to speak. These side effects are temporary and expected to last only a few days or a couple of weeks, perhaps two months at the outside, Stinnett. This effect on mentation differs sharply from the problem faced in *Kaimowitz.* The patient in that case was to be subjected to experimental psychosurgery. The effects would be irreversible and unpredictable, the dangers to the patient substantial, and the benefits uncertain, with no scientifically established therapeutic effect. More specifically as to effects on the mental processes, psychosurgery flattens emotional responses and leads to lack of abstract reasoning ability, loss of capacity for new learning, and impairment of memory. *Kaimowitz, supra* at 909. In sum, if forced medication is otherwise proper, the temporary dulling of the senses accompanying it does not rise to the level of the first amendment violations found in *Kaimowitz.*

C. THE RIGHT TO PRIVACY:
(1) Individual Interests

The court believes that any right to refuse medication in the absence of an emergency is best founded on the emerging right of privacy. The right of privacy is broad enough to include the right to protect one's mental processes from governmental interference. *Kaimowitz, supra* at 919; *Mackey v. Procunier,* 477 F.2d 877, 878 (9th Cir. 1973); *Stanley v. Georgia,* 397 U.S. 557, 565, 89 S. Ct. 1243, 22 L. Ed. 2d 542 (1969); Comment, *Advances in Mental Health, supra* at 367; Comment, *The Right Against Treatment, supra* at 785. Additionally, privacy has been used to establish an individual's autonomy over his own body. *Roe v. Wade,* 410 U.S. 113, 93 S. Ct. 705, 35 L. Ed. 2d 147 (1973); *Runnels v. Rosendale,* 499 F.2d 733, 735 (9th Cir. 1974); Comment, *Forced Drug Medication, supra* at 104. In other contexts, courts have established a constitutional right of privacy "broad enough to encompass a patient's decision to decline medical treatment under certain circumstances." *In re Quinlan,* 70 N.J. 10, 40, 355 A.2d 647, 663 (1976). This court holds that the right to refuse treatment extends to mental patients in non-emergent circumstances. *Bell v. Wayne County General Hospital at Eloise,* 384 F. Supp. 1085, 1100 (E.D. Mich. 1974) (three-judge court); DuBose, *supra* at 1160; Zander, *supra* at 50. This accords with the usual common law rule against involuntary medical treatment. *Winters v. Miller,* 446 F.2d 65, 68 (2nd Cir. 1971); *Scott v. Plante, supra.* Only where the government shows some strong countervailing interest can the right to refuse be qualified. See 1 Report and Recommendation of the President's Commission on Mental Health 44 (1978); DuBose, *supra;* Szasz, *Involuntary Psychiatry,* 45 U. of Cin. L. Rev. 347, 356-357 (1976); Zander, *supra.*

The court feels that the recognition of a right to refuse treatment

in a non-emergency situation is practical. The testimony has indicated that involuntary treatment is much less effective than the same
treatment voluntarily received. The psychiatric experts stated that it
is more likely that a patient will consent to desirable treatment
when consulted before action is taken, and when he feels that he has
some real control over his fate, than when he feels totally at the
mercy of the hospital doctors.

Furthermore, only the patient can really know the discomfort
associated with side effects of particular drugs. Again, the experts
agree that they must rely on their patients for evidence of subjective
feelings of pain associated with drug usage. Individual autonomy
demands that the person subjected to the harsh side effects of
psychotropic drugs have control over their administration.

It is also difficult for any person, even a doctor, to balance for
another the possibility of a cure of his schizophrenia with the risks
of permanent disability in the form of tardive dyskinesia. Whether
the potential benefits are worth the risks is a uniquely personal
decision which, in the absence of a strong state interest, should be
free from state coercion.

Finally, the testimony in this case underscores the fact that psychiatric diagnosis and therapy is uncertain, with great divergence of
opinion in any given case. *O'Connor v. Donaldson*, 422 U.S. 563,
579, 95 S. Ct. 2486, 45 L. Ed. 2d 396 (Burger, C.J., concurring).
This also weighs toward leaving the final decision with the patient
rather than deferring to doctors. Thus, the court concludes that it is
appropriate to recognize a right to refuse treatment.

(2) State Interest

The constitutional right to refuse treatment cannot be absolute.
Jacobson v. Massachusetts, 197 U.S. 11, 25 S. Ct. 358, 49 L. Ed.
643 (1905). The President's Commission charges all concerned with
mental health laws to pay "careful attention to the circumstances
and procedures under which the right may be qualified." Commission on Mental Health, *supra* at 44. Based on the evidence in this
case, the court has identified three factors to be considered in overriding the patient's right to refuse.

First, the state's police power is often cited as one justification for
the initial confinement of the mentally ill. The police power permits
the state to confine a mentally ill person who presents a danger to
himself or other members of society. *O'Connor v. Donaldson*, 422
U.S. 563, 575-577, 95 S. Ct. 2486, 45 L. Ed. 2d 396 (1975); Note,
Wyatt v. Stickney—A Constitutional Right to Treatment for the

Mentally Ill, 34 U. Pitt. L. Rev. 79, 82-83 (1972). The fact that the patient is dangerous in free society may give the state power to confine, but standing alone it does not give the power to treat involuntarily. *Winters v. Miller, supra* at 70. Once confined, the patient cannot hurt those outside.

However, the other patients in the hospital also have a constitutional right to protection from harm. Commission on Mental Health, *supra* at 44; *Runnels v. Rosendale, supra* at 735; *Goodman v. Parwatikar,* 570 F.2d 801, 804 (8th Cir. 1978); *Welsch v. Likins,* 373 F. Supp. 487, 503 (D. Minn. 1974). If a patient cannot be confined without endangering other patients and staff, and yet he refuses medication that would curb his dangerous tendencies, this would be one factor to weigh in overriding his decision to refuse. Comment, Forced Drug Medication, *supra* at 107.

The court found in this case that Mr. Rennie had shown frequent assaultive behavior while at Ancora. At times, this behavior led the Ancora staff to put him in restraints. Mr. Rennie has also complained bitterly about the use of restraints. However, in light of the hospital's duty to safeguard other patients and staff, plaintiff cannot both refuse his medication and be left free to inflict harm on others.

A second justification for involuntary confinement and treatment is the doctrine of parens patriae, under which the state cares for those unable to care for themselves. Note, *Wyatt v. Stickney — Constitutional Right to Treatment, supra* at 82-83. It is clear that mental illness is not the equivalent of incompetency, which renders one incapable of giving informed consent to medical treatment. *Scott v. Plante, supra;* Plotkin, *supra* at 490, 496; Comment, *Advances in Mental Health, supra* at 371; N.J.S.A. 30:4-24.2(c). Therefore, before the state can use parens patriae as a basis for medication, some hearing on the issue of competency must be held. *Scott v. Plante, supra.*

The factfinder of such a hearing must determine the extent to which the refusal of treatment is based on the underlying mental illnesses. Often, a characteristic of the illness is the inability to recognize and understand the severity of the problem. The greater the lack of insight, the stronger the impetus to override the right to individual autonomy. As stated by Judge Bazelon, "how real is the promise of individual autonomy for a confused person set adrift in a hostile world?" Bazelon, *Institutionalization, Deinstitutionalization and the Adversary Process,* 75 Colum. L. Rev. 897, 907 (1975).

If a factfinder is swayed to allow involuntary medication in part because of the patient's diminished capacity to care for himself, he should also consider the ability of the hospital to provide a reasonable full treatment plan. Since *Rouse v. Cameron,* 125 U.S. App. D.C. 366, 373 F.2d 451 (1966), courts have increasingly been recognizing a right to treatment. If a hospital cannot provide reasonable treatment services beyond the forcing of medication, one would doubt the appropriateness of allowing that institution to act in parens patriae. *Cf. Naughton v. Bevilacqua,* 458 F. Supp. 610 (D.R.I. 1978), which held that prolixin could not be used solely to control a patient's behavior, without a habilitative purpose.

In the instant case, the court has found Mr. Rennie's decision-making powers to be somewhat impaired. However, the prior refusal of lithium without an antidepressant was well-founded, and the refusal of prolixin also had a rational basis. As previously noted, prolixin has been discontinued. If the state again seeks to medicate Mr. Rennie without his consent, the court will have to evaluate the basis for using that particular drug when the occasion arises. As part of that inquiry, it will be relevant to determine if Mr. Rennie understands that the alternative to accepting treatment may be permanent custody at Ancora.

As a final consideration, many courts and commentators have employed the concept of least restrictive alternatives in regard to the choice of a custodial setting. *Welsch v. Likins, supra* at 501; *Gary W. v. State of La.,* 437 F. Supp. 1209, 1217 (E.D. La. 1976); *Eubanks v. Clarke,* 434 F. Supp. 1022, 1028 (E.D. Pa. 1977); *Bazelon, supra* at 901; *Barnett, Treatment Rights of Mentally Ill Nursing Home Residents,* 126 U. Pa. L. Rev. 578, 590 (1978); Flaschner, *Legal Rights of the Mentally Handicapped: A Judge's Viewpoint,* 60 A.B.A.J. 1371 (1974). The court feels that this concept should be extended to the choice of medications. Comment, *Advances in Mental Health, supra* at 376; Winick, *supra* at 813; Commission on Mental Health, *supra* at 44. Under this theory, a patient "may challenge the forced administration of drugs on the basis that alternative treatment methods should be tried before a more intrusive technique like psychotropic medication is used." Winick, *supra.*

In Mr. Rennie's case, psychotherapy had not proved effective. However, plaintiff's experts stated that lithium plus an antidepressant would be a reasonable therapy to which plaintiff would consent. Dr. Heller agreed that lithium and tofranil was worth a trial. Under these circumstances, the hospital is required to give Mr. Rennie a fair trial on the agreed upon lithium and tofranil regime before seeking to medicate involuntarily the plaintiff. The notion of least restrictive alternatives can also be applied to the threat of tardive dyskinesia.

If plaintiff is likely to contract tardive dyskinesia through renewed administration of psychotropic drugs, the cure would be worse than the illness, and involuntary medication would not be permitted.

Although another hearing may be required, the court does not intend to necessitate multiple hearings. The court wishes to avoid a cyclical situation where prohibition of treatment causes a patient's incompetency, upon which his doctors can then overturn his refusal and treat him with drugs, which then help him to regain competency and his refusal right. Instead, the court will, as much as possible, look to the proper treatment over the long term. Consideration of the least restrictive alternative is part of this long-term analysis.

To summarize, if the trial of lithium and tofranil has failed and the state seeks to administer another drug which is refused by the plaintiff, the drug can only be administered in an emergency. For a long range program, the state must come back to court for further hearings. On the evidence to date, the court does not believe that tardive dyskinesia is likely at this time; only a preliminary symptom *possibly* indicative of the disease has been shown. The court would find that all less restrictive alternatives have been exhausted if the lithium and tofrinil regime was given a fair trial. The court does find Mr. Rennie dangerous to others on the ward at times. Both his dangerousness and the rationality behind any new refusal would have to be evaluated at a new hearing. Furthermore, perhaps because he is a litigant, Mr. Rennie seems to be receiving an adequate treatment regime.

D. DUE PROCESS

In light of the extended nature of these hearings, Mr. Rennie certainly has received all the process to which he is due. However, in view of this court's practical experiences during this hearing, it is perhaps appropriate to comment on what the court feels are the shortcomings of the state's new Bulletin 78-3 regarding psychotropic medication, which appears as an appendix to this opinion.

First, the court finds that there is a sufficient liberty interest so that due process attaches. To go from a state of confinement to confinement plus forced medication involves a major change in the conditions of confinement, so that *Meachum v. Fano,* 427 U.S. 215, 96 S. Ct. 2532, 49 L. Ed. 2d 451 (1975) is inapposite. A drug regimen subjects a patient to harsh side effects and possible permanent disability, effects different in kind than the differences between places of confinement. Furthermore, a hearing is required to insure that the use of drugs in a particular case does not violate the first or eighth amendments or the right of privacy. Thus, in the absence of emergency, some due process hearing is required prior to the forced administration of drugs. *Scott v. Plante, supra. See also Clonce v. Richardson,* 379 F. Supp. 338, 349 (W.D. Mo. 1974); Plotkin, *supra* at 491; Winick, *supra* at 816; *Winters v. Miller, supra* at 71. *Cf.* Bazelon, *supra* at 909.

A due process hearing is also required because there is great risk of hospital error. As we have seen, hospital records are difficult even for the staff to use. Entries are sometimes missed, and the complete drug history is not always clear. This underscores the need for systematic review of the decision to medicate involuntarily.

Initially, patients must be informed of and participate in the decision-making aspects of their treatment. *In re W. S., Jr.,* 152 N.J. Super. 298, 377 A.2d 969 (Juv. and Dom. Rel. Ct. 1977).

Patients are entitled to a lawyer to assist them. Counsel is necessary to cope with the problems of law, to make skilled inquiry into the facts, and to insure proper procedures. *Bell, supra* at 1092 (quoting *In re Gault,* 387 U.S. 1, 36, 87 S. Ct. 1428, 18 L. Ed. 2d 527 (1967)); *cf.* Bazelon, *supra* at 910. It is clear in this case that without the tireless efforts of Mr. Gelman and his staff at the Public Advocate's Office, Mr. Rennie could not effectively have made an argument before a factfinder and brought his case before this court.

Independent psychiatrists are also essential to a fair hearing. Unless the state elects to set up some form of independent administrative board to review treatment decisions, the patient is entitled to an outside psychiatrist of his choice to evaluate the need for medication.

A hospital-retained psychiatrist is not sufficient. As Dr. Pepper testified, psychiatrists are as objective as lawyers when representing a client. When Dr. Pepernik and Dr. Stinnett reviewed plaintiff's files, they began with the assumption that the choice of prolixin was correct. Dr. Heller was also influenced by having the hospital doctors refer him to specific sections of the charts. Patients refusing treatment must be entitled to an outside consultant of their choice so that all of the facts can be aired.

The court also notes that once the outside consultants and hospital psychiatrists began talking, it was possible to reach areas of agreement and a fuller understanding of Mr. Rennie's problem. Thus, it believes that the presence of independent doctors will aid rather than inhibit treatment.

Finally, the patient's lawyer and psychiatrist must have access to hospital records to determine comprehensively the position of their client. Where the patient cannot reasonably afford an attorney or a psychiatrist, the state must supply them.

V. Conclusion

As the involuntary medication of prolixin was terminated, no injunction need issue on that point. Due to the time required for briefing and preparation of this opinion, over four months have passed since the parties were last in court. Accordingly, the court is not fully aware of the present status of Mr. Rennie and what effect an injunction would have.[6] Therefore, no injunction will issue at the moment. If Mr. Rennie now refuses any drug which the Ancora doctors seek to administer in a non-emergency situation, the court will upon notice restrain the administration of the drug and immediately schedule hearings to examine (1) plaintiff's physical threat to patients and staff at the institution, (2) plaintiff's capacity to decide on his particular treatment, (3) whether any less restrictive treatments exist, and (4) the risk of permanent side effects from the proposed treatment.

APPENDIX

DIVISION OF MENTAL HEALTH AND HOSPITALS ADMINISTRATIVE BULLETIN 78-3

March 1, 1978

Subject: The Administration of Psychotropic Medication to Voluntary and Involuntary Patients

I. Introduction
A. *Issue*

Division guidelines governing the administration of psychotropic medication to voluntary and involuntary psychiatric hospital patients.
B. *Objectives*

1. To fulfill our ethical, professional and statutory responsibilities in improving the condition of psychiatric hospital patients;

---

6. It is the court's understanding that as of the date of this opinion, Mr. Rennie is not receiving psychotropic drugs, and may soon be released from Ancora.

2. To provide patients with the opportunity to participate in the development of their own individual treatment plans;

3. To provide for *medical review* of the treating physician's medication determination;

4. To utilize the patient's treatment team in formulating clinical care.

C. *Legislative Parameters*

1. Every individual who is mentally ill is entitled to medical care and other professional services in accordance with accepted standards. N.J.S.A. 30:4-24.1. New Jersey courts have also recognized that a psychiatric hospital patient has an affirmative right to receive treatment and that a hospital has a correlative responsibility to attempt to improve the condition of its patients.

2. Each patient has the right to participate in planning for his own treatment to the extent that his condition permits. N.J.S.A. 30:4-24.1.

3. (a) Voluntary patients have the right to refuse medition. N.J.S.A. 30:4-24.2 d (1).

   (b) The chief executive officer of a state or county psychiatric hospital is authorized to give consent for psychiatric treatment to patients declared legally incompetent by a court or patients under the age of 21 under certain conditions. See N.J.S.A. 30:4-7.1 to 7.6.

   (c) Patients have the right to be free from unnecessary or excessive medication. N.J.S.A. 30:4-24.1 d (1) [30:4-24.2 d(1)].

   (d) Medication may not be used as punishment, for the convenience of staff, or as a substitute for a treatment program. N.J.S.A. 30:4-24.1 d (1) [30:4-24.2 d (1)].

   (e) Notation of each patient's medication shall be kept in his treatment records. At least weekly, the attending physician shall review the drug regimen of each patient under his care. All physicians' prescriptions shall be written with a termination date, which shall not exceed 30 days. N.J.S.A. 30:4-24.2 d (1).

D. *Judicial Parameters*

Although existing case law is not clear with respect to the administration of medication to involuntary patients, in December 1977 a New Jersey County District Court Judge held, in the case of, *in Re Mark B.*, that under certain conditions, "Involuntarily committed patients do not have the right to refuse medication."

II. The Involuntary Administration of Medication
Definitions

1. A patient is considered incompetent only if he has been adjudicated incompetent by a court.

2. Medication is considered a necessary part of a patient's treatment plan when either:

    (a) The patient is incapable, without medication, of participating in any treatment plan available at the hospital that will give him a realistic opportunity of improving his condition; or

    (b) Although it is possible to devise a treatment plan that is available at the hospital and will give the patient a realistic opportunity of improving his condition; either:

        (1) a treatment plan which includes medication would probably improve the patient's condition within a significantly shorter time period; or

        (2) there is a significant possibility that the patient will harm himself or others before improvement of his condition is realized, if medication is not administered.

A. *Emergency Administration of Medication*

The procedures described in this Bulletin are not intended to preclude the administration of psychotropic medication to a patient in an emergency.

Therefore, if a physician certifies that it is essential to administer psychotropic medication in order to prevent the death of or serious consequences to a patient, the Chief Executive Officer is authorized to consent to the administration of the medication recommended by the physician's certification. If it is impossible to comply with this procedure without jeopardizing the life of the patient, the medication may be administered on a physician's order.

B. If a patient refuses to take the psychotropic medication that has been prescribed for him, the attending physician shall speak to the patient and *attempt to explain:* his assessment of the patient's condition; his reasons for prescribing the medication; the benefits and risks of taking the medication; and the advantages and disadvantages of alternative courses of action.

If the patient still refuses to take the medication and the physician still believes that medication is a necessary part of the patient's treatment plan:

(a) The physician should tell the patient that the matter will be discussed at a meeting of the patient's treatment team;

(b) If the patient's clinical condition permits, the physician should invite the patient, to attend the meeting of the treatment team.

(c) The physician should suggest that the patient discuss the matter with a person of his own choosing, such as a relative or friend.

C. The treatment team shall meet to discuss the physician's recommendation and the patient's response.

(1) If the patient is present, the team shall attempt to formulate a treatment plan that is acceptable to the patient and the team. The patient may agree to take medication unconditionally or under certain conditions that are acceptable to the physician.

(2) If the patient is not present, the team and the physician shall discuss the physician's recommendation and the patient's response, and shall document their respective conclusions.

D. If, after the team meeting, the physician still believes that medication is a necessary part of the patient's treatment plan and the patient still refuses to take the prescribed medication,

Then:

Case 1: Patients Adjudicated Incompetent by a Court

(1) If there is a consensus in regard to the necessity of the medication, the physician shall attempt to secure the consent of the patient's guardian.

If the patient's guardian, after reasonable notice of the proposed action and a request for consent, refuses or neglects to execute and submit a writing expressing either the grant or denial of consent,

Then, The Chief Executive Officer may consent to the administration of medication.

(2) If there is disagreement between the team and the physician in regard to medication, then the medical director (or his designee) shall conduct a personal examination of the patient and a review of the record. If the medical director (or his designee) agrees with the physician, the physician shall attempt to secure the consent of the guardian.

If the patient's guardian, after reasonable notice of the proposed action and a request for consent, refuses or neglects to execute and submit a writing expressing either the grant or denial of consent,

Then, The Chief Executive Officer may consent to the administration of the medication.

Case 2: Patients Who Have Not Been Adjudicated Incompetent by a Court

Part I—Voluntary Patients

Medication may not be administered to a voluntary patient who refuses to accept it.

Part II—Involuntary Patients

The medical director (or his designee) must conduct a personal examination of the patient and a review of the record. If the medical director (or his designee) agrees with the necessity for medication, the medication may be administered as a part of the patient's documented individualized treatment plan.

E. *Miscellaneous*

1. *Independent Evaluations*

Whenever the medical director (or his designee) is asked to review a medication decision, the medical director shall be authorized to retain an independent psychiatric consultant to evaluate the patient's need for medication. This would be indicated particularly in cases where there is disagreement between the treating physician and the team.

If the patient is evaluated by an independent psychiatric consultant invited by the hospital and the consultant recommends a treatment plan that does not include the administration of medication, then the medical director in the report filed in the treatment record, shall address the conclusions and recommendations of the consultant.

2. *Review*

In addition to the reviews mandated by N.J.S.A. 30:24.2 d (1), the medical director (or his designee) shall review each week the treatment program of each involuntary patient, who is refusing to accept medication voluntarily, to determine:

(a) Whether the patient is still refusing his prescribed medication;

(b) Whether medication is still a necessary part of the patient's treatment plan; and

(c) Whether the other components of the patient's treatment plan are being implemented.

3. *Documentation*

Each step of the procedures outlined above shall be documented in the patient's chart.

s/ *Michail Rotov*
Michail Rotov, M.D., Director
Division of Mental Health and Hospitals

ON RENEWED MOTION FOR PRELIMINARY INJUNCTION

This is a renewed motion for a preliminary injunction pursuant to Fed. R. Civ. P. 65 by plaintiff John E. Rennie, an involuntary patient of Ancora Psychiatric Hospital. He seeks to enjoin the defendant psychiatrists and officials at Ancora from forcibly administering drugs to him in the absence of an emergency situation.

This court issued its opinion November 9, 1978. 462 F. Supp. 1131. Although the opinion discussed the facts of the case and legal issues at length, the court did not issue an injunction since the record did not reflect the plaintiff's then current status. Furthermore, the court had been informally advised by counsel that plaintiff's condition had improved substantially, and release from the hospital was contemplated. The opinion left the courthouse door open for plaintiff to reapply for immediate injunctive relief if his condition worsened and the hospital again attempted to medicate plaintiff against his will in a non-emergent situation.

Unfortunately, the plaintiff's condition has greatly deteriorated in recent weeks, and as a result the hospital on December 2, 1978 began to administer the antipsychotic drug thorazine without plaintiff's consent. Plaintiff renewed his motion for an injunction on December 6, and a hearing was held the following day. After hearing the testimony of plaintiff's witnesses and the arguments of counsel, the court denied the motion. The following are the court's findings of fact and conclusions of law, which supplement the findings and conclusions set forth in the November 9 opinion.

FINDINGS OF FACT

I. Plaintiff's Condition

Mr. Rennie's mental health began to deteriorate within a few days after the November 9 issuance of the earlier opinion. He became increasingly manic, exhibiting grandiose behaviors. By November 14, he was transferred to a closed ward and placed on homicidal precautions. His behavior has become increasingly abusive and assaultive, and he has suffered from inability to sleep and hallucinations. He has been in restraints much of the time since November 14, and is currently in a state described by his treating psychiatrist, Dr. Engrazio Balita, as floridly psychotic. Tr. 28. His physical condition has also deteriorated, and he has suffered dehydration, abnormal fluctuations in temperature, and probable infection. Dr. Balita testified that these complications have imperilled his life.

Mr. Rennie has been on a maintenance dosage of lithium carbonate. However, while on a furlough from Ancora the first week of November, he stopped taking this medication, and refused it upon returning to the hospital. However, after appeals from his counsel, Mr. Gelman, he began taking lithium November 14 and attained a maintenance level of the drug in his blood on November 24.

As the lithium failed to stabilize plaintiff's condition, Dr. Balita began emergency injections of thorazine on December 2, and at a treatment team meeting December 5 recommended that thorazine be forcefully administered in accordance with Administrative Bulletin 78-3. This recommendation was approved at the meeting, and reviewed and approved the following day by Dr. Max Pepernik, the Ancora Medical Director.

II. The Four Factors

In the November 9 opinion, the court stated four factors which must be considered in determining if an injunction should issue. These are (1) plaintiff's physical threat to patients and staff at the institution, (2) plaintiff's capacity to decide on his particular treatment, (3) whether any less restrictive treatments exist, and (4) the risk of permanent side effects from the proposed treatment. These factors will now be applied to the current situation.

Plaintiff has repeatedly threatened patients and staff during the past few weeks, and has been put on homicidal precautions by the hospital. It has often been necessary to place him in restraints to protect the plaintiff himself as well as others in the institution.

The court accepts Mr. Gelman's representation that in his current psychotic thrall Mr. Rennie has still knowingly refused to consent to injection of thorazine. But as the court indicated in its November 9 opinion, his capacity to participate in the choice of medication is limited. Plaintiff's failure to take lithium the last several weeks is additional evidence of his limited capacity to make treatment decisions, as the expert testimony is almost unanimous that lithium is a helpful drug with only minor side effects to Mr. Rennie. It should be noted that he has not only refused lithium while in his current manic state, but also early in November when his condition had markedly improved.

Analyzing plaintiff's behavior, the court concludes that while his refusal of thorazine is partly motivated by a rational desire to avoid harmful and unpleasant side effects, it is also prompted by an irrational desire to rebel against the hospital and its doctors. Therefore the court finds that plaintiff's capacity is severely limited, particularly at the present time, but also over the course of his illness. However, if plaintiff continues his present cooperation with the doctors in taking lithium for a few months, the court might reconsider this finding of lack of capacity. On the other hand, Mr. Rennie need not consent to psychotropic medication to demonstrate capacity, as his refusal of these drugs at this time has, at the least, a rational basis. The court may reconsider this finding at a later time, however.

As was stated in the court's earlier opinion, the lithium regime must be given a fair trial as a less restrictive treatment. Plaintiff's expert, Dr. William T. Carpenter, testified that lithium has not yet had a complete chance, but this is partly because plaintiff has failed to take the medication.

Even plaintiff's expert indicated that a psychotropic was essential to stabilize Mr. Rennie. He recommended that thorazine be administered for at least one week or until Mr. Rennie's condition had stabilized to the point where he could be released from restraints and lithium and psychotherapy could be effectively employed.

The court therefore finds there is currently no less restrictive alternative to thorazine, other than constant restraints, which will safeguard plaintiff and others in the hospital, and no alternative treatment which offers a reasonable chance of alleviating plaintiff's current acute psychosis. The court further finds that this situation will continue until the plaintiff's condition has stabilized and improved, and until plaintiff demonstrates a convincing willingness to participate in a lithium and psychotherapy regime.

Finally, the court must consider the risk of permanent side effects. The court is concerned about tardive dyskinesia which, as stated in the earlier opinion, is a cure worse than the mental disorder itself. While Dr. Carpenter testified that he had observed mild abnormal movements of the jaw and extremities at an August 24 examination of Mr. Rennie, plaintiff's counsel conceded that plaintiff has no symptomatic movements at this time. Dr. Carpenter concluded that Mr. Rennie may have had a very mild, reversible case of tardive dyskinesia, and at least has a predisposition to the disease. However, he also indicated that short-term use of thorazine does not pose a significant threat, though he cautioned against use of thorazine for more than four weeks, particularly if the drug does not greatly affect Mr. Rennie's psychosis. He also stated Mr. Rennie should be watched closely for manifestations of tardive dyskinesia symptoms.

The court agrees that close scrutiny is vitally necessary, but does not believe that the threat of the disease is salient enough to preclude use of thorazine at this time.

CONCLUSIONS OF LAW

As plaintiff's capacity is severely limited, and as thorazine injections provide the least restrictive means to stabilize plaintiff's condition in order that lithium and psychotherapy may be used (with or without thorazine), and in order that the hospital may safely remove plaintiff from restraints, no injunction will be issued.

The court has indicated its desire to avoid multiple hearings by examining the situation over the long term at this injunction hearing. However, the need to administer thorazine for a week or two became readily apparent, and the court did not require defendants to call their witnesses and provide their long-term treatment plan.[3] Neither did the treatment team evaluation of December 5 indicate how long thorazine will be used. Furthermore, as plaintiff's counsel, Mr. Gelman, conceded at the hearing, it was not the best time in plaintiff's view to decide his long-term care.

But consistent use of lithium for several weeks is required to demonstrate plaintiff's renewed capacity to choose his treatment, as well as to enable the hospital and this court to confidently assume that lithium and psychotherapy alone may be given a realistic trial through proper use. Therefore, this decision should be conclusive for at least two months, barring any significant evidence of tardive dyskinesia or drastic change in any other relevant factor in the court's decision. The court is still very concerned about the possibility of tardive dyskinesia and urges the hospital to monitor Mr. Rennie closely for signs of this disease. Furthermore, the court stresses that the hospital should carefully consider the need for continued administration of thorazine in light of objective medical evidence and plaintiff's refusal of the drug. The court hopes that reasoned action by both parties will preclude the need for further applications for preliminary injunctive relief.

Both parties have also asked the court to clarify the procedures for seeking an injunction established in the November 9 opinion and the definition of the term emergency used in the opinion. These procedures will apply to any later appeal by plaintiff for injunctive relief on this issue. Emergency signifies a sudden, significant change in the plaintiff's condition which creates danger to the patient himself or to others in the hospital. While restraints can always eliminate this danger, this is a realistic alternative only if a few hours' confinement are adequate to calm the plaintiff. Otherwise the hospital is not required to place the plaintiff in permanent restraints rather than forcefully medicate.

The emergency is deemed to last until the administrative procedures under Bulletin 78-3 may be followed, but no longer than 72 hours regardless. At that time, plaintiff may, if he wishes, seek a temporary restraining order by notifying the court and the state, and presenting evidence that psychotropics are being forcefully

3. A plan will be required by the pre-trial order in this case, so that long-term use of psychotropics may be fully considered when the consent to treatment issue is tried.

administered. Then the court will issue the restraining order and immediately schedule a preliminary injunction hearing, to be held within 72 hours if possible, to consider the right to refuse treatment under the four stated factors.

ORDER

Application by plaintiff on his renewed motion for preliminary injunction being heard by the court on the 7th day of December, 1978; and

The court having considered the testimony of Dr. William T. Carpenter (plaintiff's medical expert psychiatrist) and Dr. Engrazio Balita (employee of defendant and plaintiff's treating psychiatrist at Ancora), exhibits, briefs and argument of counsel; and

For the reasons stated in the court's opinion of December 12, 1978,

It is on this 12th day of December, 1978, ORDERED that the renewed motion for a preliminary injunction is denied.

RENNIE v. KLEIN

—F. Supp. —(D.N.J. 1979)

BROTMAN, District Judge.

This is a motion for a preliminary injunction by a class composed of patients in five hospitals for the mentally ill operated by the State of New Jersey. Plaintiffs seek to restrain the hospitals and their staffs from forcibly administering drugs to them unless a hearing is held and certain conditions are met. The court holds that plaintiffs do have a constitutional right to refuse medication in certain circumstances, and has fashioned a decree to enforce that right.

PROCEDURAL HISTORY

This litigation began when a complaint was filed by plaintiff John E. Rennie on December 22, 1977. The defendants were Ms. Ann Klein, Commissioner of the Department of Human Services of the State of New Jersey, Dr. Michail Rotov, Director of the Department's Division of Mental Health and Hospitals, and various officials at Ancora Psychiatric Hospital, where Mr. Rennie is an involuntarily committed patient. The complaint charged defendants with violations of four rights: (1) the right to refuse medication in non-emergent circumstances, (2) the right to treatment, (3) the right of access to counsel, and (4) the right to be free from physical abuse while in custody.

Since the complaint was filed, the litigation has focused on the right to refuse treatment, and, tangentially, on the right to counsel, while the rights to adequate treatment, safe confinement, and access to counsel generally have been reserved for later consideration. On December 20, 1978, the court imposed a temporary restraining order on defendants preventing them from medicating Mr. Rennie against his will beyond a maintenance dosage except in emergencies. Plaintiff then moved for a preliminary injunction and the court held fourteen days of hearings between January 13 and April 28, 1978. On April 18, 1978, the temporary restraining order was dissolved after a consensus was reached concerning the proper treatment for Mr. Rennie at that time. However, on May 19 the plaintiff again sought temporary relief, which was denied pending a resolution of the preliminary injunction motion.

The court issued its decision on November 9, 1978. The opinion, reported at 462 F. Supp. 1131, provides a detailed chronicle of Mr. Rennie's medical history and the litigation up to that time. It also discusses the beneficial and detrimental effects of various medications and the several legal theories asserted by plaintiff to support a right to refuse treatment.

This court concluded that a right to refuse should be recognized, based on the constitutional right of privacy. However, because of countervailing state interests, the right must be a qualified one, and the following four factors must be considered in applying the right in a given situation: (1) the patient's physical threat to other patients and staff at the institution, (2) the patient's capacity to decide on his particular treatment, (3) the existence of any less restrictive treatments, and (4) the risk of permanent side effects from the proposed treatment.

This court also stated that a mental patient has a right to procedural due process, and noted in dictum that this might include a hearing and representation by a lawyer and independent psychiatrist before drugs are forcibly administered in a non-emergent situation.

It was held that, because of the extended court hearings, Mr. Rennie had received all the process which he was due. It was also noted that Mr. Rennie was not receiving undesired medication; therefore no injunction was issued. However, Mr. Rennie's condition worsened shortly after that time and the hospital again sought to administer thorazine against the patient's will. After a hearing on December 7, 1978, the court denied Mr. Rennie's renewed motion for a preliminary injunction. In an opinion issued December 12, the court found that Mr. Rennie's capacity was severely limited at that time and that thorazine was the least restrictive means of stabilizing his condition. Therefore, the four factors indicated that an injunction should not issue.[1]

At this time plaintiff moved to enlarge his suit to a class action. By order dated March 20, 1979, the court allowed plaintiff to amend his complaint to add class action allegations, allowed various intervenors to join the action as plaintiffs and conditionally certified three subclasses pursuant to Fed. R. Civ. P. 23(b) (2). The first subclass is composed of all persons who presently are or in the future may be hospitalized at Ancora Psychiatric Hospital. This subclass, according to the amended complaint, alleged violation of the rights to adequate treatment and safe confinement. The court has not yet been asked to hear the claims of this group.

The court also conditionally certified two statewide subclasses asserting the right to refuse treatment and to due process before treatment is forcibly administered. The amended complaint focused exclusively on the forcible administration of medication. See ¶13A. One subclass is composed of all adult patients involuntarily committed to five mental health facilities operated by the Division of Mental Health and Hospitals. The other subclass is composed of voluntarily committed adult patients at the five facilities: Ancora Psychiatric Hospital, Marlboro Psychiatric Hospital, Trenton Psychiatric Hospital, Greystone Park Psychiatric Hospital, and the Glen Gardner Center for Geriatrics.[2]

After extensive discovery, these two subclasses moved for a preliminary injunction to restrain the use of psychoactive drugs without

1. After an initial regimen on the unwanted drug, thorazine, Mr. Rennie's condition again stabilized and has been generally good to date. At the present time he is voluntarily taking lithium carbonate and has been granted extended furloughs from the hospital. However, he still retains the status of an involuntary patient.

2. The statewide subclasses originally included minor as well as adult patients at the five hospitals and a sixth facility exclusively for children, the Arthur Brisbane Child Treatment Center. However, by a bench opinion on August 22, the court recertified the subclasses, creating two distinct statewide subclasses for voluntary and involuntary patients under the age of 18. The court also denied the preliminary injunction for these patients, concluding that plaintiffs, who had focused almost exclusively on the problems of adult patients during the hearings, had not provided adequate proof concerning the treatment of minors and the role of parents and guardians in determining minor patients' right to refuse.

the freely given consent of the patient and without procedural safeguards. The court held 17 days of hearings between June 13 and August 9, 1979. The parties also supplemented the record with numerous depositions and exhibits.

The court heard testimony of several patients and staff personnel from the various facilities and was provided extensive medical records. Both sides produced highly qualified experts in psychiatry, psychopharmacology and hospital administration. Numerous scholarly articles were submitted. Courtroom or deposition testimony was provided by each of the five medical directors, who are the chief psychiatrists at the hospitals and supervise medical practices. This testimony was supplemented by memoranda, records and statistical studies concerning the use of medication at the facilities. A Division attorney who has addressed these issues also testified at length.

The following are the court's findings of fact and conclusions of law pursuant to Fed. R. Civ. P. 52(a).

FINDINGS OF FACT
I. Benefits and Side Effects of Psychotropic Medication

The benefits and side effects of psychotropic drugs were discussed in Part IV of the findings of fact in the November opinion. 402 F. Supp. 1136-1138. Those findings are adopted and incorporated here. The court found that while psychotropic drug treatment had shown considerable success, recent studies had raised questions about the efficacy of using psychotropics in every case of mental illness. The present record provides additional evidence that many patients who would normally be treated with psychotropics can improve without them, and that smaller doses than are traditionally given can often be effective. Crane, Clinical Psychopharmacology in Its 20th Year, 181 Science 124 (1973); Gardos and Cole, Maintenance Antipsychotic Therapy: Is the Cure Worse than the Disease? 133 Am. J. Psychiatry 32 (1976). The drugs are most useful in diffusing schizophrenic thought patterns during acute psychotic episodes.

The evidence at the recent hearings also reconfirmed the fact that these drugs have dangerous side effects, including tardive dyskinesia. Testimony also indicated that the drugs inhibit a patient's ability to learn social skills needed to fully recover from psychosis, and might even cause cancer. Even acutely disturbed patients might have good reason to refuse these drugs.

II. The Hospitals

A. Patient Population and Staffing

Ancora Psychiatric Hospital is a state facility for the mentally ill in Hammonton, New Jersey. It houses about 1000 patients at any one time. Marlboro Psychiatric Hospital is a state facility in Marlboro, New Jersey, with a patient population of approximately 800. Greystone Park Psychiatric Hospital, in Morris Plains, New Jersey, has a population of 1100. Trenton Psychiatric Hospital in Trenton has about 1000 patients. The Glen Gardner Geriatric Center in Glen Gardner, New Jersey, has about 140 patients; all are of advanced age and have been transferred from Trenton Psychiatric Hospital.

The four large hospitals have fairly similar populations. The majority of patients in each hospital are diagnosed schizophrenic; about 25 percent are categorized as having organic brain syndrome. About five percent are diagnosed as suffering major affective disorders, and another five percent are believed to be mentally retarded. The patients at Gardner are no longer in need of acute psychiatric care, but were formerly hospitalized for mental illness and often continue to receive psychotropic medication.

The hospitals are understaffed and patients have trouble seeing psychiatrists. They generally have large, bleak and unpleasant wards, and the patients have little structured activity.

B. Use and Effect of Psychotropic Drugs

A vast majority of patients at the five hospitals receive psychotropic medications, either by pills or injection. One expert testified that drugs are the "be all and end all" at the hospitals. The medical director of Marlboro states in an office memorandum that the hospital "uses medication as a form of control and as a substitute for treatment." A 1975 study of these institutions found overuse of drugs and inadequate record-keeping. The pattern of drug usage appears to be no different than that of other large state institutions, which was described in an article by Dr. George Crane, a psychiatrist who testified at the hearings:

> Many physicians, nurses, guardians, and family members who resent the patient's behavior and are threatened by potential acts of violence fail to distinguish between manifestations of illness and reactions to frustrations. Hence, drugs are prescribed to solve all types of management problems, and failure to achieve the desired results causes an escalation of dosage, changes of drugs, and polypharmacy. It is often reported that patients refuse to ingest their pills or that relatives fail to supervise the proper administration of medicines. Less publicized is the patient's dependence on drugs. The medical

staff gains a feeling of accomplishment from the patient's adherence to a pre-scribed regime, while the nursing personnel and relatives, who are in more direct contact with the patient, derive a spurious feeling of security when the doctor's orders are carried out. Thus, the prescribing of drugs has in many cases become a ritual in which patients, family members, and physicians participate. . . . [N]euroleptics are often used for solving psychological, social, administrative, and other nonmedical problems.

Crane, supra, at 125.

This extensive use of psychotropics has caused numerous patients not only transient side effects, but permanent neurological damage including tardive dyskinesia[3] and drug-induced parkinsonism. The medical director of the Gardner Geriatric Center estimated that 35 to 50 percent of his patients—all transferred from Trenton Hospital wards—have tardive dyskinesia. The medical director of Ancora testified that the rate of tardive dyskinesia among his patients was probably between 25 to 40 percent, based on national studies, al-though he could not estimate from data generated at his own hospi-tal. In fact, none of the medical directors had a clear idea of the extent of tardive dyskinesia among their patients. Dr. Crane, a lead-ing expert in the study of tardive dyskinesia, examined patients at two of the hospitals and found a significant number of persons with tardive dyskinesia and other potentially permanent side effects which had not been diagnosed and charted in the patients' records.

Despite much criticism from outsiders, little was done by defen-dants to improve medication procedures until November 1978. At that time Commissioner Klein issued Administrative Order 2:13, and Dr. Rotov issued accompanying Administrative Bulletin 78-6. These documents provide specific guidelines to insure careful and knowl-edgeable administration of psychotropic drugs, and mandate that extrapyramidal symptoms be closely monitored. In particular, a checklist for abnormal involuntary movement syndromes, or AIMS form, must be completed every three months. The court finds that these guidelines, modeled closely after a document used by the Michigan Department of Mental Health, are well intentioned and reflect a reasoned approach to the use of psychotropic medication.

However, plaintiffs have demonstrated a widespread failure to have the guidelines implemented. For instance, while AIMS forms have

3. Doctors have recently studied ways to reverse the effects of tardive dyskinesia, and have had some tentative successes in certain types of patients. Gelenberg, Doller-Wojcik and Growdon, Choline and Lecithin in the Treatment of Tardive Dyskinesia: Preliminary Results from a Pilot Study, 136 Am. J. Psychiatry 772 (1979) (Ex. D-49); Jus, Jus and Fontaine, Long Term Treatment of Tardive Dyskinesia, 40 J. Clin. Psychiatry 72 (1979) (Ex. D-48).

been completed for most patients in the five facilities, the doctors using the forms have often failed to diagnose tardive dyskinesia and drug-induced parkinsonism. It is not always clear whether nurses are completing the forms instead of physicians.

Furthermore, the court believes that medication decisions are often left to nurses or even attendants because the doctors will ratify their recommendations without examining the patient involved. There is also overuse of medication orders which specifically leave discretion to the staff for many days, or weeks, despite hospital rules against such practice. Doctors also continue to use poor medication practices, such as unjustified polypharmacy.

The medical directors have begun to improve patient records, including pharmacy records, although there is still much to be done in this respect. There has also been an attempt to better educate physicians in the use of psychotropics.

III. Incidents Involving Individual Patients

Before turning to the general procedures concerning refusal of medication, the court will discuss the representative experiences of five of the many individual patients whose cases were brought to the court's attention during the hearings as indicative of the practices and policies of defendants Klein and Rotov and their hospitals. Although the names of all but one patient appear in the record, their names, with the exception of Mr. Rennie's, will not be used in this opinion.

The first patient is a 23-year-old woman who was involuntarily committed to Ancora in 1978. She has had a history of mental illness and hospitalization since she was ten. At Ancora she was given psychotropic drugs which often blunted her consciousness to such an extent that she would spend much of the day sleeping. Heavy doses were probably given in response to her quarrelsome and sometimes violent relationship with ward staff, which can, in large measure, be attributed to the fact that she felt unneeded and idle on the ward and was sometimes subject to physical assault from attendants.

Until January 1979 she usually took medication without objection, and, on occasion, even requested it. However, she was also threatened with forced injection of medication when she expressed reluctance to take drugs. In January she began openly resisting drugs because she had become pregnant and "did not want to hurt my baby." In disregard of her pregnancy and her opposition to drugs, the treating physician persisted in prescribing psychotropics, and the patient was forced to complain to the Public Advocate's office, which interceded. Nevertheless, with the approval of the hospital medical director, she was given haldol, a psychotropic, on March 16, 1979. One week later she ingested a small amount of detergent and was transferred to the hospital's medical unit. That unit immediately stopped her use of haldol because of her pregnancy and because her diagnosis did not require use of psychotropics. The medical unit also allowed her to do small chores on the ward. Her general condition rapidly improved and she became very cooperative with ward staff. On May 16 she was discharged and has remained off medication. Her demeanor when she testified in court was excellent.

In summary, despite the patient's hesitance and outright refusals, and her pregnancy, Ancora physicians on the psychiatric ward persisted in medicating this patient by force or intimidation when a change in environment was the least restrictive treatment indicated. A change was, in fact, quite beneficial. However, only the patient's drastic action insured the transfer she needed and an independent evaluation by another doctor.

Another woman, 66 years old, was an involuntary patient at Greystone for 10 years. Plaintiff's expert diagnosed her illness as manic-depressive psychosis. The hospital had given her diagnoses of both manic-depressive psychosis and schizo-affective schizophrenia at different times.

Recently this patient began refusing doses of thorazine, although she accepted lithium which is the drug of choice for manic-depressive illness. Her refusal was, according to plaintiffs' expert, "very good judgment." The expert credibly characterized the thorazine prescription as "grossly irresponsible," due to the reasonable success of lithium alone, her symptomatology, and particularly because the patient has tardive dyskinesia.

In fact, a neurologist's report from 1975 in her medical record indicated she had a "classical" case of tardive dyskinesia, but his report was apparently lost in her records. A January 1979 note in her record indicated that her jaw movements were "faking," although plaintiffs' expert testified that her movements were "so gross as to be unable to fake." Indeed, because of her gross mouth movements from this disease she cannot be fitted with dentures and is forced to subsist on a diet of ground food. She was also subjected to taunts from the hospital staff with the implication that the deformity was her own fault.

Not only was thorazine prescribed, but it was also forced on this patient by injection at least once, in January of this year.

Here, again, a psychotropic drug was involuntarily administered where there was little medical justification for the drug and great danger of creating or enhancing irreversible side effects. The side effects were blatantly ignored by doctors.

A third woman, a voluntary patient at Greystone, 60 years old, refused medication in August 1978 but was thrown onto a bed by attendants and given a long-acting form of prolixin by injection. The drug caused the patient severe discomfort. Plaintiff's expert credibly testified that this was improper medication in this case and that the open ward privileges then given her were inconsistent with the suicidal diagnosis appearing in the patient's record. The expert believed many of her psychotic symptoms stemmed from her frustrations with hospital staff and delays in her discharge planning.

The hospital medical director was involved in the decision to forcibly medicate this patient, and upheld the treating physician's decision based on the physician's reports. Review by an independent hearing officer before the forced injection might have aired this patient's complaints and may have prevented the questionable use of prolixin.

An intervenor in this action, age 29, was a voluntary patient at Ancora. Although the Public Advocate wrote a letter in March 1979 on the patient's behalf indicating the patient's dissatisfaction with his medication, long-acting prolixin, he continued to receive the medication. At this time the hospital had him involuntarily committed, but did not follow Division procedures for involuntary patients who refuse medication.

After several letters from the Public Advocate, the hospital responded by continuing prolixin but refusing to give cogentin, a drug which the patient wanted because it is used to alleviate certain painful side-effects of prolixin. Finally, in June of 1979 the patient was given another form of psychotropic, which caused him substantially less discomfort, and he was able to leave the hospital a few weeks later.

Here, the intervention of the Public Advocate caused reprisals against the patient. The hospital failed to follow Division procedures for reviewing the refusals of involuntary patients, and subjected him to great suffering which could have been alleviated by simply changing from one psychotropic to another.

Turning to Mr. Rennie, the original plaintiff in this action and an involuntary patient at Ancora, the court first notes the imprudent use of prolixin which caused plaintiff to experience severe side effects. During the hearings in this litigation in 1978, his condition and treatment were brought to light before the court and were subject to the evaluation of psychiatrists outside the hospital. Through this process, the hospital acknowledged Mr. Rennie's aversion to the drug and agreed to give him another psychotropic.

The court is also concerned with the hospital's treatment of Mr. Rennie's extrapyramidal side effects. One nurse, who had recorded Mr. Rennie's abnormal jaw movements, was criticized and intimidated for her actions by doctors and nursing supervisors. Mr. Rennie's case has been continuously reviewed by the medical director of Ancora since this litigation began in 1977; he has approved forced administration of psychotropics. He has failed to record jaw movements indicative of tardive dyskinesia. However, movements have been detected by other personnel and plaintiffs' highly qualified experts. The medical director's questionable judgment in failing to acknowledge Mr. Rennie's jaw movements appears to be a result of institutional self-interest. A diagnosis of possibly irreversible side effects would impugn the wisdom of previous use of psychotropics and would necessitate less reliance on drugs in treating the patient in the future. Here, the medical director's review did not serve as an independent check free of these institutional pressures which result in unnecessary and harmful use of drugs.

IV. Hospital Procedures Concerning Forced Medication

A. Adoption and Initial Implementation of Bulletin 78-3

In March 1978, Dr. Rotov issued Administrative Bulletin 78-3, which is reprinted as an appendix to the November opinion. This represented the Division's first formal attempt to deal with the problem of patients who refused medication, and was in response to the issues raised in this litigation.

The Bulletin, ¶I(C)(3)(a), acknowledges the right of voluntary patients to refuse medication, which is provided by state law. N.J. Stat. 30:4-24.2(d)(1).

For involuntary patients, the Bulletin refers to a decision of the New Jersey Superior Court, In re Hospitalization of B, 156 N.J. Super. 231, 383 A.2d 760 (Law Div. 1977), which held that involuntary patients have no right to refuse. When an involuntary patient refuses, the Bulletin provides that the treating physician shall attempt to explain the risks and benefits of the drug. If refusal persists, the issue is to be discussed at a meeting of the treatment team, which is composed of the treating physician and various other persons at the hospital who deal with the patient, including psychologists, social workers and nurses. ¶II(C). However, the team's collective opinion is only a recommendation to the treating physician. ¶II(D).

Legally competent patients may have their cases heard by the medical director of the hospital. He must conduct a personal examination of the patient before approving involuntary medication. ¶II(D). He may consult an independent psychiatrist if he wishes, and must review the patient's treatment program each week that the patient continues to protest his medication. ¶II(E). The patient may have an attorney present during this process. ¶II(B)(c).

The Office of the Commissioner also decided in March of this year that Dr. Rotov or another physician in the Division's central office should review the cases of any patient compelled to take medication by a decision of the medical director. At the time of the hearing, however, a central office representative was able to indicate with certainty that Dr. Rotov reviewed the medical charts of Mr. Rennie and only one other patient. The witness said Dr. Rotov might have reviewed "several" other cases, and examined some patients personally. The court finds that this level of review is hardly a regular procedure, and is not quickly or reliably available to patients.

The Division central office has also failed to insure that the Bulletin was rapidly implemented. The testimony shows that it was completely ignored at least at Marlboro and Greystone until December 1978. The medical director of Marlboro was not even told the document existed until November of last year.

B. Obtaining Consent and Acknowledging Refusals

A major problem in implementation of Bulletin 78-3 is identifying those patients who refuse drugs. At Marlboro Hospital about 40 to 50 patients a month have been recorded as refusing. Trenton Hospital has reported about 15 to 40 a month. Ancora Hospital has invoked the Bulletin for only Mr. Rennie and the 23-year-old woman discussed above. No other patient has been reported to have refused since the beginning of the year. Greystone has only reported three patients refusing since the beginning of the year, and the Gardner Geriatric Center has only acknowledged one refusal.

The record also reflects the fact that in a ward of 70 patients at Boston State Hospital, which has been prohibited from forcing medication by federal court order, 10 to 12 patients refuse medication at any one time. A psychiatrist with experience at state hospitals in New York testified that five percent of patients refuse medication at a given time.

The patient populations at Trenton, Marlboro and Boston State are similar to those at Greystone and Ancora. The court attributes the discrepancy in statistics to a substantial failure by staff at the latter hospitals to report refusals. Also, certain hospitals overuse the exception in the Bulletin for emergency situations.

Even if all hospitals accurately reported the number of overt refusals by patients, many patients are too intimidated to attempt to refuse medication and would still be ignored. Certainly there has been extensive use of forced injections in the hospitals when both voluntary and involuntary patients refused to take medication orally. The Marlboro medical director candidly admitted that drugs are still systematically forced on patients. Often forced injections are doses of long-acting prolixin which not only has a much longer effect than other psychotropics but usually has more immediate adverse side effects. Zander, Prolixin Decanoate: A Review of the Research, in 2 Mental Disability L. Rep. 37, 39 (1977). Therefore it would be quite rational for patients to conclude that resistance to drugs would result in their receiving a more unpleasant medication. There is little evidence that the hospitals have taken affirmative steps to inform patients of their rights, although a pamphlet for patients is being prepared by the Division central office.

Despite this situation, the hospitals only initiate review under the Bulletin where a patient affirmatively refuses to take a drug (assuming an overt refusal is acknowledged at all). Complaints or reluctance are not enough.

There has been recent discussion in the central office concerning the use of written consent forms for medication, but there are no specific plans to employ them.[4] Preparation of information pertaining to the harms, as well as benefits of drugs is also being considered in order to render medication consents informed. Indeed, Marlboro and Ancora have started drug education classes and are preparing information forms; yet these lectures and material fail to disclose fully the danger of long-term side effects including tardive dyskinesia.

Another step that the Division has taken is the appointment of "patient advocates," one each at Marlboro and Ancora. They are available to patients who have various problems, including complaints about medication. They can initiate review procedures under the Bulletin. The Marlboro advocate is responsible to that institution's

---

4. It should be noted that even at Gardner Geriatric Center, where patients are generally the most incapacitated, consent forms are successfully used for drug experimentation.

chief executive officer (a non-medical administrator who is the highest officer at the institution), while the Ancora advocate is responsible directly to the Division central office. A Division official acknowledged during her testimony that the advocate should not be responsible to hospital officials so that he can pursue his independent advocacy role. There are tentative plans to hire an advocate at each hospital.

The Division of Mental Health Advocacy, Department of the Public Advocate, which represents the plaintiffs in this litigation, has legal and paralegal representatives at different hospitals who can assist patients in asserting their rights. However, this agency lacks the resources to provide services for all patients who do not or cannot consent to medication. The Department is generally charged with representing citizens on important matters in the public interest.

It should also be noted that some patients, particularly those on geriatric wards, are permanently out of touch with their surroundings and incapable of expressing informed consent, though few of these patients have been declared legally incompetent.

C. Reviewing Refusals

Much of the evidence concerning use of Bulletin 78-3 focused on review by the medical director of refusals by involuntary patients. Few of the recorded refusals even reach that level, partly as a result of legitimate and desirable agreement by patients with their doctors or treatment team to take some medication, and partly the result of wrongful coercion of patients. The Marlboro medical director overruled three of the ten cases which reached his desk since adoption of the Bulletin. The Ancora medical director upheld the treating physician in the two cases referred to him. The same statistic applies to Greystone. At Trenton, the medical director rescinded half of the six forced medication orders she reviewed. There is no evidence of any decision reaching the medical director at Gardner.

The court does not find these statistics themselves indicative of the capability or independence of the medical directors. But these officials can be faulted for their failure to insure that the Bulletin is fully implemented, that patients' refusals are acknowledged and counted, and that force and threat of force or punishment is not used to administer medication.

The medical directors asserted in their testimony that they indeed can exercise independent and conscientious reviews. But some of the individual cases described above rebut those assertions. The Greystone medical director even delegated his responsibility to every staff psychiatrist under a clause in the Bulletin which allows another doctor to act for the medical director when he is away; however, this interpretation was later overruled by Dr. Rotov. The Ancora medical director testified that, in his opinion, an emergency justifying forced medication could last over 30 days. In fact, the medical directors have not even acknowledged a constitutional right to refuse treatment or followed the court's guidelines on the law in deciding refusal cases.

The medical directors' actions demonstrate a lack of independence and objectivity when reviewing the actions of their staffs. The court believes this stems largely from their responsibilities; they must have the support of their personnel, whose jobs are made easier when patients are subdued by medication. Unfortunately the rights and health of patients are sometimes ignored.

In many cases the patient's refusal of medication is prompted solely by the irrational components of his illness. But refusals can also be prompted by a quite rational desire to avoid unpleasant side effects and a realistic appraisal that the medication is not helping one's condition, which are both subjective factors on which the patient may be the best authority.

The author of one study of why schizophrenic patients refuse drugs concluded that "the reluctance to take chemotherapeutic agents and the dysphoric response to antipsychotic drugs are usually related to [extrapyramidal side effects]." He also noted that much of the side effects "that led to drug reluctance [were] of the 'mild' or subclinical type which is apparent only to the careful observer. . . . the subtler extrapyramidal symptoms often go unrecognized by the physician—but not by the patient!" Van Putte, Why Do Schizophrenic Patients Refuse to Take Their Drugs?, 31 Arch. Gen. Psychiatry 67, 70, 71 (1974). The same author found in another study that "the subjective response very early in chlorpromazine [thorazine, a psychotropic] treatment may predict, to a moderate degree, the symptomatic outcome after a sustained course of treatment with the drug. . . . Schizophrenics have been asked every question except, 'How does the medication agree with you?' Their response is worth listening to." Van Putten and Ray, Subjective Response as a Predictor of Outcome in Pharmacotherapy, 35 Arch. Gen. Psychiatry 477, 478-80 (1978).

The court is convinced that where patients' concerns and feelings may be more freely aired, and observable side effects are more closely monitored, medication will be used more wisely. If the refusals of involuntary patients are fairly acknowledged and independently considered in accordance with the legal criteria, a significant number of patients will receive less or no medication, frequently to their benefit.

V. Independent Review

Certain testimony concerned plaintiffs' request for independent review by some type of hearing board or examiner of decisions to forcibly medicate. The court accepts the opinions of those experts who indicated that someone outside the hospital structure would provide a fairer, more accurate review of patients' refusal rights.

The court also believes that if an independent check on forced medication is established, doctors would learn the legal limits of involuntary medication and the number of attempts to force psychotropics would eventually decrease. This would also mean that the number of cases reaching an independent decision-maker would eventually drop to a relatively small number of disputes. The court cannot specifically gauge the cost of an independent review system, but it rejects the $3 million per year figure provided by defendants, as based on overestimates of the number of reviews and the number of hours required for each hearing.

More sensitivity on the part of treating physicians would also engender better patient-doctor relations. Less use of psychotropics and more attention to patient's feelings about their treatment would likely improve patient-staff relations and foster patients' individual dignity. While the authority granted an outside review officer will initially cause resentment among many doctors and staff members of the hospital, the court believes that a carefully structured review system would eventually be accepted by most personnel, as review under the Bulletin has been accepted.

The court further finds that independent review by psychiatrists rather than by judges, lawyers or laypersons, would provide the most accurate analyses of patient interests. Review within the profession would also create far less resentment among physicians and staff whose decisions are questioned. Informal inquiries would be superior to formal procedures because the latter would require more time and resources and often be more disruptive of patient-doctor relations, but would not significantly decrease the risk of erroneous determinations.

Conclusions of Law

I. Procedures Required

The evidence produced at this hearing reinforces the court's previous conclusion that a qualified right to refuse treatment should be recognized, and that due process must be provided before drugs can be forcibly administered. The rationale for these holdings need not be repeated here.

The due process holding is also strengthened by the Supreme Court's recent decisions in Parham v. J.R., 99 S. Ct. 2493 (1979) and Secretary of Public Welfare v. Institutionalized Juveniles, 99 S. Ct. 2523 (1979). These cases, which dealt with the due process rights of juveniles who were voluntarily committed to mental institutions by their parents, or by their state as guardian, held that commitment constitutes a deprivation of a protected liberty interest. 99 S. Ct. at 2503. This court feels that forced drugging can be as intrusive as the involuntary confinement resulting from commitment, and that drugging also has the potential for permanent deprivation through long-term side effects.

After consideration of the evidence at this hearing, the court further concludes that the privacy and due process rights previously recognized in Mr. Rennie's individual case should apply to all other members of the subclass of involuntary patients.

The same reasons compel recognition of the privacy right for voluntary patients. Much of the relief which the court will afford that subclass derives from this federal constitutional right. However, all parties recognize that voluntary patients have an absolute right to refuse treatment under state law. N.J. Stat. 30:4-24.2(d)(1). This right may be enforced in a civil action. N.J. Stat. 30:4-24.2(h). One part of the order is based on this right, heard as a pendent claim.

It is not disputed that defendants acted under color of state law.

Plaintiffs do not ask the court to prohibit the administration of drugs to any particular patient. Rather they seek sweeping changes in hospital practices designed to protect their rights. Thus the crucial issue presented is what procedures are, at a minimum, required to protect the plaintiff's constitutional rights. While defendants have never acknowledged that a constitutional right to refuse exists, they also contend that procedures which have been instituted in the last year serve to meet any constitutional requirements.

In determining the procedures needed for affording members of both subclasses their constitutional right to refuse treatment, the court must consider the degree of vulnerability and helplessness of patients in the five hospitals, as well as the history of compelled medication through the use of forced injections which has created a general belief among many patients that medication cannot be refused. Given these realities—brought about by widespread improper practices on the wards—the court believes the constitutional right to refuse can be realistically afforded only if the hospitals, whenever possible, obtain specific, written consent from patients before they are medicated with any psychotropic drug. The hospitals must also inform patients of their rights and the potential side effects of medication in order that all consents be properly informed.

Both subclasses are entitled to this procedure as both hold the constitutional privacy right. Whether New Jersey law requires the same specific consent for voluntary patients need not be determined here. However, the court does construe New Jersey law to mean that once a voluntary patient withholds under this procedure, the hospital cannot medicate in a non-emergent situation. Accordingly, there is no need for a due process hearing for these patients. Of course, appeals to the voluntary patient by the treatment team or medical director in order to obtain his freely given consent are proper.

On the other hand, the informed refusal of an involuntary patient may be overridden, as these patients' right to refuse is a qualified one. Any forced medication decision must be made by considering the four factors outlined in the court's November opinion. As forced medication implicates a sufficient liberty interest, due process safeguards must be instituted as part of this determination. The court, in dictum in its November opinion, noted some of the procedures which might be necessary. See also Task Panel Reports Submitted to The President's Commission on Mental Health 1435-1436 (1978).

The Supreme Court's subsequent opinions in *Parham* and *Institutionalized Juveniles* must be considered in determining what process is due. The Court in those cases held that the district courts below had erred in requiring formal hearings before minors were committed. These holdings are not strictly applicable to the forced administration of drugs to involuntary adult patients since the Supreme Court's decision was in large part based on its great concern with governmental interference with parental decisions about their minor children. 99 S. Ct. at 2507. Even so, the Court held that a "neutral factfinder" must review the parents' commitment decision. Id. at 2506.

This court believes that a neutral, independent decision-maker is also crucial in the treatment context, and must be provided to insure the minimum quantum of due process to patients.

In *Parham* and *Institutionalized Juveniles* the Supreme Court found that review by staff physicians satisfied due process. The Court noted in *Parham* that the record provided "no support whatever" for the conclusion that staff physicians could not be neutral because of institutional pressures to admit children with no need for care. Id. at 2511.

The Court also held that a physician was an adequate decision-maker because

> [d]ue process has never been thought to require that the neutral and detached trier of fact be law-trained or a judicial or administrative officer. . . . Surely, this is the case as to medical decisions for neither judges nor administrative officers are better qualified than psychiatrists to render psychiatric judgments.

Id. at 2506-2507. Certainly this also applies to consideration of the four factors this court has held qualify the right of patients to refuse medication.

The *Parham* Court also emphasized that formal procedures are not always required:

> [D]ue process is not violated by use of informal traditional medical investigative techniques. . . . Not every determination by state officers can be made most effectively by use of the procedural tools of judicial or administrative decision-making. . . . [I]t is incumbent on courts to design procedures that protect the rights of the individual without unduly burdening the legitimate efforts of the states to deal with difficult social problems.

Id. at 2507 and n.16. The court will not require a formal hearing, or even the presence of an attorney, at the mandated independent review. Any more process than an informal inquiry may cause excessive costs to the state without significantly decreasing the risk of erroneous determinations.

In determining what unconstitutional conduct can form a basis for relief, the court must also apply the principles stated in Rizzo v. Goode, 423 U.S. 362 (1976) and Lewis v. Hyland, 554 F.2d 93 (3rd Cir.), *cert. denied,* 434 U.S. 931 (1977). Under these cases, the court may not enjoin defendants Klein and Rotov, the relevant defendants in the two statewide subclasses' right to refuse treatment claims, unless a constitutional violation is caused by their policies or deliberate indifference. Isolated incidents of improper conduct by individual psychiatrists or other staff are not sufficient to sustain class-wide relief. *Rizzo,* 423 U.S. at 373-377; *Lewis,* 554 F.2d at 98. See also Owens v. Haas, No. 825, slip op. at 3652 (2nd Cir. July 9, 1979).

Rizzo also requires a certain equitable restraint or abstention where relief is sought against a state agency. 423 U.S. at 377-380. The court is fully cognizant of the principles of federalism stated therein, and must attempt to fashion any order such that it disrupts hospital operations as little as possible. But the court must also be vigilant to insure that plaintiffs' rights are upheld. As stated by Chief Judge Lord of the Eastern District of Pennsylvania:

> Notions of comity and the limitations placed upon the use of federal equitable power restrain federal courts from intruding into daily operation of state agencies. But federal courts also have the clear obligation to terminate conditions and actions which violate constitutional rights, particularly for those who are powerless to end such abuse.

Santiago v. City of Philadelphia, 435 F. Supp. 136, 149 (E.D. Pa. 1977).

Medicine has not yet found a cure for the terrible pain of mental illness. The law cannot assist in this endeavor. But the constitution can and does prevent those who have suffered so much at the hands of nature from being subject to further suffering at the hands of man.

II. Inadequacies in Division Practices

While the Division has made certain commendable efforts to improve the procedures surrounding administration of drugs, the court holds that defendants' policies nevertheless fail to meet constitutional standards in a few critical areas. While there have been numerous acts by individual treating physicians and staff which are outside constitutional standards, the court must emphasize that the current policies and mandated procedures of defendants Klein and Rotov and their conscious and deliberate indifference to breaches of patients' rights by hospital personnel form the basis for relief in this action. Remedial action is not barred by *Rizzo* and *Lewis.*

The evidence has shown that defendants are contemplating certain steps which might correct some of the inadequacies found. However, defendants have refused to stipulate that procedures that have been mandated in writing will be fully implemented, much less that other measures contemplated will be carried out. Therefore the court must order certain procedures which might have become Division practices regardless of the court's action. The court is naturally reluctant to so order, but feels that this intervention is proper at this time because certain orders are required anyway and because defendants refuse to guarantee that such measures—which undoubtedly have been spurred by the litigation so far—will indeed be implemented. The rights at stake here are too important to wait on unsubstantiated promises of compliance.

The first major shortcoming in the hospitals' procedures is failure to adequately inform patients of their rights and the effects of drugs, particularly long-term side effects. While certain improvements are contemplated, the hospitals' current record reflects a total failure by defendants Klein and Rotov to insure that all patients are aware of the dangers of their medication, and know that they can reject or appeal medication decisions of their doctors.

Second, the hospitals have not sought written consent to specific administration of drugs. Such a step is apparently contemplated though there is no indication in the record when or whether it actually will be implemented. Neither have defendants made any provision for independent review of those patients who may be incapable of giving informed consent. All of these problems are sufficiently linked to the policies or deliberate indifference of defendants Klein and Rotov to justify classwide equitable relief because defendants have refused to implement informed consent procedures despite the atmosphere of coercion in the wards that makes such steps absolutely necessary for providing patients a realistic refusal right.

The court also finds improper the defendants' policy of limiting review of a physician's decision to forcibly medicate to informal hearings before the treatment team and hospital medical directors. This does not constitute the independent determination required by the due process clause, and the case is thus distinguishable from *Parham*. Here there are institutional pressures on treating physicians to medicate patients unnecessarily. Treatment team review is somewhat controlled by the treating physician and cannot constitute an independent determination. While the medical directors have asserted in their testimony that they are capable and willing to overrule their staff doctors when necessary, the court finds more credible the testimony of those experts who stated that the directors would inevitably be caught in a conflict between patients' interests and pressures from their staff.

The court does not impugn the good faith of the directors, who appear genuinely determined to reduce unnecessary reliance on drugs and to increase the involvement of patients in their own treatment decisions. Rather the court believes that institutional pressures—

similar to the pressures that have created the unfortunate legacy of overdrugging in state mental hospitals—make it impossible for anyone in the medical director's position to have sufficient independence, much less the appearance of fairness which due process requires. In different contexts the law has required that a decisionmaker be outside the state bureaucracy whose actions impinge on individuals' protected interests. See, e.g., Morrissey v. Brewer, 408 U.S. 471, 485-489 (1972) (parole revocation hearings). This is particularly important where informal procedures are allowed. As stated by Judge Friendly:

> [A] gencies might be offered an option of less procedural formality if the decisionmaker were not a member of the agency and still less if, as in England, he were not a full-time government employee at all.

Friendly, Some Kind of Hearing, 123 U. Pa. L. Rev. 1267, 1279 (1975).

While review by the medical director may be a prudent check inside the hospital structure, the court must hold that it does not meet the dictates of the law.

There is evidence that Dr. Rotov, the Division Director, or one of his assistants in the central office, are willing to review the medical directors' decisions to forcibly medicate. While this might provide an adequately independent decision, there is no indication in the record that Dr. Rotov or his current assistants would have the time or willingness to review the significant number of cases that may be appealed once patients are fully informed of their rights. It should also be noted that the medical directors' authorization in Bulletin 78-3 to consult an independent psychiatrist does not insure such an independent review in every case, nor are the consultant's recommendations binding on the medical record.

The court finds review by a psychiatrist, rather than a judge or administrative hearing officer, to be constitutionally adequate. Therefore, in structuring the order entered against defendants, the court will allow the independent decision-maker to be a psychiatrist, which is apparently the defendants' preference if relief must be granted on this point. Indeed, such a review would be similar to the central office review which has been proposed.

The defendants have no system for providing representation to patients who appeal the decisions of their staff psychiatrists. While the defendants have tentative plans to place a patient advocate at each hospital, there is no guarantee in the record that such a step will be taken or that representation will be assured for all who refuse.

Finally, the policies and procedures of defendants are inadequate because defendants have failed to even acknowledge and instruct their staff that involuntary patients have a qualified right to refuse.

III. Standards on a Preliminary Injunction

Four factors are considered in the application for a preliminary injunction: (1) whether the moving party has shown that it is likely to prevail on the merits, (2) whether the movant has demonstrated that he would be irreparably harmed if the preliminary injunction is denied, (3) whether the grant of the injunction would harm other interested parties to a greater extent than it would benefit movant, and (4) whether the public interest would be served. A.O. Smith Corp. v. FTC, 530 F.2d 515, 525 (3rd Cir. 1976).

After 17 days of hearings, the plaintiffs have clearly demonstrated a likelihood of prevailing on the merits on the recertified classes. It is also clear if defendants are not enjoined plaintiffs will be irreparably harmed by the transient discomfort and permanent injury caused by medication. The court finds that prevention of these harms outweighs the additional administrative costs the order may impose on the state. Finally, protection of plaintiff's constitutional rights is indisputably in the public interest.

IV. Explanation of the Decree

The court has attempted to closely tailor its order in this case to the clear violations of privacy and due process engendered by the policies of defendants. The order is designed to interfere with hospital operation as little as possible while still guaranteeing a realistic opportunity for patients to exercise their qualified right to refuse treatment. The court has also tried to include in its decree those ideas discussed by defendants themselves, but never fully implemented, which, when put into full effect, would satisfy constitutional requirements.

The order has five components. First is use of affirmative consent forms which must be signed by all patients before they are medicated. The court believes this is the least intrusive way to insure that involuntary and voluntary patients will have the opportunity to assert their constitutional rights despite the history of coercion and intimidation in the hospitals. The forms must contain the information on drugs and patient rights so that consents will be informed.

The second component is a system of Patient Advocates, which is essentially a full implementation of an idea which has been carried out by the Division in limited form only. The Advocates are given two areas of responsibility. First, they are to analyze cases where the treating physician certifies that a patient is incapable of providing informed consent. At that time an Advocate may act for the patient and obtain in-hospital and independent review, although medication is permitted during that time. The court notes that it would be unrealistic to rely on legal guardians to protect the rights of incompetent patients in this respect.

Advocates shall also serve as informal counsel to patients who wish to refuse, and, in particular, those whose cases are reviewed by an independent decision-maker.

The court believes that the Patient Advocates will play a crucial part in upholding patients' rights. It is anticipated that these individuals will be required to withstand great pressures from hospital doctors and staff. But the patients, as well as this court, will rely on their fortitude and perseverence. The Advocates are to be appointed by the Office of the Commissioner of the Department, Ms. Klein, in order to insure their independence from the hospital bureaucracy, and it is the responsibility of the Commissioner to keep the Advocates autonomous.

The court has considered requiring defendants to obtain legal representation for patients from the Division of Mental Health Advocacy or from private attorneys paid by the state on a retainer basis. This might better insure the independence of those counseling patients. However, this could only be required if the court simply prohibited all forced medication until the state legislature appropriated additional funds to the Department of the Public Advocate or for retained counsel. The court is naturally reluctant to do this when it hopes that Commissioner Klein and her successors will insure the necessary independence and qualifications of Advocates they appoint. The court believes attorneys are not necessary here, and may even be counterproductive since many compromises between patients' expressed desires and good medical practice will need to be made. The success of this aspect of the court's decree will be closely monitored during the time before a final order is entered.

The third component of the order is requirement of informal review by an independent psychiatrist before the hospital may forcibly medicate an involuntary patient. These psychiatrists will also be appointed by the Commissioner. The court believes a psychiatrist will be more effective in the role than a judge, lawyer or layperson, and that due process only requires an informal hearing which can readily be conducted by a medical person. In response to defendants' argument, the court notes that review of the medical director's decision to forcibly medicate by a panel of the Appellate Division of the Superior Court under N.J. Ct. R. 2:2-3(a)(2) does not meet due process. There is no evidence that such review has ever occurred, and almost certainly the scope of review would be restricted. See New Jersey Guild of Hearing Aid Dispensers v. Long, 75 N.J. 544, 384 A.2d 939 (1978); Parker v. Dornbierer, 140 N.J. Super. 185, 356 A.2d 1 (App. Div. 1976). Such review would also necessitate the appointment of independent counsel in every case.

The fourth part of the order is enforcement of voluntary patients' right to refuse treatment under state law, N.J. Stat. 30:4-24.2(d)(1).

The last component of the order is provision for forced medication in emergency situations, which, the court holds, not only qualifies the constitutional privacy right, but also the right of voluntary patients under state law. It also provides for the forced medication of patients involuntarily committed for short-term hospitalization under certain state statutes, but *only* in emergency situations. The court holds that the qualified privacy right is always outweighed in these emergency situations where the patient is in an acute psychotic state, has little competence but often is in great need of a psychotropic drug, and short-term use presents very little risk of permanent side effects.

The order only applies to psychotropic medication since it is the only type of drug for which there has been proof of harm to patients and overuse in the hospital.

The court has required that special reports on implementation of this decree and Department and Division orders on involuntary medication be submitted during the period before a final hearing is held and a final order is entered. However, the court relies on the Division of Mental Health Advocacy, plaintiffs' counsel, to scrutinize the implementation of the order in this case. The court will be open to further hearings if defendants fail to comply with the decree.

Finally, the court notes that while the provision of independent review here is intended to provide an efficient method for complying with due process, it does not preclude any member of the classes from bringing a civil rights action in federal court. However, appropriate deference would be given to a decision by an independent psychiatrist to allow a hospital to forcibly medicate an involuntary patient.

Preliminary Injunction

Application by the involuntary adult subclass and voluntary adult subclass of plaintiffs and intervenors for a preliminary injunction having been heard by the court; and

The court having considered the testimony, exhibits, briefs and argument of counsel; and

For the reasons stated in the court's opinion filed this day,

It is on this 14th day of September, 1979, hereby ORDERED of defendants Klein and Rotov:

A. Beginning January 7, 1980, defendants shall establish for the adult units of the Ancora Psychiatric Hospital, Greystone Park Psychiatric Hospital, Marlboro Psychiatric Hospital, Trenton Psychiatric Hospital, and Glen Gardner Geriatric Center:

1. *Consent forms.* A system of consent forms to be signed by patients before they are prescribed psychotropic drugs by hospital physicians in non-emergent situations. Such consent forms shall state in plain language the right of voluntary patients to refuse treatment and the qualified right of involuntary patients to refuse and to have their refusals reviewed within the hospital, and by the independent psychiatrist as described in this order. The forms shall also state the availability of Patient Advocates to assist patients who wish to refuse treatment. Each form shall also state all known short-term and long-term side effects of the drug to be consented to, and may be supplemented by informal discussion by hospital staff with the patient concerning the risks and benefits of the drugs. A single form may be used to obtain the consent for up to three different medications, to be used concurrently or alternatively. Information on the rights of patients and the side effects of all psychotropic drugs used in a hospital shall be posted or made available on each ward.

2. *Patient Advocate.* The Office of the Commissioner of the Department of Human Services shall hire, pay, train and supervise an adequate number of Patient Advocates in each hospital. The Patient Advocates' duties shall include those described in this order. The Patient Advocates must be supervised by an attorney and psychiatrist in the Office of the Commissioner. The Advocates may be trained attorneys, psychologists, social workers, registered nurses or paralegals, or have any equivalent experience. They must be given training in the effects of psychotropic medication and the principles of legal advocacy.

3. *Independent Psychiatrist.* The Office of the Commissioner shall hire and pay psychiatrists to review the decisions to forcibly medicate involuntary patients.

B. Beginning January 7, 1980, no voluntary or involuntary patient age 18 years or older in the five hospitals may be given any drug commonly labelled "psychotropic" by the medical profession unless the patient has signed a consent form pertaining to the specific drug. The written consent shall apply indefinitely subject to the other conditions of this order. No voluntary or involuntary patient may be given psychotropic medication if he states to a doctor or nurse that he does not want the specific drug. An injection of psychotropic medication may not be based on a prior written consent if the patient orally refuses at the time of the injection. Patient Advocates may consult with any patient and assist him in refusing medication orally. An Advocate can also require that the hospital obtain renewed written consent if a patient who has previously given written consent has since orally refused. The medical director, any treating physician or other member of the hospital staff may encourage a patient to consent to and take medication; however, force or the threat of force may not be used unless forced medication is allowed for a patient under the terms of this order.

C. Medication may be given orally or by injection without written consent and despite oral refusals in the following circumstances:

1. *Emergency Situation.* Where the treating psychiatrist certifies in a voluntary or involuntary patient's record that there is an emergency situation. An emergency is a sudden, significant change in the patient's condition which creates danger to the patient himself or to others in the hospital. Medication may then be forcibly administered for 72 hours. Certification by the medical director of the hospital may extend that period for 72 more hours if the threat to life or limb continues. Any person who is temporarily committed to a mental hospital or other institution pursuant to the procedures provided by the temporary commitment provisions of the New Jersey statutes[1] may be involuntarily medicated *only* if his condition constitutes an emergency situation as defined above, and any person who is involuntarily held in a mental hospital or institution but who has not been permanently or temporarily committed in accordance with the procedures mandated by the appli-

1. N.J. Stat. Ann. 30:4-46.1 (seven-day temporary commitment for observation); N.J. Stat. Ann. 30:4-26.3 (15-day temporary commitment for observation, examination, and treatment); and N.J. Stat. Ann. 30:4-37 and 4-38 (twenty-day temporary commitment).

cable New Jersey statutes may not be medicated against his will under *any* circumstances.

2. *Legally incompetent patient.* An involuntary patient declared legally incompetent may be medicated without written consent if proper consent is obtained in accordance with state law. However, decisions to medicate legally incompetent patients must also be referred to a Patient Advocate who may at any time assess the patient's feelings about the drug, side effects, failure to consistently take the medication and the use of force or threat of force by hospital staff to administer the drug. The Patient Advocate may then, in his discretion, initiate review under Administrative Bulletin 78-3, or similar hospital procedures succeeding that Bulletin, and may, in his discretion, seek review to the Independent Psychiatrist. The patient's guardian must be notified. Medication shall be permitted during the time period for review, which shall not exceed 15 days. A Patient Advocate shall review the treatment regime of each incompetent patient at least once every three months.

3. *Functionally incompetent.* A treating physician may certify in an involuntary patient's record that the patient is "functionally incompetent" because he is unable to provide knowledgeable consent to treatment, although he has not been declared incompetent by a court of law. These cases must also be referred to the Patient Advocate who shall review the case and initiate review in the manner described above for legally incompetent patients.

D. Except as provided in Paragraph C(1) of this order, no voluntary patient may be medicated who does not sign a consent form or who orally refuses.

E. Except as provided in Paragraphs C(1) through (4) of this order, where an involuntary patient refuses to provide consent after all in-hospital procedures are exhausted, or where an involuntary patient refuses intermittently and the hospital seeks to give medication on a continuous basis, the hospital may seek permission to involuntarily medicate by bringing the patient before the Independent Psychiatrist, in accordance with the following guidelines (the same guidelines shall apply to hearings brought by a Patient Advocate under Paragraphs C(3) and (4) of this order):

1. *Notice.* The patient must have at least five days between the first refusal to a staff nurse or physician and presentation to the Independent Psychiatrist.

2. *Advocate.* The patient shall be allowed to have an attorney and Independent Psychiatrist present at this hearing. However, the state need only supply a Patient Advocate if the patient cannot or

does not wish to have his own private counsel. The Patient Advocates at each hospital shall be notified of all refusals reaching the Medical Director under Bulletin 78-3 so that an Advocate can prepare any cases appealed to the Independent Psychiatrist.

3. *Hearing.* The Independent Psychiatrist may hold an informal proceeding. All hospital records should be made available to the Independent Psychiatrist, and he may conduct a medical examination of the patient where necessary. No compulsory access to witnesses or cross-examination need be permitted, although the Independent Psychiatrist may request hospital employees to appear if he deems this necessary.

4. *Opinion.* The Independent Psychiatrist shall issue a written determination in each case, basing any decision to override the patient's privacy right on the four factors outlined in the court's November opinion. He may also consider whether the use of the drugs in a particular case violates the principles of the first and eighth amendments as discussed in the November opinion. 462 F. Supp. at 1143-1144. He may "settle" the dispute by obtaining consent to treatment from the patient, or he may remand the case to the hospital medical director or treating physician for reformulation of a treatment plan in accordance with specific directives. He may prohibit use of psychotropic drugs altogether if required by the patient's preferences and his qualified right.

5. *Effective Period.* The Independent Psychiatrist may state a time period for which his decision allowing the hospital to forcibly medicate remains effective. This period should not exceed 60 days, and should preclude a patient from seeking review by the Independent Psychiatrist during that time. However, review may be had if the patient contends the hospital has failed to adhere to the Independent Psychiatrist's decision concerning proper treatment. The hospital may seek a rehearing in any case at any time.

F. In order to assist the court's consideration of the relief at the final hearing on the issues presented, defendants are ordered to submit monthly reports describing in reasonable detail their implementation of Administrative Order 2:13, Administrative Bulletins 78-3 and 78-6, and any other subsequent mandates on administration of psychotropic drugs, as well as their implementation of this order. The first report, covering the month of September 1979, shall be submitted on or before October 15, 1979, and each report shall be due by the 15th of the month thereafter during the period before a final order is entered.

G. Where this order specifically refers to voluntary patients, the order grants relief for that subclass, and where it specifically refers to involuntary patients it grants relief for that subclass. Where neither category is referenced, then relief is granted for both subclasses.

NOTE: READINGS ON THE RIGHT TO REFUSE MEDICATIONS

A leading discussion is Gaughan and LaRue, The Right of a Mental Patient to Refuse Antipsychotic Drugs in an Institution, 4 L. & Psychol. Rev. 43 (1978). See also Plotkin, Limiting the Therapeutic Orgy, 72 Nw. U.L. Rev. 461, 474-479 (1978), and Plotkin and Gill, Invisible Manacles: Drugging Mentally Retarded People, 31 Stan. L. Rev. 637 (1979).

A scholarly analysis of the relationships between drugs and the parens patriae approach to civil commitment is presented in Du Bose, Parens Patriae Commitment Power and Drug Treatment of Schizophrenia: Do the Benefits to the Patient Justify Involuntary Treatment?, 60 Minn. L. Rev. 1149 (1976). An extremely useful collection of materials on the side-effects of drugs and on patient reaction is Document AOR No. 31 Assembly Office of Research, California State Assembly, The Use and Misuse of Psychiatric Drugs in California's Mental Health Programs. Generally, see Note, Mental Health: A Model Statute to Regulate the Administration of Therapy Within Mental Health Facilities, 61 Minn. L. Rev. 841 (1977); Comment, Forced Drug Medication of Involuntarily Committed Mental Patients, 20 St. L. U.L.J. 100 (1975); Note, The Right to Refuse Drug Therapy Under "Emergency Restraint Statutes," 11 N.E.L. Rev. 509 (1976); Beresford, Judicial Review of Medical Treatment Programs, 12 Cal. Western L. Rev. 331 (1976); Wade, The Right to Refuse Treatment: Mental Patients and the Law, 1976 Detroit Coll. L. Rev. 53; and Perlin, The Right to Refuse Treatment in New Jersey, 6 Psychiat. Annals 300 (1976); and Michels and Himmelstein, The Right to Refuse Psychoactive Drugs, Hastings Ctr. Report 3, June, 1973, 8-11.

A debate between a psychiatrist and a lawyer is contained in German, Involuntary Treatment—Its Legal Limitations, 3 Bull. Amer. Acad. Psychiat. & L. 66 (1975) and Rachlin, One Right Too Many, 3 Bull. Amer. Acad. Psychiat. & L. 99 (1975).

A useful article dealing with the competence of the nonconsenting patient is Roth, Meisel and Lidz, Tests of Competency to Consent to Treatment, 134 Am. J. Psychiat. 279 (1977). See also Meisel, Roth and Lidz, Toward a Model of the Legal Doctrine of Informed Consent, 134 Am. J. Psychiat. 285 (1977). A useful set of guidelines is Am. Assoc. Mental Deficiency, Consent Handbook (1977).

Psychiatric analysis of how psychotropic drugs function include: Eisenberg, Psychiatric Intervention, 299 Sci. Amer. 116 (1973) and Klerman, Psychotropic Drugs as Therapeutic Agents, 2 Hastings Center Studies 81 (January, 1974).

Another significant right-to-refuse medication case is Rogers v. Okin, — F. Supp. — (D. Mass., Oct. 29, 1979) (Tauro, J.), also articulating a qualified constitutional right to refuse medications.

Pages 901-902. After Note, Shock Treatment, add:

NOTE: FURTHER NOTES ON ELECTROSHOCK THERAPY (ECT)

The literature of electroshock therapy has grown rapidly in the last several years. The most comprehensive recent study is American Psychiatric Association, Task Force Report 14, Electroconvulsive Therapy (September, 1978).

Concern about ECT has been encouraged by a number of popularistic articles which have condemned ECT as achieving results at the expense of significant cognitive and memory impairment. See, e.g., Roueché, As Empty as Eve, New Yorker, September 1974, a frequently cited piece which represents in dramatic form the case of an anonymous economist whose capacity to function was allegedly damaged after administration of ECT. The New Yorker article was responded to in Kalinowsky, "The New Yorker" on ECT: A Response, New York State District Branch Bulletin, April-May, 1975, pages 4-5.

Another influential popularistic article is Friedberg, Electroshock Therapy: Let's Stop Blasting the Brain, Psychology Today, August 1975, responded to by Avery, The Case for "Shock" Therapy, Psychology Today, August 1977.

The Friedberg article spurred the editors of the American Journal of Psychiatry to publish a symposium on the subject, entitled "Electroconvulsive Therapy—Current Perspectives," 134 Am. J. Psychiat. 991-1019. The symposium led off with a more scholarly version of Friedberg's Psychology Today article: Friedberg, Shock Treatment, Brain Damage and Memory Loss: A Neurological Perspective, 134 Am. J. Psychiat. 1010 (1977). The responding articles in the section were: Fink, Myths of Shock Therapy, 134 Am. J. Psychiat. 991 (1977); Squire, ECT and Memory Loss, 134 Am. J. Psychiat. 997 (1977); Greenblatt, Efficacy of ECT in Affective and Schizophrenic Illness, 134 Am. J. Psychiat. 1001 (1977); and Salzman, ECT and Ethical Psychiatry, 134 A. J. Psychiat. 1006 (1977).

Additional psychiatric discussions include Grossner, Pearsall, Fisher and Geremonte, The Regulation of Electroconvulsive Treatment in Massachusetts: A Follow-up, 5 Mass. J. of Mental Health 12 (Spring, 1975) and Weitzel, Changing Law and Clinical Dilemmas, 134 Am. J. Psychiat. 293 (1977). Beresford, Legal Issues Relating to Electroconvulsive Therapy, 25 Arch. Gen. Psychiat. 100 (1971) is now substantially out-of-date.

Worth reading for technical details are R. Peck, The Miracle of Shock Treatment (1974) and Kalinowsky, The Convulsive Therapies, in Freedman and Kaplan, eds., Comprehensive Textbook of Psychiatry 1279-1285 (1967).

Legal discussions include: Note, Regulation of Electroconvulsive Therapy, 75 Mich. L. Rev. 363 (1976) and Note, Informed Consent and the Mental Patient: California Recognizes a Mental Patient's Right to Refuse Psychosurgery and Shock Treatment, 15 Santa Clara Lawyer 725 (1975). See also Note, Mental Health: A Model Statute to Regulate the Administration of Therapy Within Mental Health Facilities, 61 Minn. L. Rev. 841 (1977). The entire concept of institutional review boards is analyzed in Robertson, The Law of Institutional Review Boards, 26 U.C.L.A.L. Rev. 484 (1979).

A leading case dealing with procedures for the use of electroshock therapy is Price v. Sheppard, 239 N.W.2d 905 (Minn. 1976).

Page 924. After Note, add:

NOTE: FURTHER NOTES ON PSYCHOSURGERY

The literature on psychosurgery continues to expand exponentially. One of the most valuable new documents is the Report and Recommendations Concerning Psychosurgery, National Commn. for the Protection of Human Subjects of Biomedical and Behavioral Research, December, 1976.

A number of significant new books have also appeared. Of particular importance are S. Shuman, Psychosurgery and the Medical Control of Violence (1977); W. Gaylin, J. Meister, and S. Nevill, Operating on the Mind: The Psychosurgery Conflict (1976); E. Hitchcock, L. Laitinen and K. Vaernet, eds., Psychosurgery (1972);

and S. Chavkin, The Mind Stealers: Psychosurgery and Mind Control (1978).

Among the leading law review discussions are the following: Peters and Lee, Psychosurgery: A Case for Regulation, 1978 Det. Coll. L. Rev. 383; Spoonhour, Psychosurgery and Informed Consent, 26 U. Fla. L. Rev. 432 (1974); Mearns, Law and the Physical Control of the Mind: Experimentation in Psychosurgery, 25 Case W. Res. L. Rev. 565 (1975); Gobert, Psychosurgery, Conditioning and the Prisoner's Right to Refuse "Rehabilitation," 61 Va. L. Rev. 155 (1975); Heidepriem and Resnick, Disclosure, Consent and Capacity, 1973/1974 Ann. Survey Amer. L. 87, 99-109; Shuman, The Emotional, Medical and Legal Reasons for the Special Concern About Psychosurgery, in F. Ayd, ed., Medical, Moral and Legal Issues in Mental Health Care (1974); and Hodson, Reflections Concerning Violence and the Brain, 9 Crim. L. Bull. 684 (1973). Dr. Alan Stone has written an interesting account of the Massachusetts experience in Stone, Psychosurgery in Massachusetts: A Task Force Report, 5 Mass. J. of Mental Health 26 (Spring, 1975) (including minority report, correspondence and proposed regulations). The California experience is discussed in Aden v. Younger, 129 Cal. Rptr. 535 (1976). The California statute was subsequently modified. See Cal. Welf. & Inst. Code §§5325, 5326.2-.95 (West Supp. 1977). For an excellent discussion of regulatory efforts, see Note, Mental Health: A Model Statute to Regulate the Administration of Therapy Within Mental Health Facilities, 61 Minn. L. Rev. 841 (1977).

For a polemical treatment of psychosurgery issues, see Breggin, Psychosurgery for Political Purposes, 13 Duq. L. Rev. 841 (1975). But see Koskoff, The *Kaimowitz* Case: A Short Term Legal Restraint Contrary to the Long Term Public Good, 13 Duq. L. Rev. 879 (1975); and Vaux, Look What They've Done to My Brain, Ma!: Ethical Issues in Brain and Behavior Control, 13 Duq. L. Rev. 907 (1975). The psychosurgery process is defended by Andy, The Decision-Maker Process in Psychosurgery, 13 Duq. L. Rev. 783 (1975).

Student notes include: Comment, Kaimowitz v. Dept. of Mental Health: Involuntary Mental Patient Cannot Give Informed Consent to Experimental Psychosurgery, 4 N.Y.U. Rev. of L. & Social Change 207 (1974); Comment, Prisoner Access to Psychosurgery: A Constitutional Perspective, 9 Pac. L.J. 249 (1978); and Note, Beyond the "Cuckoo's Nest": A Proposal for Federal Regulation of Psychosurgery, 12 Harv. J. Legis. 610 (1975).

A malpractice action brought against Doctors Mark and Ervin in connection with a psychosurgical operation performed by them in

1967 and described in their book, Violence and The Brain, resulted in a finding by a jury that they were not negligent. See "2 Cleared in Psychosurgery Case," New York Times, February 10, 1979, p. 12, col. 4.

The defendants had diagnosed the patient as having a form of epilepsy and had implanted electrodes in his brain to treat the illness. The patient was subsequently diagnosed as paranoid schizophrenic and described by his mother as "almost a vegetable." He has been confined in mental hospitals for most of the twelve years since the operation was performed.

The plaintiff claimed that the defendants had negligently misdiagnosed the patient, had not exhausted alternative drug therapies before turning to psychosurgery, and had not explained the risks of the procedure to the patient.

4. Behavior Modification

The use of behavior modification techniques has been analyzed in an excellent Symposium, 17 Ariz. L. Rev. 1-143 (1975). Among the lead articles are the following: Friedman, Legal Regulation of Applied Behavior Analysis in Mental Institutions and Prisons, 17 Ariz. L. Rev. 39 (1975); Goldiamond, Singling Out Behavior Modification for Legal Regulation: Some Effects on Patient Care, Psychotherapy, and Research in General, 17 Ariz. L. Rev. 105 (1975); and Wexler, Reflections on the Legal Regulation of Behavior Modification in Institutional Settings, 17 Ariz. L. Rev. 132 (1975).

An outstanding treatment of the use of behavior modification programs in hospitals and prisons is Singer, Consent of the Unfree: Medical Experimentation and Behavior Modification in the Closed Institution, 1 L. & Human Behav. 1 and 101 (parts I and II) (1977).

See also Symposium, Behavior Modification in Prisons, 13 Am. Crim. L. Rev. 1-113 (1975) (five articles and extensive bibliography). The specific articles are: Rangel, Introduction: Behavior Modification, 13 Am. Crim. L. Rev. 3 (1975); Gaylin and Blatte, Behavior Modification in Prisons, 13 Am. Crim. L. Rev. 11 (1975); Goldberger, Court Challenges to Prison Behavior Modification Programs: A Case Study, 13 Am. Crim. L. Rev. 37 (1975); Wolfe and Marino, A Program of Behavior Treatment for Incarcerated Pedophiles, 13 Am. Crim. L. Rev. 69 (1975); Serber, Hiller, Keith and Taylor, Behavior Modification in Maximum Security Settings: One Hospital's Experience, 13 Am. Crim. L. Rev. 85 (1975).

See also Symposium, Behavior Modification, 1 N.E.J. Prison L. 155-278 (1974). Of value are Whitman, Behavior Modification: Introduction and Implications, 24 De Paul L. Rev. 949 (1975); Note,

The Right Against Treatment: Behavior Modification and the Involuntarily Committed, 23 Cath. U.L. Rev. 774 (1974); Note, In Defense of Behavior Modification for Prisoners: Eighth Amendment Considerations, 18 Ariz. L. Rev. 110 (1976); and Note, Behavior Modification: Winners in the Game of Life? 24 Clev. St. L. Rev. 422 (1975).

Further discussions are: R. Schwitzgebel, Development and Legal Regulation of Coercive Behavior Modification Techniques with Offenders (1971); B. Brown, L. Wienckowski and S. Stolz, Behavior Modification: Perspective on a Current Issue (1975); R. Martin, Legal Challenges to Behavior Modification: Trends in Schools, Corrections & Mental Health (1975); and Goldiamond, Toward a Constructional Approach to Social Problems: Ethical and Constitutional Issues Raised by Applied Behavior Analysis, 2 Behaviorism 1 (1974).

A defense of behavior modification techniques in prison settings is presented in Note, In Defense of Behavior Modification for Prisoners: Eighth Amendment Considerations, 18 Ariz. L. Rev. 110 (1976).

Criminal charges were brought against a psychologist in charge of a behavior modification program at the Mendota Mental Health Institute in Madison, Wisconsin, arising from the suicide of an adolescent girl in a program that featured punishment for engaging in unacceptable behavior. In State v. Leff (Wis. Dane County Ct., filed October 25, 1977), the psychologist was charged with the crime of abusing an institutional inmate, a violation of Wis. Stats. §940.29 and 939.05.

The patient, who had earlier attempted suicide at another institution, was in a program called Training Adolescents for Community Living (TACL). Because of her misbehavior, the patient was confined to her room, and later denied visits and telephone contact with her mother. The staff theory was that the patient valued little else. The staff was "looking for something which still might hurt her to modify her behavior." This did not work. Because of subsequent additional misbehavior, the patient was later restricted to her room for two days. Her work privilege was cancelled for a week. She hanged herself and died after having been in a coma for five months. The psychologist-defendant was alleged to have said, "Maybe we went too far."

The indictment was dismissed by a county court judge on July 28, 1978.

5. Aversion Therapy

See Knecht v. Gillman, 488 F.2d 1136 (8th Cir. 1973) (apomorphine), discussed in Note, 13 Duquesne L. Rev. 621 (1975) and Nelson v. Heyne, 355 F. Supp. 451 (N.D. Inc. 1972) (tranquilizing drugs used for purpose of control in boys' school). Aversive therapy problems are discussed in Note, Aversion Therapy: Its Limited Potential for Use in the Correctional Setting, 26 Stanford L. Rev. 1327 (1974); Moya and Achtenberg, Behavior Modification: Legal Limitations on Methods and Goals, 50 Notre Dame Lawyer 230 (1974); and Note, Aversion Therapy: Punishment as Treatment and Treatment as Cruel and Unusual Punishment, 49 S. Cal. L. Rev. 880 (1976).

6. Non-psychiatric Treatment

IN RE YETTER

62 D. & C. 2d 619 (C.P. Northampton County, Pa., 1973)

WILLIAMS, J.

This matter involves the appointment of a guardian of the person for Maida Yetter, an alleged incompetent, under the Incompetent Estates Act of 1955, 50 P.S. §3101 et seq. The petition was filed by Russell C. Stauffer, her brother, and a citation issued on May 10, 1973. The citation was served on the alleged incompetent by a deputy sheriff on Lehigh County at Allentown State Hospital, Lehigh County, Pennsylvania, on May 15, 1973. A hearing was held on May 30, 1973, as specified in the petition. Present at the hearing were the petitioner and his counsel; Dr. Ellen Bischoff, a psychiatrist on the staff of the hospital; Mrs. Marilou Perhac, a caseworker at the hospital assigned to Mrs. Yetter's ward; the alleged incompetent and her counsel. Mrs. Yetter is married, although she has been separated from and has had no contact with her husband since 1947.

From the petition and the testimony it appears that the primary purpose of the appointment of a guardian of the person is to give consent to the performance of diagnostic and corrective surgery.

Mrs. Yetter was committed to Allentown State Hospital in June, 1971, by the Courts of Northampton County after hearings held pursuant to Section 406 of the Mental Health and Mental Retardation Act of 1966. Her diagnosis at that time was schizophrenia, chronic undifferentiated. It appears that late in 1972, in connection with a routine physical examination, Mrs. Yetter was discovered to have a breast discharge indicating the possible presence of carcinoma. The doctors recommended that a surgical biopsy be performed together with any additional corrective surgery that would be indicated by the pathology of the biopsy. When this recommendation was first discussed with Mrs. Yetter in December of 1972 by her caseworker, Mrs. Perhac, who had had weekly counseling sessions with Mrs. Yetter for more than a year, Mrs. Yetter indicated that she would not give her consent to the surgery. Her stated reasons were that she was afraid because of the death of her aunt which followed such surgery and that it was her own body and she did not desire the operation. The caseworker indicated that at this time Mrs. Yetter was lucid, rational and appeared to understand that the possible consequences of her refusal included death.

Mr. Stauffer, who indicated that he visits his sister regularly, and Dr. Bischoff, whose direct contacts with Mrs. Yetter have been since March 1973, testified that in the last three or four months it has been impossible to discuss the proposed surgery with Mrs. Yetter in that, in addition to expressing fear of the operation, she has become delusional in her reasons for not consenting to surgery. Her tendency to become delusional concerning this problem, although no others, was confirmed by Mrs. Perhac. The present delusional nature of Mrs. Yetter's reasoning concerning the problem was demonstrated at the hearing when Mrs. Yetter, in response to questions by the Court and counsel, indicated that the operation would interfere with her genital system, affecting her ability to have babies, and would prohibit a movie career. Mrs. Yetter is 60 years of age and without children.

Dr. Bischoff testified that Mrs. Yetter is oriented as to time, place and her personal environment, and that her present delusions are consistent with the diagnosis and evaluation of her mental illness upon admission to the hospital in 1971. The doctor indicated that, in her opinion, at the present time Mrs. Yetter is unable, by reason of her mental illness, to arrive at a considered judgment as to whether to undergo surgery.

Mr. Stauffer testified that the aunt referred to by Mrs. Yetter, although she underwent a similar operation, died of unrelated causes some 15 years after surgery. He further indicated that he has been apprised by the physicians of the nature of the proposed procedures and their probable consequences as well as the probable consequences if the procedures are not performed. He indicated that if he is appointed guardian of the person for his sister, he would consent to the surgical procedures recommended.

At the hearing Mrs. Yetter was alert, interested, and obviously meticulous about her personal appearance. She stated that she was afraid of surgery, that the best course of action for her would be to leave her body alone, that surgery might hasten the spread of the disease and do further harm, and she reiterated her fears due to the death of her aunt. On several occasions during the hearing she interjected the statements that she would die if surgery were performed.

It is clear that mere commitment to a state hospital for treatment of mental illness does not destroy a person's competency or require the appointment of a guardian of the estate or person. *In re Ryman,* 139 Pa. Super. 212. Mental capacity must be examined on a case by case basis.

In our opinion the constitutional right of privacy includes the right of a mature competent adult to refuse to accept medical recommendations that may prolong one's life and which, to a third person at least, appear to be in his best interests; in short, that the right of privacy includes a right to die with which the State should not interfere where there are no minor or unborn children and no clear and present danger to public health, welfare or morals. If the person was competent while being presented with the decision and in making the decision which she did, the Court should not interfere even though her decision might be considered unwise, foolish or ridiculous.

While many philosophical articles have been published relating to this subject, there are few appellate court decisions and none in Pennsylvania to our knowledge. The cases are collected in an annotation in 9 A.L. R. 3d 1391. Considering other factors which have influenced the various courts, the present case does not involve a patient who sought medical attention from a hospital and then attempted to restrict the institution and physicians from rendering proper medical care. The state hospital as Mrs. Yetter's custodian certainly has acted properly in initiating the present proceeding through the patient's brother and cannot be said to have either overridden patient's wishes or merely allowed her to die for lack of treatment.

The testimony of the caseworker with respect to her conversations with Mrs. Yetter in December, 1972, convinces us that at that time her refusal was informed, conscious of the consequences and would not have been superseded by this Court. The ordinary person's refusal to accept medical advice based upon fear is commonly known and while the refusal may be irrational and foolish to an outside observer it cannot be said to be incompetent in order to permit the State to override the decision.

The obvious difficulty in this proceeding is that in recent months Mrs. Yetter's steadfast refusal has been accompanied by delusions which create doubt that her decision is the product of competent, reasoned judgment. However, she has been consistent in expressing the fear that she would die if surgery were performed. The delusions do not appear to us to be her primary reason for rejecting surgery.

Are we then to force her to submit to medical treatment because some of her present reasons for refusal are delusional and the result of mental illness? Should we now overrule her original understanding but irrational decision?

There is no indication that Mrs. Yetter's condition is critical or that she is in the waning hours of life, although we recognize the advice of medical experts as to the need for early detection and treatment of cancer symptoms. Upon reflection, balancing the risk involved in our refusal to act in favor of compulsory treatment against giving the greatest possible protection to the individual in furtherance of his own desires, we are unwilling now to overrule Mrs. Yetter's original irrational but competent decision.

Since no additional reasons for the appointment of a guardian of the person are presented, we enter the following Order of Court.

AND NOW, this 6th day of June, 1973, the petition for the appointment of a guardian of the person for Maida Yetter, an alleged incompetent, is refused.

NOTE: NON-PSYCHIATRIC TREATMENT

In Superintendent of Belchertown State School v. Saikewicz, 370 N.E. 2d 417 (Mass. 1977) the Massachusetts Supreme Judicial Court affirmed the decision of a probate judge to withhold chemotherapy from a 67-year-old profoundly incompetent retarded patient suffering from leukemia. A guardian ad litem had reported that Saikewicz's illness was incurable, but that the treatment was frightening and painful. The disvalue of the treatment outweighed the value of prolonging the patient's life. Physicians also counselled against the treatment, urging that the dying are often in greater need of comfort than of treatment which may result only in trivial prolongation of life at the cost of great suffering.

The court presented an elaborate analysis of the problem of substituted consent, based on a recognized right to decline medical treatment as a function of the right of privacy. See In the Matter of Karen Quinlan, 70 N.J. 10, 355 A.2d 647 (1976).

The Saikewicz case is discussed in Kindregan, The Court as Forum For Life and Death Decisions: Reflections on Procedures for Substituted Consent, 11 Suffolk U.L. Rev. 919 (1978); Schultz, Swartz and Appelbaum, Deciding Right to Die Cases Involving Incompetent Patients: Jones v. Saikewicz, 11 Suffolk U.L. Rev. 936 (1978); and Annas, The Incompetent's Right to Die: The Case of Joseph

Saikewicz, 8 Hastings Center Report 21 (February, 1978). See also McCormick and Hellegers, The Specter of Joseph Saikewicz: Mental Incompetence and the Law, America 257 (April 1, 1978).

In Matter of Quackenbush, 156 N.J. Super. 282, 383 A.2d 785 (Morris Cty. Ct., Prob. Div. 1978), involving the refusal of a 72-year-old patient to have both his gangrenous legs amputated, the court, acknowledging that the patient would die within three weeks if he were not operated on, nevertheless ruled that, because the patient was competent, the operation should not take place. Said the court, ". . . the extensive bodily invasion involved here . . . is sufficient to make the state's interest in the preservation of life give way to Robert Quackenbush's right of privacy to decide his own future. . . ." At 789.

Chapter Sixteen

Transfers, Finances and Release

A. TRANSFERS

Page 930. To Note, add:

The transfer of an involuntary civilly committed patient from a minimum security institution to a maximum security institution usually housing criminal offenders is ruled upon in Eubanks v. Clarke, 434 F. Supp. 1022 (E.D. Pa. 1977), noted 51 Temp. L.Q. 357 (1978) (requiring a due process hearing).

Page 943. After Note, add:

The applicability of Souder v. Brennan has been eroded by the decision of the United States Supreme Court in National League of Cities v. Usery, 426 U.S. 833 (1976), ruling that the minimum wage and overtime provision of the 1974 amendments to the Fair Labor Standards Act cannot be applied to state and local governments.

The practice of providing pay to working mental patients has been attacked in Lebar, Worker-Patients: Receiving Therapy or Suffering Peonage?, 62 A.B.A.J. 219 (1976) and defended in a response, Letter, "Worker-Patient Rights," Michael Lottman, 62 A.B.A.J. 406 (1976).

A novel theory of entitlement to compensated work as therapy is presented in Perlin, The Right to Voluntary Compensated Therapeutic Work as a Part of the Right to Treatment: A New Theory in the Aftermath of Souder, 7 Seton Hall L. Rev. 298 (1976), and implemented in a pending litigation, Schindenwolf v. Klein, Docket No. L41293-75 P.W. (N.J. Super. Ct., filed Nov. 17, 1976).

Notwithstanding the possible adverse effect of the *Usery* case, there are several pending litigations on both the work stoppage and minimum wage issues. See, e.g., McKee v. Moritz, Case No. C78-40A (N.D. Ohio, filed Feb. 1, 1978) and Taylor v. Atascadero State Hospital, No. 48791 (Cal. Super. Ct., San Luis Obispo County, filed July 29, 1977). These cases (and the *Schindenwolf* case) are elaborately described in 2 M.D.L.R. 382 (1978).

Page 947. After 1., Statutory Provisions for Periodic Review, add:

2. Judicial Provisions for Periodic Judicial Review

FASULO v. ARAFEH

173 Conn. 473, 378 A.2d 553 (1977)

LONGO, Associate Justice.

The plaintiffs, Ann Fasulo and Marie Barbieri, alleging that they were illegally confined in the Connecticut Valley Hospital by the defendant superintendent, petitioned the Superior Court for writs of habeas corpus. The court denied the writs and the plaintiffs appealed.

Ann Fasulo was civilly committed to Connecticut Valley Hospital in 1951, as was Marie Barbieri in 1964. Both plaintiffs press two major claims in this appeal. First, they argue that since there is a requirement of periodic court review of the necessity for confinement of those individuals who have been acquitted of an offense on the grounds of mental disease or defect, but not for persons like themselves who are civilly committed, their continued confinement violates the equal protection guarantee of article first, §20, of the Connecticut constitution. They also claim that because their commitments are of indefinite duration and there is no procedure for periodic court review of the necessity for their confinement, their confinement is in violation of the due process guarantee of article first, §8, of the Connecticut constitution.

We consider the plaintiffs' due process claim. Though the plaintiffs do not challenge their initial involuntary commitments, the due process safeguards incorporated into that procedure help to illuminate the plaintiffs' grievances. Among the important requirements of General Statutes §17-178 are a judicial hearing initiated by the state at which the state bears the burden of proving that involuntary commitment is necessary, testimony by independent physicians who have recently examined the subject, and the rights to be represented by counsel, to present a defense and to cross-examine witnesses. Under General Statutes §17-178 the necessity for confinement is to be determined according to a legal standard as a conclusion of law. The due process clause of the Connecticut constitution shares but is not limited by the content of its federal counterpart. *Roundhouse Construction Corporation v. Telesco Masons Supplies Co.,* 168 Conn. 371, 374, 362 A.2d 778. In *O'Connor v. Donaldson,* 422 U.S. 563, 580, 95 S. Ct. 2486, 2496, 45 L. Ed. 2d 396, Mr. Chief Justice Burger in a concurring opinion spoke of the process due a person civilly committed to a mental institution: "There can be no doubt that involuntary commitment to a mental hospital, like involuntary confinement of an individual for any reason, is a deprivation of liberty which the State cannot accomplish without due process of law. *Specht v. Patterson,* 386 U.S. 605, 608, 87 S. Ct. 1209, 18 L. Ed. 2d 326 (1967). Cf. *In re Gault,* 387 U.S. 1, 12-13, 87 S. Ct. 1428, 18 L. Ed. 2d 527 (1967). Commitment must be justified on the basis of a legitimate state interest, and the reasons for committing a particular individual must be established in an appropriate proceeding. Equally important, confinement must cease when those reasons no longer exist. See *McNeil v. Director, Patuxent Institution,* 407 U.S. 245, 249-250, 92 S. Ct. 2083, 32 L. Ed. 2d 719 (1972); *Jackson v. Indiana,* 406 U.S. 715, 738, 92 S. Ct. 1845, 32 L. Ed. 2d 435 (1972)."

As recognized by General Statutes §17-178, the authority of the state to confine an individual is contingent upon the individual's present mental status, which must be one of mental illness amounting to a need for confinement for the individual's own welfare or the welfare of others or the community. See General Statutes §17-176. The original involuntary commitment proceeding can only establish that the state may confine the individual at the time of the hearing and for the period during which the individual is subject to the requisite mental illness. As the United States Supreme Court has recognized, "At the least, due process requires that the nature and duration of commitment bear some reasonable relation to the purpose for which an individual is committed." *Jackson v. Indiana,* 406 U.S. 715, 738, 92 S. Ct. 1845, 1858, 32 L. Ed. 2d 435. Once the purpose of the commitment no longer exists, there is no constitutional basis for the state to continue to deprive the individual of his liberty. See *O'Connor v. Donaldson,* supra, 422 U.S. 575, 95 S. Ct. 2486. To satisfy due process, the procedure for releasing a civilly committed patient must be adequate to assure release of those who may no longer constitutionally be confined. Due process is a flexible concept, the content of which must be renewed each time it is used to measure the adequacy of challenged procedures.

In general, "the thoroughness of the procedure by which [a] deprivation is effected must be balanced against the gravity of the potential loss and the interests at stake." *Hart Twin Volvo Corporation v. Commissioner of Motor Vehicles,* 165 Conn. 42, 45, 327 A.2d 588, 590. It is significant to this case that the process afforded an individual must be "tailored to the capacity and circumstances of those who are to be heard." *Goldberg v. Kelly,* 397 U.S. 254, 268-269, 90 S. Ct. 1011, 1021, 25 L. Ed. 2d 287.

These plaintiffs have been deprived of their liberty. Their loss is already great, but can be initially justified as a result of the legitimate exercise of the parens patriae power of the state. The plaintiffs, however, have been committed indefinitely and confined for periods of twenty-six and thirteen years respectively, thus requiring us to heed the warning of the United States Supreme Court that the longer the commitment, the greater the safeguards which are required to ensure that no one is deprived of liberty without due process. See *McNeil v. Director, Patuxent Institution,* 407 U.S. 245, 249-250, 92 S. Ct. 2083, 32 L. Ed. 2d 719. We must, therefore, review the plaintiffs' claims, in light of the important interest at stake—liberty—and the great loss which its extended deprivation constitutes.

Any procedure to allow the release of involuntarily confined civilly committed individuals must take account of the controlled and often isolated environment of the mental hospital from which the confined individuals will seek release. It must calculate the possible incompetence of those confined, their limited knowledge of release procedures, the cost of pursuing review and the amount of effort necessary to pursue review. Further, the procedure must be adapted to the possible effect of drugs or other treatment on the patient's capacity and must be formulated with consideration of institutional pressures to rely on the medical judgments of the hospital staff rather than to pursue extrainstitutional legal remedies. See note, "Civil Commitment of the Mentally Ill," 87 Harv. L. Rev. 1190, 1398.

At present, Connecticut provides several routes by which a mental patient can challenge his confinement. General Statutes §17-192 allows for release (1) by order of the Probate Court "upon application and satisfactory proof that such person has been restored to reason," or (2) "[i]f the officers, directors or trustees of a state hospital for mental illness are notified by the superintendent or other person in a managerial capacity of such institution that he has reason to believe that any person committed thereto by order of a probate court is not mentally ill or a suitable subject to be confined in such institution, such officers, directors or trustees may discharge such person." Under the second method the patient runs the risk of having his release prevented by a superintendent whose determination may later be found by a court to have been erroneous. See *O'Connor v. Donaldson,* supra; *McNeil v. Director, Patuxent Institution,* supra. Furthermore, the second procedure disregards the fundamental fact that the state's power legitimately to confine an individual is based on a legal determination under General Statutes §17-178 "that the person complained of is mentally ill and dangerous to himself or herself or others or gravely disabled" and that the commitment shall only continue "for the period of the duration of such mental illness or until he or she is discharged in due course of law." The state's power to confine terminates when the patient's condition no longer meets the legal standard for commitment. Since the state's power to confine is measured by a legal standard, the expiration of the state's power can only be determined in a judicial proceeding which tests the patient's present mental status against the legal standard for confinement. That adjudication cannot be made by medical personnel unguided by the procedural safeguards which cushion the individual from an overzealous exercise of state power when the individual is first threatened with the deprivation of his liberty. See General Statutes §17-178. In order to hold that judicial review of involuntary confinement is unnecessary, we would have to conclude either (1) that the procedural safeguards provided at the initial confinement hearing are not mandated by due process or (2) that subsequent deprivations of liberty are somehow constitutionally less serious and that the individual, therefore, can be confined with less process due. We reject both of these conclusions and hold that the due process clause of the Connecticut constitution mandates that involuntarily confined civilly committed individuals be granted periodic judicial reviews of the propriety of their continued confinement. We do not mean to suggest that a patient may not be released pursuant to the second procedure provided by General Statutes §17-192. Rather, we reject the argument that, standing alone, it is adequate to provide an involuntarily confined civilly committed individual with due process.

We also find the first method of release provided for in General Statutes §17-192 constitutionally deficient. The method allows release of a patient after he has applied to the Probate Court for discharge and has proved that he has been "restored to reason." We find this procedure inadequate on two grounds. First, it places the burden of initiating review of his status on the patient, a requirement which suffers from conceptual as well as serious practical deficiencies. As we stated previously, since the state's power to confine is premised on the individual's present mental status, the original involuntary commitment proceeding can only establish that the state may confine the individual at the time of the hearing and for the foreseeable period during which that status is unlikely to change.[1] Upon the expiration of that period, the state's power to deprive the patient of his liberty lapses and any further confinement must be justified anew. The state, therefore, must bear the burden of initiating recommitment proceedings.

This same reasoning applies to the burden of proof at the recommitment hearing. The burden should not be placed on the civilly committed patient to justify his right to liberty. Freedom from involuntary confinement for those who have committed no crime is the natural state of individuals in this country. The burden must be placed on the state to prove the necessity of stripping the citizen of one of his most fundamental rights, and the risk of error must rest on the state. Since the state has no greater right to confine a patient after the validity of the original commitment has expired than it does to commit him in the first place, the state must bear the burden of proving the necessity of recommitment, just as it bears the burden of proving the necessity for commitment.

Furthermore, to require a patient to initiate judicial review of his confinement and to bear the burden of proving the nonexistence of the necessity for that confinement ignores the practical considerations discussed above which are inherent in the mental patient's situation. Briefly, these include the difficulties of overcoming an isolated environment to initiate and coordinate a challenge to one's confinement. For instance, we cannot assume that friends and allies will always be available to secure counsel and marshal evidence on the patient's behalf. Nor can we assume that even if a patient is notified of his right to pursue any of the available remedies, he will be adequately protected. The state has suggested that the pro-

1. As the United States Supreme Court stated in *O'Connor v. Donaldson*, 422 U.S. 563, 574-575, 95 S. Ct. 2486, 2493, 45 L. Ed. 2d 396: "Nor is it enough that Donaldson's original confinement was founded upon a constitutionally adequate basis, if in fact it was, because even if his involuntary confinement was initially permissible, it could not constitutionally continue after that basis no longer existed." *Jackson v. Indiana*, 406 U.S. 715, 738, 92 S. Ct. 1845, 32 L. Ed. 2d 435; *McNeil v. Director, Patuxent Institution*, 407 U.S. 245, 249-250, 92 S. Ct. 2083, 32 L. Ed. 2d 719.

274

cedure provided in General Statutes §17-178, as amended by section 3(b) of 1976 Public Acts, No. 76-227, effective in March of 1977, met the constitutional arguments of the petitioners. That statute as amended is not now before us and we decline to rule prematurely on its provisions. We note, however, that many of the safeguards we have found necessary in this opinion are provided for in the new statute, particularly the right to a recommitment hearing with all the procedural safeguards of the initial commitment hearing at which the burden of proving the necessity for confinement rests on the state. Unfortunately, though the statute provides for annual notice to patients of their right to a hearing, the burden of requesting and, therefore, initiating review remains with the patient. The state seeks to justify this procedure by arguing that allowing the patient to choose whether to have a hearing will avoid unnecessary judicial proceedings. We doubt whether this rationale is adequate since it ignores the practical difficulties of requiring a mental patient to overcome the effects of his confinement, his closed environment, his possible incompetence and the debilitating effects of drugs or other treatment on his ability to make a decision which may amount to the waiver of his constitutional right to a review of his status. *Schneckloth v. Bustamonte,* 412 U.S. 218, 93 S. Ct. 2041, 36 L. Ed. 2d 854; *Johnson v. Zerbst,* 304 U.S. 458, 58 S. Ct. 1019, 82 L. Ed. 1461.

The second method for release is contained in General Statutes §17-178, which provides that a commiting court "may, after hearing, when it finds it to be for the best interest of the person so committed, revoke such order of commitment." This is a discretionary provision with uncertain legal standards for its administration which cannot guarantee the accuracy and fairness of the determination and which cannot substitute for periodic judicial review of commitments.

Under General Statutes §17-200, a patient may be discharged on the recommendation of a commission appointed by a Superior Court judge after receiving information that a patient is illegally confined. This type of discretionary review, while potentially of benefit to the patient, cannot take the place of regular periodic review at which the patient will enjoy procedural safeguards guaranteeing an adequate review of his condition.

Finally, a patient may challenge the legality of his confinement through a writ of habeas corpus, pursuant to General Statutes §17-201. This method of securing review falls short of the constitutional standard we have enunciated today since the burden of initiating review remains with the patient. We, therefore, conclude that the trial court erred in holding that the procedures presently available to these plaintiffs satisfy due process.

We, therefore, hold that these plaintiffs have been denied their due process rights under the Connecticut constitution by the state's failure to provide them with periodic judicial review of their commitments in the form of state-initialed recommitment hearings replete with the safeguards of the initial commitment hearings at which the state bears the burden of proving the necessity for their continued confinement.

BOGDANSKI, Associate Justice (concurring).

I agree that the present statutory scheme concerning the commitment and release of persons committed by civil process to an institution for the mentally ill is violative of the due process clause of our state constitution.

The questions presented in these proceedings are novel and unprecedented in this state. In the interests of justice they should be determined now as finally as it is possible. *Brownell v. Union & New Haven Trust Co.,* 143 Conn. 662, 672, 124 A.2d 901. I am compelled, therefore, to discuss the merits of the equal protection challenge as well and conclude that the present statutory scheme is violative of that constitutional clause also.

Few acts of the state impinge more directly and with greater finality on an individual's liberty than the act of the state in committing a person to involuntary confinement in a hospital for the mentally ill. Whether such commitment is made pursuant to civil or criminal proceedings, the ultimate effect is the same: the person loses not only his freedom, but also suffers the indignity of being treated while in confinement as something less than a normal reasoning human being.

The point sought to be stressed is twofold: first, that any involuntary commitment is a serious infringement on a person's right to liberty which should be tolerated only so long as is necessary, and second, that when any statutory scheme which significantly affects such a commitment is challenged as violative of either the due process or equal protection clauses it ought to be subjected to "strict judicial scrutiny."

The plaintiffs, civilly committed pursuant to §17-178 of the General Statutes, claim that they are deprived of equal protection of the law because of the denial to them of legal rights which are afforded to persons committed under §53a-47 after having been found not guilty of a crime by reason of insanity. They assert that while the state has provided for a comprehensive follow-up procedure, including state-initiated automatic judicial reviews, with respect to the confinement and release of persons committed pursuant to §53a-47, it has failed to provide for any similar procedure for the release of persons, such as themselves, committed pursuant to §17-178.[1] They contend that, once the state has initiated action as parens patriae to commit involuntarily persons "for the period of the duration of such mental illness," it is incumbent on the state to provide for periodic judicial review on the factual and legal question as to whether that mental illness continues; that, in essence, the state has provided for such a review procedure for persons committed pursuant to §53a-47, but not for them and for other persons similarly committed under §17-178.

An examination of §§17-178 and 53a-47 reveals that they have the same intent and purpose: (a) both provide for restraint and custody while the proceedings are pending if the court is satisfied the individual is a dangerous person;[2] (b) both require medical examinations prior to the commitment hearing; (c) both provide for a hearing at which the court determines whether or not the person is mentally ill; (d) both authorize continued commitment of the individual only as long as he or she is mentally ill; (e) both statutes provide for the right of the mentally ill person to be represented by counsel at the commitment hearing.

There are, however, important differences in the rights accorded by the statutes concerning judicial review and release from confinement. Section 53a-47, which concerns commitment after a finding of not guilty because of insanity, requires the submission to the court of a written report every six months regarding that person's mental condition, and for a copy of that report to be sent to his lawyer. It further provides that the court, either upon its own motion or at the request of the parties, shall hold a hearing to determine whether such person should be released, and that such a court hearing must be initiated by the state at least once every five

1. There are currently several different statutes which authorize a civilly committed person to initiate court proceedings to obtain his liberty. See General Statutes §§17-192, 17-200, 17-201, and 17-229a. These statutes, however, in general, place the burden on the committed person and do not provide for any periodic review as to the duration of the mental illness.

2. The standard of "dangerousness" is relevant in civil commitment procedures only insofar as temporary confinement pending a full hearing is concerned. The standard applied by the court for purposes of final commitment determination is whether "the person complained of is mentally ill and a fit subject for treatment in a hospital for mental illness or that he ought to be confined. . . ." (General Statutes §17-178).

years. Most importantly, §53a-47 requires that the state shall assume the burden of proof to show that such person's continued confinement is necessary.

By contrast a person civilly committed, pursuant to §17-178, has no automatic access to the courts. Neither he nor his attorney is entitled to periodic psychiatric reports, nor is he entitled to any state-initiated judicial review. Indeed, unless he or another interested party affirmatively seeks release from custody, he will never get one. In further contrast, if he should go to court and seek release from custody, he would have to establish before such court "satisfactory proof that . . . [he has] been restored to reason." See §17-192 of the General Statutes. In point of fact, these plaintiffs have been confined for thirteen and twenty-six years respectively, and neither has yet received any judicial review of her mental illness.

The equal protection clause of the Connecticut constitution requires that any classification affecting a fundamental right be subject to strict judicial scrutiny. *Horton v. Meskill,* 172 Conn. 615, 640, 376 A.2d 359. That constitutional provision provides in article first, §20, that "[n]o person shall be denied the equal protection of the law. . . ." Article first, §1, provides that "[a]ll men when they form a social compact, are equal in rights; and no man or set of men are entitled to exclusive public emoluments or privileges from the community." The equal protection provisions of the state and federal constitutions have the same meaning and impose similar constitutional limitations. *Horton v. Meskill,* supra, 639, 376 A.2d 359.

The equal protection clause does not prohibit a state from granting privileges to specified classes of persons where sufficient reasons exist; but where advantages are conferred upon some, the state must justify its denial to others by reference to a constitutionally recognized reason. *Thompson v. Shapiro,* 270 F. Supp. 331, 338 (D.C. Conn.), *affirmed,* 394 U.S. 618, 89 S. Ct. 1322, 22 L. Ed. 2d 600; *Sanger v. Bridgeport,* 124 Conn. 183, 189, 198 A. 746. All such classifications "must be reasonable, not arbitrary, and must rest upon some ground of difference having a fair and substantial relation to the object of the legislation, so that all persons similarly circumstanced shall be treated alike." *F.S. Royster Guano Co. v. Virginia,* 253 U.S. 412, 415, 40 S. Ct. 560, 561, 64 L. Ed. 989.

To determine whether a statutory scheme violates the equal protection clause, a court must consider three factors: "the character of the classification in question; the individual interests affected by the classification; and the governmental interests asserted in support of the classification." *Dunn v. Blumstein,* 405 U.S. 330,

335, 92 S. Ct. 995, 31 L. Ed. 2d 274. Where the "fundamental right" to education was involved, this court in *Horton v. Meskill,* supra, 649, declared that the interference with such a fundamental right requires "strict judicial scrutiny," which means that the state's action is not entitled to the usual presumption of validity. The state rather than the complainants must carry the "heavy burden of justification." *Dunn v. Blumstein,* supra, 343, 92 S. Ct. 995. It is insufficient to show that the classification is merely "reasonably related to a permissible state interest" or merely rational. Ibid.

The trial court's rationale for justifying the differences was the state's concern for public safety and the unique role of the insanity defense which requires criminal courts to remain apprised of the mental condition of the person committed after a finding of not guilty because of insanity. That rationale, however, cannot justify the disparate treatment.

In *Baxstrom v. Herold,* 383 U.S. 107, 86 S. Ct. 760, 15 L. Ed. 2d 620, the United States Supreme Court invalidated commitment procedures for a mentally ill prisoner because those procedures were not the same as those accorded to all others. The court there (p. 111, 86 S. Ct. p. 762) said: "It follows that the State, having made this substantial review proceeding generally available on this [the commitment] issue, may not, consistent with the Equal Protection Clause of the Fourteenth Amendment, arbitrarily withhold it from . . . [others]." The court further stated: "Classification of mentally ill persons as either insane or dangerously insane of course may be a reasonable distinction for purposes of determining the type of custodial or medical care to be given, but it has no relevance whatever in the context of the opportunity to show whether a person is mentally ill *at all.*" (Emphasis in original.)

Another recent United States Supreme Court case, *Jackson v. Indiana,* 406 U.S. 715, 92 S. Ct. 1845, 32 L. Ed. 2d 435, is relevant. There, the court reviewed the procedure by which a mentally defective deaf-mute was committed after having been found incompetent to stand trial for robbery. In concluding that the procedures used violated the equal protection of the law under the fourteenth amendment, the court (p. 729, 92 S. Ct. p. 1853) made the following observation: "Baxstrom did not deal with the standard for release, but its rationale is applicable here. The harm to the individual is just as great if the State, without reasonable justification, can apply standards making his commitment a permanent one when standards generally applicable to all others afford him a substantial opportunity for early release."

Other courts have struck down on equal protection grounds commitment and release procedures which denied prisoners or persons acquitted by reason of insanity the same rights as accorded to others. See *Chesney v. Adams,* 377 F. Supp. 887 (D. Conn.) (prisoner); *Cameron v. Mullen,* 128 U.S. App. D.C. 235, 387 F.2d 193 (acquittal by reason of insanity); *Bolton v. Harris,* 130 U.S. App. D.C. 1, 395 F.2d 642 (acquittal by reason of insanity); *United States ex rel. Schuster v. Herold,* 410 F.2d 1071 (2d Cir.) (prisoner).

Where the state is prohibited from denying equal rights with respect to commitment and release procedures to prisoners and persons acquitted by reason of insanity, it follows that it ought also to be prohibited from denying those same rights to persons who have committed no crimes. The burden of proof of the necessity for confinement of persons who have not been convicted of a crime should remain with the state at all times.

The state has utterly failed to show any justification for its disparate classification.

LOISELLE, J. (dissenting). It is crucial to remember that this is not an action for a declaratory judgment, but a habeas corpus proceeding. The plaintiffs alleged that they were confined pursuant to orders of the Middletown Probate Court issued in 1951 and 1964, and that their confinement was illegal because they had received no periodic review of the need for their confinement. The defendant's return admitted the first allegation and denied the second.

It is incumbent on one seeking a writ of habeas corpus to allege facts which show that he or she is illegally restrained. If the application does not set forth such facts, the court may dismiss it. *Mayock v. Superintendent, Norwich State Hospital,* 154 Conn. 704, 224 A.2d 544. The defendant may raise this objection by a motion to quash. Practice Book §453. Such a motion is equivalent to a demurrer. *Adamsen v. Adamsen,* 151 Conn. 172, 175, 195 A.2d 418. Failure so to move, however, does not cure an insufficient application if no additional allegations are made at the hearing.

In their applications, the plaintiffs did not set forth any facts showing that the orders of the Middletown Probate Court were not still valid. The court found that those orders issued in accordance with §17-178 of the General Statutes and its predecessor, §2645 (1949 Rev.). Such commitments were authorized "while such mental illness continues or until . . . discharged in due course of law." The plaintiffs did not allege that their mental illness did not continue, or that they had been discharged in due course of law. Nor did they so allege at the hearing; the court specifically found that there was no claim that they were not dangerous or that they could survive safely in a free society. Neither did they allege that if they were to be accorded due process today, they would be entitled to be released. At oral argument, counsel made it clear that the absence of such an allegation is not a mere error of pleading. These petitions have been brought not to secure the plaintiffs' immediate release but to challenge Connecticut's statutory scheme for releasing them in the event that their mental condition improves at some future date.

The burden of proof of the necessity for the confinement of one who has not been convicted of a crime should remain on the state at all times. The failure of the plaintiffs to allege facts which showed that they were illegally confined, however, meant that they were not entitled to set in motion the machinery of the court. Had they alleged that, given proper court review, they would be entitled to be released, the burden of proving the contrary would have been on the defendant.

Because the plaintiffs did not allege any facts which showed that the court orders under which they were committed were no longer valid, or that the lack of periodic court review caused their wrongful confinement, they did not make out a prima facie case of illegal confinement. The court was not in error in dismissing the applications.

NOTE: PERIODIC JUDICIAL REVIEW

For an excellent discussion of the implications of Fasulo, see Note, Procedural Safeguards for Periodic Review: A New Commitment to Mental Patients' Rights, 88 Yale L.J. 850 (1979). The implication in Fasulo that recommitment hearings should not be waivable is analyzed and criticized in Wexler, The Waivability of Recommitment Hearings, 20 Ariz. L. Rev. 175 (1978). See also Crane, Zonana and Wizner, Implications of the Donaldson Decision: A Model for Periodic Review of Committed Patients, 28 Hosp. & Commun. Psychiat. 827 (1977).

C. RELEASE

Page 951. After Note, add:

In Lewis v. Donahue, 437 F. Supp. 112 (W.D. Okla. 1977) a three-judge federal court held that Oklahoma's statute providing for revocation of out-patient status without notice or opportunity for a hearing prior to rehospitalization represents an unconstitutional deprivation of procedural due process of law. The court did not, however, indicate what specific procedures are required.

Pages 963-965. After Note, add:

For new cases, see Homere v. State, 361 N.Y.S.2d 820 (1974) (state hospital held liable for failure to reconvene a discharge panel and to reevaluate the advisability of discharging a patient subsequent to the patient's display of violent behavior) and Williams v. United States, 450 F. Supp. 1040 (D.S.D. 1978) (negligent release of mental patient by V.A. hospital). But see Johnson v. United States, 409 F. Supp. 1283 (M.D. Fla., 1976) (not negligent to release psychotic patient in remission who subsequently killed his brother-in-law.)

The standard of care imposed on community treatment centers for preventing the dangerous behavior of patients in the community is stressed in Samson v. Saginaw Professional Building, 244 N.W.2d 843 (Mich. 1975), noted 62 Va. L. Rev. 383 (1976), where the owner of a building was held liable for an attack on a female worker in that building by a mental patient at a mental clinic located in the building where the building owner had failed to take adequate "protective steps."

Page 967. After Note, add:

DIXON v. WEINBERGER

405 F. Supp. 974 (D.D.C. 1975)

AUBREY E. ROBINSON, Jr., District Judge.

This class action is brought by District of Columbia residents who are patients confined pursuant to the 1964 Hospitalization of the Mentally Ill Act, 21 D.C. Code §501 *et seq.* (hereafter referred to as the 1964 Act), in St. Elizabeths Hospital, a federally administered mental institution located in Southeast Washington. The defendants include the federal officials responsible for the administration of St. Elizabeths Hospital and District of Columbia officials responsible for implementation of the provisions of the 1964 Act. The case is currently before the Court on Plaintiffs' Motion for Partial Summary Judgment, the Federal Defendants' Motion for Summary Judgment and the District of Columbia Defendants' Opposition to Plaintiffs' Motion.

A wealth of material has been presented to the Court for assistance in resolving the motions currently pending. Although plaintiffs raise both statutory and constitutional grounds for the relief sought, the Court concludes that the statutory grounds are sufficient for resolution of this matter and this discussion is confined accordingly. The current motion is brought by the class of plaintiffs comprised of inpatients confined pursuant to the 1964 Act. In the estimation of the Hospital's clinical staff, approximately 43 percent of these inpatients currently require care and treatment in alternative facilities. Alternative facilities are defined as including but not limited to nursing homes, personal care homes, foster homes and half-way houses. Simply stated, the plaintiffs seek a judicial declaration that under the 1964 Act they have a right to treatment which includes placement in facilities outside St. Elizabeths Hospital where such placement is determined to be consistent with the rehabilitative purposes of the 1964 Act, that the federal and District of Columbia governments have a joint duty to provide for such treatment where appropriate, and that this duty has been breached because there are numerous individuals in the Hospital who have been determined in need of placement in alternative facilities but who have been denied due to a lack of same. Plaintiffs ask that this Court require defendants to initiate a plan for the development of alternative facilities and the placement of appropriate individuals therein.

Both governmental defendants oppose the requested relief. The District of Columbia defendants challenge the contention that the plaintiffs' right to treatment includes placement in alternative facilities, and, alternatively, argue that even if such a right exists, the responsibility for meeting the requirement is upon the federal government, and not the District of Columbia. The federal defendants on the other hand, deny that plaintiffs have met the burden of establishing their right to such treatment and vigorously dispute their responsibility for providing the facilities in which plaintiffs seek placement.

After extensive review of the pleadings and the record in this case, the lengthy legislative history of the 1964 Act, and the cases of this jurisdiction which have fleshed out the language of the statutory provisions in question, the Court concludes that plaintiffs' position is the correct one. In reaching this conclusion, the Court has considered two issues: Whether the right to treatment mandated by the Act includes the outpatient placement these plaintiffs seek, and if so, whether the federal or District governments, or both, are responsible for providing such facilities and effecting placement therein. The following discussion details these two considerations.

The first question is whether the 1964 Act mandates the type of treatment plaintiffs seek. The fundamental goal of the 1964 Act was to return the mentally ill through care and treatment to a full and productive life in the community as soon as possible, given the patients' conditions.[1] To implement this broad goal, Congress established a statutory right "to medical and psychiatric care and treatment." 21 D.C. Code §562. This language has been interpreted as requiring governmental authorities with respect to each patient to make a "bona fide" effort "to provide treatment which is adequate in light of present knowledge," and which must be "suited to his particular needs" as determined by a frequently evaluated, individually tailored, program. *Rouse v. Cameron,* 125 U.S. App. D.C. 366, 373 F.2d 451 at 456 (1966).

The purpose of the Act and the judicial recognition of its broad mandate are not in issue. Further the defendants do not dispute that St. Elizabeths Hospital staff are responsible for making care and treatment decisions regarding patients on the Hospital's rolls and for decisions that determine status as inpatients or outpatients.[2] Nor do they dispute that the Hospital staff has determined that plaintiffs' treatment needs include placement outside the Hospital. Yet defendants construe the above cited statutory language and the cases of this jurisdiction to conclude that plaintiffs are not entitled to the treatment sought by this action.

The District of Columbia defendants argue that 21 D.C. Code 545(b) which requires judicial consideration of any "alternative course of treatment which the court believes will be in the best interests of the person or of the public" should be applied only at the commitment stage (as the statutory scheme indicates) and not expanded to the treatment stage. These defendants assert this position despite judicial determination that "[t]he principle of the least restrictive alternative is equally applicable to alternative dispositions within a mental hospital," *Covington v. Harris,* 419 F.2d 617, at 623 (1969), and despite a declaration that "deprivations of liberty solely because of dangers to the ill persons themselves should not go beyond what is necessary for their protection." *Lake v. Cameron,* 124 U.S. App. D.C. 264, 364 F.2d 657, at 660 (D.C. Cir. 1966). These defendants construe these cases narrowly and contend that only persons criminally committed who seek removal from

1. *Covington v. Harris,* 136 U.S. App. D.C. 35, 419 F.2d 617, at 625 (1969); Hearings on the Constitutional Rights of the Mentally Ill Before the Subcomm. on Constitutional Rights of the Senate Comm. on the Judiciary, 87th Cong. 1st Sess. (1961); remarks of Senator Ervin, 110 Cong. Rec. 21346 (daily ed. Sept. 2, 1964).

2. St. Elizabeths Policy and Procedures Manual, SEH Inst. 3400.1 at 1-3.

maximum security are entitled to considerations of "least restrictive alternatives."

The federal defendants take a rather different approach. They do not dispute the fact that least restrictive alternatives must be considered in making treatment choices. However, the defendants contend that plaintiffs have failed to meet their burden of establishing that placement in the alternative facilities sought by this action is a less restrictive environment than hospitalization at St. Elizabeths for these plaintiffs. This argument is based upon the allegation that the plaintiff class includes individuals whose serious medical needs makes placement in an alternative facility most difficult.[3]

The Court finds these arguments without merit. The District of Columbia defendants' position is totally unjustified in light of the statutory language and its legislative history as recognized in the case law. And the federal defendants' contention goes more to the allocation of responsibility in an individual case, and not to the question of whether the placement is required under the Act.

The extensive legislative history of the 1964 Act as recited by plaintiffs, reviewed by the Court and referred to at length in Rouse, *supra,* clearly indicates that the "medical and psychiatric care and treatment" mandated by the Act must be broadly construed. And the record before the Court in this case convincingly demonstrates that "suitable care and treatment in light of present knowledge" includes placement in alternative facilities in numerous instances. Thus, under the statutory language as interpreted, these plaintiffs have a right to the treatment sought in this action where the Hospital has determined that such treatment is appropriate.

The underlying controversy in this case, however, arises from the statutory creation of a right to the best possible care and treatment for the mentally ill without the delineation of the responsibility for providing the full range of care and treatment mandated. The fact that Congress did fail to definitely assign responsibility makes this Court's decision a more difficult one. The statutory language clearly mandates a right to treatment for patients. And the legislative history is replete with discussions of the likelihood of placement in facilities less restrictive than a mental hospital where such is determined to be appropriate treatment. Yet a delineation of respon-

---

3. Five of the named plaintiffs are confined to wheel chairs, two are diabetic, four are epileptic, three have problems with alcohol, one suffers from mental retardation and cerebral palsy, one has glaucoma and cerebral arteriosclerosis. Defendants' Motion for Summary Judgment at 11, footnote 13.

sibility for patient needs during the course of a treatment program was only mentioned as a potential bottleneck due to the financial interrelationship between the Hospital and the District, and was deferred for study at a later time.[4]

The primary responsibility for exploring and providing alternative facilities at the commitment level is upon the District of Columbia, and other Courts have so held. *In re Johnson,* 103 Wash. Law. Rep. 505 (1975); *In re Melvin,* M.H. No. 48-74 (D.C. Sup. Ct. 1975). A recent case from Superior Court of the District of Columbia has gone even further than earlier cases and recognized the propriety of placement in a less restrictive alternative facility during the course of treatment (i.e. after an initial confinement in the Hospital) and the duty of the District of Columbia to provide promptly for such placement despite the lack of staff and facilities or budgetary limits. *In re Johnson,* 103 Wash. Law. Rep. 1913 (Nov. 10, 1975). It is beyond dispute that St. Elizabeths Hospital is responsible for providing suitable care and treatment for patients while confined in the Hospital.

Therefore, at the commitment stage and for those patients determined to be in need of only custodial care, completely independent from any care or treatment generated by St. Elizabeths, the primary responsibility is upon the District government to provide suitable alternative arrangements. But in this case the class of plaintiffs includes individuals who are in neither category and as to these persons, the responsibility cannot be the District's alone.

Although Congress failed to clearly define the responsibilities for providing the full range of treatment mandated by the Act, the Court infers the necessary Congressional intent that the responsibility be a joint one from the manner in which funds have been appropriated to St. Elizabeths for the treatment of these plaintiffs over the past years. The Hospital receives its financing from Congressional appropriations channeled through the National Institute of Mental Health. As a public facility in which individuals are confined pursuant to the 1964 Act, St. Elizabeths is responsible for providing adequate care and treatment for mentally ill patients who are on their rolls. More than 85 percent of the patient population are District of Columbia residents.[5] The cost of treating these

4. S. Rep. No. 925, 88th Cong. 2nd Session (1964) at 28, 29 and 40, U.S. Code Cong. & Admin. News, p. 597.

5. Response of Defendant Robinson to Interrogatory #189, Plaintiffs' First Interrogatories.

individuals is approximately $53 per day; of this cost the District pays approximately $25 and the Hospital pays the balance.[6] Therefore, it is obvious that the Hospital receives significant sums for treating patients confined pursuant to the 1964 Act, and, to this extent the Hospital shares the responsibilities imposed by the Act to provide a full range of treatment as required in an individual case.

The practicalities of treatment further support the Court's conclusion that Congress intended the responsibility to be a joint one. As noted earlier, one of the primary goals of the 1964 Act was to provide suitable care and treatment directed to returning individuals to the community to the extent possible. The responsibility and involvement of the Hospital in working toward this goal does not abruptly cease as a patient slowly moves from restrictive confinement in the Hospital to the less restrictive atmosphere of an alternative facility, pursuant to a plan of treatment dictated by the Hospital staff. To determine otherwise would be to disregard the fact that "housing" (as the government puts it) is integrally related to "treatment" within the purposes of the 1964 Act, and has been determined to be such by the Hospital staff.[7]

Therefore, it is concluded from the statutory scheme, the legislative history, and the Congressional intent which can be inferred from the appropriations allocated to St. Elizabeths for the care and treatment of these plaintiffs over the years, that the duty to effect placement in alternative facilities where appropriate is a joint one. The Court makes this determination with a realization that the division of responsibility will vary in an individual case and that the Hospital's primary responsibility is for psychiatric care and treatment. But as an individual's need for such treatment decreases and need for mere custodial care increases, the Hospital's responsibilities will correspondingly decrease. Individuals who are determined to be solely custodial cases, without need for psychiatric care or treatment in the broadest sense and for whose care the Hospital receives no funds, are more properly the responsibility of the District of Columbia government.

The record before the Court indicates that there are many individuals currently confined in the Hospital who are desperately

6. Affidavit of Dr. Luther Robinson, Attachment #5; 1973 House Appropriations Hearings at 301, 308.

7. The Hospital places patients in alternative facilities as part of the patient's treatment plans in order to reintegrate the patient into the community and to develop self-reliance and self-determination. Response of Defendant Robinson to Interrogatory #90(a).

in need of care and treatment which the Hospital staff has determined includes placement in facilities outside St. Elizabeths Hospital. The record further reflects that the named plaintiffs, at the very least, are among the individuals who are still in need of psychiatric care despite their readiness for placement in alternative facilities. Thus as to these individuals and others like them, the duty to provide such treatment by placement in alternative facilities is a joint one.

Upon the foregoing, it is this 23 day of December, 1975,

Ordered that Plaintiffs Motion for Partial Summary Judgment be, and hereby is, granted; and it is further

Adjudged and decreed that the 1964 Hospitalization of the Mentally Ill Act requires that patients confined in St. Elizabeths Hospital pursuant to the 1964 Act receive suitable care and treatment under the least restrictive conditions as such conditions are required in an individual case consistent with the purposes of the Act; that the District of Columbia and the Federal Government defendants have a joint duty to provide such care and treatment where appropriate; that both defendants have violated the 1964 Act by failing to place plaintiffs and members of their class, who are inpatients at St. Elizabeths Hospital and who have been determined suitable for placement in alternative facilities in proper facilities that are less restrictive alternatives to the Hospital, as it is presently constituted, such alternatives including but not being limited to nursing homes, foster homes, personal care homes and half-way houses; and that, therefore, such failure is unlawful and invalid; and it is further

Ordered that, forty-five (45) days from the date of this Order, the defendants shall submit to the Court an outline of a plan which shall detail the manner in which and the timetable by which defendants will meet their duty to provide plaintiffs who are and who will be inpatients at the Hospital with care and treatment in suitable residential facilities under the least restrictive conditions consistent with the purpose of the 1964 Act; that the outline shall include but shall not be limited to:

(a) a statement of the number of inpatients confined at the Hospital pursuant to the 1964 Act who require alternative placement at the time the outline is submitted and the type and reasons for alternative care required;

(b) a statement of the estimated number of inpatients who are or who will be confined pursuant to the 1964 Act who will need alternative placement in the next six months, twelve months and eighteen months, in addition to the patients identified in (a), and the type of alternative care required;

(c) a statement of the major problems inhibiting alternative placement of those plaintiffs who are or who will be inpatients at the Hospital confined pursuant to the 1964 Act on the date the outline is submitted;

(d) a statement of the tentative solutions to the problems inhibiting alternative placement which defendants will propose in the completed plan;

(e) a tentative statement of the standards that will govern the care and treatment and the conditions in the various types of alternative facilities to which the inpatients identified in (a) and (b) will be outplaced;

(f) a tentative statement of the procedures and personnel to be used in monitoring the care and treatment and conditions in the various types of alternative facilities to which the inpatients identified in (a) and (b) will be outplaced;

(g) a statement describing tentative changes in budgetary patterns and/or sources of funding for implementing the solutions and aspects of the treatment process identified in (d-f);

(h) a tentative timetable for implementing the solutions identified in (d);

(i) a statement of the respective roles to be played by the Federal and District of Columbia defendants in preparation of the plan, including specification of the type and number of personnel to be provided by each of the defendants;

(j) a tentative statement of the respective responsibilities of the Federal and District of Columbia defendants in implementing the plan, i. e. in providing suitable, least restrictive care and treatment in alternative facilities to the inpatient plaintiffs; and it is further

Ordered that, after submission of the outline by defendants, after any further submissions by plaintiffs, and after approval of the outline of the plan by the Court, defendants shall, four (4) months from the date of the Court's order approving the outline of the plan, submit a final plan; and it is further

Ordered that the Court shall retain jurisdiction over this action to consider appropriate measures to be taken for the implementation of the plan submitted.

NOTE: DE-INSTITUTIONALIZATION

Several years following the decision in Dixon v. Weinberger the issues of that case have still not been resolved.

More recently the U.S. District Court for the Eastern District of

Pennsylvania has decided Halderman v. Pennhurst State School and Hospital, 446 F. Supp. 1295 (E.D. Pa. 1977), *stay denied*, 451 F. Supp. 233 (E.D. Pa. 1978), *appeal docketed*, No. 78-148 (2d Cir. Apr. 25, 1978). In the Pennhurst case the court found that Pennhurst, a large and isolated state institution for the mentally retarded, was inherently incapable of providing its residents with minimally adequate habitation. Instead of ordering improvements in staffing, funding, and programming, the court ordered that Pennhurst be closed and that alternative suitable facilities in the community be provided for its residents. The Pennhurst case is discussed in Note, 57 N.C.L. Rev. 336 (1979) and in Ferleger and Boyd, Anti-Institutionalization: The Promise of the Pennhurst Case, 31 Stanford L. Rev. 717 (1979).

Page 967. After Note, add:

NOTE: EXPUNGEMENT OF RECORDS

The developing issue of expungement of records is treated in Note, Expungement of Mental Health Records in the Civil Commitment Context: A Remedy in Search of a Right, 19 Ariz. L. Rev. 377 (1977). See Wolfe v. Beal, 353 A.2d 481 (Comm. Ct. Pa. 1976) (refusal to expunge where commitment was voided; two dissents).

In Souder v. Watson, Civ. Act. No. 74-279 (M.D. Pa. Dec. 20, 1977), a Pennsylvania court refused to expunge the records of a prisoner whose earlier civil commitment to Farview Hospital had been declared unconstitutional. The court reasoned that presentation of the records was more important both to the state and to the former patient than the value to him of their destruction. Should the former patient ever be re-committed, the records would be useful. The court commented on the fact that new Pennsylvania statutory provisions effectively prevented use of the records for any purpose other than legitimate future treatment.

Chapter Eighteen

Contracts, Torts, and Testimonial Capacity

Pages 1003-1004. After 4., Reading on Torts, add:

See Picker, The Tortious Liability of the Insane in Canada. . . . With a Comparative Look at the United States and Civil Law Jurisdictions and a Suggestion for an Alternative, 13 Osgoode Hall L.J. 193 (1975).

Pages 1016-1017. After Readings on Psychiatric Evaluations of Credibility of Witnesses, add:

See O'Neale, Court Ordered Psychiatric Examination of a Rape Victim in a Criminal Rape Prosecution—Or How Many Times Must a Woman Be Raped?, 18 Santa Clara L. Rev. 119 (1978) and Comment, Pre-Trial Psychiatric Examination as Proposed Means for Testing the Complainant's Competency to Allege a Sex Offense, 1957 U. Ill. L.F. 651. In State v. Looney, 294 N.C. 1, 240 S.E.2d 612 (1978), the North Carolina Supreme Court ruled, in a murder case, that a key prosecution's witness' right to privacy was more important than defendant's right to a psychiatric evaluation of the witness' credibility. Said the Court, ". . . the possible benefits to an innocent defendant, flowing from such a court ordered examination of the witness, are outweighed by the resulting invasion of the witness' right to privacy and the danger to the public interest from discouraging victims of crime to report such offenses and other potential witnesses from disclosing their knowledge of them." At

627. The suggestion that such court-ordered examinations may never be justified is criticized in Note, 57 N.C.L. Rev. 448 (1979).

Page 1021. After (2), Acting on Behalf of a Retardate, add:

See Lausier v. Pescinski, 67 Wis. 2d 4, 226 N.W.2d 180 (1975), discussed in Robertson, Organ Donations by Incompetents and the Substituted Judgment Doctrine, 76 Colum. L. Rev. 48 (1976).

Pages 1017-1021. After (1) Competence to Hold a Job, add:

Data concerning discrimination against former mental patients is beginning to build up. An excellent general treatment of one aspect of discrimination is R. Plotkin, Constitutional Challenges to Employment Disability Statutes (National Clearinghouse on Offender Employment Restrictions, undated). See also Olshansky, et al., Employers' Attitudes and Practices in the Hiring of Ex-Mental Patients, 42 Mental Hygiene 391 (1958); Farina, Reactions of Workers to Male/Female Mental Patients Job Applicants, 41 J. Consult. & Clin. Psych. 363 (1973); and Farina v. Felner, Employment Interviewer Reactions to Former Mental Patients, 82 J. Abn. Psych. 268 (1973).

Spencer v. Toussaint, 408 F. Supp. 1067 (E.D. Mich. 1976) deals with the application for the job of bus driver made by a previously hospitalized woman. See also Beazer v. New York City Transit Authority, 399 F. Supp. 1032 (S.D.N.Y. 1975) (a methadone maintenance case), rev'd, 99 S. Ct. 1355 (1979).

In Tolbert v. McGriff, 434 F. Supp. 682 (M.D. Ala. 1976) the court ruled that an Alabama statute which permitted the suspension of a driver's license on the basis of mental or medical incompetence, but without a due process hearing, was unconstitutional. The plaintiff, an epileptic truck driver who maintained himself on medication, was deprived of his license following a departmental investigation which included an interview with the driver as well as with his doctor. The license was then suspended without a hearing. The court held that the driver had not only been deprived of a hearing, but also had not been notified of available statutory appeal procedures.

The court acknowledged the need for the suspension of a license without a hearing in an emergency situation where the continued driving of an incompetent driver presents an immediate threat to the lives of other motorists and pedestrians. The court expanded on emergency issues in a companion case, Smith v. McGriff, 434 F. Supp. 673 (M.D. Ala. 1977), which involved an alcoholic driver.

Page 1023. After Note, add:

(4) Competence to Have Children: Sterilization

See Burgdorf and Burgdorf, The Wicked Witch Is Almost Dead: Buck v. Bell and the Sterilization of Handicapped Persons, 50 Temp. L.Q. 995 (1977); Recent Development, Sterilization of Mental Incompetents, 44 Tenn. L. Rev. 879 (1977); Note, Sterilization of Mental Defectives, 3 Cumb.-Sam. L. Rev. 458 (1972); Murdock, Sterilization of the Retarded: A Problem or a Solution?, 62 Calif. L. Rev. 917 (1974) and Note, Addressing the Consent Issue Involved in the Sterilization of Mentally Incompetent Females, 43 Albany L. Rev. 322 (1979). See also Gaylin, Sterilization of the Retarded: In Whose Interest?, 8 The Hastings Center Report 28 (June, 1978); Thompson, The Behavioral Perspective, id. at 29; Neville, The Philosophical Arguments, id. at 33; and Bayles, The Legal Precedents, id. at 37. The cases are collected in Annot., Validity of Statutes Authorizing Asexualization or Sterilization of Criminals or Mental Defectives, 53 A.L.R.3d 960.

(5) Competence to Vote.

See Klein and Grossman, Voting Competence and Mental Illness, 127 Am. J. Psychiat. 1562 (1971); Howard and Anthony, The Right to Vote and Voting Patterns of Hospitalized Psychiatric Patients, 49 Psychiat. Q. 124 (1977); Klein and Grossman, Voting Competence and Mental Illness, 3 Pro. of the 76th Annual Com. of the Am. Psychol. Assoc. 701; Anno., Voting Rights of Persons Mentally Incapacitated, 80 A.L.R.3d 1116; Plotkin, Too Crazy to Vote? Disenfranchisement of the Mentally Handicapped Citizen, 2 Mental Health Law Project Summary 1 (Fall, 1976) (with chart of state statutory provisions).

An excellent new discussion is Note, Mental Disability and the Right to Vote, 88 Yale L.J. 1644 (1979).

(6) Competence to Be a Juror.

See Note, Judgment By Your Peers? The Impeachment of Jury Verdicts and the Case of the Insane Juror, 21 N.Y.L. Forum 57 (1975).

(7) Miscellaneous Discrimination.

See Greenley, Abel and Small, Availability of Health and Life Insurance for Persons With a History of Mental Illness, Alcoholism, Drug Abuse or Criminal Record (Center for Public Representation, Madison, Wis., November, 1978).

Chapter Nineteen

Divorce and Child Custody

Page 1035. After Note, add:

The right of the mentally disabled to marry is discussed in Linn and Bowers, The Historical Fallacies Behind Legal Prohibitions of Marriages Involving Mentally Retarded Persons—The Eternal Child Grows Up, 13 Gonzaga L. Rev. 625 (1978), with a wealth of reference to both legal and non-legal material, and in Murray, Marriage Contracts for the Mentally Retarded, 21 Cath. Lawyer 182 (1975). See also Note, The Right of the Mentally Disabled to Marry: A Statutory Evaluation, 15 J. Fam. L. 463 (1976-1977). Thirty-eight states and the District of Columbia either limit or prohibit marriages of the mentally disabled. For an annotation dealing with the power of an incompetent's guardian, committee, or next friend to sue for an annulment, see Annot., 6 A.L.R.3d 681.

Page 1067. After Note, add:

Although the Goldstein, Freud and Solnit book has been influential, it has also drawn vigorous criticism. See, e.g., Dembitz, Book Review, Beyond Any Discipline's Competence, 83 Yale L.J. 1304 (1974); Strauss and Strauss, Book Review, 74 Colum. L. Rev. 996 (1974); Katkin, Bullington and Levine, Above and Beyond the Best Interests of the Child: An Inquiry Into the Relationship Between Social Science and Social Action, Law and Society, Summer, 1974, p. 669; Lennon, Book Review, Juvenile Justice, February, 1976, p. 39; Foster, Book Review, 2 Bull. Amer. Acad. Psychiat. & L. 46 (1974); and Foster, Book Review, 12 Willamette L.J. 545 (1976). A powerful critique from the social work perspective is presented in Kadushin, Beyond the Best Interests of the Child: An Essay Review, 48 Social Service Rev. 508 (1974).

See also Bates, Expert Evidence in Cases Involving Children, 12 West. Australia L. Rev. 139 (1975); Mnookin, Child-Custody Adjudication Judicial Functions in the Face of Indeterminacy, 39 Law & Contemp. Prob. No. 3 at 226 (1975); Batt, Child Custody Disputes: A Developmental-Psychological Approach to Proof and Decisionmaking, 12 Will. L.J. 491 (1976); Okpaku (now Rush), Psychology: Impediment or Aid in Child Custody Cases?, 29 Rutgers L. Rev. 1117 (1976).

Page 1073. After Note, add:

See further In the Matter of Stephen B., 60 Misc. 2d 662, 664-666, 303 N.Y.S.2d 438, 441-443 (Fam. Ct. 1969), *aff'd mem. sub nom.* In re Behrman, 34 App. Div. 2d 527, 309 N.Y.S.2d 864 (1970) where custody was transferred because of the mother's hospitalization for mental illness, and Matter of Diane Millar, 40 App. Div. 637 (N.Y. 1972), *aff'd* 35 N.Y.2d 767 (1974). See also In Re Appeal in Pima County, 543 P.2d 809 (Ariz. Ct. App. 1975), noted 15 J. Fam. L. 366 (1976-1977) (termination of parental rights) and In Re David B., 5 Fam. L. Rep. 253 (Cal. 5th Dist. Ct. App. March 28, 1979) where the California Court of Appeal affirmed a lower court decision terminating a mentally ill mother's parental rights very shortly after the child was born. The court ruled that a showing of actual harm to the child is not necessary. See, e.g., In Re William L., 383 A.2d 1228 (1978), *cert. denied,* 99 S. Ct. 216.

The hospitalization of a parent may have a significant consequence. See Annot., Parent's Involuntary Confinement or Failure to Care for Child as Result Thereof as Permitting Adoption Without Parental Consent, 78 A.L.R.3d 712 and Annot., Parent's Involuntary Confinement, or failure to care for child as a result thereof, as evincing neglect, unfitness, or the like in dependency or divestiture proceeding, 79 A.L.R.3d 417.

Part 5

The Psychiatrist - Patient Relationship

Chapter Twenty

Privilege, Confidentiality, and Abuses

A. ABUSES OF THE PSYCHIATRIST-PATIENT RELATIONSHIP: MALPRACTICE

Page 1079. Before Note: Malpractice, add:

ROY v. HARTOGS

381 N.Y.S.2d 587 (1976)

PER CURIAM:

A complaint should not be dismissed on the opening statement of counsel unless, accepting as true all facts stated in the opening and resolving in plaintiff's favor all material facts in issue, plaintiff nevertheless is precluded from recovery as a matter of law. Counsel asserted in the opening statement that the defendant, a psychiatrist, had treated the plaintiff, as his patient, during the period March, 1969 through September, 1970. It was further averred that, during the last thirteen months of her treatment, plaintiff was induced to have sexual intercourse with the defendant as part of her prescribed therapy. As a result of this improper treatment, counsel alleged that the plaintiff was so emotionally and mentally injured that she was required to seek hospitalization on two occasions during 1971.

The right of action to recover a sum of money for seduction has been abolished by Article 8 of the Civil Rights Law and the predecessor legislation found in Article 2-A of the Civil Practice Act. These statutes were passed, as a matter of public policy, so that marriages should not be entered into because of the threat or danger of an action to recover money damages and the embarrassment and humiliation growing out of such action. However, this legislation did not abolish all causes of action wherein the act of sexual intercourse was either an "incident of" or "contributed to" the ultimate harm or wrong. In this proceeding, the injury to the plaintiff was not merely caused by the consummation of acts of sexual intercourse with the defendant. Harm was also caused by the defendant's failure to treat the plaintiff with professionally acceptable procedures (cf. *Zipkin v. Freeman*, 436 S.W.2d 753, 761, 762 [Mo. 1969] ; cf. *Anclote Manor Foundation v. Wilkinson*, 263 So. 2d 256, 257 [Fla. App. 1972]). By alleging that his client's mental and emotional status was adversely affected by this deceptive and damaging treatment, plaintiff's counsel asserted a viable cause of action for malpractice in his opening statement.

Generally, evidence of other acts or transactions, even of a similar nature, are not admissible where such acts can only be deemed relevant through the inference that the party would follow the same course in the transaction in issue. However, the physicial condition of the defendant in this appeal became relevant when he stated that he did not have sexual intercourse after 1965 because of a hydrocele. At that juncture, the testimony of witness Stern was correctly received in rebuttal on defendant's physical condition in 1969 and 1970 when he was treating the plaintiff. Because witnesses Cuttler and Sherwood were unaware of defendant's physical capability during the period in issue, their testimony was properly stricken by the court below. In the context of this protracted trial, the jurors were not so unduly influenced by this stricken testimony as to warrant a reversal on this ground.

The award of $50,000 in compensatory damages for defendant's aggravation of plaintiff's pre-existing mental disorders, is, however, in our opinion excessive. Plaintiff's condition was of long standing, and began years before she became defendant's patient. There is no evidence to support a permanent worsening of the condition by defendant's acts; nor is there proof demonstrating a permanent impairment of her ability to work in a position comparable to that she had before or during the period she was defendant's patient. Given the fact that she may recover only for the aggravation of her condition by defendant (*Schneider v. New York Telephone Co.*, 249 App. Div. 400, 292 N.Y.S. 399), we conclude that an award of more than $25,000 would be excessive.

The jury's finding, implicit in its award of punitive damages, that the defendant was actuated by evil or malicious intentions when the parties had sexual intercourse was against the predominating weight of the credible evidence. Viewing all the facts and circumstances incident to the occurrences most favorably to the plaintiff as disclosed in this record (*Sanders v. Rolnick,* 188 Misc. 627, 67 N.Y.S.2d 652, *affd.* 272 App. Div. 803, 71 N.Y.S.2d 896), the weight of the evidence did not justify the jury's finding that defendant's conduct, while inexcusable, was so wanton or reckless as to permit an award for punitive damages.

Judgment, entered July 29, 1975 (Myers, J. and jury); reversed and new trial ordered limited to the issue of compensatory damages, with $30 costs to appellant to abide the event that plaintiff recovers less than $25,000 in compensatory damages, unless respondent within ten days after service of a copy of the order entered hereon with notice of entry, stipulates to reduce the recovery to $25,000, in which event judgment modified accordingly and as modified, affirmed without costs.

MARKOWITZ, Presiding Justice (concurring):

I concur in the Per Curiam but would like to add the following observations.

The subject matter of this case was highly sensational forcing the participants to operate in a charged atmosphere rather than the calm almost cloistered climate of the routine civil courtroom. However, since this State has not closed the door on all actions merely because sexual relations are part of the core facts, and does permit civil prosecutions where the wrong alleged is grounded on conventional tort (*Tuck v. Tuck,* 14 N.Y.2d 341, 251 N.Y.S.2d 653, 200 N.E.2d 554) there is no question that the facts adduced in this record were properly presented to the jury as a possible basis for malpractice which had a causal connection to plaintiff's subsequent psychotic episodes.

While cultists expound theories of the beneficial effects of sexual psychotherapy, the fact remains that all eminent experts in the psychiatric field including the American Psychiatric Association abjure sexual contact between patient and therapist as harmful to the patient and deviant from accepted standards of treatment of the mentally disturbed.

Dr. Ernest Jones, in his encyclopedic treatment of "The Life and Word of Sigmund Freud" (New York, Basic Books, Inc. 1953) sets forth (Vol. 3, p. 163) a letter written by Freud to a colleague which is relevant to the discussion here.

It reads in pertinent part as follows:

Lieber Freund:

. . . You have not made a secret of the fact that you kiss your patients and let them kiss you; . . .

Now I am assuredly not one of those who from prudishness or from consideration of bourgeois convention would condemn little erotic gratifications of this kind. . . . But that does not alter the facts . . . that with us a kiss signifies a certain erotic intimacy. We have hitherto in our technique held to the conclusion that patients are to be refused erotic gratifications. You know too that where more extensive gratifications are not to be had milder caresses very easily take over their role, in love affairs, on the stage, etc.

Now picture what will be the result of publishing your technique. There is no revolutionary who is not driven out of the field by a still more radical one. A number of independent thinkers in matters of technique will say to themselves: why stop at a kiss? Certainly one gets further when one adopts "pawing" as well, which after all doesn't make a baby. And then bolder ones will come along who will go further to peeping and showing—and soon we shall have accepted in the technique of analysis the whole repertoire of demiviergerie and petting parties, resulting in an enormous increase of interest in psychoanalysis among both analysts and patients. The new adherent, however, will easily claim too much of this interest for himself; the younger of our colleagues will find it hard to stop at the point they originally intended, and God the Father Ferenczi gazing at the lively scene he has created will perhaps say to himself: may be after all I should have halted in my technique of motherly affection *before* the kiss.

Sentences like "about the dangers of neocatharsis" don't get very far. One should obviously not let oneself get into the danger. I have purposely not mentioned the increase of calumnious resistances against analysis the kissing technique would bring, although it seems to me a wanton act to provoke them.

With cordial greetings
Your
Freud"

Thus from the font of psychiatric knowledge to the modern practitioner we have common agreement of the harmful effects of sensual intimacies between patient and therapist.

Of interesting note is an annotation entitled Civil Liability of Doctor or Psychologist for Having Sexual Relationship With Patient (33 A.L.R.3d 1393), in which the notewriters state: "Apart from *Nicholson v. Han* [12 Mich. App. 35, 162 N.W.2d 313, 33 A.L.R.3d 1386, a case whose facts are not applicable here] research has failed to disclose any case in which the courts have discussed or passed upon the civil liability of a doctor or a psychologist, as such, who while the doctor-patient relationship substituted, had established a sexual relationship with a patient." However, where the sexual contacts are themselves the prescribed course of treatment and where such treatment is outside of accepted professional standards, what remains is a simple malpractice action as to which research would be merely cumulative.

On the question of punitive damages, such recovery is allowed in cases where the wrong complained of is morally culpable, or is actuated by evil and reprehensible motives, not only to punish the defendant but to deter him as well as others, from indulging in similar conduct in the future.

In the instant case all that has been established is professional incompetence. It was established that plaintiff was influenced to participate on a theory that it would solve her problems.

Sex under cloak of treatment is an acceptable and established ground for disciplinary measures taken against physicians either by licensing authorities or professional organizations. Whether defendant acted in such manner as to seriously affect his performance as a practitioner in the psychiatric field should be left to these more competent fora, rather than by seeking deterrence by way of punitive damages. The only thing that the record herein supports is that his prescribed treatment was in negligent disregard of the consequences. For that, and that alone, he must be held liable.

RICCOBONO, Justice (dissenting):

The plaintiff pursued her action for malpractice by alleging that over a period of some 13 months the defendant made sexual advances towards her with a lewd and lascivious motive and that he did in fact engage in sexual intercourse and other acts of carnal knowledge with her, in a purported furtherance of psychiatric treatment. Plaintiff further asserts that instead of assisting and curing her, the defendant's therapeutic methods caused her permanent mental and emotional harm. This harm, it is alleged, was caused by the defendant's failure to treat the plaintiff by acceptable medical procedures.

The right of action to recover a sum of money for seduction was abolished by virtue of former Article 2-A of the Civil Practice Act, now Civil Rights Law, section 80-a et seq. Article 8 of the Civil

Rights Law must be liberally construed to effectuate this purpose (Civil Rights Law, §84). This legislation was passed as a matter of public policy because of the threat or danger of an action to recover money damages and the embarrassment and humiliation emanating from such scandalous causes of action.

In the case at bar, although the plaintiff was suffering from a number of emotional problems her competency was never placed in issue. Is it not fair to infer, therefore, that she was capable of giving a knowing and meaningful consent? For almost one and a half years while this "meaningful" relationship continued, the plaintiff was not heard to complain. Upon the defendant terminating the relation, this lawsuit evolves.

The defendant obviously did not help his cause by denying what the jury found to be the fact, viz., that the defendant did have sexual relations with the plaintiff. Nevertheless, however ill-advised or ill-conceived was the choice of his defense, in my view this did not constitute malpractice. The plaintiff was still obliged to prove her case by the preponderance of the credible evidence, regardless of the defendant's defense.

I neither condone the defendant's reprehensible conduct, nor maintain that it was not violative of his professional ethics and Hippocratic oath. If, however, the defendant has committed a crime, let him be brought before the criminal halls of justice. For violation of his Hippocratic oath, if there be any, let him suffer the sanctions of the Medical Ethics Board or other appropriate medical authority. But let him not be convicted of his acts of misfeasance and malfeasance by virtue of an action in malpractice. I might parenthetically add, that if the plaintiff is to succeed I am in total agreement with my colleagues that the plaintiff is not entitled to punitive damages and am likewise in full accord that her recovery should not exceed $25,000.

The relief sought by this plaintiff constitutes the closest approach to a conventional action for seduction, and hence must be treated as such. This is barred by section 80-a of the Civil Rights Law (*Fernandez v. Lazar,* N.Y.L.J., September 15, 1971, p. 19, col. 6, N.Y. Supreme Ct., *Leff, J.; Nicholson v. Han,* 12 Mich. App. 35, 162 N.W.2d 313 [1968]). As so inextricably intertwined, I would reverse and dismiss the complaint.

Pages 1079-1080. After Note: Malpractice, add:

For additional general materials on psychiatric malpractice, see D. Hogan, The Regulation of Psychotherapists, Vol. III: A Review of

Malpractice Suits in the United States (1979); Slawson, Psychiatric Malpractice: The California Experience, 136 Am. J. Psychiat. 650 (1979); Slawson, Psychiatric Malpractice: A State-Wide Survey, 6 Bull. Am. Acad. Psychiat. & L. 58 (1978); Note, Tort Liability of the Psychotherapist, 8 U.S.F. L. Rev. 405, 425-434 (1973); Rothblatt and Leroy, Avoiding Psychiatric Malpractice, 9 Cal. W. L. Rev. 260 (1974); Note, Psychiatric Negligence, 23 Drake L. Rev. 640 (1974); and Robey, Getting Caught in the "Open Door": Psychiatrists, Patients and Third Parties, 1 Mental Disab. L. Rep. 220 (1976). See also Annot., Patient Tort Liability of Rest, Convalescent, or Nursing Homes, 83 A.L.R.3d 871.

A new theory of recovery for defective psychiatric treatment for a mental condition is advanced in Furrow, Defective Mental Treatment: A Proposal for the Application of Stict Liability to Psychiatric Services, 58 B.U.L. Rev. 391 (1978). See also Note, Injuries Precipitated by Psychotherapy: Liability Without Fault as a Basis for Recovery, 20 S. Dak. L. Rev. 401 (1975) and Fishalow, The Tort Liability of the Psychiatrist, 3 Bull. Am. Acad. of Psychiat. & L. 191 (1975).

An interesting case involving the failure to prevent a suicide is Haines v. Bellissimo, 82 D.L.R.3d 215 (Ontario High Court of Justice, 1977). See also Chatwin v. Millis, 517 S.W. 504 (Ark. 1975) (is a psychiatrist or psychologist liable in malpractice for the expression of a negligently formed opinion concerning a person not his patient?).

NOTE: SEX RELATIONS BETWEEN PSYCHOTHERAPISTS AND PATIENTS

As the *Hartogs* case indicates, the long suppressed problem of sexual relations between therapist and patient has finally surfaced. The literature on the subject is growing rapidly, both on the professional side and in the popular press, although little meaningful research has as yet been done about the validity of such practices, where it is alleged that they have therapeutic value.

From a psychiatric, psychological, and psychoanalytic perspective, consult Stone, The Legal Implications of Sexual Activity Between Psychiatrist and Patient, 133 Am. J. Psychiat. 1138 (1976); Perr, Legal Aspects of Sexual Therapies, J. Legal Med., January, 1975, p. 33; Kardener, Fuller and Mensh, Characteristics of "Erotic" Practitioners, 133 Am. J. Psychiat. 1324 (1976); Perry, Physicians' Erotic and Nonerotic Contact with Patients, 113 Am. J. Psychiat. 838

(1976); Dahlberg, Sexual Contact Between Patient and Therapist, 6 Contemp. Psychoanal. 107 (1970); Holroyd and Brodsky, Psychologist's Attitudes and Practices Regarding Erotic and Nonerotic Physical Contact With Patients, 32 Am. Psychologist 843 (1977); Marmor, Sexual Acting Out in Psychotherapy, 32 Am. J. Psychoanal. 3 (1972); Finney, Therapist and Patient After Hours, 75 Am. J. Psychotherapy 593 (1975); Voth, Love Affair Between Doctor and Patient, 26 Am. J. Psychotherapy 395 (1972); Elias, Stand In for Eros, 6 Hum. Behav. No. 3 at 17 (1977); Jacobs, Thompason and Truxaw, The Use of Sexual Surrogates in Counseling, 5 The Counseling Psychol. 73 (1975); and Davidson, Psychiatry's Problem With No Name: Therapist-Patient Sex, 37 Am. J. Psychoan. 43 (1977).

The subject has, oddly enough, not yet been widely discussed in the legal literature. See, e.g., Leroy, The Potential Criminal Liability of Human Sex Clinics and Their Patients, 16 St. Louis U.L.J. 602 (1972). An excellent and comprehensive legal study of therapist-patient sexual relations, with recommendations for control and regulation for experimental purposes, is Riskin, Sexual Relations Between Psychotherapists and Their Patients: Toward Research or Restraint, 67 Calif. L. Rev. 1000 (1979).

The *Hartogs* case is the one most significant recently reported case involving an action in tort, although there appear to be other cases either brought to conclusion or settled which alleged tortious sexual relations between therapists and patients. See, e.g., the case of Hoey and Buckingham v. Trahms, reported in Pacific Sun, Sept. 9-15 (1977) at 5.

In addition to actions in tort, criminal prosecutions may be brought for proscribed sexual relations between therapists and patients. See, e.g., People v. Bernstein, 171 Cal. 2d 279, 340 P.2d 299 (Cal. Dist. Ct. App. 1959), affirming a psychiatrist's conviction for the statutory rape of a 16-year-old female patient whose presenting problem was sexual promiscuity. A fascinating criminal prosecution of a doctor who ran a camp for emotionally disturbed boys, and who claimed that his sexual relations with them were intended as therapy, is State v. Martin (a fictitious name), reported and discussed in J. Goldstein, A. Dershowitz, and R. Schwartz, Criminal Law: Theory & Process 3-31 (1974).

Professor Riskin points out that criminal prosecutions based on sexual offense statutes are not likely, in the main, to be successful inasmuch as most rape statutes apply only if there is force and the act is against the will of the patient, facts unlikely to occur in most therapist-patient sexual encounters.

Some specific criminal statutes do provide protection. See, e.g., Mich. Comp. Laws Ann. §750.90 (1978), which provides:

> Any person who shall undertake to medically treat any female person and while so treating her, shall represent to such female that it is, or will be, necessary or beneficial to her health that she have sexual intercourse with any man, and any man, not being the husband of such female, who shall have sexual intercourse with her by reason of such representation shall be guilty of a felony. . . .

State licensing agencies have acted in some cases to revoke the license of a physician or psychologist for unprofessional conduct, malpractice, or for conviction of a crime involving moral turpitude. See, e.g., Bernstein v. Bd. of Medical Examiners, 22 Cal. Rptr. 419 (Dist. Ct. App. 1962) and Morra v. St. Bd. of Examiners of Psychologists, 212 Kan. 103, 510 P.2d 614 (1973).

Some psychotherapists insist that sexual relations of one sort or another between therapists and patients can be significantly therapeutic, and that it would be unwise to ban all such contacts. Professor Riskin agrees and offers recommendations that would encourage legitimate sexual contacts based on a research/experimentation model. He urges the collection of research data about such relations under conditions that would be protective of the patient against abuse. The main feature of Riskin's protective model would be an institutional review board which would determine whether research protocols are acceptable, in terms of research legitimacy and protection of the patient.

The plaintiff in the *Hartogs* case has written up her story in L. Freeman and J. Roy, Betrayal (1976). In Mason and Stitham, The Expensive Dalliance: Assessing the Cost of Patient-Therapist Sex, 5 Bull. Am. Acad. Psychiat. & L. 450 (1977) there is an evaluation of the Roy v. Hartogs case together with an estimate of its costs.

Page 1084. After 2., The Patient in Therapy, add:

NOTE: A CONSTITUTIONAL PSYCHOTHERAPIST-PATIENT PRIVILEGE

In In Re B, Appeal of Dr. Loren Roth,—Pa.—, 394 A.2d 419 (1978) the Pennsylvania Supreme Court, over two dissents, ruled that ". . . an individual's interest in preventing the disclosure of information revealed in the context of a psychotherapist-patient relationship has deeper roots than the Pennsylvania doctor-patient privilege statute, and that the patient's right to prevent disclosure of such information is constitutionally based." At 425. The Court relied heavily on the right to privacy, citing Roe v. Wade, 410 U.S. 113 (1973), Griswold v. Connecticut, 381 U.S. 479 (1965) and numerous other cases, as well as a series of Pennsylvania constitutional provisions. The case arose in the context of the dispositional stage of juvenile proceeding in which the juvenile court judge sought psychiatric records and testimony concerning inpatient psychiatric treatment received by the juvenile's mother. The Court pointed out that the mother "might have voluntarily submitted to psychiatric examination by a court-appointed psychiatric expert who could evaluate her ability to provide a proper home for her child, or who could, based on the findings of such examination, recommend alternative placement." At 426. The Court regarded the Pennsylvania doctor-patient privilege statute as inadequate in that it applied the privilege only to "communications" which would "blacken the character of the patient." The Court concluded that the definitions of "communications" and of what would "blacken" a patient's character were too narrowly applied to be of value in this case.

Two dissenters rejected the constitutional right to privacy argument, as did one concurring justice who argued that the doctor-patient privilege did cover the situation. One other concurring justice did not give reasons for his concurrence.

A constitutional psychotherapist-patient privilege was rejected in Caesar v. Mountanos, 542 F.2d 1064 (9th Cir. 1976), cert. denied, 430 U.S. 954, 97 S. Ct. 1598, 51 L. Ed. 2d 804 (1977), discussed in Note, 10 Loyola L.A.L. Rev. 695 (1977). See also Note, Psychotherapy and Griswold: Is Confidence a Privilege or Right?, 3 Conn. L. Rev. 599 (1971).

For further privilege cases see Roberts v. Superior Court, 9 Cal. 3d 330, 508 P.2d 309, 107 Cal. Rptr. 309 (1973), noted in 62 Calif. L. Rev. 604 (1974) and Schaffer v. Spicer, 215 N.W.2d 134 (S.D. 1974).

In Allred v. State, 554 P.2d 411 (Ala. 1976) the Alaska Supreme Court established a common law psychotherapist-patient privilege which applies where the communications are made either to a psychiatrist or to a licensed psychologist either in the course of psychotherapeutic treatment or in the course of diagnostic interviews which might reasonably lead to psychotherapeutic treatment.

Page 1088. After Note, add:

Proposed Federal Rule of Evidence 504 was not adopted by Congress.

Page 1092. After 3., Readings on Privilege, add:

A comprehensive treatment of privilege law is Note, Protecting the Confidentiality of Pretrial Psychiatric Disclosures: A Survey of Standards, 51 N.Y.U.L. Rev. 409 (1976). Other worthwhile studies include Note, The Psychotherapist-Patient Privilege: Are Some Patients More Privileged Than Others?, 10 Pac. L.J. 801 (1979), emphasizing the California privilege; Dickens, Legal Protection of Psychiatric Confidentiality, 1 Intl. J. L. & Psychiat. 255 (1978); Note, The Psychotherapist's Privilege, 12 Washburn L. Rev. 297 (1973); Sadoff, Informed Consent, Confidentiality and Privilege in Psychiatry: Practical Applications, 2 Bull. Amer. Acad. Psychiat. & L. 101 (1974); Slovenko, Psychotherapist-Patient Testimonial Privilege: A Picture of Misguided Hope, 23 Cath. U.L. Rev. 649 (1974); March, The Connecticut Confidentiality Statutes, 39 Conn. Med. 108 (1975); and Meyer and Smith, A Crisis in Group Therapy, Ann. Psychol., Aug. 1977, p. 638.

See also Curran, et al., Protection of Privacy and Confidentiality, 182 Science 797 (1973); Dubey, Confidentiality as a Requirement of the Therapist: Technical Necessities for Absolute Privilege in Psychotherapy, 131 Am. J. Psychiat. 1093 (1974); and Slovenko, Psychotherapy and Confidentiality, 24 Clev. St. L. Rev. 375 (1975).

C. CONFIDENTIALITY IN THE PSYCHIATRIST-PATIENT RELATIONSHIP

Page 1097. Before Clark v. Geraci, add:

Access to Patients' Own Records.

A leading case is Gotkin v. Miller, 514 F.2d 125 (2d Cir. 1975), holding that there is no consitutional right of access to psychiatric hospital records. Compare Pyramid Life Ins. Co. v. Masonic Hosp. Assn. of Payne County, 191 F. Supp. 51 (W.D. Okla. 1961), and see Sprankle v. Pennsylvania, 88 Dauph. 372, 94 D. & C. 2d 431 (1967) holding the complaint defective for failing to set forth reasons for seeking access.

Articles include Stein, Furedy, Simonton and Neufer, Patient Access to Medical Records on a Psychiatric Inpatient Unit, 136 Am. J. Psychiat. 327 (1979); Note, Access to Medical and Psychiatric Records: Proposed Legislation, 40 Albany L. Rev. 580 (1976); Kaiser, Patients' Right of Access to Their Own Medical Records: The Need for New Law, 24 Buffalo L. Rev. 317 (1975); and Shenkin,

Giving the Patient His Medical Record: A Proposal to Improve the System, 289 New Engl. J. Med. 688 (1973). An important but as yet unpublished paper is Roth and Meisel, Patient Access to Records— "Tonic" or "Toxin," paper presented to American Psychiatric Association, Annual Meeting, May, 1977.

Pages 1097-1100. After Clark v. Geraci, add:

NOTE: COMPUTERIZED MENTAL HEALTH RECORDS

An excellent discussion of problems arising from the computerization of mental health records is Gobert, Accommodating Patient Rights and Computerized Mental Health Systems, 54 N.C.L. Rev. 153 (1976). See also Furner and Thomason, Physician-Patient Confidences: Legal Effects of Computerization of Records, 31 Ala. Law. 193 (1970). A comprehensive study which presents a great deal of data is Westin, Computers, Health Records, and Citizen Rights (1976).

In Volkman v. Miller, 52 A.D.2d 146, 383 N.Y.S.2d 95 (1976), the New York Appellate Division, Third Department, ruled that the keeping of computerized psychiatric records does not violate right of privacy or doctor-patient privilege.

Page 1100. Replace the *Tarasoff* Case with the following:

TARASOFF v. REGENTS OF THE UNIVERSITY OF CALIFORNIA

131 Cal. Rptr. 14 (1976)

TOBRINER, Justice.

On October 27, 1969, Prosenjit Poddar killed Tatiana Tarasoff. Plaintiffs, Tatiana's parents, allege that two months earlier Poddar confided his intention to kill Tatiana to Dr. Lawrence Moore, a psychologist employed by the Cowell Memorial Hospital at the University of California at Berkeley. They allege that on Moore's request, the campus police briefly detained Poddar, but released him when he appeared rational. They further claim that Dr. Harvey Powelson, Moore's superior, then directed that no further action be taken to detain Poddar. No one warned plaintiffs of Tatiana's peril.

Concluding that these facts set forth causes of action against neither therapists and policemen involved, nor against the Regents of the University of California as their employer, the superior court sustained defendants' demurrers to plaintiffs' second amended complaints without leave to amend. This appeal ensued.

Plaintiffs' complaints predicate liability on two grounds: defendants' failure to warn plaintiffs of the impending danger and their failure to bring about Poddar's confinement pursuant to the Lanterman-Petris-Short Act (Welf. & Inst. Code, §5000ff.) Defendants, in turn, assert that they owed no duty of reasonable care to Tatiana and that they are immune from suit under the California Tort Claims Act of 1963 (Gov. Code, §810ff.).

We shall explain that defendant therapists cannot escape liability merely because Tatiana herself was not their patient. When a therapist determines, or pursuant to the standards of his profession should determine, that his patient presents a serious danger of violence to another, he incurs an obligation to use reasonable care to protect the intended victim against such danger. The discharge of this duty may require the therapist to take one or more of various steps, depending upon the nature of the case. Thus it may call for him to warn the intended victim or others likely to apprise the victim of the danger, to notify the police, or to take whatever others steps are reasonably necessary under the circumstances.

In the case at bar, plaintiffs admit that defendant therapists notified the police, but argue on appeal that the therapists failed to exercise reasonable care to protect Tatiana in that they did not confine Poddar and did not warn Tatiana or others likely to apprise her of the danger. Defendant therapists, however, are public employees. Consequently, to the extent that plaintiffs seek to predicate liability upon the therapists' failure to bring about Poddar's confinement, the therapists can claim immunity under Government Code section 856. No specific statutory provision, however, shields them from liability based upon failure to warn Tatiana or others likely to apprise her of the danger, and Government Code section 820.2 does not protect such failure as an exercise of discretion.

Plaintiffs therefore can amend their complaints to allege that, regardless of the therapists' unsuccessful attempt to confine Poddar, since they knew that Poddar was at large and dangerous, their failure to warn Tatiana or others likely to apprise her of the danger constituted a breach of the therapists' duty to exercise reasonable care to protect Tatiana.

Plaintiffs, however, plead no relationship between Poddar and the police defendants which would impose upon them any duty to Tatiana, and plaintiffs suggest no other basis for such a duty. Plaintiffs have, therefore, failed to show that the trial court erred in sustaining the demurrer of the police defendants without leave to amend.

1. *Plaintiffs' complaints.*

Plaintiffs, Tatiana's mother and father, filed separate but virtually identical second amended complaints. The issue before us on this appeal is whether those complaints now state, or can be amended to state, causes of action against defendants. We therefore begin by setting forth the pertinent allegations of the complaints.

Plaintiffs' first cause of action, entitled "Failure to Detain a Dangerous Patient," alleges that on August 20, 1969, Poddar was a voluntary outpatient receiving therapy at Cowell Memorial Hospital. Poddar informed Moore, his therapist, that he was going to kill an unnamed girl, readily identifiable as Tatiana, when she returned home from spending the summer in Brazil. Moore, with the concurrence of Dr. Gold, who had initially examined Poddar, and Dr. Yandell, assistant to the director of the department of psychiatry, decided that Poddar should be committed for observation in a mental hospital. Moore orally notified Officers Atkinson and Teel of the campus police that he would request commitment. He then sent a letter to Police Chief William Beall requesting the assistance of the police department in securing Poddar's confinement.

Officers Atkinson, Brownrigg, and Halleran took Poddar into custody, but, satisfied that Poddar was rational, released him on his promise to stay away from Tatiana. Powelson, director of the department of psychiatry at Cowell Memorial Hospital, then asked the police to return Moore's letter, directed that all copies of the letter and notes that Moore had taken as therapist be destroyed, and "ordered no action to place Prosenjit Poddar in 72-hour treatment and evaluation facility."

Plaintiffs' second cause of action, entitled "Failure to Warn On a Dangerous Patient," incorporates the allegations of the first cause of action, but adds the assertion that defendants negligently permitted Poddar to be released from police custody without "notifying the parents of Tatiana Tarasoff that their daughter was in grave danger from Posenjit Poddar." Poddar persuaded Tatiana's brother to share an apartment with him near Tatiana's residence; shortly after her return from Brazil, Poddar went to her residence and killed her.

Plaintiffs' third cause of action, entitled "Abandonment of a Dangerous Patient," seeks $10,000 punitive damages against defendant Powelson. Incorporating the crucial allegations of the first cause of action, plaintiffs charge that Powelson "did the things herein alleged with intent to abandon a dangerous patient, and said acts were done maliciously and oppressively."

Plaintiffs' fourth cause of action, for "Breach of Primary Duty to Patient and the Public," states essentially the same allegations as the first cause of action, but seeks to characterize defendants' conduct as a breach of duty to safeguard their patient and the public. Since such conclusory labels add nothing to the factual allegations of the complaint, the first and fourth causes of action are legally indistinguishable.

As we explain in part 4 of this opinion, plaintiffs' first and fourth causes of action, which seek to predicate liability upon the defendants' failure to bring about Poddar's confinement, are barred by governmental immunity. Plaintiffs' third cause of action succumbs to the decisions precluding exemplary damages in a wrongful death action. (See part 6 of this opinion.) We direct our attention, therefore, to the issue of whether plaintiffs' second cause of action can be amended to state a basis for recovery.

2. *Plaintiffs can state a cause of action against defendant therapists for negligent failure to protect Tatiana.*

The second cause of action can be amended to allege that Tatiana's death proximately resulted from defendants' negligent failure to warn Tatiana or others likely to apprise her of her danger. Plaintiffs contend that as amended, such allegations of negligence and proximate causation, with resulting damages, establish a cause of action. Defendants, however, contend that in the circumstances of the present case they owed no duty of care to Tatiana or her parents and that, in the absence of such duty, they were free to act in careless disregard of Tatiana's life and safety.

In analyzing this issue, we bear in mind that legal duties are not discoverable facts of nature, but merely conclusory expressions that, in cases of a particular type, liability should be imposed for damage done. As stated in *Dillon v. Legg* (1968) 68 Cal. 2d 728, 734, 69 Cal. Rptr. 72, 76, 441 P.2d 912, 916: "The assertion that liability must . . . be denied because defendant bears no 'duty' to plaintiff 'begs the essential question—whether the plaintiff's interests are entitled to legal protection against the defendant's conduct. . . . [Duty] is not sacrosanct in itself, but only an expression of the sum total of those considerations of policy which lead the law to say that the particular plaintiff is entitled to protection.' (Prosser, Law of Torts [3d ed. 1964] at pp. 332-333.)"

In the landmark case of *Rowland v. Christian* (1968) 69 Cal. 2d 108, 70 Cal. Rptr. 97, 443 P.2d 561, Justice Peters recognized that liability should be imposed "for an injury occasioned to another by his want of ordinary care or skill" as expressed in section 1714 of the Civil Code. Thus, Justice Peters, quoting from *Heaven v. Pender* (1883), 11 Q.B.D. 503, 509 stated: "'whenever one person is by circumstances placed in such a position with regard to another . . . that if he did not use ordinary care and skill in his own conduct . . . he would cause danger of injury to the person or property of the other, a duty arises to use ordinary care and skill to avoid such danger.'"

We depart from "this fundamental principle" only upon the "balancing of a number of considerations;" major ones "are the foreseeability of harm to the plaintiff, the degree of certainty that the plaintiff suffered injury, the closeness of the connection between the defendant's conduct and the injury suffered, the moral blame attached to the defendant's conduct, the policy of preventing future harm, the extent of the burden to the defendant and consequences to the community of imposing a duty to exercise care with resulting liability for breach, and the availability, cost and prevalence of insurance for the risk involved."

The most important of these considerations in establishing duty is foreseeability. As a general principle, a "defendant owes a duty of care to all persons who are foreseeably endangered by his conduct, with respect to all risks which make the conduct unreasonably dangerous." As we shall explain, however, when the avoidance of foreseeable harm requires a defendant to control the conduct of another person, or to warn of such conduct, the common law has traditionally imposed liability only if the defendant bears some special relationship to the dangerous person or to the potential victim. Since the relationship between a therapist and his patient satisfies this requirement, we need not here decide whether foreseeability alone is sufficient to create a duty to exercise reasonable care to protect a potential victim of another's conduct.

Although, as we have stated above, under the common law, as a general rule, one person owed no duty to control the conduct of another, nor to warn those endangered by such conduct, the courts have carved out an exception to this rule in cases in which the defendant stands in some special relationship to either the person whose conduct needs to be controlled or in a relationship to the foreseeable victim of that conduct. Applying this exception to the present case, we note that a relationship of defendant therapists to either Tatiana or Poddar will suffice to establish a duty of care; as explained in section 315 of the Restatement Second of Torts, a duty of care may arise from either "(a) a special relation ... between the actor and the third person which imposes a duty upon the actor to control the third person's conduct, or (b) a special relation . . . between the actor and the other which gives to the other a right of protection."

Although plaintiffs' pleadings assert no special relation between Tatiana and defendant therapists, they establish as between Poddar and defendant therapists the special relation that arises between a patient and his doctor or psychotherapist. Such a relationship may support affirmative duties for the benefit of third persons. Thus, for example, a hospital must exercise reasonable care to control the behavior of a patient which may endanger other persons. A doctor must also warn a patient if the patient's condition or medication renders certain conduct, such as driving a car, dangerous to others.

Although the California decisions that recognize this duty have involved cases in which the defendant stood in a special relationship *both* to the victim and to the person whose conduct created the danger, we do not think that the duty should logically be constricted to such situations. Decisions of other jurisdictions hold that the single relationship of a doctor to his patient is sufficient to support the duty to exercise reasonable care to protect others against dangers emanating from the patient's illness. The courts hold that a doctor is liable to persons infected by his patient if he negligently fails to diagnose a contagious disease, or, having diagnosed the illness, fails to warn members of the patient's family.

Since it involved a dangerous mental patient, the decision in *Merchants Natl. Bank & Trust Co. of Fargo v. United States* (D.N.D. 1967), 272 F. Supp. 409 comes closer to the issue. The Veterans Administration arranged for the patient to work on a local farm, but did not inform the farmer of the man's background. The farmer consequently permitted the patient to come and go freely during nonworking hours; the patient borrowed a car, drove to his wife's residence and killed her. Notwithstanding the lack of any "special relationship" between the Veterans Administration and the wife, the court found the Veterans Administration liable for the wrongful death of the wife.

In their summary of the relevant rulings Fleming and Maximov conclude that the "case law should dispel any notion that to impose on the therapists a duty to take precautions for the safety of persons threatened by a patient, where due care so requires, is in any way opposed to contemporary ground rules on the duty relationship. On the contrary, there now seems to be sufficient authority to support the conclusion that by entering into a doctor-patient relationship the therapist becomes sufficiently involved to assume some responsibility for the safety, not only of the patient himself, but also of any third person whom the doctor knows to be threatened by the patient." (Fleming and Maximov, *The Patient or His Victim: The Therapist's Dilemma* (1974), 62 Cal. L. Rev. 1025, 1030.)

Defendants contend, however, that imposition of a duty to exercise reasonable care to protect third persons is unworkable because therapists cannot accurately predict whether or not a patient will resort to violence. In support of this argument amicus representing the American Psychiatric Association and other professional societies cites numerous articles which indicate that therapists, in the present state of the art, are unable reliably to predict violent acts; their forecasts, amicus claims, tend consistently to overpredict violence, and indeed are more often wrong than right. Since predictions of violence are often erroneous, amicus concludes, the courts should not render rulings that predicate the liability of therapists upon the validity of such predictions.

The role of the psychiatrist, who is indeed a practitioner of medicine, and that of the psychologist who performs an allied function, are like that of the physician who must conform to the standards of the profession and who must often make diagnoses and predictions based upon such evaluations. Thus the judgment of the therapist in diagnosing emotional disorders and in predicting whether a patient presents a serious danger of violence is comparable to the judgment which doctors and professionals must regularly render under accepted rules of responsibility.

We recognize the difficulty that a therapist encounters in attempting to forecast whether a patient presents a serious danger of violence. Obviously we do not require that the therapist, in making that determination, render a perfect performance; the therapist need only exercise "that reasonable degree of skill, knowledge, and care ordinarily possessed and exercised by members of [that professional specialty] under similar circumstances." Within the broad range of reasonable practice and treatment in which professional opinion and judgment may differ, the therapist is free to exercise his or her own best judgment without liability; proof, aided by hindsight, that he or she judged wrongly is insufficient to establish negligence.

In the instant case, however, the pleadings do not raise any question as to failure of defendant therapists to predict that Poddar presented a serious danger of violence. On the contrary, the present complaints allege that defendant therapists did in fact predict that Poddar would kill, but were negligent in failing to warn.

Amicus contends, however, that even when a therapist does in fact predict that a patient poses a serious danger of violence to others, the therapist should be absolved of any responsibility for failing to act to protect the potential victim. In our view, however, once a therapist does in fact determine, or under applicable professional standards reasonably should have determined, that a patient poses a serious danger of violence to others, he bears a duty to exercise reasonable care to protect the foreseeable victim of that danger. While the discharge of this duty of due care will necessarily vary with the facts of each case, in each instance the adequacy of the therapist's conduct must be measured against the traditional negligence standard of the rendition of reasonable care under the circumstances. As explained in Fleming and Maximov, *The Patient or His Victim: The Therapist's Dilemma* (1974), 62 Cal. L. Rev. 1025, 1067: ". . . the ultimate question of resolving the tension between the conflicting interests of patient and potential victim is one of social policy, not professional expertise. . . . In sum, the therapist owes a legal duty not only to his patient, but also to his patient's would-be victim and is subject in both respects to scrutiny by judge and jury."

Contrary to the assertion of amicus, this conclusion is not inconsistent with our recent decision in *People v. Burnick, supra,* 14 Cal. 3d 306, 121 Cal. Rptr. 488, 535 P.2d 352. Taking note of the uncertain character of therapeutic prediction, we held in *Burnick* that a person cannot be committed as a mentally disordered sex offender unless found to be such by proof beyond a reasonable doubt. (14 Cal. 3d at p. 328, 121 Cal. Rptr. 488, 535 P.2d 352.) The issue in the present context, however, is not whether the patient should be incarcerated, but whether the therapist should take any steps at all to protect the threatened victim; some of the alternatives open to the therapist, such as warning the victim, will not result in the drastic consequences of depriving the patient of his liberty. Weighing the uncertain and conjectural character of the alleged damage done the patient by such a warning against the peril to the victim's life, we conclude that professional inaccuracy in predicting violence cannot negate the therapist's duty to protect the threatened victim.

The risk that unnecessary warnings may be given is a reasonable price to pay for the lives of possible victims that may be saved. We would hesitate to hold that the therapist who is aware that his patient expects to attempt to assassinate the President of the United

States would not be obligated to warn the authorities because the therapist cannot predict with accuracy that his patient will commit the crime.

Defendants further argue that free and open communication is essential to psychotherapy; that "Unless a patient . . . is assured that . . . information [revealed by him] can and will be held in utmost confidence, he will be reluctant to make the full disclosure upon which diagnosis and treatment . . . depends." The giving of a warning, defendants contend, constitutes a breach of trust which entails the revelation of confidential communications.

We recognize the public interest in supporting effective treatment of mental illness and in protecting the rights of patients to privacy, and the consequent public importance of safeguarding the confidential character of psychotherapeutic communication. Against this interest, however, we must weigh the public interest in safety from violent assault. The Legislature has undertaken the difficult task of balancing the countervailing concerns. In Evidence Code section 1014, it established a broad rule of privilege to protect confidential communications between patient and psychotherapist. In Evidence Code section 1024, the Legislature created a specific and limited exception to the psychotherapist-patient privilege: "There is no privilege . . . if the psychotherapist has reasonable cause to believe that the patient is in such mental or emotional condition as to be dangerous to himself or to the person or property of another and that disclosure of the communication is necessary to prevent the threatened danger."

We realize that the open and confidential character of psychotherapeutic dialogue encourages patients to express threats of violence, few of which are ever executed. Certainly a therapist should not be encouraged routinely to reveal such threats; such disclosures could seriously disrupt the patient's relationship with his therapist and with the persons threatened. To the contrary, the therapist's obligations to his patient require that he not disclose a confidence unless such disclosure is necessary to avert danger to others, and even then that he do so discreetly, and in a fashion that would preserve the privacy of his patient to the fullest extent compatible with the prevention of the threatened danger. (See Fleming and Maximov, *The Patient or His Victim: The Therapist's Dilemma* (1974) 62 Cal. L. Rev. 1025, 1065-1066.)

The revelation of a communication under the above circumstances is not a breach of trust or a violation of professional ethics; as stated in the Principles of Medical Ethics of the American Medical Association (1957), section 9: "A physician may not reveal the confidence entrusted to him in the course of medical attendance ... *unless he is required to do so by law or unless it becomes necessary in order to protect the welfare of the individual or of the community.*" (Emphasis added.) We conclude that the public policy favoring protection of the confidential character of patient-psychotherapist communications must yield to the extent to which disclosure is essential to avert danger to others. The protective privilege ends where the public peril begins.

Our current crowded and computerized society compels the interdependence of its members. In this risk-infested society we can hardly tolerate the further exposure to danger that would result from a concealed knowledge of the therapist that his patient was lethal. If the exercise of reasonable care to protect the threatened victim requires the therapist to warn the endangered party or those who can reasonably be expected to notify him, we see no sufficient societal interest that would protect and justify concealment. The containment of such risks lies in the public interest. For the foregoing reasons, we find that plaintiffs' complaints can be amended to state a cause of action against defendants Moore, Powelson, Gold, and Yandell and against the Regents as their employer, for breach of a duty to exercise reasonable care to protect Tatiana.

Finally, we reject the contention of the dissent that the provisions of the Lanterman-Petris-Short Act which govern the release of confidential information prevented defendant therapists from warning Tatiana. The dissent's contention rests on the assertion that Dr. Moore's letter to the campus police constituted an "application in writing" within the meaning of Welfare and Institutions Code section 5150, and thus initiates proceedings under the Lanterman-Petris-Short Act. A closer look at the terms of section 5150, however, will demonstrate that it is inapplicable to the present case.

Section 5150 refers to a written application only by a professional person who is "[a] member of the attending staff ... of an evaluation facility designated by the county," or who is himself "designated by the county" as one authorized to take a person into custody and place him in a facility designated by the county and approved by the State Department of Mental Hygiene. The complaint fails specifically to allege that Dr. Moore was so empowered. Dr. Moore and the Regents cannot rely upon any interference to the contrary that might be drawn from plaintiff's allegation that Dr. Moore intended to "assign" a "detention" on Poddar; both Dr. Moore and the Regents have expressly conceded that neither Cowell

Memorial Hospital nor any member of its staff has even been designated by the County of Alameda to institute involuntary commitment proceedings pursuant to section 5150.

Furthermore, the provisions of the Lanterman-Petris-Short Act defining a therapist's duty to withhold confidential information are expressly limited to "information and records *obtained in the course of providing services* under Division 5 (commencing with Section 5000), Division 6 (commencing with Section 6000), or Division 7 (commencing with Section 7000)" of the Welfare and Institutions Code (Welf. and Inst. Code, §5328). (Emphasis added.) Divisions 5, 6 and 7 describe a variety of programs for treatment of the mentally ill or retarded. The pleadings at issue on this appeal, however, state no facts showing that the psychotherapy provided to Poddar by the Cowell Memorial Hospital falls under any of these programs. We therefore conclude that the Lanterman-Petris-Short Act does not govern the release of information acquired by Moore during the course of rendition of those services.

Neither can we adopt the dissent's suggestion that we import wholesale the detailed provisions of the Lanterman-Petris-Short Act regulating the disclosure of confidential information and apply them to disclosure of information *not governed by the act.* Since the Legislature did not extend the act to control all disclosures of confidential matter by a therapist, we must infer that the Legislature did not relieve the courts of their obligation to define by reference to the principles of the common law the obligation of the therapist in those situations not governed by the act.

Turning now to the police defendants, we conclude that they do not have any such special relationship to either Tatiana or to Poddar sufficient to impose upon such defendants a duty to warn respecting Poddar's violent intentions. Plaintiffs suggest no theory, and plead no facts that give rise to any duty to warn on the part of the police defendants absent such a special relationship. They have thus failed to demonstrate that the trial court erred in denying leave to amend as to the police defendants.

3. *Defendant therapists are not immune from liability for failure to warn.*

We address the issue of whether defendant therapists are protected by governmental immunity for having failed to warn Tatiana or those who reasonably could have been expected to notify her of her peril. We postulate our analysis on section 820.2 of the Government Code. That provision declares, with exceptions not applicable here, that "a public employee is not liable for an injury resulting from his act or omission where the act or omission was the result of the exercise of the discretion vested in him, whether or not such discretion [was] abused."

Noting that virtually every public act admits of some element of discretion, we drew the line in *Johnson v. State of California* (1968), 69 Cal. 2d 782, 73 Cal. Rptr. 240, 447 P.2d 352, between discretionary policy decisions which enjoy statutory immunity and ministerial administrative acts which do not. We concluded that section 820.2 affords immunity only for "*basic* policy decisions." (Emphasis added.)

We also observed that if courts did not respect this statutory immunity, they would find themselves "in the unseemly position of determining the propriety of decisions expressly entrusted to a coordinate branch of government." It therefore is necessary, we concluded, to "isolate those areas of quasi-legislative policy-making which are sufficiently sensitive to justify a blanket rule that courts will not entertain a tort action alleging that careless conduct contributed to the governmental decision." After careful analysis we rejected, in Johnson, other rationales commonly advanced to support governmental immunity and concluded that the immunity's scope should be no greater than is required to give legislative and executive policymakers sufficient breathing space in which to perform their vital policymaking functions.

Relying on Johnson, we conclude that defendant therapists in the present case are not immune from liability for their failure to warn of Tatiana's peril. Johnson held that a parole officer's determination whether to warn an adult couple that their prospective foster child had a background of violence "present[ed] no . . . reasons for immunity," was "at the lowest, ministerial rung of official action," and indeed constituted "a classic case for the imposition of tort liability." Although defendants in Johnson argued that the decision whether to inform the foster parents of the child's background required the exercise of considerable judgmental skills, we concluded that the state was not immune from liability for the parole officer's failure to warn because such a decision did not rise to the level of a "basic policy decision."

We also noted in Johnson that federal courts have consistently categorized failures to warn of latent dangers as falling outside the scope of discretionary omissions immunized by the Federal Tort Claims Act.

We conclude, therefore, that the therapist defendants' failure to warn Tatiana or those who reasonably could have been expected to notify her of her peril does not fall within the absolute protection afforded by section 820.2 of the Government Code. We emphasize that our conclusion does not raise the specter of therapists employed by the government indiscriminately being held liable for damage despite their exercise of sound professional judgment. We require of publicly employed therapists only that quantum of care which the common law requires of private therapists. The imposition of liability in those rare cases in which a public employee falls short of this standard does not contravene the language or purpose of Government Code section 820.2.

4. *Defendant therapists are immune from liability for failing to confine Poddar.*

We sustain defendant therapists' contention that Government Code section 856 insulates them from liability under plaintiffs' first and fourth causes of action for failing to confine Poddar. Section 856 affords public entities and their employees absolute protection from liability for "any injury resulting from determining in accordance with any applicable enactment . . . whether to confine a person for mental illness." Since this section refers to a determination to confine "in accordance with any applicable enactment," plaintiffs suggest that the immunity is limited to persons designated under Welfare and Institutions Code section 5150 as authorized finally to adjudicate a patient's confinement. Defendant therapists, plaintiffs point out, are not among the persons designated under section 5150.

The language and legislative history of section 856, however, suggest a far broader immunity. In 1963, when section 856 was enacted, the Legislature had not established the statutory structure of the Lanterman-Petris-Short Act. Former Welfare and Institutions Code section 5050.3 (renumbered as Welf. & Inst. Code §5880; repealed July 1, 1969) which resembled present section 5150, authorized emergency detention at the behest only of peace officers, health officers, county physicians, or assistant county physicians; former section 5047 (renumbered as Welf. & Inst. Code §5551; repealed July 1, 1969), however, authorized a petition seeking commitment by any person, including the "physician attending the patient." The Legislature did not refer in section 856 only to those persons authorized to institute emergency proceedings under section 5050.3; it broadly extended immunity to all employees who acted in accord with "any applicable enactment," thus granting immunity not only to persons who are empowered to confine, but also to those authorized to request or recommend confinement.

The Lanterman-Petris-Short Act, in its extensive revision of the procedures for commitment of the mentally ill, eliminated any specific statutory reference to petitions by treating physicians, but it did not limit the authority of a therapist in government employ to request, recommend or initiate actions which may lead to commitment of his patient under the act. We believe that the language of section 856, which refers to any action in the course of employment and in accordance with any applicable enactment, protects the therapist who must undertake this delicate and difficult task. (See Fleming & Maximov, *The Patient or His Victim: The Therapist's Dilemma* (1974) 62 Cal. L. Rev. 1025, 1064.) Thus the scope of the immunity extends not only to the final determination to confine or not to confine the person for mental illness, but to all determinations involved in the process of commitment. (Cf. *Hernandez v. State of California* (1970) 11 Cal. App. 3d 895, 899-900, 90 Cal. Rptr. 205.)

Turning first to Dr. Powelson's status with respect to section 856, we observe that the actions attributed to him by plaintiffs' complaints fall squarely within the protections furnished by that provision. Plaintiffs allege Powelson ordered that no actions leading to Poddar's detention be taken. This conduct reflected Powelson's determination not to seek Poddar's confinement and thus falls within the statutory immunity.

Section 856 also insulates Dr. Moore for his conduct respecting confinement, although the analysis in his case is a bit more subtle. Clearly, Moore's decision that Poddar be confined was not a proximate cause of Tatiana's death, for indeed if Moore's efforts to bring about Poddar's confinement had been successful, Tatiana might still be alive today. Rather, any confinement claim against Moore must rest upon Moore's failure to overcome Powelson's decision and actions opposing confinement.

Such a claim, based as it necessarily would be, upon a subordinate's failure to prevail over his superior, obviously would derive from a rather onerous duty. Whether to impose such a duty we need not decide, however, since we can confine our analysis to the question whether Moore's failure to overcome Powelson's decision realistically falls within the protection afforded by section 856. Based upon the allegations before us, we conclude that Moore's conduct is protected.

Plaintiffs' complaints imply that Moore acquiesced in Powelson's countermand of Moore's confinement recommendation. Such acquiescence is functionally equivalent to determining not to seek Poddar's confinement and thus merits protection under section

856. At this stage we are unaware, of course, precisely how Moore responded to Powelson's actions; he may have debated the confinement issue with Powelson, for example, or taken no initiative whatsoever, perhaps because he respected Powelson's judgment, feared for his future at the hospital, or simply recognized that the proverbial handwriting was on the wall. None of these possibilities constitutes, however, the type of careless or wrongful behavior subsequent to a decision respecting confinement which is stripped of protection by the exception in section 856. Rather each is in the nature of a decision not to continue to press for Poddar's confinement. No language in plaintiffs' original or amended complaints suggests that Moore determined to fight Powelson, but failed successfully to do so, due to negligent or otherwise wrongful acts or omissions. Under the circumstances, we conclude that plaintiffs' second amended complaints allege facts which trigger immunity for Dr. Moore under section 856.

5. *Defendant police officers are immune from liability for failing to confine Poddar in their custody.*

Confronting, finally, the question whether the defendant police officers are immune from liability for releasing Poddar after his brief confinement, we conclude that they are. The source of their immunity is section 5154 of the Welfare and Institutions Code, which declares that: "[t]he professional person in charge of the facility providing 72-hour treatment and evaluation, his designee, *and the peace officer responsible for the detainment of the person* shall not be held civilly or criminally liable for any action by a person released at or before the end of 72 hours. . . ." (Emphasis added.)

Although defendant police officers technically were not "peace officers" as contemplated by the Welfare and Institutions Code, plaintiffs' assertion that the officers incurred liability by failing to continue Poddar's confinement clearly contemplates that the officers were "responsible for the detainment of [Poddar]." We could not impose a duty upon the officers to keep Poddar confined yet deny them the protection furnished by a state immunizing those "responsible for . . . [confinement]." Because plaintiffs would have us treat defendant officers as persons who were capable of performing the functions of the "peace officers" contemplated by the Welfare and Institutions Code, we must accord defendant officers the protections which that code prescribed for such "peace officers."

6. *Plaintiffs' complaints state no cause of action for exemplary damages.*

Plaintiff's third cause of action seeks punitive damages against defendant Powelson. The California statutes and decisions, however, have been interpreted to bar the recovery of punitive damages in a wrongful death action.

7. Conclusion.

For the reasons stated, we conclude that plaintiffs can amend their complaints to state a cause of action against defendant therapists by asserting that the therapists in fact determined that Poddar presented a serious danger of violence to Tatiana, or pursuant to the standards of their profession should have so determined, but nevertheless failed to exercise reasonable care to protect her from that danger. To the extent, however, that plaintiffs base their claim that defendant therapists breached that duty because they failed to procure Poddar's confinement, the therapists find immunity in Government Code section 856. Further, as to the police defendants we conclude that plaintiffs have failed to show that the trial court erred in sustaining their demurrer without leave to amend.

The judgment of the superior court in favor of defendants Atkinson, Beall, Brownrigg, Hallernan, and Teel is affirmed. The judgment of the superior court in favor of defendants Gold, Moore, Powelson, Yandell, and the Regents of the University of California is reversed, and the cause remanded for further proceedings consistent with the views expressed herein.

MOSK, Justice (concurring and dissenting).

I concur in the result in this instance only because the complaints allege that defendant therapists did in fact predict that Poddar would kill and were therefore negligent in failing to warn of that danger. Thus the issue here is very narrow: we are not concerned with whether the therapists, pursuant to the standards of their profession, "should have" predicted potential violence; they allegedly did so in actuality. Under these limited circumstances I agree that a cause of action can be stated.

Whether plaintiffs can ultimately prevail is problematical at best. As the complaints admit, the therapists did notify the police that Poddar was planning to kill a girl identifiable as Tatiana. While I doubt that more should be required, this issue may be raised in defense and its determination is a question of fact.

I cannot concur, however, in the majority's rule that a therapist may be held liable for failing to predict his patient's tendency to violence if other practitioners, pursuant to the "standards of the profession," would have done so. The question is, what standards? Defendants and a responsible amicus curiae, supported by an impressive body of literature discussed at length in our recent opinion in *People v. Burnick* (1975), 14 Cal. 3d 306, 121 Cal. Rptr. 488, 535 P.2d 352, demonstrate that psychiatric predictions of violence are inherently unreliable.

In Burnick, at pages 325-326, 121 Cal. Rptr. at page 501, 535 P.2d at page 365, we observed: "In the light of recent studies it is no longer heresy to question the reliability of psychiatric predictions. Psychiatrists themselves would be the first to admit that however desirable an infallible crystal ball might be, it is not among the tools of their profession. It must be conceded that psychiatrists still experience considerable difficulty in confidently and accurately diagnosing mental illness. Yet those difficulties are multipled manyfold when psychiatrists venture from diagnosis to prognosis and undertake to predict the consequences of such illness: '"A diagnosis of mental illness tells us nothing about whether the person so diagnosed is or is not dangerous. Some mental patients are dangerous, some are not. Perhaps the psychiatrist is an expert at deciding whether a person is mentally ill, but is he an expert at predicting which of the persons so diagnosed are dangerous? Sane people, too, are dangerous, and it may legitimately be inquired whether there is anything in the education, training or experience of psychiatrists which renders them particularly adept at predicting dangerous behavior. Predictions of dangerous behavior, no matter who makes them, are incredibly inaccurate, and there is a growing consensus that psychiatrists are not uniquely qualified to predict dangerous behavior and are, in fact, less accurate in their predictions than other professionals.'" (*Murel v. Baltimore City Criminal Court* (1972) . . . 407 U.S. 355, 364-365, fn. 2, 92 S. Ct. 2091, 32 L. Ed. 2d 791, 796-797 (Douglas, J., dissenting from dismissal of certiorari).)" (Fns. omitted.) (See also authorities cited at p. 327 and fn. 18 of 14 Cal. 3d, 121 Cal. Rptr. 488, 535 P.2d 352.)

The majority confidently claim their opinion is not offensive to Burnick, on the stated ground that Burnick involved proceedings to commit an alleged mentally disordered sex offender and this case does not. I am not so sanguine about the distinction. Obviously the two cases are not factually identical, but the similarity in issues is striking: in Burnick we were likewise called upon to appraise the ability of psychiatrists to predict dangerousness, and while we declined to bar all such testimony (*id.* at pp. 327-328, 121 Cal. Rptr. 488, 535 P.2d 352) we found it so inherently untrustworthy that we would permit confinement even in a so-called civil proceeding only upon proof beyond a reasonable doubt.

I would restructure the rule designed by the majority to eliminate all reference to conformity to standards of the profession in predicting violence. If a psychiatrist does in fact predict violence, then a duty to warn arises. The majority's expansion of that rule will take us from the world of reality into the wonderland of clairvoyance.

CLARK, Justice (dissenting).

Until today's majority opinion, both legal and medical authorities have agreed that confidentiality is essential to effectively treat the mentally ill, and that imposing a duty on doctors to disclose patient threats to potential victims would greatly impair treatment. Further, recognizing that effective treatment and society's safety are necessarily intertwined, the Legislature has already decided effective and confidential treatment is preferred over imposition of a duty to warn.

The issue whether effective treatment for the mentally ill should be sacrificed to a system of warnings is, in my opinion, properly one for the Legislature, and we are bound by its judgment. Moreover, even in the absence of clear legislative direction, we must reach the same conclusion because imposing the majority's new duty is certain to result in a net increase in violence.

The majority rejects the balance achieved by the Legislature's Lanterman-Petris-Short Act. (Welf. & Inst. Code, §5000 et seq., hereafter the act.) In addition, the majority fails to recognize that, even absent the act, overwhelming policy considerations mandate against sacrificing fundamental patient interests without gaining a corresponding increase in public benefit.

STATUTORY PROVISIONS

Although the parties have touched only briefly on the nondisclosure provisions of the act, amici have pointed out their importance. The instant case arising after ruling on demurrer, the parties must confront the act's provisions in the trial court. In these circumstances the parties' failure to fully meet the provisions of the act would not justify this court's refusal to discuss and apply the law.

Having a grave impact on future treatment of the mentally ill in our state, the majority opinion clearly transcends the interests of the immediate parties and must discuss all applicable law. It abdicates judicial responsibility to refuse to recognize the clear legislative policy reflected in the act.

Effective 1 July 1969, the Legislature created a comprehensive statutory resolution of the rights and duties of both the mentally infirm and those charged with their care and treatment. The act's purposes include ending inappropriate commitment, providing prompt care, protecting public safety, and safeguarding personal rights. (§5001.) The act applies to both voluntary and involuntary commitment, and to both public and private institutions; it details legal procedure for commitment; it enumerates the legal and civil rights of persons committed, and it spells out the duties, liabilities and rights of the psychotherapist. Thus the act clearly evinces the Legislature's weighing of the countervailing concerns presently before us—when a patient has threatened a third person during psychiatric treatment.

Reflecting legislative recognition that disclosing confidences impairs effective treatment of the mentally ill, and thus is contrary to the best interests of society, the act establishes the therapist's duty to not disclose. Section 5328 provides in part that "[a]ll information and records obtained in the course of providing services . . . to either voluntary or involuntary recipients of services *shall* be confidential." (Italics added.) Further, a patient may enjoin disclosure in violation of statute and may recover the greater of $500 or three times the amount of actual damage for unlawful disclosure. (§5330.)

However, recognizing that some private and public interests must override the patient's, the Legislature established several limited exceptions to confidentiality. The limited nature of these exceptions and the legislative concern that disclosure might impair treatment, thereby harming both patient and society, are shown by section 5328.1. The section provides that a therapist may disclose "to a member of the family of a patient the information that the patient is presently a patient in the facility or that the patient is seriously physically ill . . . if the professional person in charge of the facility determines that the release of such information is in the best interest of the patient." Thus, disclosing even the fact of treatment is severely limited.

As originally enacted the act contained no provision allowing the therapist to warn anyone of a patient's threat. In 1970, however, the act was amended to permit disclosure in two limited circumstances. Section 5328 was amended, in subdivision (g), to allow disclosure *"[t]o governmental law enforcement agencies* as needed for the protection of federal and state elective constitutional officers and their families." (Italics added.) In addition, section 5328.3 was added to provide that when "necessary for the protection of the patient or *others* due to the patient's disappearance from, without prior notice to, a designated facility and his whereabouts is unknown, notice of such disappearance *may* be made to *relatives and governmental law enforcement agencies* designated by the physician in charge of the patient or the professional person in charge of the facility or his designee." (Italics added.)

Obviously neither exception to the confidentiality requirement is applicable to the instant case.

Not only has the Legislature specifically dealt with disclosure and warning, but it also has dealt with therapist and police officer liability for acts of the patient. The Legislature has provided that the therapist and the officer shall not be liable for prematurely releasing the patient. (§§5151, 5154, 5173, 5278, 5305, 5306.)

Ignoring the act's detailed provisions, the majority has chosen to focus on the "dangerous patient exception" to the psychotherapist-patient privilege in Evidence Code sections 1014, 1024 as indicating that "the Legislature has undertaken the difficult task of balancing the countervailing concerns." (Ante, p. —, p. 26 of 131 Cal. Rptr., p. — of — P.2d.) However, this conclusion is erroneous. The majority fails to appreciate that when disclosure is permitted in an evidentiary hearing, a fourth interest comes into play—the court's concern in judicial supervision. Because they are necessary to the administration of justice, disclosures to the courts are excepted from the nondisclosure requirement by section 5328, subdivision (f). However, this case does not involve a court disclosure. Subdivision (f) and the Evidence Code sections relied on by the majority are clearly inapposite.

The provisions of the act are applicable here. Section 5328 (see fn. 2, *supra*) provides, *"All information and records obtained in the course of providing services under Division 5 . . . shall be confidential."* (Italics added.) Dr. Moore's letter describing Poddar's mental condition for purposes of obtaining 72-hour commitment was undisputedly a transmittal of information designed to invoke application of division 5. As such it constituted information obtained in providing services under division 5. This is true regardless of whether Dr. Moore has been designated a professional person by the County of Alameda. Although section 5150 provides that commitment for 72 hours' evaluation shall be based on a statement by a peace officer or person designated by the county, section 5328 prohibits disclosure of all information, not just disclosure of the committing statement or disclosure by persons designated by the county. In addition, section 5330 gives the patient a cause of action for disclosure of confidential information by "an individual" rather than the persons enumerated in section 5150.

Moreover, it appears from the allegations of the complaint that

Dr. Moore is in fact a person designated by the county under section 5150. The complaint alleges that "On or about August 20, 1969, defendant Dr. Moore notified Officers Atkinson and Teel, he would give the campus police a letter of diagnosis on Prosenjit Poddar, so the campus police could pick up Poddar and take him to Herrick Hospital in Berkeley where Dr. Moore would assign a 72-hour Emergency Psychiatric Detention on Prosenjit Poddar." Since there is no allegation that Dr. Moore was not authorized to sign the document, it must be concluded that under the allegations of the complaint he was authorized and thus a professional person designated by the county.

Whether we rely on the facts as stated in the complaint that Dr. Moore is a designated person under section 5150 or on the strict prohibitions of section 5328 prohibiting disclosure of "all information," the imposition of a duty to warn by the majority flies directly in the face of the Lanterman-Petris-Short Act.

Under the act, there can be no liability for Poddar's premature release. It is likewise clear there exists no duty to warn. Under section 5328, the therapists were under a duty to not disclose, and no exception to that duty is applicable here. Establishing a duty to warn on the basis of general tort principles imposes a Draconian dilemma on therapists—either violate the act thereby incurring the attendant statutory penalties, or ignore the majority's duty to warn thereby incurring potential civil liability. I am unable to assent to such.

If the majority feels that it must impose such a dilemma, then it has an obligation to specifically enumerate the circumstances under which the Lanterman-Petris-Short Act applies as opposed to the circumstances when "general tort principles" will govern. The majority's failure to perform this obligation—leaving to the therapist the subtle questions as to when each opposing rule applies—is manifestly unfair.

DUTY TO DISCLOSE IN THE ABSENCE OF CONTROLLING STATUTORY PROVISION

Even assuming the act's provisions are applicable only to conduct occurring after commitment, and not to prior conduct, the act remains applicable to the most dangerous patients—those committed. The Legislature having determined that the balance of several interests requires nondisclosure in the graver public danger commitment, it would be anomalous for this court to reweigh the interests, requiring disclosure for those less dangerous. Rather, we should follow the legislative direction by refusing to require disclosure of confidential information received by the therapist either before or in the absence of commitment. The Legislature obviously is more capable than is this court to investigate, debate and weigh potential patient harm through disclosure against the risk of public harm by nondisclosure. We should defer to its judgment.

COMMON LAW ANALYSIS

Entirely apart from the statutory provisions, the same result must be reached upon considering both general tort principles and the public policies favoring effective treatment, reduction of violence, and justified commitment.

Generally, a person owes no duty to control the conduct of another. (*Richards v. Stanley* (1954), 43 Cal. 2d 60, 65, 271 P.2d 23; *Wright v. Arcade School Dist.* (1964), 230 Cal. App. 2d 272, 277, 40 Cal. Rptr. 812; Rest. 2d Torts (1965) §315.) Exceptions are recognized only in limited situations where (1) a special relationship exists between the defendant and injured party, or (2) a special relationship exists between defendant and the active wrongdoer, imposing a duty on defendant to control the wrongdoer's conduct. The majority does not contend the first exception is appropriate to this case.

Policy generally determines duty. (*Dillon v. Legg* (1968), 68 Cal. 2d 728, 734, 69 Cal. Rptr. 72, 441 P.2d 912.) Principal policy considerations include foreseeability of harm, certainty of the plaintiff's injury, proximity of the defendant's conduct to the plaintiff's injury, moral blame attributable to defendant's conduct, prevention of future harm, burden on the defendant, and consequences to the community. (*Rowland v. Christian* (1968), 69 Cal.2d 108, 113, 70 Cal. Rptr. 97, 443 P.2d 561.)

Overwhelming policy considerations weigh against imposing a duty on psychotherapists to warn a potential victim against harm. While offering virtually no benefit to society, such a duty will frustrate psychiatric treatment, invade fundamental patient rights and increase violence.

The importance of psychiatric treatment and its need for confidentiality have been recognized by this court. (*In re Lifschutz* (1970), 2 Cal. 3d 415, 421-422, 85 Cal. Rptr. 829, 467 P.2d 557.) "It is clearly recognized that the very practice of psychiatry vitally depends upon the reputation in the community that the psychiatrist will not tell." (Slovenko, *Psychiatry and a Second Look at the Medical Privilege* (1960), 6 Wayne L. Rev. 175, 188.)

Assurance of confidentiality is important for three reasons.

DETERRENCE FROM TREATMENT

First, without substantial assurance of confidentiality, those requiring treatment will be deterred from seeking assistance. (See Sen. Judiciary Comm. comment accompanying §1014 of Evid. Code; Slovenko, *supra,* 6 Wayne L. Rev. 175, 187-188; Goldstein and Katz, *Psychiatrist-Patient Privilege: The GAP Proposal and the Connecticut Statute* (1962), 36 Conn. Bar J. 175, 178.) It remains an unfortunate fact in our society that people seeking psychiatric guidance tend to become stigmatized. Apprehension of such stigma —apparently increased by the propensity of people considering treatment to see themselves in the worst possible light—creates a well-recognized reluctance to seek aid. (Fisher, *The Psychotherapeutic Professions and the Law of Privileged Communications* (1964) 10 Wayne L. Rev. 609, 617; Slovenko, *supra,* 6 Wayne L. Rev. 175, 188; see also Rappeport, *Psychiatrist-Patient Privilege* (1963) 23 Md. L.J. 39, 46-47.) This reluctance is alleviated by the psychiatrist's assurance of confidentiality.

FULL DISCLOSURE

Second, the guarantee of confidentiality is essential in eliciting the full disclosure necessary for effective treatment. (*In re Lifschutz, supra,* 2 Cal. 3d 415, 431, 85 Cal. Rptr. 829, 467 P.2d 557; *Taylor v. United States* (1955), 95 U.S. App. D.C. 373, 222 F.2d 398, 401; Goldstein and Katz, *supra,* 36 Conn. Bar J. 175, 178; Heller, *Some Comments to Lawyers on the Practice of Psychiatry* (1957), 30 Temp. L.Q. 401; Guttmacher and Weihofen, *Privileged Communications Between Psychiatrist and Patient* (1952), 28 Ind. L.J. 32, 34.) The psychiatric patient approaches treatment with conscious and unconscious inhibitions against revealing his innermost thoughts. "Every person, however well-motivated, has to overcome resistances to therapeutic exploration. These resistances seek support from every possible source and the possibility of disclosure would easily be employed in the service of resistance." (Goldstein and Katz, *supra,* 36 Conn. Bar J. 175, 179; see also, 118 Am. J. Psych. 734, 735.) Until a patient can trust his psychiatrist not to violate their confidential relationship, "the unconscious psychological control mechanism of repression will prevent the recall of past experiences." (Butler, *Psychotherapy and Griswold: Is Confidentiality a Privilege or a Right?* (1971) 3 Conn. L. Rev. 599, 604.)

SUCCESSFUL TREATMENT

Third, even if the patient fully discloses his thoughts, assurance that the confidential relationship will not be breached is necessary to maintain his trust in his psychiatrist—the very means by which treatment is effected. "[T]he essence of much psychotherapy is the contribution of trust in the external world and ultimately in the self, modelled upon the trusting relationship established during therapy." (Dawidoff, *The Malpractice of Psychiatrists,* 1966 Duke L.J. 696, 704.) Patients will be helped only if they can form a trusting relationship with the psychiatrist. (*Id.* at p. 704, fn. 34; Burham, *Separation Anxiety* (1965), 13 Arch. Gen. Psychiatry 346, 356; Heller, *supra,* 30 Temp. L.Q. 401, 406.) All authorities appear to agree that if the trust relationship cannot be developed because of collusive communication between the psychiatrist and others, treatment will be frustrated. (See, e.g., Slovenko (1973), Psychiatry and Law, p. 61; Cross, *Privileged Communications Between Participants in Group Psychotherapy* (1970), Law and the Social Order, 191, 199; Hollender, *The Psychiatrist and the Release of Patient Information* (1960), 116 Am. J. Psychiatry 828, 829.)

Given the importance of confidentiality to the practice of psychiatry, it becomes clear the duty to warn imposed by the majority will cripple the use and effectiveness of psychiatry. Many people, potentially violent—yet susceptible to treatment—will be deterred from seeking it; those seeking it will be inhibited from making revelations necessary to effective treatment; and, forcing the psychiatrist to violate the patient's trust will destroy the interpersonal relationship by which treatment is effected.

VIOLENCE AND CIVIL COMMITMENT

By imposing a duty to warn, the majority contributes to the danger to society of violence by the mentally ill and greatly increases the risk of civil commitment—the total deprivation of liberty —of those who should not be confined. The impairment of treatment and risk of improper commitment resulting from the new duty to warn will not be limited to a few patients but will extend to a large number of the mentally ill. Although under existing psychiatric procedures only a relatively few receiving treatment will ever present a risk of violence, the number making threats is huge, and it is the latter group—not just the former—whose treatment will be impaired and whose risk of commitment will be increased.

Both the legal and psychiatric communities recognize that the process of determining potential violence in a patient is far from exact, being fraught with complexity and uncertainty. (E.g., *People' v. Burnick* (1975), 14 Cal. 3d 306, 326, 121 Cal. Rptr. 488, 535 P.2d 352, quoting from *Murel v. Baltimore City Criminal Court* (1972), 407 U.S. 355, 364-365, fn. 2, 92 S. Ct. 2091, 32 L. Ed.

2d 791 (Douglas, J., dissenting from dismissal of certiorari); Ennis and Litwack, *Psychiatry and the Presumption of Expertise: Flipping Coins in the Courtroom,* 62 Cal. L. Rev. 693, 711-716; Rector, *Who Are the Dangerous?* (July 1973), Bull. of Amer. Acad. of Psych. & L. 186; Kozol, Boucher & Garofalo, *The Diagnosis and Treatment of Dangerousness* (1972), 18 Crime & Delinquency 371; Justice and Birkman, *An Effort to Distinguish the Violent From the Nonviolent* (1972), 65 So. Med. J. 703.) In fact precision has not even been attained in predicting who of those having already committed violent acts will again become violent, a task recognized to be of much simpler proportions. (Kozol, Boucher and Garofalo, *supra,* 18 Crime & Delinquency 371, 384.)

The predictive uncertainty means that the number of disclosures will necessarily be large. As noted above, psychiatric patients are encouraged to discuss all thoughts of violence, and they often express such thoughts. However, unlike this court, the psychiatrist does not enjoy the benefit of overwhelming hindsight in seeing which few, if any, of his patients will ultimately become violent. Now, confronted by the majority's new duty, the psychiatrist must instantaneously calculate potential violence from each patient on each visit. The difficulties researchers have encountered in accurately predicting violence will be heightened for the practicing psychiatrist dealing for brief periods in his office with heretofore nonviolent patients. And, given the decision not to warn or commit must always be made at the psychiatrist's civil peril, one can expect most doubts will be resolved in favor of the psychiatrist protecting himself.

Neither alternative open to the psychiatrist seeking to protect himself is in the public interest. The warning itself is an impairment of the psychiatrist's ability to treat, depriving many patients of adequate treatment. It is to be expected that after disclosing their threats, a significant number of patients, who would not become violent if treated according to existing practices, will engage in violent conduct as a result of unsuccessful treatment. In short, the majority's duty to warn will not only impair treatment of many who would never become violent but worse, will result in a net increase in violence.

The second alternative open to the psychiatrist is to commit his patient rather than to warn. Even in the absence of threat of civil liability, the doubts of psychiatrists as to the seriousness of patient threats have led psychiatrists to overcommit to mental institutions. This overcommitment has been authoritatively documented in both legal and psychiatric studies. (Ennis and Litwack, *Psychiatry and the*

Presumption of Expertise: Flipping Coins in the Courtroom, supra,
62 Cal. L. Rev. 693, 711 et seq.; Fleming and Maximov, *The Patient
or His Victim: The Therapist's Dilemma,* 62 Cal. L. Rev. 1025,
1044-1046, Am. Psychiatric Assn. Task Force Rep. 8 (July 1974)
Clinical Aspects of the Violent Individual, pp. 23-24; see Livermore,
Malmquist and Meehl, *On the Justifications for Civil Commitment,*
117 U. Pa. L. Rev. 75, 84.) This practice is so prevalent that it has
been estimated that "as many as twenty harmless persons are incarcerated for every one who will commit a violent act." (Steadman
and Cocozza, *Stimulus/Response: We Can't Predict Who is Dangerous* (Jan. 1975), 8 Psych. Today 32, 35.)

Given the incentive to commit created by the majority's duty, this
already serious situation will be worsened, contrary to Chief Justice
Wright's admonition "that liberty is no less precious because for-
feited in a civil proceeding than when taken as a consequence of a
criminal conviction." (*In re W.* (1971), 5 Cal. 3d 296, 307, 96
Cal. Rptr. 1, 9, 486 P.2d 1201, 1209.)

CONCLUSION

In adopting the act, the Legislature fully recognized the concerns
that must govern our decision today—adequate treatment for the
mentally ill, safety of our society, and our devotion to individual
liberty, making overcommitment of the mentally ill abhorrent.
(§5001.) Again, the Legislature balanced these concerns in favor of
nondisclosure (§5328), thereby promoting effective treatment,
reducing temptation for over-commitment, and ensuring greater
safety for our society. Psychiatric and legal expertise on the subject
requires the same judgment.

The tragedy of Tatiana Tarasoff has led the majority to disregard
the clear legislative mandate of the Lanterman-Petris-Short Act.
Worse, the majority impedes medical treatment, resulting in increased violence from—and deprivation of liberty to—the mentally
ill.

We should accept legislative and medical judgment, relying upon
effective treatment rather than on indiscriminate warning.

The judgment should be affirmed.

McCOMB, J., concurs.

NOTE: THE TARASOFF CASE

The *Tarasoff* opinion set forth here is sometimes referred to as
Tarasoff II. It is the second decision of the California Supreme Court
on *Tarasoff,* following a rehearing granted after *Tarasoff I* had been

decided. The caption of the first *Tarasoff* case is Tarasoff v. Regents of University of California, 13 Cal. 3d 177, 529 P.2d 533, 118 Cal. Rptr. 129 (1974).

The *Tarasoff* case has generated a substantial flow of commentary. Influential in determining the *Tarasoff* outcome was Fleming and Maximov, The Patient or His Victim: The Therapist's Dilemma, 62 Calif. L. Rev. 1025 (1974), published while the California court was considering the case. A well-presented psychiatric view of the implications of Tarasoff is Stone, The Tarasoff Decisions: Suing Psychotherapists to Safeguard Society, 90 Harv. L. Rev. 358 (1976). The Stone view is countered in Wexler, Patients, Therapists, and Third Parties; The Victimological Virtues of Tarasoff, 2 Intl. J.L. & Psychiat. 1 (1979). See also Gurevitz, Tarasoff: Protective Privilege Versus Public Peril, 134 Am. J. Psychiat. 289 (1977). Other discussions worth consulting include Brooks, Mental Health Law, 4 Admin. in Mental Health 94 (1976); and Roth and Meisel, Dangerousness, Confidentiality and the Duty to Warn, 134 Am. J. Psychiat. 508 (1977). See also Latham, Liability of Psychotherapist for Failure to Warn of Homicide Threatened by Patient, 28 Vand. L. Rev. 631 (1975); Ayres and Holbrook, Law, Psychotherapy & the Duty to Warn: A Tragic Trilogy, 27 Baylor L. Rev. 677 (1975); Annas, Confidentiality and the Duty to Warn, 6 Hastings Ctr. Report 6 (December, 1976); Gurevitz, Tarasoff: Protective Privilege Versus Public Peril, 134 Am. J. Psychiat. 289 (1977); Leonard, A Therapist's Duty to Potential Victims: A Nonthreatening View of Tarasoff, 1 L. and Human Behav. 309 (1977); and Griffith and Griffith, Duty to Third Parties, Dangerousness and the Right to Refuse Treatment: Problematic Concepts for Psychiatrist and Lawyer, 14 Cal. W. L. Rev. 241 (1978).

A significant number of student notes have discussed the case. See, e.g., Notes, 44 U. Cin. L. Rev. 368 (1975); 12 Hous. L. Rev. 986 (1975); 6 Golden Gate L. Rev. 229 (1975); see also 37 U. Pitt. Rev. 155 (1975); 6 Seton Hall L. Rev. 536 (1975); 12 San Diego L. Rev. 932 (1975); 9 Akron L. Rev. 191 (1975); 15 Washburn L.J. 496 (1976); 22 N.Y.L.S.L. Rev. 1011 (1977); 48 U. Colo. L. Rev. 2831 (1977); and 29 Hastings L.J. 179 (1977).

See also Annot., Liability of One Treating Mentally Afflicted Patient for Failure to Warn or Protect Third Persons Threatened by Patient, 83 A.L.R.3d 1201. An analysis of the impact of Tarasoff is presented in a news story, McDonald, *Tarasoff:* The Consequences Emerge, Psychiatric News, December 3, 1976.

In Bellah v. Greenson, 73 Cal. App. 3d 911, 141 Cal. Rptr. 92 (1st Dist. 1977), *modified on rehearing,* 81 Cal. App. 3d 614, 146

Cal. Rptr. 535 (1978), the California Court of Appeal, refusing to extend the *Tarasoff* rationale to a suicide case, affirmed the dismissal of an action brought by parents following the suicide of their daughter. The psychiatrist had concluded that his patient was suicidal but had not informed the parents. The parents argued that the psychiatrist not only had the duty of disclosure but also had the obligation to attempt to restrain the patient from committing suicide. The court distinguished *Bellah* from *Tarasoff,* ruling that Tarasoff did not apply to cases of self-inflicted harm or suicide.

A New Jersey Superior Court is the first to adopt the Tarasoff rationale. See McIntosh v. Milano, 168 N.J. Super. 466, 403 A.2d 500 (Law Div. 1979) concerning the murder by a patient in treatment of a young woman who had been his next-door neighbor and with whom he claimed to have had a sexual relationship. Although the patient had expressed great hostility to the victim, he apparently had never told the doctor he would kill her.

Page 1122. After Problem, add:

DOE v. ROE

400 N.Y.S.2d 668 (1977)

MARTIN B. STECHER, Justice:

This action for an injunction and for damages for breach of privacy is a matter of first impression in this State, and so far as I am able to ascertain, a matter of first impression in the United States. It arises out of the publication, verbatim, by a psychiatrist of a patient's disclosures during the course of a lengthy psychoanalysis. I have made and filed detailed findings of fact which are briefly summarized here.[1]

Dr. Joan Roe is a physician who has practiced psychiatry for more than 50 years. Her husband, Peter Roe, has been a psychologist for some 25 years. The plaintiff and her late, former husband were each patients of Dr. Roe for many years. The defendants, eight years after the termination of treatment, published a book which reported verbatim and extensively the patients' thoughts, feelings, and emotions, their sexual and other fantasies and biographies, their most intimate personal relationships and the disintegration of their mar-

1. By prior order this file has been sealed from indiscriminate viewing and pseudonyms have been used in the title of the action and in the other documents. I see every reason to continue that arrangement [*cf. Munzer v. Blaisdell,* 268 App. Div. 9, 48 N.Y.S.2d 355].

riage. Interspersed among the footnotes are Roe's diagnoses of what purport to be the illnesses suffered by the patients and one of their children.

The defendants allege that the plaintiff consented to this publication. This defense is without substance. Consent was sought while the plaintiff was in therapy. It was never obtained in writing. In Dr. Roe's own words consent "was there one day and not there another day. That was the nature of the illness I was treating, unreliable." I need not deal with the value of an oral waiver of confidentiality given by a patient to a psychiatrist during the course of treatment. It is sufficient to conclude that not only did the defendants fail to obtain the plaintiff's consent to publication, they were well aware that they had none.

The plaintiff seeks to prevail on any or all of four theories: that violation of subdivision (a) of Section 4504 CPLR gives rise to a cause of action;[2] that the provisions of the Education Law [§6509] and the Regulations of the Commissioner of Education [8 NYCRR 60.1, subd. (d)(3)][3] establish a public policy whose breach gives rise to a cause of action in tort; that the physician-patient relationship is contractual and in it there is implied the physician's promise to obey the Hippocratic Oath[4] whose violation gives rise to a cause of action for breach of contract; and, finally, "in light of the expanding recognition of privacy actions" a separate cause of action exists for unreasonably publicizing elements of plaintiff's life which ought to have been left in confidence.

The defendants contend not only that there was no unlawful disclosure, the patient's identity having been fully concealed, but that no right of action exists even if the plaintiff is recognizable in

2. CPLR 4504(a) provides in part: "Unless the patient waives the privilege, a person authorized to practice medicine . . . shall not be allowed to disclose any information which he acquired in attending a patient in a professional capacity, and which was necessary to enable him to act in that capacity."

3. Subd. 9, §6509 of the Education Law provides: "Each of the following is professional misconduct: . . . (9) Committing unprofessional conduct, as defined by the board of regents in its rules or by the commissioner in regulations approved by the board of regents." 8 NYCRR 60.1 subd. (d)(3) provides in part, "Unprofessional conduct in the practise of medicine shall include . . . the revealing of facts, data or information obtained in a professional capacity relating to a patient or his records without first obtaining the consent of the patient. . . ."

4. Every physician is presumed to have taken the Oath of Hippocrates [460?-377? B.C.] which states in part, "I will abstain [in treating patients] . . . from whatever is deleterious and mischievous. . . . Whatever, in connection with my professional practise, or not in connection with it, I may see or hear in the lives of men which ought not to be spoken abroad I will not divulge, as reckoning that all such should be kept secret."

this volume. The defendants assert that neither the "evidentiary privilege" contained in CPLR 4504(a) nor the regulations of the Commissioner of Education, by their history, are intended to give rise to a cause of action for their violation; that the only cause of action for invasion of privacy recognized in the state of New York is the statutory cause of action set forth in Sections 50 and 51 of the Civil Rights Law; that the invasion of privacy concept as developed in the Federal Courts and elsewhere is a constitutional guarantee of a right to privacy against intrusion by governments and has no reference to non-state action; that the volume in question is of such scientific merit that the professional need which it fills transcends the patient's right of non-disclosure; that the plaintiff is guilty of laches in bringing this action; and, finally, that the defendants' right to publication is protected by the first amendment to the United States Constitution.

The few New York cases dealing with a physician's unauthorized disclosure of a patient's confidences usually turn on other issues, restrict themselves for the most part to a discussion of the effect of the current evidentiary statute [CPLR 4504(a)] or its predecessor [CPA 352] and in their dicta reach contradictory conclusions. In *Munzer v. Blaisdell,* 183 Misc. 773, 49 N.Y.S.2d 915, *aff'd as modified,* 269 A.D. 970, 58 N.Y.S.2d 359, a patient in a State psychiatric institution sued its director for unauthorizedly releasing his case record in violation of the Mental Hygiene Law. The cause of action founded on CPA §352 was dismissed because there was no physician-patient relationship between the parties. The court did, however, offer the opinion [p. 775, 49 N.Y.S.2d p. 917] that

. . . where the statutory duty is violated, the patient is entitled to redress; for it is well settled that, where a positive duty is imposed by statute, a breach of that duty will give rise to a cause of action for damages on the part of the person for whose benefit the duty was imposed; and, in such cases, if the statute itself does not provide a remedy, the common law will furnish it. This principle was recognized by the decision of the Appellate Division in the case at bar [see *Munzer v. Blaisdell,* 268 App. Div. 9, 48 N.Y.S.2d 355].

In *Clark v. Geraci,* 29 Misc. 2d 791, 208 N.Y.S.2d 564, the court found that the patient had waived the privilege and stated in a dictum that CPLR 4504(a), the Education Law [§6509] and the Regulations issued thereunder [8 NYCRR 60.1(d)(3)] provided no cause of action for breach of confidentiality. *Felis v. Greenberg,* 51 Misc. 2d 441, 273 N.Y.S.2d 288, on the other hand expresses the view that such disclosure gives rise to a cause of action but turns on the sufficiency of a pleading alleging the publication of false information. *Curry v. Corn,* 52 Misc. 2d 1035, 277 N.Y.S.2d 470, suggests that violation of CPLR 4504(a) was not intended by the Legislature to create an independent cause of action; but there the physician's disclosure was to the plaintiff's husband and the court held that a husband is entitled, as a matter of right, to be informed of his wife's medical condition. In *Hammer v. Polsky,* 36 Misc. 2d 482, 233 N.Y.S.2d 110, the court, in a dictum, said that neither CPA 352 nor the Regulations issued under the Education Law will support a cause of action; but as in *Munzer v. Blaisdell, supra,* 183 Misc. 777, 49 N.Y.S.2d 918, recovery was denied on the ground that no physician-patient relationship was alleged to have existed.

The most frequently cited cases arising in other jurisdictions suffer from the same limitations. Although in *Smith v. Driscoll,* 94 Wash. 441, 162 P. 572 [1917], the court said 162 P. p. 572, that "for so palpable a wrong the law provides a remedy," the case turned on a question of pleading. A dictum in *Simonsen v. Swenson,* 104 Neb. 224, 177 N.W. 831 [1920], suggests the availability of a remedy for violation of the duty of secrecy, but the issue involved what the court held to be a limited right of disclosure of the existence of a communicable disease. The court in *Berry v. Moench,* 8 Utah 2d 191, 331 P.2d 814 [1958], expressed the opinion that violation of evidentiary statutes gives rise to a cause of action, but like *Felis v. Greenberg, supra,* the action was for libel, the issue turning on whether or not the physician's disclosures were truthful. *Alexander v. Knight,* 197 Pa. Super. 79, 177 A.2d 142 [1962], similarly contains such dicta, but the action was for personal injuries sustained in an automobile accident.

In *Hague v. Williams,* 37 N.J. 328, 181 A.2d 345 [1962], the Court, 181 A.2d at 349 states that despite the absence of a common law physician-patient privilege "a patient should be entitled to freely disclose his symptoms and condition to his doctor in order to receive proper treatment without fear that those facts may become public property" and that a physician "was under a general duty not to disclose frivolously the information received from (the patient) or from an examination of the patient." The court, however, concluded that a physician was perfectly justified in disclosing to an insurer the heart condition of a child whose parents had applied for a policy of life insurance on that child's life.

None of the post Civil Practice Act cases had considered the effect of the repeal of Section 354 CPA. Section 352 CPA which prohibited disclosure, was carried forward verbatim into the new statute [CPLR 4504(a)]. Section 354 CPA limited the application of Section 352

CPA providing in part that it applied "to any examination of a person as a witness," but this language was excluded from the new statute leaving only the broad prohibition without limitation that "a person authorized to practice medicine . . . shall not be allowed to disclose any information which he acquired in attending a patient in a professional capacity, and which was necessary to enable him to act in that capacity."

Were this case to turn exclusively on the application of CPLR 4504(a) it might be argued that had the Legislature intended, on adoption of the Civil Practice Law and Rules, to create a new cause of action where none existed before, it would have said so explicitly. Obviously, this case does not depend on so limited an approach; but I am of the opinion that the Legislature, in excluding from the new statute the opening words of CPA 354 [quoted supra], intended to reinforce the public policy of this state expressed in numerous statutes and regulations prohibiting physicians, persons in allied fields and medical institutions from disclosing without authorization of the patient, information discovered in attending the patient. I believe it clear, from the statutory and regulatory schemes set forth above that the Legislature did not intend to confine the prohibition to trials and other formal hearings whose proceedings are governed by a practice act but intended that "'the statute [CPLR 4504(a)] should have a broad and liberal construction to carry out its policy.'"

As hereafter indicated there are theories on which liability may be predicated other than violation of the CPLR [4504(a)], the licensing and disciplinary statutes [Ed.L. 6509 et seq.] and what I perceive as this State's public policy. In two of the very few cases which have come to grips with the issue of wrongful disclosure by physicians of patients' secrets [*Hammonds v. Aetna Casualty & Surety Company*, 243 F. Supp. 793 [N.D. Ohio, 1965]; and *Horne v. Patton*, 291 Ala. 701, 287 So. 2d 824 [1973] the courts predicated their holdings on the numerous sources of obligations which arise out of the physician-patient relationship. In Hammonds, *supra,* an insurance carrier, defending an action brought by a patient of the physician, tricked the physician into revealing confidential data by telling him that the patient intended a medical malpractice action. Both physician and insurance carrier were held liable in damages for the wrongful disclosure on theories of public policy;[5] the privileged

5. "When a course of conduct is cruel or shocking to the average man's conception of justice, such course of conduct must be held to be obviously contrary to public policy, though such policy has never been so written in the bond, whether it be Constitution, statute or decree of court." [p. 796].

communication statute; the state licensing statute; the implied covenant not to disclose whose breach is a contractual violation[6]; invasion of privacy and breach of a fiduciary duty to which a trust doctrine should be applied. The court was "of the opinion that the preservation of the patient's privacy is no mere ethical duty upon the part of the doctor; there is a legal duty as well. The unauthorized revelation of medical secrets, or any confidential communication given in the course of treatment, is tortious conduct which may be the basis for an action in damages" [pp. 801-802].

Horne v. Patton, supra, was a case of first impression in Alabama, a state without a testimonial privilege statute, but which had a licensing statute [Title 46 §257(21) Code of Alabama] which, like our own statute [Ed. Law 6509 et seq.] and regulations [8 NYCRR 60.1(d)(3)] permitted revocation of the physician's license for "betrayal of a professional secret." The court, 287 So. 2d at p. 830, sustained the complaint seeking an injunction and damages and recognized the "right of a person to be free from unwarranted publicity or unwarranted appropriation or exploitation of one's personality, publicization of one's private affairs with which the public has no legitimate concern, or the wrongful intrusion of one's private activities in such a manner as to outrage or cause mental suffering, shame or humiliation to a person of ordinary sensibilities." Its conclusions were also based on obligations arising from the Hippocratic Oath and the Principles of Medical Ethics of the American Medical Association[7]; the state licensing and disciplinary statute; the fiduciary nature of the relationship; and the implied covenant of secrecy in the contract between the parties. It held that "the public policy in Alabama requires that information obtained by a physician in the course of a doctor-patient relationship be maintained in confidence . . ." The court "concluded that a medical doctor is under a general duty not to make extra judicial disclosures of information acquired in the course of the doctor-patient relationship and that a breach of that duty will give rise to a cause of action." 287 So. 2d pp. 829-830.

6. "Almost every member of the public is aware of the promise of discretion contained in the Hippocratic Oath, and every patient has a right to rely upon this warranty of silence. The promise of secrecy is as much an express warranty as the advertisement of a commercial entrepreneur." [p. 801].

7. "A physician may not reveal the confidences entrusted to him in the course of medical attendance, or the deficiencies he may observe in the character of patients, unless he is required to do so by law or unless it becomes necessary in order to protect the welfare of the individual or of the community." American Medical Association, Principles of Medical Ethics, 1957, §9.

I too find that a physician, who enters into an agreement with a patient to provide medical attention, impliedly covenants to keep in confidence all disclosures made by the patient concerning the patient's physical or mental condition as well as all matters discovered by the physician in the course of examination or treatment. This is particularly and necessarily true of the psychiatric relationship, for in the dynamics of psychotherapy "(t)he patient is called upon to discuss in a candid and frank manner personal material of the most intimate and disturbing nature. . . . He is expected to bring up all manner of socially unacceptable instincts and urges, immature wishes, perverse sexual thoughts—in short the unspeakable, the unthinkable, the repressed. To speak of such things to another human being requires an atmosphere of unusual trust, confidence and tolerance.

"Patients will be helped only if they can form a trusting relationship with the psychiatrist." [Melvin S. Heller, M.D., *Some Comments to Lawyers on the Practice of Psychiatry*, 30 Temple L.R. 401, 405-406 (1957)].

There can be little doubt that under the law of the State of New York and in a proper case, the contract of private parties to retain in confidence matter which should be kept in confidence will be enforced by injunction and compensated in damages. [Cites.]

The contract between the plaintiff and Dr. Roe is such a contract. The contention that such enforcement of a private agreement not to disclose information received in confidence somehow offends the United States Constitution would seem to be disputed by implication in *Kewanee Oil Co. v. Bicron Corp.*, 416 U.S. 470, 94 S. Ct. 1879, 40 L. Ed. 2d 315. The cases cited by the defendants in support of their theory that First Amendment rights are somehow involved do not support their contention. *Time Inc. v. Hill*, 385 U.S. 374, 87 S. Ct. 534, 17 L. Ed. 2d 456, involves a right to publish a matter of general public interest. *New York Times Company v. Sullivan*, 376 U.S. 254, 84 S. Ct. 710, 11 L. Ed. 2d 686, involved the right to publish matters critical of, or even offensive to, public officials. Reliance on the defamation cases [*New York Times v. Sullivan, supra; Garrison v. Louisiana*, 379 U.S. 64, 85 S. Ct. 209, 13 L. Ed. 2d 125; *Curtis Publishing Co. v. Butts*, 388 U.S. 130, 87 S. Ct. 1975, 18 L. Ed. 2d 1094; *St. Amant v. Thompson*, 390 U.S. 727, 88 S. Ct. 1323, 20 L. Ed. 2d 262; *Gertz v. Robert Welch, Inc.*, 418 U.S. 323, 94 S. Ct. 2997, 41 L. Ed. 2d 789; *Cox et al. v. Cohn*, 420 U.S. 469, 95 S. Ct. 1029, 43 L. Ed. 2d 328; *Time, Inc. v. Firestone*, 424 U.S. 448, 96 S. Ct. 958, 47 L. Ed. 2d 154; *Chapadeau v. Utica*

Observer-Dispatch, Inc., 38 N.Y.2d 196, 379 N.Y.S.2d 61, 341 N.E.2d 569] would appear to be misplaced. In none of them is a contractual duty to maintain a confidence involved. On the other hand, in *United States v. Marchetti,* 466 F.2d 1309, 4 Cir., *cert. den.,* 409 U.S. 1063, 93 S. Ct. 553, 34 L. Ed. 2d 516, an agreement by an agent of the Central Intelligence Agency not to disclose information acquired during his service with the Agency was sufficient to enjoin the publication in a book by Marchetti of matter reasonably deemed by the CIA to be in violation of that contract.

The complaint alleges a cause of action for breach of privacy under the Civil Rights Law [§§50, 51]. These statutes have not been violated for the defendants did not use the plaintiff's "name, portrait or picture" in their book. We are not, of course, limited to the theory set forth in the complaint, but may consider any cause of action revealed by the pleadings and proof [*Diemer v. Diemer,* 8 N.Y.2d 206, 203 N.Y.S.2d 829, 168 N.E.2d 654] and can even amend the pleadings on the court's own motion after trial [*Princiotto v. Materdomini,* 45 A.D.2d 883, 358 N.Y.S.2d 13]. A motion to amend this cause of action has been granted and a cause of action for breach of privacy has been established—if such a cause of action is recognized in this state apart from the Civil Rights Law.

The expression "right of privacy" is not without confusion and has been applied to varying rights and causes of action. Among the cases cited by the plaintiff in support of its contention are *Roe v. Wade,* 410 U.S. 113, 93 S. Ct. 705, 35 L. Ed.2d 147, *Griswold v. Connecticut,* 381 U.S. 479, 85 S. Ct. 1678, 14 L. Ed. 2d 510, and *Drake v. Covington,* 371 F. Supp. 974 [D.C.]. In each of these cases there is a judicial recognition that the individual has rights of privacy which may not be infringed upon by a government. Such right of privacy, of course, is not involved in this litigation.

In *Nader v. General Motors,* 25 N.Y.2d 560, 307 N.Y.S.2d 647, 255 N.E.2d 765, a case decided under the law of the District of Columbia, Judge [now Chief Judge] Breitel, in a concurring opinion p. 572, 307 N.Y.S.2d p. 657, 255 N.E.2d p. 772, said that "scholars in trying to define the elusive concept of the right of privacy, have, as of the present, subdivided the common law right into separate classifications, most significantly distinguishing between unreasonable intrusion and unreasonable publicity [Restatement, 2d Torts, Tent. Draft No. 13 (April 27, 1967), sects. 652A, 652B; 652D Prosser, Torts (3d ed.), pp. 832-837]. This does not mean, however, that the classifications are either frozen or exhausted, or that several of the classifications may not overlap." The Nader case is a classic case of "unreasonable intrusion." At bar is a claim of "unreasonable publicity" [cf. Time v. Hill, supra].

Ever since Roberson v. Rochester Folding Box Co., 171 N.Y. 538, 64 N.E. 442, the courts of this state have held uniformly [cf. Waters v. Moore, 70 Misc. 2d 372, 334 N.Y.S.2d 428] that no cause of action for invasion of privacy will be recognized apart from that authorized by Sections 50 and 51 of the Civil Rights Law. Only this year the Appellate Division, First Department reaffirmed this view [Wojtowicz v. Delacorte Press et al., 58 A.D.2d 45, 395 N.Y.S.2d 205].[8] Stated differently, to date there has not been recognized in this State a common law right of privacy. The right of privacy urged here, however, is not a common law right. The right of privacy with which we deal arises from two other sources: the public policy [discussed supra] of the State of New York proclaimed by statute [CPLR 4504(a), 4507, 4508; Ed. L. 6509-6511; MHL 15.13 subds. (c) and (d), 35.11; PHL 2803-c subd. 3(f), 2805-e subd. 3, 3371] and Regulation [8 NYCRR 60.1 subd. (d)(3)] which bars a physician from disclosing a patient's confidences; and the implied promise of confidentiality which every physician makes to his patient. It is in this context that the Appellate Division, 1st Department, upheld and expanded the preliminary injunction previously granted in this case saying "(i)n light of the expanding recognition of invasion of privacy actions [citing cases] and in view of the confidentiality accorded the physician-patient relationship, we believe that plaintiff has alleged a cognizable claim for relief. . . ." [Doe v. Roe, 42 A.D.2d 559, 560, 345 N.Y.S.2d 560, 562].

Every patient, and particularly every patient undergoing psychoanalysis, has such a right of privacy. Under what circumstances can a person be expected to reveal sexual fantasies, infantile memories, passions of hate and love, one's most intimate relationship with one's spouse and others except upon the inferential agreement that such confessions will be forever entombed in the psychiatrist's memory, never to be revealed during the psychiatrist's lifetime or thereafter? The very needs of the profession itself require that confidentiality exist and be enforced. As pointed out in Matter of Lifschutz, 2 Cal. 3d 415, 85 Cal. Rptr. 829, 467 P.2d 557 [1970] "a large segment of the psychiatric profession concurs in Dr. Lifschutz's strongly held belief that an absolute privilege of confidentiality is essential to the effective practice of psychotherapy" [cf. Annotation, 20 A.L.R.3d,

8. It has been predicted [Galella v. Onassis, 487 F.2d 986, 995, 2d Cir. 1973] that the New York Court of Appeals when again faced with the issue, will abandon Roberson v. Rochester Folding Box Co., supra, but this case need not turn on such prediction.

1109, 1112]. Despite the fact that in no New York case has such a wrong been remedied due, most likely, to the fact that so few physicians violate this fundamental obligation, it is time that the obligation not only be recognized but that the right of redress be recognized as well.

What label we affix to this wrong is unimportant [although the category of wrong could, under certain circumstances—such as determining the applicable statute of limitations—be significant]. "It is generally accepted that 'There is no necessity whatever that a tort must have a name. New and nameless torts are being recognized constantly'. [Prosser, Torts (2d ed.), p. 3]. What is important is that there must be the infliction of intentional harm, resulting in damage, without legal excuses or justification. [Cites.]

The defendants contend that the physician's obligation of confidentiality is not absolute and must give way to the general public interest. The interest, as they see it in this case, is the scientific value of the publication.

It is not disputed that under our public policy the right of confidentiality is less than absolute. The evidentiary statute itself [CPLR 4504(a)] contains its own exceptions. Despite the duty of confidentiality courts have recognized the duty of a psychiatrist to give warning where a patient clearly presents a danger to others [*Tarasoff v. Regents of the University of California,* 13 Cal. 3d 177, 118 Cal. Rptr. 129, 131, 529 P.2d 553, at p. 555, 1974], to disclose the existence of a contagious disease [P.H.L. 2101; *Hofmann v. Blackmon,* 241 So. 2d 752 [Fla. App. 1970]; *Wojcik v. Aluminum Co. of America,* 18 Misc. 2d 740, 183 N.Y.S.2d 351], to report the use of "controlled substances" in certain situations [P.H.L. 3355, 3373], and to report gunshot and other wounds [PL 265.25]. In no case, however, has the curiosity or education of the medical profession superseded the duty of confidentiality. I do not reach the question of a psychiatrist's right to publish case histories where the identities are fully concealed[9] for that is not our problem here, nor do I find it necessary to reach the issue of whether or not an important

9. It is interesting to observe that a leading professional organization, The Group for the Advancement of Psychiatry, in its report No. 45 [New York, N.Y., 1960] concurs in the conclusion that conflicts between ethical obligations and scientific advance must be resolved in favor of the ethical consideration. It said, "When the psychiatrist describes the details of the life history of his patient, his job problems, et cetera, the possibility of recognition is very high.

"For this reason clinical data may have to be disguised with consequent impairment of the objective scientific value. Sometimes material may be so impossible to camouflage that it should not be published at all, in spite of its scientific value.

"Such ethical requirements take priority over research objectives."

scientific discovery would take precedence over a patient's privilege of nondisclosure. I do not consider myself qualified to determine the contribution which this book may have made to the science or art of psychiatry. I do conclude, however, that if such contribution was the defendants' defense they have utterly failed in their proof that this volume represented a major contribution to scientific knowledge. The evidence is to the contrary and this defense must necessarily fail.

Nor is the argument available that by enjoining the further distribution of this book the court will be engaging in a "prior restraint" on publication. The Supreme Court long ago recognized that "Liberty of speech and of the press is . . . not an absolute right, and the state may punish its abuse" [*Near v. Minnesota,* 283 U.S. 697, 708, 51 S. Ct. 625, 628, 75 L. Ed. 1357]. That the action contemplated here is not a "prior restraint" is clear. In *Kingsley Books Inc. v. Brown,* 354 U.S. 436, 77 S. Ct. 1325, 1 L. Ed. 2d 1469. Justice Frankfurter distinguished prior restraint from the situation at bar. Contrasting the unconstitutional statute in *Near v. Minnesota, supra,* with the New York statute [22A CCP, now CPLR 6330], Justice Frankfurter said, "The two cases are no less glaringly different when judged by the appropriate criteria of constitutional law. Minnesota empowered its courts to enjoin the dissemination of future issues of a publication because its past issues had been found offensive. In the language of Mr. Chief Justice Hughes, 'This is of the essence of censorship.' [283 U.S. at 713, 51 S. Ct. at 625]. As such, it was found unconstitutional. This was enough to condemn the statute wholly apart from the fact that the proceeding in Near involved not obscenity but matters deemed to be derogatory to a public officer. Unlike Near, §22-a is concerned solely with obscenity and, as authoritatively construed, it studiously withholds restraint upon matters not already published and not yet found to be offensive."

There is no prior restraint in the case at bar. The book has been published and it does offend against the plaintiff's right of privacy, contractual and otherwise, not to have her innermost thoughts offered to all for the price of this book. There is no prior restraint and, therefore, no censorship within constitutional meaning.

As I have indicated in the separately filed findings of facts, the defense of laches is groundless. Publication occurred ten years after Dr. Roe last discussed the book with the plaintiff, eight years after treatment stopped. As soon as the plaintiff heard of the impending publication, she protested, orally through a mutual friend and in writing through her attorney. Dr. Roe's evasive and misleading answer to the attorney should serve to still any claim of laches.

The liability of Dr. Roe to respond in damages is clear; and Mr. Poe's liability is equally clear. True, he and the plaintiff were not involved in a physician-patient relationship and he certainly had no contractual relationship to her. But, the conclusion is unassailable that Poe, like anyone else with access to the book, knew that its source was the patient's production in psychoanalysis. He knew as well as, and perhaps better than Roe, of the absence of consent, of the failure to disguise. If anyone was the actor in seeing to it that the work was written, that it was manufactured, advertised and circulated, it was Poe. He is a co-author of the and a willing, indeed avid, co-violator of the patient's rights and is therefore equally liable [*Hammonds v. Aetna Casualty & Surety Company*, 243 F. Supp. 793, D.C., *supra*].

The plaintiff seeks punitive damages and suggests that a proper measure of those damages, in addition to compensatory damage, is approximately $50,000, the sum plaintiff has thus far expended on and incurred for attorney's fees. [Given the history of this action with appeals to the United States Supreme Court, it is reasonable to assume that she shall continue to incur expenses]. Under the English rule, an allowance of costs to the prevailing party includes attorney fees assessed by the court. Early in the judicial history of the United States, this country and nearly all, if not all, jurisdictions within it, determined that except for extraordinary circumstances, attorneys' fees were not a proper element of costs unless provided for by statute. It has been held that in the federal courts where jurisdiction is attained other than by diversity of citizenship, attorneys' fees may be awarded under general federal equity jurisdiction where a losing litigant has acted "in bad faith, vexatiously, wantonly or for oppressive reasons." It would appear that as punitive damages or otherwise, attorneys' fees are not available in this case there being no statutory authority providing for them.

In order to warrant an award of punitive damages, it must have been affirmatively demonstrated that the wrong committed was willful and malicious, that the act complained of was "morally culpable or . . . actuated by evil and reprehensible motives, not only to punish the defendant but to deter him, as well as others. . . ." [*Walker v. Sheldon*, 10 N.Y.2d 401, 223 N.Y.S.2d 488, 179 N.E.2d 497]. Where the act complained of is willful, malicious and wanton, punitive damages are sometimes available to "express indignation at the defendants' wrong rather than a value set on plaintiff's loss" [*Gostowski v. Roman Catholic Church, etc.,* 262 N.Y. 320, 324, 186 N.E. 798, 800]. Certainly, the acts of the defendants here are such as to warrant an expression of indignation and punishment for the purpose of deterring similar acts by these defendants or others. The difficulty, however, is that the defendants' acts were not willful, malicious or wanton—they were merely stupid. I have no doubt that the defendants were of the opinion that they had sufficiently concealed the identity of the plaintiff and her family. I have no doubt that in addition to the commercial success they hoped to have, they believed that they were rendering a public service in publishing what they considered an indepth description of the plaintiff's family. But there was no motive to harm. Under these circumstances, punitive damages are not available.

On turning to compensatory damages, we are confronted by the defendants' contention that the information concerning the book acquired by the plaintiff's university students and colleagues be excluded from consideration. They argue that these people acquired their information as a consequence of newspapers reported the filing of this suit. They say, inferentially, that had plaintiff not brought this action she would have been spared that particular embarrassment, and therefore, having brought the action, she must bear its consequences.

This argument must be rejected for the same reason we reject the demand for attorneys fees. An underlying principle of American law is that a person having a cognizable claim is entitled or even encouraged to pursue that claim in the courts and that which discourages a person from seeking redress, such as the imposition of substantial costs as a penalty for losing his suit, is rejected. [*Cf. Alyeska Pipeline Service Co. v. Wilderness Society, supra,* 421 U.S. at 251, 95 S. Ct. 1612]. So it is here. The plaintiff clearly had a meritorious cause of action and we encourage her to assert her rights. If a consequence of that assertion of rights was further damaging publicity, the loss must fall, not on the plaintiff, but on the defendants, whose conduct made this law suit necessary. The wrongful publication and not the commencement of suit was the proximate cause of the damage.

The plaintiff has suffered damage as a consequence of this publication. She suffered acute embarrassment on learning the extent to which friends, colleagues, employer, students and others, had read or read of the book. Her livelihood, as indicated in the findings, was threatened; but fortunately, the actual cash loss was only some $1,500. Medical attention, principally treatment with Dr. Lowenfeld, cost an additional $1,400. But beyond these sums the plaintiff suffered in health. She had insomnia and nightmares. She became reclusive as a consequence of the shame and humiliation induced by the book's publication and her well-being and emotional health were significantly impaired for three years. In my opinion the fair and reasonable value of the injury she sustained—to the extent it can be compensated in damages—is $20,000.

Damages, of course, do not provide an adequate remedy; for should the book circulate further, beyond the 220 copies already sold, the damage must accrue anew. The plaintiff is entitled to a judgment permanently enjoining the defendants, their heirs, successors and assigns from further violating the plaintiff's right to privacy whether by circulating this book or by otherwise disclosing any of the matters revealed by the plaintiff to Dr. Roe in the course of psychotherapy. On settlement of the judgment suggestions will be entertained concerning the disposition of any remaining volumes or parts thereof.

NOTE: CONFIDENTIALITY

See Note, Roe v. Doe: A Remedy for Disclosure of Psychiatric Confidences, 29 Rutgers L. Rev. 190 (1975).

A valuable bibliography of confidentiality studies is contained in National Commission on Confidentiality of Health Records, Health Records and Confidentiality: An Annotated Bibliography With Abstracts (1977).

See, in particular, Noll and Hanlon, Patient Privacy and Confidentiality at Mental Health Centers, 133 Am. J. Psychiat. 11 (1976); Shah, Privileged Communications, Confidentiality and Privacy, 1 Prof. Psychol. 159 (1970); Grossman, Insurance Reports as a Threat to Confidentiality, 128 Am. J. Psychiat. 96 (1971); Note, Psychotherapy and Griswold: Is Confidence A Privilege or a Right?, 3 Conn. L. Rev. 559 (1971); and Grossman, Confidentiality in Medical Practice, 28 Ann. Rev. Med. 28 (1977).